Books on
American Indians
and Eskimos

Books on

American Indians
and Eskimos

A selection guide
for children and young adults

MARY JO LASS-WOODFIN, Editor

AMERICAN LIBRARY ASSOCIATION

Chicago 1978

Library of Congress Cataloging in Publication Data

Main entry under title:

Books on American Indians and Eskimos.

    Includes index.
    1. Indians of North America—Juvenile literature—
Bibliography. 2. Eskimos—Juvenile literature—
Bibliography. I. Lass-Woodfin, Mary Jo.
Z1209.2.U5B66 [E77.4] 016.97'0004'97 77-17271
ISBN 0-8389-0241-3

Printed in the United States of America

Contents

=====

Children's and Young People's Literature on American Indians and Eskimos

Annotated Bibliography

=====

Preface

This bibliography is designed to help librarians, parents, educators, and others concerned with books for young people make intelligent choices among the many book selections now available on American Indians and Eskimos.

To this end, the books reviewed in this volume represent a complete continuum of philosophy, thought, style, political outlook, attitudes, conclusions, and opinions reflective of the field as a whole. Each review summarizes content; comments on possible uses; lists strengths and weaknesses in writing, accuracy, format, and feel; estimates grade levels for most appropriate use; and rates the books according to these criteria:

> GOOD—Buy; better than average in writing and accuracy of contents.
> ADEQUATE—Buy; however, be aware of flaws and/or errors in writing and/or accuracy.
> POOR—Think before buying; seriously flawed in writing and/or accuracy of material.

The grade level estimates provided for each book are based on the reviewers' experience gained through working with young people at diverse age levels; on their familiarity with various readability formulas; on their judgment of book format, layout, and concept difficulty levels; and on their perceptions of the varying purposes books serve. Consequently, each grade level estimate includes a range. Within the suggested range, most readers should be able to read the material with little difficulty. In addition, slower readers at the lower grade levels of a particular range can often benefit from studying the pictures or from hearing portions of the book read aloud, while the more advanced readers in primary grade levels can profit from the challenge of reading a book with a range that begins at their grade level and continues upward. At the upper reaches of each range (although these books are appropriate for all levels of reader ability within the given span), slower upper-grade readers may find these books easy to read without being insultingly juvenile in format. These differences are discussed in the separate reviews.

Every book listed in this bibliography was read by at least two reviewers, and the resulting comments summarize their thoughts. In a few instances (see James Houston's books), the reviewers perceived such differences in the material that both are included.

Only books written about Indians and Eskimos found within the boundaries of the continental United States and Hawaii are included in this bibliography. Other groups from Canada, Mexico, and Central and South America were excluded in order to keep the final publication within a reasonable format and working frame. The cutoff deadline for books to be included was January 1, 1977, and the reviews are limited to texts generally available at that time.

It is hoped that this bibliography will offer guideposts in the selection of material, and the reviews are written in a style designed to facilitate this choice. As it seemed insufficient to recommend some books without providing some examples of inappropriate choices, the books reviewed in this volume represent all levels of quality. In fact, readers may wish to buy books rated as *Poor* for many reasons. College instructors may wish to use concrete examples of such writing in the training of prospective educators, librarians, and writers (and, indeed, prospective parents!) in the recognition of the distortions and inaccuracies to be found in written material. Educators and librarians may use such books to illustrate critical reading skills, the detection of propaganda techniques, and the recognition of author bias and assumptions.

Books were not rated as *Poor* because they contained an unpopular point of view, because the reviewer disagreed with the author, or because the material was controversial. Such books were rated

Poor because they tended to give readers impressions that the viewpoint the author presented is the only possible viewpoint, that it is, indeed, not opinion, but fact. They were also rated as *Poor* if the writing craftsmanship, organization, and format seemed less than professional, or if they led to conclusions based on selective or biased presentation of facts and events.

Readers at any grade level should be capable of making intelligent choices when given sufficient information. For example, a book that purports to deal with Navajo history should incorporate the event known as "The Long Walk," and a book on Sequoyah is incomplete without reference to the "Trail of Tears." Not only is it important to refer to such critical events, but references to historical episodes should also be formed through a comparison of several accounts. A child with access to only one book on a crucial period, especially a book lacking breadth or access to other ideas or thoughts, will therefore be subjected to unacceptable simplification. And, just as an author certainly has the right to include or exclude any facts, a reviewer certainly has the obligation to bring such shortcomings to the attention of the reader.

Acknowledgments

Reviewing several hundred children's books is humbling, some-times panic-producing, and always time-consuming experience. Special thanks are due the following individuals for their assist-ance:

Paul Agriesti, New Mexico State Library, Santa Fe, New Mexico: for clearing the way.

Jean Atwood and Staff, County Clerk, Catron County, New Mexico: for clerical assistance.

Herbert Bloom, Senior Editor, American Library Association: for confi-dence that reviewing is difficult, but possible.

Renee Broughton and Ron Gardner, students, California State Univer-sity, Long Beach: for research assistance.

Carol Byers and Laurel McCarthy: for typing, proofing, and working late hours.

Helen Cline, Managing Editor, ALA: for editing assistance and needed encouragement.

Octavia Fellin, Public Library, Gallup, New Mexico: for generous shar-ing of her resources and background.

Doris Gregor, New Mexico State Library, Santa Fe, New Mexico: for suggestions, ideas, and views far beyond any reasonable ex-pectation, all the while insisting that "This is what a library person is for."

Karen Lass: for help with some of the more tedious aspects of writing and research.

Enid D. McCargish, Judge Magistrate, Catron County, New Mexico, retired: friend, listener, and critic.

Harry E. Schwartz: for logistics and support.

David Shapiro, the Ecker Foundation, Chicago: for encouragement of earlier work that sparked this project.

ACKNOWLEDGMENTS

Linda Sneed: for research assistance.

O. T. Ventress, late Chairman of the Department of Indian Studies,
California State University, Long Beach: for encouragement,
humorous critiques, and belief in the importance of scholarship.

STAFFS OF THE FOLLOWING LIBRARIES:

The Library at California State University, Long Beach: Charles T.
Taylor, Head, Education Library; Judy Bell, Assistant.
The elementary and high school libraries of the Catron County, New
Mexico, School District: Chuck Ellis, Superintendent; Chuck
Dimwitty, High School Principal; Myrna Christiansen, School
Secretary; and Arkie Kiehne, Reserve Grade School Principal.
The Gallup, New Mexico, Public Library.
The Laguna Beach Branch of the Orange County, California, Public
Library System.
The Long Beach Unified School District Professional Library; Margaret
Dunne, Librarian.
The Los Angeles County Library System.
The New Mexico Public Library System.
The Riverside County, California, Library System.
The Springerville, Arizona, Public Library.

MARY JO LASS-WOODFIN
Editor

Reviewers

Marion Neal Faustman, Ph.D.

Administrative Consultant, California State Department of
Education, Sacramento.

Born in Cameroon, West Africa, Ms. Faustman worked her
way through college writing for the *Portland Oregonian* and published
a book of poetry early in her career. She has served throughout the state
of California as consultant for Indian educational programs, for Indian
councils, and for Indian parent organizations, including the Hupa,
Witchipick, Chumash, Miwok, and Smith River groups. She teaches
courses on psycholinguistics and educational diagnosis and prescription
at various campuses of the University of California.

Juliana Townsend Gensley, Ed.D.

Professor, School of Education, California State University,
Long Beach.

Ms. Gensley lives on a 40-acre ranch in the Santa Monica
Mountains near Calabasas, California, where she often finds artifacts
and the same plants and animals used and described by the Chumash
Indians. She published her first book, a book of poetry, at age nine, and
writes a regular feature article for the *Gifted Child Quarterly*. Her university assignments include teaching classes in early childhood education, language arts, and social studies, where she emphasizes methods
for working with gifted children and developing creative abilities. She
was active in planning the Calabasas Bicentennial celebration and frequently lectures to high school classes and other interested groups on
the Chumash culture.

Sandra L. Lass, M.A., Ph.D. Candidate

Research Associate, Department of Medical Education, School of
Medicine, University of Southern California.

Sandra Lass began her writing career at 16 with a story she sold to *Seventeen* magazine. A specialist in research and testing procedures, she works with minority students in the USC School of Medicine. Ms. Lass has served as a research consultant in medical education for numerous hospitals throughout the country. Her minor for her Ph.D. program is English, with emphasis on American Literature.

Mary Jo Lass-Woodfin, Ed.D.
　　　　Professor, School of Education, California State University,
　　　　Long Beach.
　　　　Born in Cement, Oklahoma, of mixed Scot-Irish-German and American Indian background, Ms. Woodfin directed the American Indian Heritage Project for Teachers, funded by the Ecker Foundation, Chicago, Illinois, at California State University, Long Beach, in 1974–75. As a consultant to numerous educational, governmental, and business organizations, she has given workshops in group process, creativity, teaching methodology, and teaching-learning styles. She is currently finishing a book on creative process in reading and has published numerous articles, including a photo-essay on Catron County, New Mexico, women for *Ms.* magazine.

Helen Newcastle, Ph.D.
　　　　Associate Professor, School of Education, California State
　　　　University, Long Beach.
　　　　The review editor for the campus literary magazine when she attended Duquesne University, Ms. Newcastle's career includes such diverse elements as supervising teachers and student teachers of Yaqui students near Tucson, Arizona, and devising assessment techniques of competencies for teachers training to become reading specialists. She reviews proposed books for several publishing companies and has conducted research on children's problems with written directions. Her academic teaching specialties include reading methodology, educational psychology, and educational diagnosis.

Doris Dee Tabor, Ed.D.
　　　　Professor, School of Education, California State University,
　　　　Long Beach.
　　　　Ms. Tabor has been a teacher at all grade levels from preschool to the university level. She taught Indian children in Omaha, Nebraska, and currently supervises student teachers working in classes containing Indian children. Her present university assignment includes working with the reading specialist credential program at Long Beach State, where she uses her background in speech, English, music, and

drama to advantage in teaching Ethnic Literature as part of her reading methods courses. The field of reading comprehension is one of her special concerns.

Norma Bernstein Tarrow, Ph.D.
          Professor, School of Education, California State University,
          Long Beach.

          As coordinator of foreign students in Israel for the California State University system, Ms. Tarrow lives in Jerusalem, where she continues to pursue her interest in Bedouin children. Her academic specialties include early childhood education, reading methodology and diagnosis, children's literature, and compensatory education design. She has served as a consultant for the United States Office of Education for experimental Head Start projects in New Mexico and has conducted research on children's language patternings, working with ethnic groups of all backgrounds. At present she is completing a book on early childhood education.

Introduction

Selecting books for young people is a process requiring thoughtful reflection, and questions abound to haunt the conscientious purchaser. For instance, what is a good book? What is good writing? What is a believable plot? What is a suitable illustration? What should be done about a book that is dry, but accurate; beautifully crafted, but stereotyped; well written, but poorly illustrated; movingly illustrated, but lacking in the niceties of elementary grammar and punctuation? And, of course, does anyone merit self-appointment as the one and only evaluator of the truth and the word?

When dealing with one of the most controversial, emotion-provoking, and guilt-producing subjects in today's literature—American Indians and Eskimos—the doubts increase geometrically. Indeed, many of the educators, librarians, parents, authors, and illustrators contacted in the course of writing these reviews were almost immobile in their fear of buying or producing a book that was "inaccurate" in portraying Indians and Eskimos. Realistically so, as anyone who has plowed through past and current children's books on these subjects can attest.

This immobility stems from the necessity of making hard choices. Even minor details in format can make a difference. Oftentimes, critics look first for possible errors, then allow even minor deviations in detail or format to override the general literary quality of the book; for example, the reader would almost have to be a botanist or a reservation resident to know that the ocotillo and other plant life featured prominently in the fine illustrations for Miska Miles' *Annie and the Old One* are more likely to be encountered in southern Arizona than on the Navajo Reservation.

1

Disagreements on accuracy of detail between equally knowledgeable groups are also common. For example, do Navajos will property, as detailed in *Annie and the Old One*, or not? Even Navajos
disagree as customs change. Or, would a Pueblo population ostra-
cize a small child because his mother was from a different tribe,
as Eileen Thompson suggests in *The Golden Coyote*?

Another controversy revolves around the question of "who is
the real Indian." Peter Collier, in *When Shall They Rest? The
Cherokee's Long Struggle with America*, feels that a listing on the
tribal rolls is not enough to establish one as a Cherokee; one must
be "full blood." He implies, further, that not only must the individual be of full blood but a member of one particular Cherokee
organization and not of another, to establish true "Indianness."

The stereotyping of groups in the abstract is obviously incorrect,
but what should be done about books that (1) stereotype in a positive manner, as in Ann Nolan Clark's *Circle of Seasons*: "Pueblo
Indians are gentle, kindly, laughter-loving people" (p.41); (2)
stereotype in a way that is generally acceptable today, as in Peter
Collier's *When Shall They Rest?*: (in speaking of whites) "Is it just
obsessive greed? Or is it the dangerous jealousy of people who
suspect that their way of relating to their fellow men is drastically
limited in comparison with the Indians'" (p.146); (3) stereotype
by expressing personal opinion as fact, as in Erna Fergusson's
otherwise fine and scholarly analysis of Indian dance, *Dancing
Gods*, in which she characterizes the whites as follows: "Every
year more white visitors crowd the villages, threatening the frail
roofs, making crude and loud comments, squirming in an agony of
pleasant horror to see men handle venomous snakes" (p.148) and
says of Apaches:

> Apaches are defeated. Pueblos move smoothly be-
> tween an outward conciliatory conformity to Amer-
> ican ways and an inner adherence to their customs;
> Navajos yield nothing of their own integrity as they
> slowly adopt certain mechanical aspects of white
> civilization, but the Apache seems completely con-
> quered. Even the casual observer gets the impres-
> sion that his capitulation is deeper than any
> military surrender. His savage spirit is broken . . .
> Now he is sullen and uncommunicative, often
> drunken and lazy. [p.249];

2

or (4) stereotype through the use of synonyms, using *white* as synonymous with *American*, as in the Fergusson and Collier selections, and *savage* as synonymous with *Indian*. Where does such stereotyping leave nonwhite Americans?

If, however, the buyer was determined to purchase only those books on Indians and Eskimos that were written by knowledgeable tribal members, that never used stereotyping, that contained illustrations showing in exact and minute detail the dress, life, and environment of the group depicted, and that were, in equal measure, well written, well illustrated, and accurate in every word, the final collection would be small indeed.

What is the solution to this problem? Buy every book in a spirit of "freedom of expression"? Or buy only books that come with a certificate attesting to genuine "Indianness" or "Eskimoness"? (And who'll give out the seals?) The only logical answer is to follow the same criteria in choosing books on American Indians and Eskimos that are used in purchasing books in less controversial fields:

1. Expect controversy. It is an impossible task to select a book on any subject agreeable to all readers, even in less controversial areas than the literature about American Indians and Eskimos. In addition, pressures to remove books dealing with beliefs that differ from those of an individual, a particular group of readers, or with unpopular points of view are always present. Reader access to a collection well rounded in terms of opinions, life styles, and philosophies can, to some extent, override many objections, as can intelligent discussions with young readers about controversies raised by some of the available literature. It is impossible, however, to do away entirely with controversy. In the process of bringing many points of view to the attention of young readers it must be clearly understood that, although the resultant controversies can be helpful in teaching children to understand the power of literature, there are times when disagreements cannot be resolved, times when compromise is not possible, times when the person responsible for choosing books has to say that young readers need access to this or that book even though an individual, a group, or the majority of the population feels it should not have been purchased. The decision to be the purchaser carries with it the certainty that any choices will, in fact should, be debated.

2. Become more knowledgeable about Native Americans and

3

Eskimos. Read the children's books you buy, read adult books, become more and more knowledgeable about your subject. Two good books that can help are Vine Deloria's *Custer Died for Your Sins* and Fred Bruemmer's *Seasons of the Eskimo*. Deloria presents a literate, humorous, and biting coverage of Indian/non-Indian relations, past and present. This is perhaps the most comprehensive book to date written by an Indian about Indian concerns. Bruemmer's book combines prose and photography in a poetic summary of past and present Eskimo life.

Remember, truths come in many packages, and to find the quintessence of Indian experience is an unceasing goal. To be a Navajo is not to be a Nez Percé is not to be a Creek. To live in Canyon de Chelly in 1865 is not to live in Canyon de Chelly in 1935 is not to live in Canyon de Chelly in 1985. Two Shoshone Indians living in Fort Washakie, Wyoming, in 1965 will have two different experiences to report. In short, with changes in cultural patterns an ongoing process since history began, it is difficult to know what one individual from a group will or will not do. George A. Boyce states this well in *Some People Are Indians*:

> As Indians come into contact with non-Indian ways,
> conditions change so rapidly that no one can say all
> Navajos behave in a particular manner. Nor can it
> be said that no Navajos behave in certain ways.
> [p.x]

There is a need for books written by Indians, part-Indians, and non-Indians alike. For, while it is true that no one knows an experience as deeply as one who has lived it, it is equally true that an observer can sometimes see processes that the person involved in the events cannot see until later, if ever. Many of the Indian and Eskimo legends, myths, and speeches would have been lost forever if non-Indian anthropologists, writers, and ethnologists had not recorded them; in fact the Bureau of American Ethnology was responsible for preserving many of these accounts until Indian and Eskimo writers had received sufficient education and achieved sufficient proficiency in written English to take over.

3. Read other opinions. Consult bibliographies and book reviews from a diversity of sources to learn what others see in a book under consideration. Several state departments of education publish

annotated bibliographies and selected references on American Indians and Eskimos. Especially thorough material is available from the state superintendents of public instruction of Montana, Minnesota, Massachusetts, Arizona, and Alaska, among others.

4. Use a good rating scale. Various rating scales have been developed by Native American and Eskimo groups to help evaluate children's books. The scale in *A Guide to Text Book Evaluation* (Task Force for Evaluation of Instructional Materials, P.O. Box 4003, Stanford, California, 94305) is thorough, easy to use, and helpful in choosing books that do not discriminate by age, background, race, sex, or religion.

5. Balance errors in minor details against other redeeming qualities, judging the book on the basis of overall literary quality. Even the most painstakingly researched book will often include conjecture or surmise based on the author's best hypotheses about materials, dates, or events, especially in cases where there are no living witnesses, where the details were never written down, or where the details have been altered because of hindsight, changed values, or customs. Even in books concerned with current events and issues, witnesses will differ as to the details and facts, following a Rashoman pattern of perceiving their own separate truths. A book should be purchased, then, in spite of inevitable minor errors or controversial elements that may be included, if the overall design includes a convincing reconstruction of the life of the Indian or Eskimo group depicted or believable characterization, which includes a complexity of qualities and traits, or if the background information is generally sound, the writing of high quality, and the scholarship competent. To be weighed equally is the possibility of purchasing a book characterized by factual accuracy but poor overall design, inadequate character development, awkward writing style, or weak plot development.

6. Choose selections in accordance with a specific purpose. Is the book to form the beginning of a collection? To stand alone? To round out a relatively large, but unbalanced, collection? To add a different viewpoint to a collection? Is it chosen as a gift? As a reference for an accomplished young archaeologist, historian, or writer? To present a more accurate picture of sex roles? For a young reader, for the sake of its rousing good story? The purpose, in short, should determine the selection.

Children's and Young People's Literature on American Indians and Eskimos

The literature contains few examples that show American Indians, non-Indians, or Eskimos as rounded individuals. While in former years Indians were frequently portrayed as feathered, war-whooping savages, the present trend is to portray them as silent, strong, good, pain-bearing, noble "supermen." (The word is used advisedly; there are still few stories on real life women other than the omnipresent boarding-house ones.) An exception to this trend is Bales' *Kevin Cloud,* the story of a young Ojibwa boy learning to be a person in the slums of Chicago, living a solid, close, family life full of a variety of feelings, including hope. A straightforward account of a life that is good but tough, *Kevin Cloud* is unique for many reasons. Kevin is pictured as an individual not doomed by the system, but instead having some control over his life. The reader perceives that poverty is bad, but that a child raised in poverty is not necessarily fated to accept either a poor family life, defeat, or constant struggle. This is a rare book, one that neither apologizes for the system responsible for such poverty, nor abandons its characters to a life of eternal dreariness.

EITHER/OR

Many authors apparently have a tendency to take an either/or position on Indian, as opposed to white, values, standards, and cultures (other nonwhite American groups are apparently lumped under white in this category). Peter Collier has already been cited in this regard. Even as thorough a researcher as Paul I. Wellman falls into this trap:

> From the wide view—the view of the human race as a whole—it is not right for a vast area of productive land to be kept as an unused wilderness. Too badly does the world need food and material. Where they are, men will go and make that land productive, at any cost. It has been so since history began. (p.180)

This is not to suggest that writers should adopt an "everything is wonderful in both worlds" stance, but it is the rare author today who does not extol one culture over another. And today the choice is usually in favor of the Indian.

For years, Indians were stereotyped as a group of warlike, feathered, cruel savages living in tepees. Equally disturbing was the treatment of Indians as a single people, sharing the same customs and looking alike, as, for example, in Margaret Friskey's Indian Two Foot series. Recently a more subtle prejudice has developed that portrays Indians and Eskimos as super beings from superior cultures who disdain the crassness of "white" ways. This attitude depicts the Indian who wants centralized heat or new, stylish clothes as "selling out." Indians and Eskimos who choose to cut their hair or operate gas stations or beauty parlors now run the risk of being described as cultureless creatures; they may be subjected to pressures to stay as they are, without the options for cultural change all the rest of us have. Someday, no doubt, purist writers will lament the loss of that traditional Indian mode of transportation—the pickup.

For the most part, current literature does a poor job of portraying the motivation of whites, Eskimos, and Indians alike. It is, perhaps, easier for authors to picture Indians as warriors, Eskimos as concerned only with filling their stomachs, and whites as land-hungry villains. Consider, for instance, prevalent assumptions found in most books dealing with white-Indian or white-Eskimo relations. Whites are portrayed as powerful, with no hint that governmental policies were equally unjust for them at times, as in the cases of southern reconstruction policy, denial of woman suffrage, and religious persecution, for example. Non-Indians are usually portrayed as possessing the basic comforts such as home, family, food, and power, even though they could have been the descendants of the Irish fleeing a famine; indentured servants; groups escaping religious persecution; men displaced by the European industrial revolution; southerners, black or white, fleeing a South in chaos; fugitives from the French Revolution; Mexicans who came then (as today) to improve their lives; slaves; Orientals impressed into duty on California railroads or Hawaiian pineapple fields; and the like. In reality, a poor Scandinavian immigrant who spoke little or no English had little choice; he or she could not pack up and go home to a welcoming, wealthy family in Stockholm or Copenhagen.

It is unjust to demand that one group have a right to maintain its religion and way of life, while, at the same time, demanding that another group change. For a long time, the American Indians and Eskimos were subjected to this treatment in literature; now whites, especially Christians, are on the firing line. For example, the Quakers and other denominations who managed some reservations in the past are justly faulted for their insistence that Indians become "white" in language, occupation, religion, and culture. Perhaps far worse was these agents' naïveté in business and their lack of education that delayed Indians under their jurisdiction from acquiring the know-how to get what they wanted in goods, ideas, education, and power from the majority culture.

Perhaps authors should not always sketch well-rounded characters or see all points of view. The extinction of angry authors, presenting a picture of injustice, would be a great loss, even if, in their indignation, they choose their facts accordingly. However, the adult selecting books for children needs to choose carefully, so that the child will understand that there is a wide diversity of both indignant authors and angry points of view.

The generally inadequate treatment of Eskimos and American Indians in children's literature is, of course, one of the central subjects of this entire presentation. If one specific fault could be singled out, however, it is the assumption, even by some authors who are Indian or "friendly" to the Indians' cause, that Indians are helpless. That the Indians have been and are victims is well documented; that they are not helpless or lacking in the ability to take what they want from the dominant culture is not. Tribal cooperatives, organizations of silversmiths, the sophisticated fight for Blue Lake, the organization of model school districts, well-documented court suits, successful students in graduate schools, well-run Indian centers in some cities—all need attention. Not to the exclusion of deserved attention to the inequities, injustices, prejudices; but sufficient attention to let both Indian and non-Indian readers know that there are plenty of Indians and Eskimos who have carved out a life for themselves, that they are not "helpless victims," that they do not have to depend on the cultural, emotional, and material castoffs and charities from others, that they can be in charge of their lives—or in as much charge as any other American in an increasingly complex and proscribed society. In short, the literature now available fails to give Indians and Eskimos who have made a satisfactory life for themselves their due.

Also deserving of condemnation is the use of the word *white* as synonymous with *Americans*. The groups who marched into Santa Fe and Los Angeles pueblos included few red-haired Spanish conquistadores in full armor (the heat and cold alone would have prevented the armor); most were part Indian and black, with some Spanish blood, looking for a better life. To refer to these groups as white only is inaccurate. Afro-Americans, Oriental-Americans, Hawaiian-Americans are equally ignored. Perhaps a better term would be *non-Indian*.

TECHNIQUE

A well-crafted but inaccurate book may actually be more harmful to a reader's developing of accurate pictures of Indian and Eskimo life than a poorly written one. Such books may be far more convincing because of their precision. For example, John Tomerlin's *Prisoner of the Iroquois*, a beautifully executed story based on a false assumption, that a white accepted as a tribal member would continue to be subject to harassment and torture, provides an unrealistic portrait of the Iroquois women as servile.

How far the reader's suspension of belief can be carried is another point of controversy. In E. C. Foster and Slim Williams' *The Friend of the Singing One* and its sequel, *The Long, Hungry Night*, the reader is asked to believe that an Eskimo boy shares his last bite of fish with a wolf, survives a dunking in water that would surely freeze him in seconds, and brings meat to starving Eskimos who then take time to cook it; all possible, but highly improbable.

A third problem involves the often disconcerting and time-consuming lack of page numbers or a table of contents, especially in books for primary children. Many of these are nonfiction or reference books, and it is difficult to teach library or reference skills without using page numbers. Educators even need page numbers in books of fiction for teaching such skills as vocabulary development (to refer to particularly well-written passages), or comprehension (to allow a student to refer to a page by number).

Finally, and especially in books containing legends and myths, the author fails to inform the reader about certain important details of setting or the tribe involved, thus contributing to reader confusion and stereotyping of characters. A short introductory statement or prologue providing such information could eliminate this problem.

Illustrations should also be mentioned. Occasionally a book's illustrations convey a mood unrelated to the text, to the extent of being at cross-purposes with the plot, as in Thomas Falls' *Jim Thorpe*, Frances Farnsworth's *Winged Moccasins*, and John Jakes' *Mohawk*. Before purchasing any book, careful attention to the illustrations and the format of the book as a whole should be given.

MULTIPURPOSE BOOKS

Many books offer instructional possibilities beyond pleasure or research purposes. William Wondriska's *The Stop* is a great tool for teaching such visual perception skills as form constancy and visual discrimination. Constantine Aiello's *Oo-oónah Art: Taos Indian for Child* provides fine examples to spark art students in new uses of crayons and felt markers, and illustrations such as "The Invisible Horses" on page 14 could be used to develop such basic reading skills as visual figure-ground. Another good book for teaching visual figure-ground is Fred Bruemmer's *Seasons of the Eskimos*, which includes pictures of Arctic birds almost impossible to detect against their setting. Aline Amon's *Talking Hands* provides a method for incorporating more perceptual motor training into teaching reading through the use of stories told in sign language, as well as data on every aspect of sign language. In the bibliography reviewers will point out many of these dual uses.

GENRE

Anyone wishing to choose books on American Indians and Eskimos from among those now available for children and young people needs to consider carefully the present state of the field.

Within the genres listed below, purchasers will find variations in thoroughness of coverage and ranges of opinion. To help in the selection process, the current state of each genre is summarized.

Fiction

Books on the Navajo dominate the fiction scene and have done so since Laura A. Armer's books, written in the 1930s. Other highly visible groups in fiction include the Dakota (or Sioux), the Iroquois, the Cherokee, and the Pueblo. In no instance, however, is the literature on any one tribe voluminous, complete, or exhaustive. Books on less publicized tribes may be snapped up even though they represent a highly specialized viewpoint, as in the case of the Catholic-oriented book on the Hurons by Laura N. Baker, *O Children of the Wind and Pines*, simply because there are so few.

A majority of stories about Indians are set in the past, and may give the impression that Indians are a people of the past. Those books available that concentrate on current Indian and Eskimo life styles tend to follow a limited number of themes: (1) The "boarding school" theme, in which a young person, sent to boarding school, faces the problems involved in consolidating old and new cultures (actually, boarding schools are less prevalent now, but a considerable amount of fiction is still concerned with them); (2) a sort of "Jim and Judy Visit _____land" book, in which visitors comment on "quaint" Indian customs and scenes; (3) the "life is real and earnest" theme, with a resultant lack of humor (Credit Evelyn S. Lampson and Vine Deloria with successfully injecting humor—in two entirely different ways.); (4) "Navajos (or Eskimos, or Shoshones) are just like you" books, in which cultural commonality is often reduced to cultural banality; (5) fiction in which Indians or Eskimos are incidental to the story, and the main focus is on non-Indians, as in Betty Baker's *Do Not Annoy the Indians*; and (6) stories about going back to the reservation to visit grandparents, causing a sense of déjà vu among readers who remember the farm of Dick and Jane's grandparents.

One must be careful about lumping books into categories (it would be possible to reject *Romeo and Juliet* on the basis that it is just another boy-girl love story), but it is the rare author who can use one of these themes in a fresh manner.

Fiction concerned with a young person's conflict as he or she learns to deal with two cultures represents some of the finest writing in the field, as found, for instance, in Hal Borland's *When the Legends Die* and Christie Harris' *Ravens Cry*. When successfully done, such books detail the agonies, decisions, counter-decisions, and indecisive choices young Indians and Eskimos often face.

Nonfiction

Perhaps the single most devastating criticism to be made of the nonfiction currently available is its inadequate treatment of Indian and Eskimo women. Many authors accept the thesis that war and hunting are the most exciting, productive, and important aspects of Indian life; and, since most authors evidently do not realize that women participate in these activities, as well as in all others of Indian life, they portray the women's role as an unexciting one.

In fact, most historical writing is based on artifacts and battles, with little attention directed toward the everyday lives of the peoples involved. Byrd Baylor Schweitzer's *One Small Blue Bead* is an important exception. While a fictionalized account, perhaps therefore running the risk of extrapolating beyond the available data (a danger any writer in the field of archaeology runs), the book conveys a sense of reality, that real people with real dreams and goals used the objects mentioned in the book.

Nonfiction themes also fall into patterns. Many traditional history texts follow the "Columbus gave the wrong name to Indians, and they have much to teach us" patterns. A second, favored by modern activists, is the "Columbus didn't discover us, we were already here, and when will they realize we don't all live in tepees or wear feathers" pattern. A third, used by some white authors who have lived near or visited Indian settlements, presents the "I am a friend of the Indians and share their secrets, mystical experiences, and greater wisdom." A final theme, the "Indians' greatest sport was war and hunting, women didn't count" idea, is usually employed by those authors who think history is composed merely of wars and dates.

The format of books dealing with eastern Indian tribes is often so similar that the books seem to share a common source. Such books uniformly start with a statement that Columbus mistakenly named the people he encountered *Indians*, imply that war was the greatest glory of these tribes, describe the chiefs (most of whom

13

were part white), list any wars fought between Indians and whites, and end with a few paragraphs on modern tribal conditions, the accuracy of which is subject to the publication date, the space allowed, and the author's perceptive abilities.

Autobiography and Biography

Few biographies or autobiographies feature Indian women or elaborate upon the role played by women in the lives of famous Indian men. In fact, biographies on such prominent Indian women as Pocahontas and Sacajawea usually offer a slanted portrayal of them as women who betrayed their fellow tribesmen to help the whites, whether or not this was actually the case. An important exception is Marion Gridley's *American Indian Women*, which deals more realistically with women's roles.

Most biographies of Indian men depict carefree, happy childhoods, with the individual showing great ingenuity and strength at an early age (the episode of killing a bear in hand-to-hand combat is a common theme, found in nearly identical language from biography to biography). These men invariably end up defeated, driven, and deflated in their later years, described as ineffectual, weak (if not retarded or senile) old men. In addition, few biographies deal with Indian leaders before the coming of non-Indian settlers. Such leaders either appear in legends and myths or apparently have been forgotten.

Legends and Myths

Unfortunately, the purpose of legends and myths is often confused in books dealing with storytelling available at present. Charles A. Eastman and Elaine Goodale in *Wigwam Evenings* commented on this tendency as far back as 1909. Such books often make the assumption that a myth, legend, or story must be written for children when, in reality, many were designed for adult listeners. Consequently, the concepts and language patterns of Indian or Eskimo myths and legends are often more appropriate for older readers than the book format or illustrations would suggest. In addition, the same myths and legends recur in a variety of books, as many used the same basic sources for ideas, such as the collec-

14

tions of Frank Boas or Schoolcraft, or the material collected by the Bureau of Ethnology at the end of the nineteenth and beginning of the twentieth century. Purchasers should look for the format and illustrations that suit them, as these elements apparently vary more than text.

The writing style used to retell these legends and myths seems to change over the years, from a form similar to European and Asian fairy tales and fables to the more realistic translations now available. Most are edited to delete repetition, reconcile differences between an oral form and a written one, and to facilitate the understanding of the young reader. Also, most can be read aloud with great effectiveness, a feature that speech and drama teachers can use profitably, and that will help librarians to design educational programs for their readers.

Poetry

The assumption that poems for primary-age children must be short is prevalent in many young people's books about Indian and Eskimo poetry. Consequently, poems similar to these are often found:

> The wolves are howling.
> Let this be a pleasant day.

or

> Who is my equal or can compare with me?
> I have forty whales on my beach

(from Theodore Clymer's *Four Corners of the Sky*, recommended for young children). Shortness, as evident in these selections, is not necessarily equivalent to simplicity, and should not be limited to primary grade books, as underlying the shortness and simplicity of such poems is often an intricacy of thought suitable for all. The seemingly too complex structures of some of the longer chants and poems which, at first reading, would appear too adult for primary-age children can, because of repetition of design, pleasing sound pattern combinations, and appealing rhythmic undercurrents, delight young readers. The thought and concept processes of the same poem can also furnish older readers with material for meditation, insight, and/or enjoyment of the complexities of the language used. Many chants and poems were parts of religious cere-

15

monies or tribal oral history traditions, and can provide material for laughter or thought or enjoyment at many stages of personal growth, regardless of age. In fact, grade level placement for books on Indian poetry is an especially difficult matter to decide.

Captivities

One area often found in children's literature on American Indians that causes special need for buyer introspection is that of the stories of white captives. A case in point is Evelyn Lampson's *White Captives*, the story of the Oatman children captured by the Apaches and Mojaves. Whether the treatment given the children was cruel is a controversial point; most whites would find the life of even the most providentially provided Mojave of that time difficult at best. Does this portray Indians realistically? Should there be books showing some Indians as cruel? Many people feel that this book exceeds the bounds of propriety by dealing with the subject at all; others feel that the account may very well be valid, but should not be purchased because "it doesn't do any good, anyway."

One of the subtle problems of books dealing with captivities is that they may, indeed, be some of the best written and the most delicious to read. The suspense and action often engulf the reader. That they can imply treatment that may or may not be true confuses an already complex issue. Such books do seem to follow a pattern: the happy pioneer family, the sudden killing of part of that family, the hardships of the captives as the Indians flee pursuers, the initial bewilderment due to lack of language and culture commonalities, the adoption into the tribe, the taking on of the Indian cultural characteristics, the wrenching decision to go or stay—all ingredients that make for a good story of conflict.

The perfect world for some would be one in which authors write perfect books for perfect readers who understand perfectly what the author is communicating. For the rest of us, the better world would have books of diverse opinions against whose ideas we could compare our own, to include or exclude whatever we choose to make ourselves better people, thinkers, readers. Perhaps young people's literature on Indians and Eskimos will present in the future a wider diversity of geography, tribes, and ideas to help us adults help children do this very thing.

16

Annotated Bibliography

1. Abisch, Roz, adaptor.
   'TWAS IN THE MOON OF WINTERTIME.
   Englewood Cliffs, N.J.: Prentice-Hall,
   1969. (K–3)
   The illustrations by Boche Kaplan are
   excellent, and the format is designed to
   appear as if the book were written on
   buckskin in this retelling of the Christmas
   nativity story in a Huron setting. Hurons
   are pictured as shepherds; Manitou is
   equated with God. This primary level story
   of Father Jean de Brebeuf's Christmas
   carol, reportedly the first written in the
   New World, depicts Christianity as an extension of the Huron's original religious
   practices. This is a highly specialized book
   and should be purchased accordingly; its
   prevailing Christian theme limits its usefulness. Within this limitation, the book
   is well done. Adequate.

2. Acker, Helen.
   LEE NATONI: YOUNG NAVAJO.
   New York: Abelard-Schuman, 1958.
   (4–6)
   This book contains black-and-white
   line drawings by Richard Kennedy that
   demonstrate good technique but do not especially look like Navajo children. They illustrate a story about a Navajo boy caught
   between non-Indian and Navajo values:
   The father, a "code talker" for the Army,
   wants to take his family away from the
   reservation to a better life, while his son,
   looking for a blue flower to heal a sick
   friend, finds a trailer school where he can

have the benefits of both cultures. Several
translations of Navajo chants are included in the text. New medicines are
shown as better than the Navajo healing
traditions in an "either/or" pattern. While
revealing some of the changes that are
occurring in reservation life, the book resolves its conflict in a rather facile ending.
Adequate.

3. Adams, Audrey.
   KARANKAWA BOY.
   San Antonio, Tex.: Naylor, 1965.
   (4–6)
   The author's feelings about the Karankawas is vividly revealed in the book's foreword: "You may even learn to love him,
   which would be an unusual twist of fate.
   Lovable was not a term applied to this
   irresponsible, vagabond tribe of early
   Texas Indians. Their cruel, heathenistic
   customs gave little advantage in meriting
   friendship or favor from any of their ac-
   quaintances. But then, no one is totally
   bad—not even a Kronk" (p.x). Because
   children's books on the Karankawas are
   so scarce, a buyer might purchase this
   book to round out a collection. Consider
   this carefully: the author's bias, stereotyping language, and cliché-filled writing
   overwhelms the scarcity factor. Poor.

4. Agnew, Edith J.
   NEZBAH'S LAMB.
   New York: Friendship Pr., 1954.
   (K–3)

This is a routine basal-reader type of story of a Navajo girl's anxieties about visiting a nurse. The illustrations by Jean Martinez depict the Navajo lifestyle in a kind of Navajo "Dick and Jane" fashion, as does the writing: "Nezbah had a little pet lamb. The lamb was black. Wherever the lamb went, Nezbah went, and wherever Nezbah went, the lamb went" (p.7). Adequate.

5. Aiello, Constantine, ed.
   OO-OO'NAH ART: TAOS INDIAN
   FOR CHILD; by 7th- and 8th-grade
   students of Taos Pueblo School.
   Taos, N. Mex.: Taos Pueblo Governor's
   Office, 1970. (K and up)

The Indian children writers and illustrators chosen for inclusion in this outstanding book are given by-lines and picture credits by their art teacher, Constantine Aiello. Examples of various art techniques make this book as interesting for its art instruction possibilities as for its detailing of Indian art and Pueblo children. Effective use of such simple media as crayon and felt-tip pens create unusual color results; for example, the Invisible Horses on page 14, composed of black, white, and brown patterns, would be good for teaching such basic reading skills as visual figure-ground. Good.

6. Alderman, Clifford Lindsey.
   JOSEPH BRANT: CHIEF OF THE
   SIX NATIONS.
   New York: Messner, 1958. (6–8)

This biography of Joseph Brant, a chief of the Six Nations, portrays him as a sycophant to the whites of his time, a chief who brands as traitors all who disagree with him, and a Christian with little tolerance for those of the "Long House" religion, including his own son. Brant, a complex man living in a bewildering time, deserves better than this. The simplistic, moralistic tone of the writing can be judged on the following: "You and your braves will go with Colonel Williams, Teoniakigarawe" (p.9); "There was much to talk over with his sister, for he had been

away two years" (p.63); "Could he be of more help to his people by going back to work with Mr. Stuart at Fort Hunter or by remaining with Guy Johnson?" (p.93); "Then, with black looks, the traitors slunk away" (p.178); "As though the evil fates that had dealt the war chief so many blows were satisfied at last, the peaceful years began" (p.181). The book includes a bibliography and an index. **Poor.**

7. Alderman, Clifford Lindsey.
   OSCEOLA AND THE SEMINOLE WARS.
   New York: Messner, 1973. (5–7)

In a stilted fashion (e.g., "As the American troops marched out of Fort Brooke that December 23, they made a brave show in their dark-blue, gilt-buttoned coats and sky-blue trousers, with sharply contrasting white cross-belts" [p.75]), this book follows the career of Osceola from his boyhood, through the Seminole migrations, as a warrior, and finally as a prisoner. The author brings unusual facts to the attention of the reader, such as the Black Drink for warriors and the Red Sticks versus the White Sticks in Creek tribal disputes. Osceola is portrayed throughout as a brilliant commander. An interesting sidelight is Alderman's apologies for the Seminoles' practice of slavery: "And, although the red men themselves sometimes enslaved the runaways, they were benevolent masters" (p.10)—the excuse used throughout history to justify withholding freedom. The book includes an index and a bibliography. Adequate.

8. Alexander, C. I.
   AN INTRODUCTION TO NAVAJO
   SAND PAINTINGS.
   Santa Fe: New Mexico Museum of
   Navajo Ceremonial Arts, 1967.
   (7 and up)

This scholarly introduction to Navajo sand painting links history, linguistics, legends, and religion to the basic purposes for sand painting—healing ceremonies and illustrations of Navajo mythology. The book mentions several little-known points, such as the fact that sand painting, "in simplified form, is practiced today by Australian aboriginees" (p.12). A publication of the Museum of Navajo Ceremonial Arts, the book includes an adequate bibliography. Not a book for casual reading; it would have profited from the inclusion of more sand painting illustrations. Good.

9. Allen, Leroy.
SHAWNEE LANCE.
New York: Delacorte Pr., 1970. (6–8)
Allen writes well, capturing the reader's interest and moving the story along briskly. Some of the assumptions in the basic story, which involves a captive white boy of 14, suffering from discrimination from the Shawnee because he is white, in his attempt to decide whether to go back to the whites or stay with the Indians, may be hard to accept. White captives, after being accepted into the tribe, usually were treated as well as Shawnee children of the same age; this treatment, however, may have seemed unusually harsh to captives who had known easier prior lives. The author does not resolve the main character's dilemma at the end, leaving readers a chance to use their own imagination. Adequate.

10. Allen, T. D.
NAVAHOS HAVE FIVE FINGERS.
Norman: Univ. of Oklahoma Pr., 1963. (9–12)
A young white couple, volunteers at a clinic on the Navajo Reservation, produced this personal interpretation of Navajo history and customs. Flip section headings such as "Don't Take Any Wooden Indians" and "Navahos in Labor" seem at variance with the rest of the text. The writing, while not exemplary, is interesting: "The Army called on Kit Carson, a man wise in the ways of Indian warfare. He bribed Utes, Mexicans, Pueblos, Hopis to help. To receive pay for robbing your arch-enemy struck them as good strategy" (p.7). The photographs accompanying the text help provide further understanding of the experiences described. Educators, librarians, parents, and other purchasers may wish to supplement this with other books featuring Indians helping whites. Good.

11. Allen, T. D.
TALL AS STANDING ROCK.
Philadelphia: Westminster, 1963. (6–8)
The writing, competent, but not exceptional, carries the reader along, especially in the dialogues between the main character and his girl when they decide to get an education before they marry. The hero is a Navajo boy who dropped out of school after the sixth grade, caught between his desire to become a singer and his family's real need for medical care. The story does not take into account some recent cooperative efforts between hospitals and Navajo medicine men. Occasional asides unintentionally reflect the author's condescension: "Nonie's husband had gone to Illinois to work on the railroad, so he wasn't there ironing or weaving a bead belt the way he would be again, after he had earned enough to live on unemployment pay awhile" (p.11), or "She's [Nonie] pretty now, Ann thought, but she's going to get fat. Too bad. Still, she reminded herself, mutton stew and 'fry' bread aren't carrot sticks" (p.65). Adequate.

12. Allen, T. D., ed.
THE WHISPERING WIND: POETRY BY YOUNG AMERICAN INDIANS.
Garden City, N.Y.: Doubleday, 1972. (7 and up)
A collection of poetry by young Indian writers, this book includes brief biographies of the contributors that furnish insights into their lives. The preface contains an interesting history of American Indian literature, occasionally reflecting the authors' point of view, as in the use of the word *adaptable* in the following quote: "Following World War II, cultural isolationism gave way and the adaptable Navajo clamored for schools" (p.xiv). The authors give unusual praise to the Bureau

of Indian Affairs* for the Institute of American Indian Arts at Santa Fe, New Mexico, where the contributors attended school. The poems, while reflecting Indian thought, also often stress themes familiar to young non-Indians, which serve to strengthen the book even further. Good.

13. Amon, Aline.
TALKING HANDS: INDIAN SIGN LANGUAGE.
Garden City, N.Y.: Doubleday, 1968. (2–4)
Comments on contemporary sign language, such as that used by umpires or drivers, discussions of sentence patterning, and inclusion of stories in sign language all provide unusual instructional possibilities for this book: for example, English teachers at appropriate grade levels could teach syntax and structure utilizing these perceptual-motor techniques. The book may be too complicated in parts for unsupervised use by elementary children, as in the discussion of possessives on page 11 and the various definitions for the same sign, given as *before*, *ahead*, and *future time*. The black-white-blue illustrations by the author do show Indians wearing the archetypal feather, and the book is directed to boys: "It can even help you make secret plans with a friend when your little sister will not leave you alone" (p.8). The book would be stronger and more useful if it were rewritten to include girls as well as boys, both in illustrations and in content, and the rating reflects this omission. Adequate.

14. Anderson, LaVere.
QUANAH PARKER: INDIAN WARRIOR FOR PEACE.
Champaign, Ill.: Garrard, 1970. (2–4)
Illustrated by numerous pictures and the drawings of Russell Hoover, this is a fictionalized account of the Comanche chief Quanah Parker. The writing is routine, and the author adds motivating facors that do not always ring true. For in-

*Hereinafter referred to as the BIA.

stance, the idea that Quanah would be plagued by other Comanches about his white blood simply ignores reality: " 'Look at Quanah!' Little Cloud shouted. 'He is trying to wash away his white man's smell' " (p.15). The photograph of Quanah Parker opposite the frontispiece is good. Adequate.

15. Anderson, La Vere.
SITTING BULL: GREAT SIOUX CHIEF.
Champaign, Ill.: Garrard, 1970. (2–5)
In a simply written story beautifully illustrated by Casy, the author proposes another series of explanations for Sitting Bull's childhood and how he received his famous name. According to this account, he was originally named Slow, first because "he took time to think before he acted" and, second, "a boy needed to think carefully and to be on his guard in the Dakota Country in 1843." Sitting Bull acquired his new name from his father, Jumping Bull, when he struck the enemy and counted coup at a very young age. The author tells how Sitting Bull became a leader of his people and describes several Indian wars on the prairie, including the battle at the Little Big Horn. A rather bizarre inclusion is the description of Sitting Bull's death, in which his horse, presented to him by Buffalo Bill when he left the Wild West Show, begins to do his tricks, cued by the same gunfire that killed his master. Apparently the horse was one of the few survivors. Adequate.

16. Anderson, Susanne.
SONG OF THE EARTH SPIRIT.
A Friends of the Earth Series.
New York: McGraw-Hill, 1973. (6 and up)
The author-photographer accompanies each of her photographs of the Navajo in this volume with a personally oriented explanatory text. A skilled craftsman, her photographs are different from those illustrating most books on the Navajo. Some of her portraits of Navajo women catch a unique spirit of independence, as well as the more customary sense of strength.

Other compositions demonstrating her unique viewpoint include views of sheep and a pickup (p.28), snow (p.47), a Navajo boy on a motorcycle (p.45), the transition in dress patterns (p.85), and the Indian hard-hat worker (p.103). This book represents more than three years' work in remote parts of the reservation. The author never falls into the fallacy of believing that she knows the Navajo; she tells what happened to her without added, undue generalization. Photographers, as well as readers interested in the Navajo, will find this book a source for ideas. Good.

17. Andrist, Ralph K.
THE LONG DEATH: THE LAST DAYS OF THE PLAINS INDIANS.
New York: Collier Book, 1969.
(8 and up)
Beginning and ending with the massacre at Wounded Knee, the last major battle between the Plains Indians and the United States, this excellent book tells the story of the conquering of the Plains. The author's description of these wars is in contrast to the high-adventure style of writing frequently indulged in by writers describing this era:

> The wars of the plains [were] not clean, crisp little tableaux of cavalry with singing trumpets and snapping guidons meeting thundering charges of Sioux and Cheyenne warriors against a backdrop of grass bending in waves to the horizon and thunderheads piling up against a western sky. They were not that kind of conflict at all. As in all wars, men died unpleasantly, and often in extreme agony. Women and children suffered along with the warrior and the soldier, and the Army made it a part of strategy to destroy the enemy's food and possessions in order to leave him cold, hungry, and without the will to resist. [p.3]

Andrist draws a fascinating picture of the differences between the surrender at Appomattox and that at Wounded Knee, although the southerners did not get off as lightly as he describes. The small type makes the book difficult to read and look

more forbidding than it is. An excellent source book for adults, as well as a reference for advanced junior high and high school readers, the book contains a middle section of photographs, a bibliography, and an index. A classic. Good.

18. Annixter, Jane, and Annixter, Paul.
WHITE SHELL HORSE.
New York: Holiday House, 1971.
(7 and up)
Set against the background of the Long Walk, this story of a boy and his horse demonstrates Navajo customs and pride. The illustrations by Andy Tsinahjinnie are outstanding. Well written, the book sweeps the reader along in a satisfying story. The "chief" may be given more power in the story than was customary at that time. A short glossary of Navajo and Spanish words is found at the end of the book. Good.

19. Antell, Will.
WILLIAM WARREN: THE STUDY OF AN AMERICAN INDIAN.
Minneapolis, Minn.: Dillon Pr., 1973.
(4-6)
Antell achieves an excellent blend of simple language and good writing in this book:

> It is impossible to understand Indian history by looking at the shape of a moccasin. An arrowhead found on a lonely beach will not give you a true picture of Indian life. You will not know the real feelings of an Indian by riding in a birch bark canoe. [p.1]

This is the story of William Warren, the son of an American fur trader and a French-Ojibwa mother, who was elected to the Minnesota Territorial Legislature at a time when Indians did not vote, and who is famous for his *History of the Ojibways*, published posthumously. The author makes use of unusual facts: for instance, details of Warren's clan, fasting as a means for children to learn about—and to better—themselves, and Warren's statement of prophecy about Duluth and Superior. Black-and-white pictures by different artists add greatly to the reader's enjoyment. This book is as much about Ojibwas as about William Warren. Good.

20. Anton, Ferdinand, and Dockstader, Frederick J.
PRE-COLUMBIAN ART AND LATER INDIAN TRIBAL ARTS.
New York: Abrams, 1968. (7 and up)
This book includes a short, highly selective account of the artistic history of the Indians in pre-Columbian Arctic America, the Northwest Coast, the Prairies, the Woodlands, and the Southwest. Although too brief, the section concerned with the selected American Indian and Eskimo groups does put their art into perspective, and the authors make the interesting generalization that Indian art was not "free"; that it had specific functions and duties. Not all art historians would agree with this theory. The illustrations are good, particularly those in color, and the art examples chosen are representative and well done. The book includes a bibliography and an index. Adequate.

21. Appleton, LeRoy H.
AMERICAN INDIAN DESIGN AND DECORATION.
New York: Dover, 1971. (5 and up)
Although the reading level for this book is grade five and above, it can easily be used at all levels. The design presentations could spark primary children's art work; some of the stories could be read aloud to middle graders; and the material could be used by advanced readers in grades three and four. Art, as broadly defined by this author, includes painting, building, and storytelling; consequently, poetry and legends are as much a part of the text as design motifs. The illustrations are excellent, and the publisher gives readers permission for up to ten reproductions of each. The format, contents, and illustrations depict the universality of Indian art; the author, however, limits this universality in scope and gender in his writing: "His [the Indian's] art is social" (p.1). The book includes a bibliography and an index. Good.

22. Archer, Jules.
INDIAN FOE, INDIAN FRIEND.
New York: Crowell-Collier, 1970.
(7–12)
The life of Lieutenant General William Selby Harney is used as a focal point for a delineation of Indian wars and atrocities against Indians committed by whites. General Harney fought Indians and then fought for them with the United States government, aborting his own career in the process. The book details the numerous law cases involving Indians and whites over the years to the present. In the discussion of contemporary events, the author occasionally overstates his case. For instance, he generalizes that most Americans did not know of the discrimination against Indians in his description of the Poor People's Campaign of June, 1968:

> The appearance of Indians in this demonstration startled most Americans viewing the event on television. It was common knowledge that the other groups were being discriminated against under the American system. But Indians? Surely any injustices *they* had suffered had long since been made up to them! [p.1]

His occasional use of the term *red men* may offend some Indian and/or feminist readers. These problems are relatively minor, however, in this a monumental, well-researched volume by a very angry author. The middle section contains an interesting selection of black-and-white photos, prints, and paintings, and there is a bibliography and an index. Good.

23. Armer, Laura Adams.
DARK CIRCLE OF BRANCHES.
New York: Longman, 1933. (6–8)
From its black-and-white illustrations of slender figures in old-fashioned dress that remind the reader that Art Deco can look Indian, to the variations from the usual spelling of Navajo words (*Shama, Tinneh, Pelicanos, Nakai*), this book is a constant surprise. The story of a crippled Navajo boy at the time of Canyon de Chelly and the Long Walk, the author's reverence for her subjects emerges con-

stantly. Her gentleness toward her characters even extends to Kit Carson, who probably never had a more sympathetic portrayal:

> She sat on the floor near the fire, cooking her corn bread. The small, red haired Pelicano stood beside her. Despite his deep frown and peering eyes, he looked at her kindly. He had orders from Washington to treat women and children considerately, but Kit Carson needed no orders for that. He knew Indian women. Two of them had been wife to him. [p.152]

Readers will enjoy the book's unexpected phrasing; for example, "Few Navahos understood why they must leave the home of their mothers" (p.163). Good.

24. Armer, Laura Adams.
IN NAVAJO LAND.
New York: McKay, 1962. (4 and up)
In this book, Laura Adams Armer provides a diary-type record of her journeys among the Navajo. Privileged to attend sacred ceremonials, to witness the execution of traditional sand paintings, and to observe the elaborate tribal dances, the author's spiritual kinship with the Navajo permeates the text. Photographs enhance the text. The book may be supplemented with others that provide a Navajo view of white customs. Good.

25. Armer, Laura Adams.
WATERLESS MOUNTAIN.
New York: McKay, 1931. (5–8)
Little Singer, a young boy born in the early 1900s into a traditional Navajo family, gains a great deal of wisdom from the wonders around him. He especially learns from his uncle, a medicine man, and wishes to become one himself. Throughout the book Navajo legends are used, crossing reality and fantasy, making the book more interesting and enjoyable. This story would be a good focus for a discussion of the differences between reality and fantasy in teaching critical reading skills. The illustrations are excellent. Good.

26. Armstrong, Virginia Irving.
I HAVE SPOKEN: AMERICAN HISTORY THROUGH THE VOICES OF THE INDIANS.
New York: Pocket Books, 1972.
(4 and up)
A chronological compilation of both famous and unfamiliar Indian speeches from the seventeenth to the twentieth century, this book begins with Powhatan's statement in 1609: "Will you take by force what you may obtain by love? Why will you destroy us who supply you with food?" (p.1), and ends on page 188 with a speech by an unknown Indian grandfather: "I believe that we will survive, I still believe we will survive. That is our dream." Some white speeches and documents are included, such as Judge Dundy's decision in 1879 on the Standing Bear versus George Crook case. The preface is scholarly and informative, and the notes section is thoroughly done. Many of the speeches could be read aloud with profit to elementary grade children. Speech and drama teachers, as well as English and social science teachers, will find this book invaluable. The bibliography and index are well done. Good.

27. Arnold, Elliott.
BROKEN ARROW.
New York: Duell, 1954. (6–9)
Well written by a master craftsman, this is a rewrite of *Blood Brother* in more elementary language, and is the story of the relationship between Cochise and Tom Jeffords. It concentrates on Cochise's sons, and indicates a great deal of research on the author's part. Cochise may, in fact, be given more power in the book than he had in reality. The story concerns two remarkable men, and although somewhat romanticized, the fiction does them both justice. The book ends at a happy time, when Jeffords becomes agent to the Chiricahuas, before his resignation because the treaty provisions were violated and the Apaches were mistreated. It does not include the romance between Jeffords and the Apache girl that held such a prominent position in the adult edition. Fascinating reading provided by a dependable writer. Good.

28. Arnold, Elliott.
THE SPIRIT OF COCHISE.
New York: Scribner, 1972. (7 and up)
This is the story of an Indian man who comes home from Vietnam to a reservation that hasn't changed. He opens an Apache cooperative general store, closing down the dishonest white trader. The author obviously has done his research. While the writing is not up to Arnold's usual standard, and some of the character portrayals are excessively stereotyped, the book does show that Indians can help themselves. Adequate.

29. Arnold, Elliott.
WHITE FALCON.
New York: Knopf, 1955. (7 and up)
This book relates the story of a white man held captive by the Indians during the fight for control of the fur trade by the North West and Hudson's Bay companies, and shows evidence of solid author research. It is well written, but the technically excellent illustrations by Frederick T. Chapman, primarily of the "horses, war, and feathers" variety, are of limited value. The portrayal of the captive's life seems unrealistic: "His life was brutal from the start. He was hated as a stranger and as a white man" (p.13); "And the more Indian he became, the more the Indians hated him" (p.15). Most captives were treated as well as the tribe's children of the same age, once they had been adopted. The book won a William Allen White Award in 1958. Good.

30. Arnold, Owen.
SAVAGE SON.
Albuquerque: Univ. of New Mexico Pr., 1951. (6–8)
This story of an Apache child, kidnapped by Pimas when he was six, who became a leading society doctor in Chicago at age 31 seems incredible, but the author documents his presentation with interviews and newspaper accounts. The first part of the book is written in the form of a novel; the second half is documentary. The author writes well: "There are two or three known ways to catch mice.

Pondering them now, the lad decided to try yet a new method" (p.1). His explanation for the main character's motives as he withered away into an unfought death, however, do not seem adequate or thorough. Appendixes include a biography of Charles Gentile, who bought Montezuma, the Apache boy, from the Pimas; a discussion of Pima calendar sticks; a review of Montezuma's relatives; and an explanation for Montezuma's motives for his actions. Good.

31. Atkinson, M. Jourdan.
INDIANS OF THE SOUTHWEST.
San Antonio, Tex.: Naylor, 1963.
(6–8)
Concentrating on the Indians of Texas rather than the entire Southwest, as stated in the title, this book is uneven and jerky in its language. Unrelated, poorly written episodes characterize the writing and organization, with numerous stereotypes: "Superficially speaking, the Comanche women, according to many chroniclers, were a lousy lot. Nevertheless, they are admitted to have been industrious, learned in their arts, and accredited, even by fastidious white men, with a large amount of family affection and family pride" (p.287). The reader would probably not suspect that a section entitled "The Social Whirl" would include a discussion of the laws of hospitality, the caste system, and Indian orchestras. Other chapter headings are equally obscure and banal, such as "Garden Patch" or "The Riders of the Plains." The author's kind words for the Old Spanish and English chroniclers of Indian history and culture are not echoed by many other writers. Poor.

32. Aubry, Claude.
AGOUHANNA.
Garden City, N.Y.: Doubleday, 1972.
(6 and up)
Aubry's plot, while exciting, does not indicate that boys had options other than to become warriors in Iroquois life before the coming of the whites. Agouhanna is the gentle, peace-loving son of Black Eagle, chief of the Iroquois. His love of

nature, preference for the protection of the fort rather than the adventures of the hunt, and his hatred of violence and bloodshed set him apart from his peers and make him a source of concern to his father. Agouhanna manages to survive the hunting and endurance tests required of future warriors through the help of his best friend and luck. During his final test (to live in the forest alone without food) he overcomes his fears, saves his tribe from a surprise attack, and is judged worthy to be the successor to his father, leader of the tribe. The Iroquois are not portrayed as preferring violence and bloodshed, but even the daily hunting and sporadic fights with tribal enemies are abhorred by Agouhanna. This story is so well written and moves along so briskly that it seems overly particular to remind the reader that chieftainships are not necessarily hereditary and that the usual Indian system is to allow children to develop their own patterns. The descriptions of Iroquois customs and life styles are vivid and interesting. The fact that Iroquois children are rarely punished and have relatively more freedom than white children is brought out. The main character, because he is pictured as being so different from the others, might cause a stereotype of opposite character traits to develop. The black-and-white illustrations by Julie Brinkloe are well done. Good.

33. Averill, Esther.
KING PHILLIP: THE INDIAN CHIEF.
New York: Harper, 1950. (5–9)
Told from the point of view of a young Pilgrim growing up shortly after King Philip's death, the story provides an interesting contrast in cultures and cultural conflicts, not only between the Indian and white cultures, but also between whites (e.g., Plymouth Colony versus Rhode Island Colony). The book is written with clarity and sensitivity. Most of the characters are fully developed, but none seem so fictionalized as to become either superheroic or mysterious. The customs and beliefs of the Algonquin tribes are described in great detail. The inability of these tribes

to unite and move as one cohesive group to withstand the constant wave of white settlers who invaded and populated Indian lands is documented. Black-and-white illustrations by Vera Belsky include maps identifying both white and Indian settlements. A brief but helpful pronouncing dictionary identifying Indian names and places is included at the end of the book. Good.

34. Bahti, Tom.
SOUTHWESTERN INDIAN
CEREMONIALS.
Flagstaff, Ariz.: KC Publications,
1970. (5 and up)
Noteworthy illustrations by modern Indian artists and photographs by K. C. Den Dooven combine with the sensitive writing of Tom Bahti to give the reader an understanding and feel for the ceremonials of many Southwestern tribes including the Navajo, Pueblo, Zuñi, Hopi, Apache, Papago, and Yaqui. The author reminds the reader that "superstition, it should be recalled, is the other man's religion" (p.2) and that "no [Indian] group presumed its religion to be superior to that of another and certainly no tribe ever conducted warfare against another for the purpose of forcing its religious beliefs upon them" (p.3). A history of non-Indian suppression of Indian religions is provided, and a calendar of Southwestern ceremonials is included. Good.

35. Bahti, Tom.
SOUTHWESTERN INDIAN TRIBES.
Flagstaff, Ariz.: KC Publications,
1968. (4 and up)
Tom Bahti has a sensitivity for Indian heritage and a thorough background in research; he writes well; and he tries to provide a balanced account of white-Indian cultural clashes. Every once in a while, however, his anger at the way Indians have been treated lashes out. For example, he writes sarcastically of the belief held by some whites of a future "golden cultural sunset" in which "the Indian may remain quaint in his crafts, colorful in his religion, and wise in his

philosophy–*but* still reasonable enough in his relations with us (the superior culture) to see things our way" (back cover). Bahti is wise enough to realize that the Indians' submission was and is often more apparent than real:

> The Spaniards also imposed the law of the Indies which decreed that each [Indian] village elect a governor, lieutenant governor and other officials to handle secular affairs. The Indians obligingly added this new political system to their theocratic form of government and the cacique or priest-chief continued to function as the real head of the village. [pp.4–5]

This book is filled with facts, many of them unpleasant; for example, under Spanish rule the Pueblos were reduced in population by one-half. Fine color and black-and-white pictures supplement the author's commentary. This is an unusually thorough, survey type of volume; it is a good reference and travel book for vacationers who want more than pleasant pap for holiday reading. Good.

36. Bailey, Paul.
GHOST DANCE MESSIAH.
Los Angeles: Westernlore Pr., 1970.
(6–9)

This book is about Wovoka, a remarkable Paiute who, in the space of three years, initiated a religious movement that spread from tribe to tribe in the West, culminating in the massacre at Wounded Knee. Wovoka was not above using the tricks of the shaman to convince those who followed him, as well as skeptics, that he, indeed, possessed supernatural powers. He is, nevertheless, depicted as sincerely dedicated to the betterment of his people. The author succeeds in bringing out Wovoka's human qualities, and dramatizes events to an extent improbable in a strictly historical approach. Good.

37. Bailey, Ralph Edgar.
THE STORY OF NELSON A. MILES:
INDIAN FIGHTER.
New York: Morrow, 1965. (7 and up)

Except for the first chapter, describing Miles's career as an officer in the Union Army, this book presents the story of one white man's relationship with Indians at the close of the Indian wars from his own, personal point of view. Although an antagonist and a fighting man, Miles is portrayed as an individual who thoroughly understood and sometimes sympathized with his Indian enemies. He fought the Kiowas, Comanches, Sioux, Cheyenne, and chiefs Sitting Bull and Crazy Horse, as well as Chief Joseph and the Nez Percés. The book is extremely well written and well balanced, but is most definitely directed toward an audience who understands and enjoys reading about wars, military forces, battle strategies, and the geography of the Southwest. A series of maps is included, illustrating the Civil War and the Indian campaigns in which Miles participated. Miles's wife, Mary, is the only woman in the book described in any detail. Despite its limitations, the book is clearly written and elaborates upon the brilliant military strategies of Sitting Bull, Crazy Horse, and Chief Joseph who, until completely overwhelmed, managed to keep the U.S. Army at bay in a period of history when Indians lost more battles than they won. Good.

38. Baker, Betty.
AND ONE WAS A WOODEN INDIAN.
New York: Macmillan, 1970. (5–9)

Betty Baker attempts a difficult feat: a comic story of Apache life in the late 1850s. The plot involves two boys and their manhood tests. The main character has poor eyesight; in the course of his trials, however, he learns the importance of inner, rather than external, sight and decides to become a shaman. The book is sometimes difficult to read, in part because the author uses so much dialogue that the reader often loses track of the speaker. The Afterwards section is well done. Adequate.

39. Baker, Betty.
AT THE CENTER OF THE WORLD.
New York: Macmillan, 1973. (3–6)

This book is a well-written collection of creation myths of the Pima and Papago. Because the author is aware that "modern collections of myths show little resemblance to those recorded almost a hundred years ago" (p.52), she has combined several of the earliest versions of each myth extant. This is a good book to read aloud to young children and could serve as a model for creative writing students interested in children's books. Good.

40. Baker, Betty.
THE BIG PUSH.
New York: Coward-McCann, 1972. (1–3)
This story, based on a true incident, details Hopi life in the early 1900s; it depicts the forced entry of the Hopi into the white world. References are made to Hopi ceremonies. Navajos are presented from what the author apparently believes to be the Hopi point of view. In using this book with children, give them access to other books on Hopi-Navajo relations to provide young readers a chance to learn the various sides of this intertribal controversy. Adequate.

41. Baker, Betty.
DO NOT ANNOY THE INDIANS.
New York: Macmillan, 1968. (4–6)
This is a well-told, funny story, primarily focused on a white family that comes to Yuma to manage the stagecoach line in 1857. The Yuma Indians are a part of the plot, but are not analyzed in any great depth. They do serve to teach the family about the West and about prejudice, as the young son, especially, learns to deal with his feelings. For example:
Tebarro rubbed a scratch on his ankle. After a moment he said, "Only true men dream. Kwanami say white men do not dream." "We do so," Jeff said. "Where do you think the cities and boats and stage coaches come from?" "Those real." "They come from dreams." [pp.93–94]
Story line: Good. Incidental portrayal of Yuma Indians: Adequate.

42. Baker, Betty.
KILLER-OF-DEATH.
New York: Harper, 1963. (5–7)
Betty Baker has obviously done her research for this book and it is well written, although in a more flowery style than customary: "Tight against the Divide on the east flows the Rio Grande and beyond that stretches the dreaded White Sands" (p.1). The story concerns the feud and subsequent friendship of two Apache boys who lived at the time the whites were moving in. Baker defines the authority of Apache chiefs well: "Everyone knows that with age comes wisdom, so his order was obeyed" (p.4). Historical events form part of the plot, but she did not use actual place names, which could have served to orient the reader. John Kaufman's black-and-white illustrations are good and deserve more prominence, as they lose impact in the small space they are allotted. Good.

43. Baker, Betty.
LITTLE RUNNER OF THE LONGHOUSE.
New York: Harper, 1962. (K–2)
The story of a young Iroquois boy of the past, this book is simplistic fiction that tells little of Iroquois life. The cherubic Indian children that dominate Arnold Lobel's illustrations show his artistic ability but do not add to the story. The whole effect of the illustrations and the text is affected. An easy book for a young reader to enjoy, it is not heavy enough for learning or inspiring thoughtfulness. Adequate.

44. Baker, Betty.
THE SHAMAN'S LAST RAID.
New York: Harper, 1963. (3–6)
This is the story of a modern Apache family who live in Arizona. The children's great-grandfather, an Indian shaman, comes to visit, and they are shocked and displeased when the dignified old man decides that many of their ways are "not Indian," including eating hamburger and sleeping in a house. In the process of learning more about their Indian culture to please great-grandfather, the children begin to appreciate the values of the Apache way. When a television company

comes to Arizona to film a movie about Indian life, great-grandfather gets to make his "last raid," and the children take pride in all that he represents. A well-paced story with interesting characterizations, a new look at cultural conflict and understanding between the generations, and a touch of humor, this book is designed to be read by intermediate grade children. The book is marred somewhat by stereotyping of the sexes; for instance, the boy, not the girl, has the insight that he must learn to be his own kind of Indian and make a unique place of his own in the world. Good.

45. Baker, Betty.
A STRANGER AND AFRAID.
New York: Macmillan, 1972. (7–8)
In a good story filled with interest and adventure, this book tells of Sopete and Zabe, young Pawnee boys taken captive and living among the Zuñi. The younger brother, Zabe, has learned to enjoy life after his three years of captivity; the older brother, Sopete, yearns to return to his life with the Prairie Indians. As the Spanish invaders approach the Cicuye pueblo, Sopete sees an opportunity to escape and return to his people. Although Baker focuses on male characters, she includes enough women to provide a balance. A map of Coronado's route from Mexico through Kansas is included. Good.

46. Baker, Betty.
THREE FOOLS AND A HORSE.
New York: Macmillan, 1975. (1–2)
These are Apache tall tales about a tribe of Indians the Apaches invented as a brunt for their humorous stories. Excellent use of repetition by the writer gives opportunities for teaching primary reading vocabulary, yet also preserves a valid language pattern in which the repetition forms an integral part of the story and not a basal-text wording exercise. In using this book with children, either as a read-aloud book or as an enjoyable silent reading item, discussion time should be scheduled to explore the concept that this book shows some ways Apaches joke, and that these are a type of tall tale, not a factual account

of how Apache people behave. The color illustrations by Glen Rounds are particularly good. Good.

47. Baker, Betty.
WALK THE WORLD'S RIM.
New York: Harper, 1965. (5–8)
In this well-written book, Betty Baker uses as background the story of Cabeza de Vaca, Esteban, and the three other Spaniards who survived of some 600 who began the expedition. The Spaniards were captured and lived among Gulf Coast Indians for seven years. In the story another captive, a Cheyenne Indian boy, helps Cabeza de Vaca and the others escape, goes with them to Mexico, and brings back horses to the Cheyenne. Esteban is portrayed more sympathetically here than he usually is; in this book he dies to help the boy. The author includes a bibliography. Good.

48. Baker, Laura Nelson.
O CHILDREN OF THE WIND AND PINES.
Philadelphia: Lippincott, 1967. (2–4)
One of the few available stories about the Huron Indians, this book is based on materials gathered by the Jesuits in the early days of French colonization and is, therefore, highly Catholic-oriented. A fictionalized account of Father de Brébeuf and a little Huron girl named Atatase, the plot centers around her conversion to Christianity, setting up a conflict situation that places conversion in the best light. The author's writing style and religious bias is obvious: " 'Who was right?' Atatase wondered. She admired her father very much. He was the bravest and best hunter in their village. Still, he didn't seem as powerful as the Frenchmen [priests]" (p.16). The illustrations by Inez Storer contain small, undetailed figures suggested through an interesting art technique using a minimum of lines. Adequate.

49. Balch, Glenn.
HORSE OF TWO COLORS.
New York: Crowell, 1969. (5–9)

This book provides historical and cultural information in fictionalized form as it develops the story of the Nez Percé and their spotted horses. Two captive Nez Percé boys are traded to the Spaniards in New Mexico at the start of the colonial period. They escape with a spotted horse. The horse dies of wounds, but not before siring a colt. The story moves slowly, and the writing is adequate but not especially inspired. Lorence Bjorklund's black-and-white illustrations are well done. Adequate.

50. Balch, Glenn.
INDIAN PAINT.
Binghampton, N.Y.: Scholastic, 1972. (7–9)
Plot lines of this story center around Little Falcon, son of the great Chief War Cloud, who disappoints his father when he selects a mare as his horse. The story details Little Falcon's pride and problems in training his horse. A good tale of adventure and achievement over adversity, this will appeal to intermediate-grade and older readers. Although the main character is a boy, often the case in books about Indians, it is possible to use this book as a starting point for a discussion of the customs of Indian children; it also seems to be designed with non-Indian rather than Indian readers in mind. Adequate.

51. Balch, Glenn.
INDIAN SADDLE-UP.
New York: Apollo, 1970. (6–8)
Accurate but stilted writing characterizes this story of how the Indians got horses. An "adventure" tale for boys, the book has all the drawbacks and advantages this term implies, including extensive stereotyping, especially of women. Adequate.

52. Baldwin, Gordon C.
AMERICA'S BURIED PAST: THE STORY OF NORTH AMERICAN ARCHAEOLOGY.
New York: Putnam, 1962. (5–8)
The why, how, when, and where of archaeology are presented in a style that will appeal to children and young people.

Discoveries in the Ohio, Mississippi, and Missouri river valleys and in the Southwest are described in detail. The book is illustrated with photographs, some of actual sites, others of dioramas that recreate scenes of ancient Indian life. This book is interesting and accurate, presenting methods of discovery in an exciting but factual style. Written for children in grades five and above, the book would be valuable for the teacher's library as well. Good.

53. Baldwin, Gordon C.
THE ANCIENT ONES: BASKETMAKERS AND CLIFF DWELLERS OF THE SOUTHWEST.
New York: Norton, 1963. (7 and up)
One of the few references about prehistoric Indians for young readers, this book traces the history of the Anasazi, or ancient ones, of the Southwest. Using his own photographs, the author provides sixty-five illustrations to demonstrate where and how the ancient ones lived; their art, clothing, food, and how they buried their dead. The book is exceptionally well written, although some archaeologists might not agree with some of the author's dates and his chronology of events. The young reader interested in archaeology will find the book most informative. Good.

54. Baldwin, Gordon C.
HOW THE INDIANS REALLY LIVED.
New York: Putnam, 1967. (5–9)
This book presents a comprehensive overview of Indian and Eskimo life through the author's photographs and clear, easily understood writing. In fact, the writing is so clear that, at times, it seems unnecessarily simplistic, and the author's summary statements appear superficial: "Warfare was the major sport of most Southeastern tribes" (p.69); "Five hundred years ago California must have been an Indian paradise. Indians migrated there from all over the country" (p.146); or "Today reservations are not concentration camps. The Indians are free to come and go as they please" (p.210). A book that would serve best as a beginning refer-

ence, the text also includes a section on Eskimos. For this reason, the title choice was an unfortunate one. Adequate.

55. Baldwin, Gordon C.
INDIANS OF THE SOUTHWEST.
New York: Putnam, 1970. (4–7)

In this concisely and clearly written book, Baldwin's background in anthropology and archaeology is evident as he presents the reader with an unusually detailed setting of the geography and plant and animal life found in the land of the Southwestern tribes. "Some Indians have managed to achieve a happy balance between their culture and that of the white man. Others have been badly bent, but not quite broken, under the burden of the meeting of such greatly different civilizations" (p.165) is one of a series of vignettes that lift this book well above average. Black-and-white pictures, maps, and good writing suit this book for reference work and for a vacation travel guide. Good.

56. Baldwin, Gordon C.
RACE AGAINST TIME: THE STORY OF SALVAGE ARCHAEOLOGY.
New York: Putnam, 1966. (5 and up)

Salvage archaeology is the rescuing of irreplaceable clues to ancient cultures before the onslaught of modern progress. Construction companies discovering something of archaeological interest in their excavations are required, under federal law, to notify the proper authorities. Baldwin writes of the hundreds of archaeologists who have been salvaging as many prehistoric remains as possible before projects of the present, such as dams and highways, sweep the sites into oblivion. This account covering some twenty years of archaeological work, will capture the imagination of boys and girls in upper elementary grades, junior high, and high school. Good.

57. Bales, Carol Ann.
KEVIN CLOUD: CHIPPEWA BOY IN THE CITY.
Chicago: Reilly & Lee, 1972. (K–3)

This book celebrates surviving. Kevin Cloud is an Ojibwa boy living in an impoverished part of Chicago. He talks matter-of-factly about his broken family: "My father doesn't live with us. I haven't seen him for a long time" (not paged). He then turns and teases his mother:

I was born on Thanksgiving Day in Cook County Hospital in Chicago. I suddenly popped out and started flying around the room. Mama says she doubts that I flew, but I did. I like to tease like that. I tease everybody. Sometimes when I tease Mama, she pretends to beat me up. I like that. [np]

Carol Bales has captured a fascinating image of an Indian boy living a tough but good life in a straightforward text illustrated by her own color and black and white photographs. She talks to her young readers without condescension, in language that uses primary-level words in a nonsimplistic fashion; as, for example, when she states in the foreword,

When you read this book, you will see that Kevin is a lot like you. But you also will see, if you read carefully, that Kevin knows about some things and does some things that have been passed down to him from a long time ago.

Her pictures catch the feeling of the boy's life: real, tough, but full of satisfactions as well. And, although his family is a broken one, it is a strong one; when Kevin was teased at school for being an Indian, his mother took action: "Mama was mad. She took off work and went to school the next day. The ones who chased us got in trouble. The principal suspended them, and Grandma started walking us home from school. I hated school last year" (np). An outstanding book for any collection. Good.

58. Barbour, Philip L.
POCAHONTAS AND HER WORLD.
Boston: Houghton, 1970. (7 and up)

Written by a historian, this book includes all the characteristics of careful, although somewhat tedious, and accurate research. To enjoy this book, the young reader will need to be fairly well versed in

English and early American history. The book is technical, thoroughly documented, and most definitely written from the point of view of an English or American scholar, rather than that of an Indian historian. However, the author makes no pretense at being well versed in Indian history and attitudes, except as reflected by early documents and sources. He merely speculates about what his characters "must have felt" or "might have done," based upon the historical information available. He offers a variety of alternative interpretations where information is limited or obscure. Reproductions of an engraving of Pocahontas, said to be the only likeness done in her lifetime, as well as other portraits from the early seventeenth century are included in the book. The first chapter provides background on "the great family now called Algonkians," as well as a map of "Powhatan's empire." Good.

59. Barnett, Franklin.
DICTIONARY OF PREHISTORIC INDIAN ARTIFACTS OF THE AMERICAN SOUTHWEST.
Flagstaff, Ariz.: Northland Pr., 1973. (4 and up)
This is an illustrated dictionary defining terms, words, and objects relating to prehistoric artifacts of the Southwest. Photographs by the author provide the reader with easy identification and a way of comparing objects to the ones described in the text. The book is scientific in style, yet can easily be read by an average reader in grade four (except for the preface and use statement, both written on a higher reading level). The author obviously believes in restoring damaged artifacts, a process not all archaeologists are in favor of; and the book does not include some important types of artifacts, such as ceramic wares, weaving, or baskets. There is a glossary, a contributors' list, and a short bibliography. Good.

60. Barnouw, Victor.
DREAM OF THE BLUE HERON.
New York: Delacorte Pr., 1966. (2–6)

This is the story of a young Ojibwa boy in 1905, caught between his traditional grandparents and his father, who works in a lumber mill. The black-and-white drawings by Lynd Ward are excellent and effectively add to the story. Barnouw writes well, although occasionally his dialogue seems strained. He has a good grasp of Ojibwa customs, and often surprises his readers, as in first presenting the white school disciplinarian, Mr. Wickham, as a stereotype of brutality, only to allow him later on to tell the main character that he feels Indians have a better life, one he envies. Barnouw's description of the differences between Indians and whites in hunting lice is unexpected, and the reason he has one character give for opposing formal education for girls, "school was bad for girls and made their muscles soft" (p.78), was true for some Indian groups who depended on the physical strength of their women to find and prepare food. This is one of the few good fiction books about the Indians of the northern border. Good.

61. Bateman, Walter L.
THE NAVAJO OF THE PAINTED DESERT.
Boston: Beacon, 1970. (5 and up)
This book describes life among the Navajos as it might have been before 1890 reservation life. The author artfully interweaves daily life customs and legends into a cohesive, interesting history book. He begins the text with the sights a ten-year-old Navajo boy might see first thing in the morning through the smokehole in the roof of the hogan as he got up from his sheepskin bed. He describes the family unit, cultural expectations for boys and girls, and the legends the Navajos use to explain tribal customs, as well as natural and physical phenomena. Customs and legends associated with marriage, birth, death, and the creation of life are described in the book:
Marriage is based on the solid judgment of older people, not the dreams of romantic young people. How many sheep does this family have? Can the girl cook? Do they eat a lot of mutton?

31

Does the girl weave well? Does she work hard?" [p.51]
The book is illustrated with photographs, as well as many black-and-white illustrations by Richard C. Bartlett. It includes two short pages on Navajos today. Good.

62. Bauer, Helen.
CALIFORNIA INDIAN DAYS.
Garden City, N.Y.: Doubleday, 1963. (4 and up)
Designed as a supplementary state textbook for California schools, this book contains authentic information about the various Native American cultures in California. The style appeals to children. For any class studying California Indians, it is essential. Helen Bauer has researched many aspects of California history. She has included charts and a glossary of Indian words, as well as a list of places still bearing Indian names, including translations for these place names, and the name of the language group from which they came. The book is carefully indexed and illustrated with maps, photographs, and sketches. Good.

63. Baylor, Byrd.
BEFORE YOU CAME THIS WAY.
New York: Dutton, 1969. (1–5)
In poetic form, this story of the designs of ancient Indian pictographs and petroglyphs has been woven into a brief, unforgettable book that can be enjoyed by all ages, especially if read aloud. The Indian author selects words that help the reader feel kinship with the unknown artists who recorded their marks on canyon walls. The illustrator is also Indian, and the illustrations are inspired by ancient designs. The author creates an atmosphere such that readers "ALMOST hear the echoes of those voices still in the wind." Text and illustrations complement each other in artistic unity. Good.

64. Baylor, Byrd.
THE DESERT IS THEIRS.
New York: Scribner, 1975. (2–4)

The author emphasizes the relationship between the Papago Indians, or Desert People, and the animals with which they share the land as she develops her main message to the reader: the land belongs to no one, yet to everyone. She tells how hardships (adverse weather, for example) affect both people and animals, and how the desert, in particular, demands great discipline from all living things, as well as the ability to endure. A Caldecott Honor Book, this is a story with a message, but one told from a more practical and logical than pedantic point of view. The illustrations by Peter Parnall are colorful, imaginative, and appropriate. His line drawings are developed using unusual lines and shapes and often include an x-ray view of some animal in its burrow underground. Good.

65. Baylor, Byrd.
THEY PUT ON MASKS.
New York: Scribner, 1974. (1–4)
It would seem almost impossible to create a memorable book about masks that provides primary-age children with a mystical experience, but author Byrd Baylor and illustrator Jerry Ingram manage to do just that in this book. It is impossible to separate the effects that are the result of Baylor's words from the effects of Ingram's forms, so complementary are they. The beautiful and simply written text tells of the uses of masks and ceremonial dances for healing, ceremonials, and celebration. Ingram's illustrations use the same design layout and picture format throughout the book, varying only colors and masks from page to page. Design students in higher grades will appreciate the effectiveness of this and find ideas for their own study. Younger children may enjoy finding the natural materials described in the text and designing masks and ceremonials of their own as a part of their social studies activities. The book is invaluable for children whose vacation plans include a trip through a reservation. Indian children can see in print an important part of their heritage. Good.

66. Baylor, Byrd.
WHEN CLAY SINGS.
New York: Scribner, 1972. (2–6)

Byrd Baylor and illustrator Tom Bahti have combined rhythmic prose and designs from ancient pottery in a book that will appeal to all ages. The book is of interest for all who wish to know more about original Americans, and can be used as a read-aloud book for the youngest children. Bahti has selected designs from fragments of pottery of the Anasazi (Utah, Arizona, New Mexico, and Colorado), the Hohokam (New Mexico and Arizona), the Mogollon (Arizona and New Mexico), and the Mimbres (New Mexico) prehistoric cultures. With words as beautiful as they are simple, Baylor makes the designs come alive so that the reader can envision the lives of the potters who made clay "sing." This book is a must for every school library. Good.

67. Beal, Merrill D.
"I WILL FIGHT NO MORE FOREVER":
CHIEF JOSEPH AND THE
NEZ PERCÉ WAR.
Seattle: Univ. of Washington Pr., 1971. (8 and up)

This is an excellent biography of Chief Joseph and a fine delineation of the Nez Percés. The author's careful documentation even includes such details as the lists of killed or wounded for several major battles, such as the Bear Paw Battlefield and the earlier Battle of Camus Meadows. The book begins with a condensed history of the Nez Percés, then launches into the Indian wars, focusing upon the campaign in Idaho, crossing the Bitterroot Ranges, the flight toward Canada, and the last battles. The book ends with the final subjugation of the tribe and Chief Joseph's futile attempt to buy back part of his homeland, the Wallowa Valley. Not a story to be skimmed, the reader will need some background in the post-Civil War period of Western American history. The author provides adequate examples, little is left to conjecture, and an extensive bibliography is included, in addition to chapter-by-chapter notation. Good.

68. Bealer, Alex W.
ONLY THE NAMES REMAIN: THE
CHEROKEES AND THE TRAIL OF TEARS.
Boston: Little, 1972. (4–6)

An in-depth story of the Cherokee Nation from its origin to the present, this book contains extensive historical data as well as Cherokee legends. William Bock's line drawing illustrations add equal portions of reality and fantasy. The book format is excellent and adds to reader interest. While detailing the more well-known episodes in Cherokee history, the author also includes such little known items as the facts that the Cherokee peace chiefs were usually women and that Cherokees captured by the colonists during the revolutionary war were often shipped to the West Indies as slaves. The author includes a thorough index. Good.

69. Beals, Frank I.
CHIEF BLACK HAWK.
Chicago: Wheeler, 1960. (4–6)

This is a textbook, with questions at the end of some chapters. It is divided into five sections and, except for a few chapters in the beginning, deals mainly with Black Hawk after he became war chief. The book is replete with stereotypes, both white and Indian. The author speaks of the "streets of Saukenuk," Black Hawk's village, and implies the chiefs of the tribe had absolute ruling powers. Unfortunately, some of the questions at the end of the chapters tend to reinforce the stereotypes: "What was the duty of a Sauk war chief?" A quotation found at the end of the book, although not attributed to Black Hawk, suggests the type of nationalism that prevailed in the literature of the early 1940s, the first printing date of the book: "Go, my braves, and defend with your lives the freedom of our country. Fight beside your white brothers. Point your guns with theirs." Illustrations by Jack Merryweather are too small to be either informative or interesting. Poor.

70. Beatty, Patricia.
THE SEA PAIR.
New York: Morrow, 1970. (5–8)

The author draws a parallel between

the lives of two sea otters and a young Quileute Indian boy in this story, set in the 1940s when conservationists were trying to save the remaining sea otters. The boy wants to be an auto mechanic, and, although this is a "white teacher saves him" type story, it is done more in the spirit of the normal desire of any teacher to assist than in the "white man to the rescue" mode. The author's use of a lot of adjectives and analogies is better done than in most nature books:

> Today the calm Pacific water seemed a mile-deep gelatin. The thousand tangles, the top branches of the kelp forest, were motionless on the scarcely moving water and from above resembled a thick brown embroidery on a blue-green tapestry background. [p.11]

Her writing is characterized by unusual phrasing that might be offensive in less skillful hands, such as her use of *squaw*: "Yeah, a squaw was driving it all right yesterday. That wasn't any news. Roy continued to hold Mrs. Benson's eyes. Sometimes if he did that to *oquats*, they got nervous and started to talk more" (p.56) and other emotionally loaded words: "Jack Adams is no more typical of Quileute than any mean, lazy bum is typical of any ethnic group, including whites" (p.222). The black-and-white line drawings by Franz Altschuler are excellent and appropriate. Good.

71. Beckhard, Arthur J.
    BLACK HAWK.
    New York: Messner, 1957. (5–9)
    This book fairly drips with male and female stereotypes. From the first page most young readers will be put off by the stilted, unimaginative dialogue. For example, Black Hawk and a friend are out hunting when the sister of Black Hawk's friend drops a bird with her own arrow after both boys had shot and missed. The girl is chastised for "not helping with the spring plowing, cooking . . . and tanning hides," as well as for "chasing after" the two boys, "even though Black Hawk" is her "hero." Although included as characters throughout the book, outspoken women are repeat-

edly put into their place by the author in such an offensive manner that, despite the book's strengths, objective reviewing is most difficult. The author's descriptions of places and events are well done and seem accurate. He includes an extensive bibliography and index. He describes the sensitive and explosive situation between white and Indian characters in a thoughtful, plausible manner. The book is not illustrated. Adequate.

72. Bell, Corydon.
    JOHN RATTLING-GOURD OF BIG COVE.
    A COLLECTION OF CHEROKEE
    INDIAN LEGENDS.
    New York: Macmillan, 1955. (4–5)
    Corydon Bell has written and illustrated an excellent collection of Cherokee legends and myths (and he knows the difference). The stories are woven together by means of a continuing commentary on Cherokee history and customs: "Every storyteller maintains a mood of his own whether he tells an original story or retells an old one" (p.xi). The book includes good pictures of reservation life at the time of publication and a glossary of Cherokee words. An excellent publication for its time, if it were revised to include more current data, it would continue to be a major contribution to children's literature. Good.

73. Bell, Margaret E.
    KIT CARSON: MOUNTAIN MAN.
    New York: Morrow, 1952. (2–5)
    Indians are portrayed as antagonists, and not too successful ones at that, in this biography of Kit Carson: "This was not the last engagement Kit had with the unrelenting Blackfoot, but he always succeeded in outwitting, outfighting, or outretreating this wiliest tribe of all" (p.58). Even in defeat, the Indians are given short shrift by the author: "He was held in such respect by the Indians, even this fierce and barbarous tribe [Apache], that he was able to sit in council with them . . . hundreds of miles from any possible aid if he needed it" (p.70). No mention of Carson's activities at Canyon de Chelly is made at all,

leaving out an important chunk of the subject's life, not to say of Navajo history. The black-and-white illustrations by Harry Daugherty are good but wasted in this poorly written, slanted, incomplete biography. Poor.

74. Belting, Natalia.
THE EARTH IS ON A FISH'S BACK: TALES OF BEGINNINGS.
New York: Holt, 1965. (4–9)
This book contains twenty-one tales collected from Africa, Asia, South America, Europe, and the United States; a unique and diverse collection. Although each is a "tale of beginning," each has local color and accent. Some tell of the supernatural; some have a practical theme such as building houses and developing a corn culture. One tale that will appeal to youthful readers as well as adults is entitled "Why Dog Has a Fur Coat and Woman Has Seven Tempers (and Nine Moods)." The black-and-white illustrations by Esta Nesbitt add interesting dimensions to the book. Use this collection to teach students to observe similarities as well as differences among cultures. Good.

75. Belting, Natalia.
THE LONG-TAILED BEAR.
Indianapolis, Ind.: Bobbs-Merrill, 1961. (4–6)
Natalia Belting demonstrates a scholar's attention to fact in this book, illustrated by Louis Cary. In 100 pages the author recounts 22 tales of the Creeks, Cherokees, Tewas, Pawnees, Shawnees, and Indian tribes of the Mackenzie River area. Many of the legends account for characteristics of animals and birds, such as how they acquired long tails, flat feet, brown spots. Adequate.

76. Belting, Natalia.
OUR FATHERS HAD POWERFUL SONGS.
New York: Dutton, 1974. (2–5)
Poems and chants from a diversity of tribes have been selected by the author for this book. The black-and-white illustrations by Laszlo Kubinyi are superb; indeed, they are the best part of a fine book.

The selections lend themselves well to reading aloud. Art teachers may wish to use this book as an example of effective illustrative technique for children's literature. Good.

77. Benchley, Nathaniel.
ONLY EARTH AND SKY LAST FOREVER.
New York: Harper, 1972. (7 and up)
This is the story of Dark Elk, a young Cheyenne adopted by Sioux parents, who tries to live the free life of a warrior on rapidly diminishing Indian land. Somewhat romanticized, the story nevertheless provides interest and information about the desires and life of a young Indian man growing up in the late 1800s. The author contrasts the agency Indian or "Loaf-About-the-Forts" with other Indians such as Crazy Horse and Sitting Bull. He describes various other Indian individuals who seem to fall between the two extremes. The women in the story do not fare as well, with the exception of Lashuha, the love object, and her grandmother, who are a study in contrasts on their own. The white men in the story are all depicted as evil or sinister. However, the author reminds us that "eyewitness versions of the same event often contradict one another, and are bewildering to anyone trying to find out the truth" (author's note, beginning of story). He gives careful attention to the authenticity of small details: "The fish hooks were made from the ribs of field mice, and the matter of tying them to the horsehair leader was a delicate one" (p.3) and includes a bibliography. Good.

78. Benchley, Nathaniel.
RED FOX AND HIS CANOE.
New York: Harper, 1964. (K–3)
If all references to Indians were taken out of this book, it would perhaps be acceptable as a story for young children. The illustrations by Arnold Lobel feature cute, greeting-card type Indians. The author uses unimaginative dialogue: " 'I need a new canoe. Will you make me a bigger one?' 'Sure,' said his father. 'How big a one do you want?' " (p.9) and exaggera-

tions obviously intended, but failing, to be clever: "He fished for a long time and was nearing the half million mark" (p.21). From beginning to end, this story about an Indian boy (tribe unspecified) who wants the biggest canoe in the world but settles for a small one adds little to the literature about Indians. Poor.

79. Benchley, Nathaniel.
SMALL WOLF.
New York: Harper, 1969. (K–2)
Nathaniel Benchley retells in primary language the story of the Dutch purchase of Manhattan Island and the consequent moving of the Indians as they continued to lose their land:

> So they went to a white man, who looked startled to see them. He raised his gun and held it ready . . . "You'd better go along. This land is ours now. We paid for it. . . ." "What Indians did he pay?" Small Wolf asked, as they paddled away. "The Canarsees," said his father, "and they did not even live there." [pp. 36–40]

The text is easy for young children to read for themselves; however, the writing and Joan Sander's illustrations are pedestrian. Adequate.

80. Bennett, Kay.
KAIBAH: RECOLLECTION OF A
NAVAJO GIRLHOOD.
Los Angeles: Westernlore Pr., 1964.
(6 and up)
This is an uneven book. The author writes with love and understanding of her years as a young girl on the Navajo Reservation from 1928 to 1935 as only a tribal member could. She makes it clear that she is writing about a definite period, time, and family; and she presents unusual happenings of which a non-Navajo might never be aware, such as her account of the mother taking the whole family home from a sing, in disgrace because her daughter chewed tobacco and became sick in public. At the same time, however, the illustrations are not particularly good, and at times the writing is ungrammatical and full of rather inappropriate pop sociology

terms: "Life on the Navajo Reservation did not provide all the luxuries of a city, but the people were happy. They lived an uncomplicated existence, free from the worries which beset most people who live and work in urban communities" (p.11) and generalizations which few would agree with: "At the time of this story their [the Navajo] growth had become so rapid that they almost destroyed themselves" (introductory statement). Still, the book has a unique statement to make. Adequate.

81. Bennett, Kay, and Bennett, Russ.
A NAVAJO SAGA.
San Antonio, Tex.: Naylor, 1969.
(7 and up)
This story of Kay Bennett's Navajo grandmother, who kills herself in despair at the end of the book, fluctuates in its construction from very good to very bad. The authors make a genuine effort to write fairly of an era about which they both obviously feel great emotion, but their fury still shows:

> Fortunately, thousands, perhaps even a million, Navajos escaped from bureaucratic control. The offspring of Navajo slaves throughout the Southwest who speak Spanish or English are considered to be Spanish Americans or English Americans, and are therefore not in need of the guardianship provided by the United States government. On the other hand, thousands of the descendants of the Spanish people who were slaves of the Navajos and who preferred to stand with the Navajos, now live in Navajoland and help to swell the number of Indians being helped by the Bureau of Indian Affairs. . . . One wonders why there has never been a Bureau of African Affairs, or Asiatic Affairs. [pp.viii–ix]

Many authorities would question the use of the phrase "even a million" in the above quotation. Women are described in accurate and sympathetic fashion, perhaps the best feature of the book. The illustrations by Kay Bennett are interesting, but amateurish. The writing is uneven—sometimes poorly constructed, sometimes bringing forward a new insight that other authors have overlooked. The controversy this book evokes makes it well worth shelf room. Adequate.

82. Bennett, Noël.
THE WEAVER'S PATHWAY:
A CLARIFICATION OF THE "SPIRIT TRAIL" IN NAVAJO WEAVING.
Flagstaff, Ariz.: Northland Pr., 1974. (7 and up)
A scholarly, readable, and thorough discussion of the Spirit Line or Devil's Pathway, "a line passing from the background to the selvage in bordered rugs" (p.xi), in Navajo rug weaving. This is a fascinating book. Weaving is analyzed in terms of this line, its relationship to Navajo culture, technical aspects of making the line, various methods of weaving it into a rug, and descriptions of unusual pathway designs, often in the words of the weaver; all incredibly precise and complete. For instance, the book even describes pathways that cannot be seen: "Visibility, then, is not a necessity—the point being it's for the weaver and she knows it's there" (p.20). There is much to be learned here about rugs, culture, and the pride of working with one's hands. Various scholarly appendixes, notes, and a most complete bibliography end the book. Younger children will enjoy the diagrams and illustrations of Navajo rugs. Good.

83. Bennett, Noël, and Bighorse, Tiana.
WORKING WITH WOOL: HOW TO WEAVE A NAVAJO RUG.
Flagstaff, Ariz.: Northland Pr., 1971. (6 and up)
This is a veritable encyclopedia about Navajo weaving. It includes descriptions of equipment, weaving basics, what to do when things go wrong, supply rooms, and step-by-step instructions. There are several appendixes concerned with technical weaving data, a glossary, and a suggested reading list. The two coauthors make a good team; Bennett has an unusual re-search and scholastic background, and Bighorse is an expert weaver and designer. The black-and-white drawings by Robert Jacobson are unobtrusive and helpful. Good.

84. Berger, Thomas.
LITTLE BIG MAN.
New York: Dial, 1964. (7 and up)
Thomas Berger is an incredibly good writer, as is evident in his handling of humor, irony, and dialogue in this story of Little Big Man. He tells inside jokes that flatter the reader who understands: "As to Crazy Horse's not wearing feathers, we know that statement to be erroneous—his war bonnet, as mentioned in the Preface, presently reposes in my own collection; the dealer who sold it to me is a man of the highest integrity" (p.440). This book pokes gentle fun at traditional captive stories (Little Big Man begins his Indian life as a captive) as it tells its story of the last free days of the Plains Indians. A classic. Good.

85. Bernstein, Margery, and Kobrin, Janet.
COYOTE GOES HUNTING FOR FIRE:
A CALIFORNIA INDIAN MYTH.
New York: Scribner, 1974. (2–3)
In a book young children can read for themselves, Bernstein and Kobrin retell Yana Indian stories of Coyote. Well written in simple language, the book contains black-and-white illustrations by Ed Heffernan. Teachers and parents may want to supplement this book with additional background for child readers, since the story is presented as is, without explanation. While it is a delightful tale in itself, children who have some understanding of the culture from which the story came may appreciate it even more. Books of this type are a good way to show Indian children some of the rich literature their cultures produced; children of other tribal backgrounds may want to examine likenesses and differences between tales from their own particular Indian culture and this one. Good.

86. Bernstein, Margery, and
Kobrin, Janet.
EARTH NAMER.
New York: Scribner, 1974. (1-3)
This book is unique in that it contains stories retold by two teachers to children who cannot read. Simple line drawings by Ed Heffernan enliven each page of the text. The stories are basically creation tales and, like all legends, call for a vivid imagination. Well written, this book will appeal to all ages, particularly primary grade children. Good.

87. Berry, Rotha McClain.
SWIFT DEER—THE NAVAJO.
San Antonio, Tex.: Naylor, 1953.
(4-6)
This story illustrates the author's views about Navajo culture. A boy, son of a Navajo father and Blackfoot woman captive, journeys with his grandfather for three years, learning wisdom. He goes East to study, but enlists in World War II instead of completing his work for a degree in medicine. The writing is strained: "They [the Navajo] are unique and picturesque in native costumes" (p.xii); contains inappropriate words and condescending phraseology: "Much to the surprise of government officials, these redskins showed up the next day with guns—yes, their own rifles—ready to fight beside the whites for the Great White Father" (p.99); and places an unfair burden of behavior on the main character. As the boy prepares to leave for school, his white companion tells him he represents his entire race and his people will be judged by his actions: "At all times he must be the purest, truest type of Navajo that had ever gone into the white man's profession of medicine" (p.96). The black-and-white pictures in the book are interesting, but small and not well reproduced. Poor.

88. Bierhorst, John, ed.
IN THE TRAIL OF THE WIND:
AMERICAN INDIAN POEMS AND
RITUAL ORATIONS.
New York: Farrar, 1971. (7 and up)
This is a good, representative sample of poems and speeches from many Native American tribal groups, including Eskimo examples. The book contains a brief history and review of Indian thought and an informative discussion of the problems encountered in translating the oral literature of one language into the written literature of another. The author is knowledgeable and not afraid to put forward controversial opinions: "How fragile these cultures were, on one hand, is readily suggested by the history of their submission. . . . Indian people and Indian lifestyles have, on the other hand, shown remarkable powers of endurance" (introduction). Some of the selections can be read aloud to primary children. The book ends with a section of author's notes, a glossary, and suggestions for further study. Good.

89. Bierhorst, John.
THE RING IN THE PRAIRIE:
A SHAWNEE LEGEND.
New York: Dial, 1970. (1-4)
First recorded more than 100 years ago by Henry Rowe Schoolcraft, who preserved many legends and probably added the format, this is the legend of a man who loved a woman from the sky. The color illustrations by Leo and Diane Dillon show considerable technical skill, but all the women are pictured as pretty girls in modern, Indian-style costumes. The editor's note at the back of the book is helpful in establishing the setting and explaining the author's choices. Good.

90. Bierhorst, John.
SONGS OF THE CHIPPEWA.
New York: Farrar, 1974. (4-6)
Fine illustrations by Jo Servello are the best part of this book. Musical notations appropriate for unskilled pianists are given. The reader should be aware that many Native Americans of this tribe would rather be called Ojibwa than Chippewa. Although the recommended grade level for this book is four through six, many andvanced second and third grade students will also enjoy it. Good.

91. Bierhorst, John, ed.
THE FIRE PLUME: LEGENDS OF THE
AMERICAN INDIANS.
Collected by Henry Rowe Schoolcraft.
New York: Dial, 1969. (2-6)
Henry Rowe Schoolcraft was an explorer who lived from 1793-1864. During his travels he recorded numerous American Indian legends and myths, adapting and interpreting them according to the fashion of his time. As Bierhorst states, "Schoolcraft did not merely translate, he interpreted. The result is a story form that is loosely knit, often poetic, highly romantic, and thoroughly American" (p.3). This process is apparent in the stories: "There was once a very beautiful young girl, who died suddenly on the day she was to have been married to a handsome young man" (p.29). Not often is a writer as candid about his process as is Bierhorst; but then, not often is a writer such a scholar. The black-and-white line and point drawings by Alan E. Cober are good, particularly those featuring his cross-hatching technique. The foreword is written for children, and Indian terms are defined in the back of the book. Good.

92. Biesterveld, Betty.
SIX DAYS FROM SUNDAY.
Chicago: Rand McNally, 1973. (6-8)
Willy Littlehorse, a Navajo schoolboy, is forced to make a decision: if he leaves home to attend boarding school he may lose touch with the Navajo way. Willy goes through six days of adventure that cause continual confusion involving his choice. When the sixth day arrives, Willy is still confused and afraid, but is able to make the best decision. The book is well written, and the author accurately portrays the dilemma many young Navajos face when adolescence is approached. A controversy among reviewers involves the appropriateness of the young boy's final decision. Adequate.

93. Bird, Traveller.
THE PATH TO SNOWBIRD MOUNTAIN.
New York: Farrar, 1972. (3-6)
These sixteen Eastern Cherokee legends are recounted by Traveller Bird, who intersperses personal reminiscences and recollections throughout, adding immeasurably to the effectiveness of the book. As a small child he heard the tales told during tribal reunions at his grandfather's home near Snowbird Creek and Snowbird Mountain in North Carolina. Here in the land of "The Sky People," according to legend, a giant white snowbird once lived. The stories date from 1838, when the federal government drove the Cherokees from their homes. Although a compromise was affected which permitted some Cherokees to live in a restricted area, the Indians never lost their fear of eviction. These legends reflect the insecurities and difficulties they experienced. Each short tale has an appropriate black-and-white illustration. A classic. Good.

94. Blassingame, Wyatt.
OSCEOLA: SEMINOLE WAR CHIEF.
Champaign, Ill.: Garrard, 1976. (2-5)
As in all books in the Garrard series, this book begins with a brief history of the Seminoles. Some background information about chickees, Seminole houses, is provided by the author; however, he includes little about the Florida plains or Everglades and nothing about the relationship between the Seminoles and the black slaves. Few women are mentioned. The author notes that Osceola had two wives and several children, but does not elaborate. The illustrations by Al Fiorentino are colorful, and the book contains a map showing various forts in Florida where major Seminole battles took place, and where Osceola died in 1838. Adequate.

95. Blassingame, Wyatt.
SACAJAWEA: INDIAN GUIDE.
Champaign, Ill.: Garrard, 1965. (2-5)
One of the better books about famous Indian leaders published by Garrard, this story of Sacajawea begins with her capture by the Minnetarees, covers her adventures with Lewis and Clark, and offers some theories regarding her fate after returning to St. Louis following the expedition. Garrard's standard single page of

background information and map are provided at the beginning of the book to give the uninformed reader some knowledge of Shoshone life, Lewis and Clark's route, and highlights of Sacajawea's experiences on the expedition. The Sacajawea in this story is portrayed as a rather accommodating, resigned, and meek individual. The author presents Charbonneau, the French fur trapper who bought Sacajawea and presumably was the father of her son, Little Pomp, as a rather ignorant and self-centered person. Edward Shenton's colorful illustrations add to the book's effectiveness. Good.

96. Bleeker, Sonia.
THE APACHE INDIANS: RAIDERS OF
THE SOUTHWEST.
New York: Morrow, 1951. (3-6)
A simplistic, basal reader type of writing is used to tell the story of 100 years of Apache history. The contemporary material reflects 1951 events (the publication date) and is in need of updating. Althea Karr's black-and-white illustrations picture people who do not look Apache or, for that matter, particularly Indian. Uninspired section headings such as "Apache on the Move" and "The Apache at Home" set the pace of the rest of the writing. Adequate.

97. Bleeker, Sonia.
THE CHEROKEE INDIANS OF
THE MOUNTAINS.
New York: Morrow, 1952. (4-6)
This book interweaves the story of a runner making his way from his home village to challenge the chief of another village to a ball game with descriptions of Cherokee marital customs, nature rites, hunting, shamens and their functions, and finally the ball game itself. References to Sequoyah, John Ross, and the framing of the constitution for the Cherokee Nation are included. The combination of legend, history, and detailed daily life make the book both interesting and worthwhile, although much of the material on current affairs is dated. The illustrations

by Althea Karr are in typical social studies textbook style. Good.

98. Bleeker, Sonia.
THE CHIPPEWA INDIANS: RICE
GATHERERS OF THE GREAT LAKES.
New York: Morrow, 1955. (4-6)
Using a fictional Chippewa family as a narrative pivot, the author describes their customs, practices, and legends in fictionalized form, focusing on the Chippewa's dependence upon seasonal travel in order to live. Consistent with most of her books about Indian tribes, the author emphasizes that the natural resources available dictated to a great extent the manner in which the tribe lived. In this case she follows Chippewa movement from maple-sugar groves in the spring, to lake shores in the summer, rice fields in the autumn, and finally to the forest in the winter. Patricia Boodell's black-and-white sketches provide sufficient detail for the young reader to understand more of the old Chippewa way of life. The author devotes the last chapter to the modern Chippewa, although the early publication date causes this material to be dated now. Good.

99. Bleeker, Sonia.
THE CROW INDIANS: HUNTERS OF THE
NORTHERN PLAINS.
New York: Morrow, 1953. (4-6)
This is a readable and engaging story in which Sonia Bleeker paints a vivid picture of Crow character and daily life as it was before the white man, through the eyes of Crow children of different ages who are in various stages of growing up. How they learn the homemaking and warrior skills of their elders through observation and imitation; their strong sense of family; the values of courage, generosity, cooperation, and gratitude to family and spirits; the legends; the buffalo hunt and war parties; and the games which prepare them for adult survival are all told with warmth and impressive detail. Good.

100. Bleeker, Sonia.
THE DELAWARE INDIANS: EASTERN
FISHERMEN AND FARMERS.
New York: Morrow, 1953. (4-6)

A journeyman job by a writer who researches her subjects carefully, this book is a fictionalized account of a Delaware family that serves to clarify customs of the past. Their life along the ocean and the rivers of the East is presented in detail. The black-and-white illustrations by Patricia Boodell give the reader a sense of dress, housing, and the like, but are few and portray the Delaware in a cute, childish style. Much of the material on modern-day Delaware Indians is now dated. Adequate.

101. Bleeker, Sonia.
THE ESKIMO: ARCTIC HUNTERS AND TRAPPERS.
New York: Morrow, 1959. (4-6)
Information about the life of the Eskimo before non-Eskimo immigrants changed the culture is presented in a style appropriate for elementary classes. The 1959 publication date of this book must be kept in mind by the reader, since Eskimo life is changing, and much of Bleeker's information has become outdated. By today's standards, Bleeker's attitude would be considered sexist. For example: "Although women lack the strength to cut the huge snow blocks, they have built igloos for themselves when male help was unavailable." Nevertheless, by 1959 standards she has tried to maintain authenticity, and has provided useful information about how Eskimos lived and about Arctic exploration. Adequate.

102. Bleeker, Sonia.
HORSEMEN OF THE WESTERN PLATEAUS: THE NEZ PERCÉ INDIANS.
New York: Morrow, 1957. (3-6)
Fictional excerpts are used by the author to make the life and history of the Nez Percé more vivid to the reader. For the most part she presents a fair, well-researched picture, subject to the limitations of such an early publication date. Bleeker is more optimistic about present-day majority culture intentions than are most writers:

Today perhaps, Joseph's fate and that of his people would have been a happier

one. We have learned, at great cost of lives and property, to respect treaties and to respect the rights of people, even if the people are neither numerous nor strong. It is sufficient for us to know that they have needs. [pp.130–31]

The illustrations by Patricia Boodell are black-and-white line drawings typical of social studies textbooks. The author includes a short index. Adequate.

103. Bleeker, Sonia.
INDIANS OF THE LONG HOUSE.
New York: Morrow, 1950. (4-6)
This is an interesting, factual account of the Iroquois Indians, past and present. With the exception of some broad generalizations and a few questionable value judgments, the book is a good reference and enrichment reading source for use in a social studies Northeastern Indian unit. In a readable and straightforward manner, questions about the following topics are answered and often illustrated: food, ceremonies, shelter, clothing, seasonal activities, religion, government, community life, games, festivals, hunting, planting and harvesting, tool making, and weapons. The last chapter briefly traces the history of the Iroquois League from the 1600s to the present. It includes a discussion of treaty problems, the taking of Indian land, and the establishment of reservations. It points out that the Iroquois of today are engaged in a wide variety of occupations and professions including medicine, law, farming, and steel construction work. Dated. Good.

104. Bleeker, Sonia.
MISSION INDIANS OF CALIFORNIA.
New York: Morrow, 1956. (4-6)
This fictionalized account of the life of a Southern California Indian who lived to be ninety includes much factual material such as dates and historical events. *Mission Indians* is a misleading title, suggesting a more factual volume. The mixture of pure fiction and historical summaries distracts from the continuity of either. Poor.

105. Bleeker, Sonia.
THE NAVAJO: HERDERS, WEAVERS,
AND SILVERSMITHS.
New York: Morrow, 1958. (4-6)
The author uses the fictional story of a
thirteen-year-old Navajo boy, Slim Runner, to present aspects of Navajo life and
culture. The main character spends long
months in the white man's hospital where
he learns the joy of drawing and painting.
When he returns home, he has to choose
between his new-found dreams of art
school and his responsibility to his family.
The only part of the story not written in
fictional form is the section on contemporary (1958) Navajos. The book presents
a detailed account of the defeat of the
Navajo at Canyon de Chelly. The illustrations are by Patricia Boodell. Adequate.

106. Bleeker, Sonia.
THE PUEBLO INDIANS: FARMERS OF
THE RIO GRANDE.
New York: Morrow, 1955. (4-6)
Sonia Bleeker uses the format of a fictional account of a Pueblo Indian family
as a way to describe Pueblo practices, customs, and daily life of four hundred years
ago. In addition, she includes some historical information. Her emphasis is upon
the relationship between the Pueblo and
the environment. The last chapter brings
the Pueblo Indians to the near present
(1955). The black-and-white illustrations
by Patricia Boodell complement the story
and are detailed enough for the young
reader to appreciate. As in her other books,
a map of some of the old pueblos along the
Rio Grande River is included. Good.

107. Bleeker, Sonia.
THE SEA HUNTERS: INDIANS OF THE
NORTHWEST COAST.
New York: Morrow, 1951. (4-6)
In this story the author describes the
customs, ceremonies, and life patterns of
the Pacific Coast Indians, specifically
those who lived along the western coast of
Canada, southern archipelago of Alaska,
and Vancouver Island in prehistoric times.
She provides extensive detail about roles,
customs, tools, and practices. The black-

and-white illustrations by Althea Karr that
include sketches of fishing tools, baskets,
jewelry, floats, boats, oars, and knives, are
equally as detailed and fit the mood of the
text. In the last chapter the author deals
with the arrival of the Russians, the first
Europeans to make contact with these Indians. This book provides a good beginning overview. Good.

108. Bleeker, Sonia.
THE SEMINOLE INDIANS.
New York: Morrow, 1954. (4-6)
Beginning with Osceola's boyhood, the
author traces the movement of the Creeks
from their homeland (now southern Georgia and Alabama) to Florida. The author
explains how Florida became the home of
the Seminoles; the relationship between
whites, blacks, and Indians; and provides
some details about Seminole customs and
practices. She reserves the last chapter to
describe the reservation life of present-day
Seminoles; much of this material is now
dated. The black-and-white illustrations
by Althea Karr are adequate but not as
detailed as they might be. Adequate.

109. Bleeker, Sonia.
THE SIOUX INDIANS: HUNTERS AND
WARRIORS OF THE PLAINS.
New York: Morrow, 1962. (4-6)
An unusually good description of travel
on the Great Plains in the nineteenth century is a highlight of this book describing
the past and present life of the Sioux.
Bleeker details how many travelers almost
lost their minds because they doubted they
were moving at all through the monotony
of the landscape, and how Indians shot
arrows to find their way. Bleeker's writing
is clear with a basic social studies text type
of expression: "Their beautiful, bountiful
lands, with clear lakes, rivers, and
streams, had sufficient game and fish for
everyone, but warring seemed also to be
a part of the Indians' way of life" (p.14).
She describes coming of age rites for boys
and girls and other facets of Plains life in
the 1800s, often presenting a superhuman, warlike picture. Her description of
modern-day Sioux life is limited, and she

sometimes oversimplifies: "At present the problems that face these Sioux are the same problems that face any people whose means are limited" (p.154). Kisa Sasaki's black-and-white illustrations are detailed, adequate textbook pictures. Adequate.

110. Blood, Charles L., and Link, Martin.
    THE GOAT IN THE RUG.
    New York: Parents' Magazine Pr.,
    1976. (K-3)
This is a charming, nonsensical treatment of Navajo rug making that is fun to read. A goat narrates the story of what happens to his wool from the time it is sheared until it becomes a rug, and the process is sufficiently well-detailed to give children a feel for its intricacy. The illustrations by Nancy Winslow Parker, in color and black-and-white, fit the writing beautifully; the whimsical touch of a "shopping list" as the goat and the weaver look for dye plants is typical. The book is easy for primary age children to read for themselves. Good.

111. Bodo, Murray.
    WALK IN BEAUTY: MEDITATIONS FROM
    THE DESERT.
    Cincinnati, Ohio: St. Anthony
    Messenger Pr., 1974. (3 and up)
Four lengthy poems comprise the body of this book about Navajo land, people and songs, and the Franciscan missionaries who came in 1898 from Cincinnati to Gallup to teach them. The story is told from a knowledgeable observer's point of view. It is an explanation of the present based upon the past. The emphasis or tone concentrates on nature, tranquility, and religion (Christianity as well as the Navajo stance toward life). The author includes several poems and prose pieces by other authors, as well as numerous black-and-white photographs by Gregory Fryzel. Good.

112. Bonham, Barbara.
    THE BATTLE OF WOUNDED KNEE:
    THE GHOST DANCE UPRISING.
    Chicago: Reilly & Lee, 1971. (6-8)
The book describes the events leading up to the massacre at Wounded Knee (to call it a *battle,* as in the title, is inaccurate). There are some fascinating insights here into the people, events, and complexities of the time, such as the army surgeon, accustomed to death, who faints when he sees wounded and dying Indian women and children, and the author's description of one soldier:

> As the squad turned to leave, Blacksmith Carey noted some movement and said, "Hey, this man ain't dead." As Carey made the statement, he put the muzzle of his rifle to the Indian's head and pulled the trigger. Turning the body over, the squad saw that it was a boy of fourteen or fifteen.
>
> Captain Godfrey was upset and asked Carey why he had shot the boy. Carey, upset, too, and frightened, began to cry. "I had been warned not to trust a wounded Indian, or take any chances with one. I shot without thinking." Carey later recalled he had been a soldier for only a few weeks at the time of the battle. [p.137]

The research is thorough, the writing done well, and the author is scrupulously fair to all participants. Occasionally it is possible to disagree with her conclusions; for example, she perhaps gives too much emphasis to the Ghost Dance as the major cause of the events (it, too, was merely a symptom); and some of her generalizations about the Sioux could be contested: "Next to hunting, the most important activity of the Sioux was war" (p.3), or "Indians showed their children great affection and indulged their every whim" (p.3). The illustration on the cover of the book is unfortunate; it gives the impression that this is a "blood and thunder" fiction story about Indians. The author includes a bibliography. Good.

113. Borland, Hal.
    WHEN THE LEGENDS DIE.
    New York: Bantam Pathfinder Ed.,
    1969. (7 and up)
An extremely well-written study of characterization, certainly one of the best written about Indians and Indian life on

the reservation. A summary of the story cannot begin to do justice to its effectiveness. It involves a young Indian boy who, when his father fears prosecution for killing another Indian, flees with his family to the forest and lives the old Indian way of life until he is captured and brought back to the reservation some ten years later, after his parents' deaths. The contrast the author presents between reservation life and life in the forest is devastating; the young reader cannot help but deplore the ignorance that existed among both Indians and whites during the 1900s. Poor communication between individuals and groups is a constant factor throughout the book, to the point that the young reader may feel futility at such waste and may need to share these feelings—the book is that moving. This is, indeed, fiction, highly romanticized fiction. Still, it offers views of Indian life that surpass the accuracy of most non-fiction books. A classic. Good.

114. Bounds, Thelma V.
THE STORY OF THE MISSISSIPPI
CHOCTAWS.
Chilocco, Okla.: Interior-Chilocco Pr.
for U.S. Dept of Interior, Bureau of
Indian Affairs, 1958. (2–4)
This presentation of present-day life (1958) of the Mississippi Choctaw was designed as a reader for Indian children; consequently, the language reflects a basal-reader style: "The Choctaws were a peaceful tribe and never started wars with their white neighbors" (p.9). Descriptions of the history, educational practices, health services, and industry of the Mississippi Choctaw Agency are given. Students at the Conehatta School at the agency illustrated the book. If the book is ever updated, it would be of interest to non-Indian students as well, because it describes many aspects of Indian life not often included in social studies texts. Adequate.

115. Bowman, James Cloyd.
WINABOJO: MASTER OF LIFE.
Chicago: Albert Whitman, 1941.
(4–7)

This retelling of the legend of Winabojo is presented in a typical 1940s format. The color and black-and-white illustrations are similar to those characteristic of children's books of the era—small, realistic, yet romanticized. The writing style is stiff but acceptable; the introduction is too brief to offer the reader enough feel for the setting. Adequate.

116. Boyce, George A.
SOME PEOPLE ARE INDIANS.
New York: Vanguard, 1974.
(7 and up)
This is an outstanding book, with its black-and-white drawings by Yeffe Kimball, its series of short stories about real persons, places, and events known to the author, and the section of cultural and historical comments at the end. The author reminds us that "as Indians come into contact with non-Indian ways, conditions change so rapidly that no one can say all Navajos behave in a particular manner. Nor can it be said that no Navajos behave in certain ways" (p.x). Boyce deals with the feelings of the Navajo about darkness, ghosts, courtship, pride, witches, rewards, and the whites authentically and convincingly. He writes well, making good use of setting, customs, language, and details to catch the reader up in Navajo life. For instance, he uses believable names such as Gold Tooth's Daughter, George None Smith, Badge Wearer, and includes such details as the casual mention of a younger wife; a realistic picture of a trading post, including chest-high counters; Navajos pointing with their chins; rocks in sacks of wool and of piñones to increase the sense of authenticity. This is a good resource book for teachers unacquainted with Navajo history and ways, as well as a good book for reading aloud and for pleasure reading. Young Navajo readers may find the book an inspiration for their own creative writing, since it will remind them of the details of their own lives. Statements such as "she should have set his things outside the door long ago" (p.33) will be a source for class discussions. Be prepared. Parents who have instituted read-

ing aloud in their families will find this a good book for older children and teen-agers. Good.

117. Brandon, William, Ed.
THE MAGIC WORLD: AMERICAN INDIAN SONGS AND POEMS.
New York: Morrow, 1971. (K and up)
A thorough, complete coverage of Indian poetry and songs—Modoc to Cochití—makes this book a valuable addition to any library. The book is designed for adults, but could be used, in a selective fashion, with young children. For example, the Mandan bedtime song for children on page 90 is suitable to read aloud to primary children. A literate introductory section presents a good discussion of the purpose of oral literature:

> Much of it was only for fun and entertainment, in which poetry added the joyous dimension of fantasy for which seemingly, the day-to-day American Indian life was lived. It was a life that appeared (to European eyes) to consist overwhelmingly of play taken seriously. If the Pawnees had operated a General Motors, each worker would have had his time-clock-punching song, and so on, and the management would have been at least as attentive to the songs as to the rate of production, probably more so. [p.xii]

Good.

118. Brewster, Benjamin [Mary Elting].
THE FIRST BOOK OF ESKIMOS.
New York: Watts, 1952. (4-6)
All Eskimos from Siberia to Alaska are the subject of this book, providing intermediate grade readers with a feel for the diversity of the Eskimo population of the world. A fictionalized story of an Eskimo boy and girl is used by the author to present Eskimo life and customs. At times, the text is overgeneralized: "An Eskimo laughed more in a day than anyone else did in a week." A section deals with Eskimo inventions such as snow goggles and shoes for dogs. Including a polar projection map is a good touch; most maps in books for elementary children are the

standard Mercader. The illustrations by Ursula Koering are greeting-card cute and unfortunately, the section on modern-day life is dated. Adequate.

119. Brewster, Benjamin [Mary Elting].
FIRST BOOK OF INDIANS.
New York: Watts, 1950. (2-4)
Perhaps the easiest way to describe this book is to allow some of the section headings to speak for themselves: "There Were Tribes and More Tribes" (p.8); "They Knew All Sorts of Things" (p.12); "The Zunis Helped Each Other" (p.53). The rest of the book reflects this same simplistic, textbook tone. William Moyer's color and black-and-white illustrations continue the same pattern. Dated. Poor.

120. Brindze, Ruth.
THE STORY OF THE TOTEM POLE.
New York: Vanguard, 1951. (4-6)
History, legends, and facts about totems are skillfully blended in this narrative. The reader should have a clear concept of this unique art form when he finishes this book. Told in an appealing style and brightened by illustrations in the best totem pole tradition, the book should motivate students to learn more about the culture that produced these spectacular carvings. Good.

121. Bringle, Mary.
ESKIMOS.
New York: Watts, 1973. (4-7)
Packed with accurate information, illustrated with a map, photographs, and drawings, this book is a must for a social studies unit on Eskimos. The people, the land, the way of life are all related; and this book brings together the old and the new. The old way of life is pictured as producing a vigorous, resourceful people, and the new way as preserving life: the Eskimo population is growing in number. Good.

122. Broun, Emily.
A BALL FOR LITTLE BEAR.
Eau Claire, Wisc.: Hale, 1955. (K-3)

The author provides no introduction or explanation to this Ojibwa legend; consequently, the young reader may well wonder what Indians are doing in it. An animal tale, it tells about the bear that stole the sun. The color illustrations by Dick Mac-Kay are adequate, but not exceptional. The story is really rather good, but the lack of grounding or explanation about the background handicaps the book. Adequate.

123. Brown, Dee.
WOUNDED KNEE.
New York: Holt, 1974. (5–7)
Adapted for young readers by Amy Ehrlich from Dee Brown's *Bury My Heart at Wounded Knee,* this is basically a conflict and war history from the Indians' viewpoint. It examines little-known incidents of Indian/non-Indian struggles, as well as such better known examples as Wounded Knee. Black-and-white illustrations and pictures, an Indian calendar, and an excellent bibliography contribute to the effectiveness of the book. This treatment is primarily concerned with confrontation; consequently, it does not concentrate on customs. As a presentation of the Indian side, it is an effective book; however, non-Indians are stereotyped as one-dimensional, routinely insensitive villains. Perhaps the authors felt the non-Indian side had been examined thoroughly in other books; even so, it would be well to supplement this with books written by other authors, Indian and non-Indian, who hold different views of the same events. Good.

124. Brown, Evelyn N.
KATERI TEKAKWITHA: MOHAWK MAID.
New York: Farrar, 1958. (5–7)
This story has been written for "Catholic readers" from nine- to fifteen-years-old, and may be too sectarian for some children. The book is replete with religious interpretations, practice, and dogma. A woman's role as a Mohawk is described as *either marry or starve.* At the end, when Kateri decides to devote herself to the Catholic church, she literally starves herself to death. There are other religious overtones that may offend some non-Catholic readers. In all, the emphasis is not upon Mohawk customs and life, except as they relate to Christianity, but rather the author synchronizes actual events in Kateri's life with tribal customs and superstitions, "in order to paint her against her own crude and colorful background." Adequate.

125. Brown, Vinson.
GREAT UPON THE MOUNTAIN: THE STORY OF CRAZY HORSE, LEGENDARY MYSTIC AND WARRIOR.
New York: Macmillan, 1975.
(6 and up)
This is a fictionalized account of Crazy Horse's visions and how they influenced his life as a warrior. One of the few biographies that acknowledges the assistance of Indian contributors, whose ancestors passed down from generation to generation some of the stories included and referred to in the story, this book seems a curious mixture of past and present. Early in the book, discussing a vision, the author infuses a little modern anger into Crazy Horse's dream of "the two-leggeds, white man and red, yellow man and black alike, [who] have killed too much of life, and made the world ugly with smog and pollution, wars and lies." This is a book of sadness and cynicism. There is also an element of guilt, characteristic of some books about Indians written by white authors. It includes a foreword written by Red Dawn, a Santee Sioux; an introduction by the author, who describes a vision of his own; an annotated map of major events in the life of Crazy Horse; and a brief glossary of the Lakota language. For the rest, the book includes comprehensive legends, stories, and quite a bit of background information explaining Lakota religion and mysticism. Good.

126. Brown, Vinson, and
Andrewes, Douglas.
THE POMO INDIANS OF CALIFORNIA AND THEIR NEIGHBORS.
Healdsburg, Calif.: Naturegraph, 1969. (4 and up)

A scholarly, thorough work which includes such items as the language, background, history, physical characteristics, and foods of the Pomo Indians, this book may put off younger readers by its adult-like format. Actually, the words are not that difficult and the text, itself, is interesting; but such section headings as "Divisions, Habitats, and Physical Characteristics" appear drier than necessary. Consequently, middle graders will perhaps find the charts more appealing. And there are charts on everything: a plant chart on page 17; a cooking chart on page 25 that shows the various ways the Pomos cooked (in holes, baskets, etc.). The authors also offer some interesting philosophy:

> Even the term "civilized" can have many meanings. If by "civilized" we mean having many gadgets and comforts, then we are more civilized than any Indian people of the past. But if we mean people able to get along together in comparative peace, with little or no war or crime, without a polluted atmosphere and water or other destruction of the environment, and with a close understanding between members of the society, then California Indians had a superior civilization. [pp.5–6]

The volume includes an appendix on place names and meanings, a bibliography for older readers, an index, and maps and illustrations by Douglas Adams. The book deserves a better printing and format. Good.

127. Bruchac, Joseph.
TURKEY BROTHER: AND OTHER TALES IROQUOIS FOLK STORIES.
Trumansburg, N.Y.: Crossing Pr., 1975. (4–6)
A collection of nine Iroquois tales in which subtle morals are drawn for the listener, these stories deal with both animals and people. Kahonhe's black-and-white line drawings are suitably and appropriately done. The author describes his stories as "never moralistic or tiresome in the way that some stories written FOR children can be, perhaps because too many stories written FOR children are actually written

AT children" (p.11). The stories are short and succinct, and the author reminds the reader that they are designed to be read aloud. Adequate.

128. Bruemmer, Fred.
SEASONS OF THE ESKIMO.
Greenwich, Conn.: New York Graphic Soc., 1971. (6 and up)
Exquisite text and photographs combine to tell the story of a year in the life of the Eskimo. A thorough, well-written introduction describes past and modern Eskimo life. The photographs, in color and black-and-white, would make this a fine gift for young people interested in either photography or Eskimos, or both. Much of the text is written on too high a conceptual level for young children, but they would enjoy the photographs. A classic. Good.

129. Budd, Lillian.
FULL MOONS: INDIAN LEGENDS OF THE SEASONS.
Chicago: Rand McNally, 1971. (4–6)
This book contains thirteen Indian legends about the seasons, corresponding to each of the thirteen full moons in a year. Each of these "moons" was given a name: the worm moon, the planters' moon, the flower moon, and the like. The story of the worm moon, for example, relates how the Panamint Indians selected this name from the inchworm. The introductory sections are helpful; the author sets a good stage for his tales. George Armstrong's illustrations are outstanding and indicate a great deal of research on his part. In green, brown, and charcoal, they used mixed art media to achieve an effect that enhances the text presentation immensely. Two minor criticisms: not all tribes called the moons by the same name, as some readers could mistakenly deduce from this book; and the table of contents would be more helpful if it included the name of the tribe from which each legend came. Good.

130. Buff, Mary, and Buff, Conrad.
DANCING CLOUD, THE NAVAJO BOY.
New York: Viking, 1957. (2–5)
Each chapter in this story comprises a

47

complete incident in the life of the Navajos Dancing Cloud and his sister, Lost Tooth. The illustrations by Conrad Buff are good; the writing is rather strained and awkward. Occasionally the story deviates from usual Navajo customs as, for example, when the two children are depicted as collecting prehistoric pottery bits—even many modern Navajos would avoid the places of the "Old Ones." In considering this book, allow also for the 1957 publication date. Although the story is useful to portray a point in time, stories of other, more modern, adjustments to cultural change are now available. Adequate.

131. Buff, Mary, and Buff, Conrad.
HAH-NEE OF THE CLIFF DWELLERS.
Boston: Houghton, 1965. (3-5)
This is an unusual book. It builds a plausible and interesting story around what is known about the life of prehistoric Cliff Dwellers, a task that requires a great deal of research and extrapolation. The story is centered around a boy who is different—a Ute raised by Cliff Dweller parents as their own. The story explores prejudice, growing old, and death as it tells of the boy's feeling of rejection and his final acceptance as he finds a way for the pueblo to survive the drought. The authors may make more of the rejection theme than necessary; an adopted boy with two Cliff Dweller parents would have a range of relatives as part of his extended family. The phrasing of the prologue and epilogue in poetic form is a good touch. The illustrations of a Mesa Verde-like environment add greatly to the books effectiveness. Good.

132. Buff, Mary, and Buff, Conrad.
KEMI: AN INDIAN BOY BEFORE THE
WHITE MAN CAME.
Pasadena, Calif.: Ritchie, 1966. (4-6)
Writing that adheres closely to known facts about Southern California Indians makes this book a valuable introduction for children to the cultures along the Southern California coast before the coming of Europeans. Beautifully illustrated with Conrad Buff's lithographs, the story of Kemi includes much information about pre-Cabrillo life. Kemi travels with his father from their foothill village to a coastal village, where island traders came with soapstone (steatite). The day of trading between inlanders and islanders makes an interesting sequence. Apparently Kemi spoke Shoshone, for he was able to converse with the boy from the island of soapstone (Santa Catalina). The story involves ethics. Good.

133. Bulla, Clyde R.
EAGLE FEATHER.
New York: Crowell, 1953. (K-3)
In this descriptive story of a young Navajo boy and his life on the reservation, the author has included Navajo customs and two Navajo songs to add to the setting. The boy's decision to attend school is a subject of controversy among Indian readers. Supplement with more recent material. Adequate.

134. Bulla, Clyde R.
INDIAN HILL.
New York: Crowell, 1963. (2-4)
This is a sensitive story of an eleven-year-old Navajo boy's difficult acceptance of life in the city. The father moves his family to the city where he can use the trade he learned in school. The gentleness and strength of the boy's family and his own reactions are perceptively and honestly presented. Good.

135. Bulla, Clyde R.
POCAHONTAS AND THE STRANGERS.
New York: Crowell, 1971. (5-7)
In this sensitive, well-written story about the relationship between Pocahontas and the English settlers, the author infuses depth into his characters. Pocahontas, as presented here, lacks neither spirit nor initiative. Her relationship with other members of her tribe is realistically portrayed. The reader will feel the power of tribal law; although not enforced in an authoritative manner, it affected equally all members of the tribe. In this story Pocahontas invokes an old law whereby "if a prisoner is to be killed, a woman may say,

'Give me this man. He is mine.' " In this manner she was able to save the life of Captain John Smith, although historians disagree as to the accuracy of this episode. Describing her as probably the first Indian woman to visit England, the author speculates in a plausible manner on how Pocahontas must have felt and reacted when she, her husband, John Rolfe, and her son visited London. The author also implies what many other historians believe, that Pocahontas deeply loved John Smith but believed him to be dead when she married John Rolfe. The shaded black-and-white illustrations by Peter Burchard lend a dreamy quality to the characters, further emphasizing the tenuousness of the relationships between the Indians and the early English settlers. Good.

136. Bulla, Clyde R.
SQUANTO: FRIEND OF THE WHITE MEN.
New York: Crowell, 1954. (3-6)
The Squanto of this book has depth and will seem real to the young reader. The story concentrates on Squanto's adventures with, in order, the English Captain Weymouth, Charles Robbins and his family, Captain John Smith, Thomas Hunt, John Slanie, and Captain Thomas Dermer. The well-known tale of Squanto and the Pilgrims and the settlement of Plymouth is not so romanticized as to mislead the young reader. Squanto's trips to England and Spain are described. The simplicity of Peter Burchard's black-and-white illustrations adds to the book. Good.

137. Bunting, Eve.
THE ONCE-A-YEAR DAY.
Chicago: Childrens Pr., 1974. (4-6)
The "Once-a-Year Day" of the title is the day the barges come in through the sea to the Eskimo village to deliver supplies and mail. This story is based on a non-Eskimo assumption that a child would hesitate to share her home, her toys, and her food with an orphan cousin girl; more likely the cousin would be regarded as her sister. In the story the girl is resentful of her cousin, but soon realizes that the cousin is like an orange, with the best part

inside and the tart part outside. This story is well developed and written and would be more effective if the Eskimo identity of the characters were changed to other backgrounds where the main thesis would be more in keeping with the cultural pattern. The black-and-white illustrations by W. T. Mars are well done and follow the spirit of the story. Adequate.

138. Bureau of Indian Affairs.
INDIAN AND ESKIMO CHILDREN.
Washington, D.C.: U.S. Government Printing Office, 1969. (1-3)
This book is uneven in its design. The format consists of photographs followed by short explanations in an effective pattern. Fine black-and-white photographs of Eskimo children present unusual views of their lives, such as the Eskimo boy with his front teeth missing (p.3) and the Alaskan Indian mother and baby on page 4. Parts of the text show Eskimos and Indians working at modern jobs, although all of them are men. Charles Curtis, part-Indian vice-president of the United States, is mentioned. A good feeling for the changes taking place in Eskimo life is presented: "Some Eskimos also drive snowmobiles or fly airplanes" (p.17). Counterbalancing this is the pedantic wording of the text: "The costumes the boy and these men are wearing are symbols of the history of native Alaskans" (p.39); the tendency to stereotype on a sexist basis: "Mothers are the same everywhere. This Alaskan mother loves her baby very much" p.4); to overgeneralize: "In the Northwest, Indians are fishermen" (p.21); and to lump all Indian groups together. Adequate.

139. Burrows, Don.
INDIAN NAMES.
(no place): Keller Printing Service, 1976. (1 and up)
This is an alphabetically arranged educational reference book giving the names of Indian tribes of North America, with cross-references and alternate spellings, as well as identification of clans for some of the more widely known tribes. For ex-

ample, some forty-one families in the Apache tribe are specified. The book is useful as a reference, although it consists solely of lists of names, with no information or description provided. Writers, anthropologists, and students will find it helpful for identification purposes. Good.

140. Burt, Jesse, and
   Ferguson, Robert B.
   INDIANS OF THE SOUTHEAST: THEN
   AND NOW.
   Nashville, Tenn.: Abingdon Pr., 1973.
   (5 and up)
This is an exhaustive, thorough reference, almost encyclopedic in nature, with dictionary overtones. Among other subjects it reviews the peoples, religions, ceremonials, foods, dance, music, child-rearing practices, and Indian traders of the Southeastern Indian tribes. It includes such information as geographic data, descriptions of clans, analysis of language patterns, and carefully described diagrams. The writing is scholarly in tone: "Vanderbilt University anthropologist Ronald Spores points out, however, that Indians and Mongoloids do tend to diverge rather markedly in blood type relative frequencies, a fact not yet explained by anthropologists" (p.16); and the explanations of tribal customs are carefully researched: "Women were influential in council, and in some places they cast the deciding vote for war or peace" (p.69). The last section on Indian young people is contemporary and informative; the quotes from Indian youths indicate a wide variety of lifestyles. Good.

141. Callan, Eileen T.
   A HARDY RACE OF MEN: AMERICA'S
   EARLY INDIANS.
   New York: Harcourt, 1970. (7 and up)
Beginning with the Age of Reptiles, the author traces life changes on earth, then explores the clues that help archaeologists piece together information about ancient civilizations. Illustrated with photographs, sketches, and maps, this book gives a panoramic view of the early inhabitants of the Americas. The work of noted archaeologists is carefully described, with special attention given to landmark discoveries. Most interesting are the descriptions of the lifestyles of various groups of prehistoric Americans, as indicated by the findings of archaeologists. Good.

142. Campbell, C. W.
   SEQUOYAH: THE STORY OF AN
   AMERICAN INDIAN.
   Minneapolis, Minn.: Dillon Pr., 1973.
   (5-9)
An extremely well-documented book for the target age group, this story of Sequoyah includes a nice mixture of photographs, portrait reproductions, a map, and the complete Cherokee syllabary. The author presents several theories regarding Sequoyah's early life, including those about the identity of his father and the cause of his lameness, allowing even the youngest reader either to choose from the theories given or simply to speculate, thus helping them develop a scientific attitude. The writing style and format are very similar to short biographies that appear in magazines and journals. In other words, this author does not talk down to his readers. He presents his characters in an objective but entirely human fashion, and describes Cherokee philosophy and practices in a rich, complete manner. Although he fought with the white Americans in the War of 1812, Sequoyah's interest in Indian languages, "talking leaves" (books), and his development of the Cherokee syllabary (which led to the creation of the Cherokee newspaper, *Cherokee Phoenix*) are emphasized as Sequoyah's leadership contribution. Good.

143. Carlson, Natalie S.
   THE TOMAHAWK FAMILY.
   New York: Harper, 1960. (2-6)
This story concerns contrasts between the old Indian traditions and modern Indian life. The young children portrayed attend school and are not always in sympathy with the ideas of their grandmother. The Indian boy Frankie tricks his grandmother into coming to a PTA meeting with surprising results. Well balanced between

the sexes, the book is clearly written and would be interesting for both girls and boys. Good.

144. Carlson, Vada F.
COCHISE: CHIEF OF THE CHIRICAHUAS.
New York: Harvey House, 1973. (5–9)
One of the better-written biographies of Indian leaders, this book traces Cochise's life from his youth until his death. Although the emphasis is upon the role and activities of young men, their preparation for manhood, and expectations of their tribe, the role and activities of women are developed as carefully and in an interesting fashion; hence, the reader has a sense of a more complete society, peopled with both males and females, old and young. The story lacks depth of characterizations and some characters are introduced and then dropped, which may lead the young reader to wonder what happened to them. The black-and-white illustrations by William Odd complement the tone of the biography. A brief glossary is included, as well as a list of the author's sources. Good.

145. Carlson, Vada F.
HIGH COUNTRY CANVAS.
Flagstaff, Ariz.: Northland Pr., 1972. (5 and up)
This is a collection of approximately fifty short, simply written poems describing the land, animals, and climate, as well as the people of the high deserts of Arizona and New Mexico. Six poems describe Indians, specifically. In these, the author concentrates upon the Navajo. The black-and-white sketches by Joe Rodriguez greatly enhance the author's poems; in fact, the illustrations could stand on their own merit. Adequate.

146. Carlson, Vada, and
    Witherspoon, Gary.
BLACK MOUNTAIN BOY.
Rough Rock, Ariz.: D.I.N.E., 1970. (2–4)
Written for use by Navajo boys and girls as they learn to read, this is an outstanding book. The description of Navajo family life and customs is superb. In spite of the authors' having to use a controlled vocabulary, the wording, particularly the dialogue, sounds incredibly real. The book describes the importance of small happenings, the beauty to see if one but looks, the sense of expectancy of childhood as vividly for all children as it does for the target audience of Navajo youngsters. The touching moment when the Navajo boy goes to live with his older sister and her husband, not because his parents do not want him or feel they are losing him, but because "they have given you to me to raise because I have no children of my own" (p.47) is typical of the sharing spirit of many Navajo families. Andy Tsinajinnie's black-and-white illustrations fit beautifully with the story. Do not fail to buy this. Good.

147. Carpenter, Edmund, ed.
THE STORY OF COMOCK THE ESKIMO.
New York: Simon & Schuster, 1968. (5 and up)
This story has an interesting history. It was told by Comock to Robert Flaherty in 1912, who, many years later, wrote it down and shared it with Carpenter, who edited and illustrated the book. Comock's story tells, in his own words, of the survival of a family on an isolated Arctic island for ten years. A dramatic story, it is climaxed by the family's decision to return to the mainland and their ingenious ways of solving Arctic problems. Besides Carpenter's illustrations of Arctic life, there are a few line drawings of Eskimo artifacts. Good.

148. Carroll, Ruth, and Carroll, Latrobe.
TOUGH ENOUGH'S INDIANS.
New York: Walck, 1960. (4–6)
About a group of young mountain children saved by a Cherokee Indian family, the story is more concerned with mountain life than Cherokee life. The drawings serve to move the story along, but primarily illustrate the white family's life. The book does talk about scalping, raising controversy in some quarters (Who intro-

duced scalping to America? Should it be mentioned at all? Does it belong in children's books, and the like). Story design: Adequate. Portrayal of Indians: Poor.

149. Chafetz, Henry.
THUNDERBIRD AND OTHER STORIES.
New York: Pantheon, 1964. (3–5)
This book contains legends about Thunderbird, Bat, and the Peace Pipe that explain natural phenomena and the history and use of the peace pipe. The format, layout, and art work are especially fine. Ronni Solbert's black-white-red drawings look like a combination of Navajo sand paintings and Northwest Indian design motifs, a pleasing combination that may not be particularly apt for illustrating legends of Eastern American Indian groups, but is beautiful. The book is well written, and the text flows: however, the whole treatment would benefit from an introductory section to set the stage and give information on the "Indians" whose legends these were, as the term *Indians* is used in a nondifferentiated way. Adequate.

150. Chandler, Edna Walker.
ALMOST BROTHERS.
Chicago: Albert Whitman, 1971.
(3–5)
There is much to commend in this book: it presents American Indians as professionals—M.D. and nurse; it tells of a successful Sioux family; it shows that a young Sioux boy could be as uninformed as any other child about Yaqui customs; and it has the type of story that keeps youngsters interested. The young Sioux boy comes to Arizona with his M.D. father and nurse mother when they take charge of a hospital. Lonely, he meets Yaqui and Mexican-American friends. He also finds an old mine that will help his new-found friends economically. There are features that weaken the book: the author follows the usual father—M.D., mother—nurse pattern, although it is refreshing to meet a Sioux M.D.; the plot follows the same lines of the familiar "white saves the native" pattern, except here it's a Sioux boy who saves the natives (again, an improve-

ment); and the text and passages of dialogue are awkwardly constructed:
"Why did my dad come to Arizona?" Benjie asked himself. "Sure, he can be head of the hospital here. But this is an awful place! It's a desert. Nothing grows here but a lot of prickly cactus. It's hot and I hate it. And now I'm going to be all alone after Charlie goes." [p.6]
The writing is the main drawback to the book. Adequate.

151. Chandler, Edna Walker.
INDIAN PAINTBRUSH.
Chicago: Albert Whitman, 1975.
(6–8)
The feelings of many Indians forced by economic conditions to travel back and forth between reservation and city are well described in this story of a half-breed Sioux girl who has trouble adjusting to life on a reservation, where she does not know the customs or the language. The author describes the essence of reservation life for some youths: "She didn't see Billy Lone Deer. He was probably at the gas station throwing dice with the other big boys" (p.17); the reaction of some half-breeds: "Francie—half white, half Indian—looked Indian, and most of the time she used her Indian name, Frances White Rabbit. But when it made a difference, she called herself Francie Morris" (p.18); and the agonies for an Indian child who could not speak her native language and was ignored by those who could: "They looked through her, over her, around her, as if she were a rock or a tree" (p.19)—anyone who has ever been ignored by an Indian can relate to this last quote. A particularly touching moment comes when Maria, the leading character, stands gazing silently at the new teacher's pretty laundry on the clothesline. The feelings described by the author in this story are honest and strong; they will, no doubt, arouse equally strong feelings in the reader. Adults should be prepared for emotional discussions on this book, particularly if there are Indian students in the group. The girl's mother allows her to make her own decision about

going to school, a matter that may puzzle readers who are not familiar with Indian child-raising patterns. The black-and-white illustrations of Lee Fitzgerrell-Smith are appropriate and well done, and the story can be used profitably with both Indian and non-Indian readers. Good.

152. Cheney, T. A.
LAND OF THE HIBERNATING RIVERS:
LIFE IN THE ARCTIC.
New York: Harcourt, 1968. (5 and up)
T. A. Cheney accompanied Byrd on his Antarctic expedition, and has also participated in Arctic expeditions; hence, his description of life in the Arctic is from personal experience. Photographs of Arctic life and scenes, many of them taken by Cheney, illustrate the beauty and ruggedness of the Far North. Eskimos and their culture are described in detail. Cheney also tells about the reindeer people, the people of the taiga, and the Yakuts. He makes the problems and the problem-solving of adapting to extreme cold interesting. Good.

153. Chisholm, Matt.
INDIANS.
Translated from the French by Claude Appell.
Chicago: Follett, 1965. (4–6)
A book about American Indians written for French children, this volume concentrates primarily on the Plains culture, although it does refer to other Indians at times. The full color illustrations by several artists are good, the best part of the book, in fact; but most of them are of Plains Indians, almost entirely of men, and concentrate on horses, hunting, and fighting. The picture caption on page 29 is interesting: "A modern Indian artist's picture of buffalo being led and driven into a catch-pen. Why the hunters did not kill them from the saddle is not clear"; it is obvious that a catch-pen is easier than shooting from horseback, not the position for the most accurate shooting of either bows or guns. The organization of the book is completely different from most American books, indicating a fresh view-

point, not necessarily a better one. There is a whole section on Indian slaves. Some of the wording is objectionable, such as a section headed "The Work of the Squaws," and some of the author's conclusions are subject to debate, such as his opinion of Comanches in this excerpt: "They varied from the tall, dignified Cheyenne and the fine Blackfoot to the short, stocky Comanche of the Plains who only looked good on a horse" (p.9). The book is limited in scope, both in coverage and concepts. Adequate.

154. Clark, Ann Nolan.
ALONG SANDY TRAILS.
New York: Viking, 1969. (K–5)
Fine color photographs by Alfred A. Cohn add authenticity and beauty to the story of a Papago girl and her grandmother who walk together in the Arizona desert. The grandmother helps her see the beauty around her—the photographs show what she sees. One tremendous shot shows her looking at bird eggs in a cactus nest. The language patterns add to the feelings of exploration and wonderment. Good.

155. Clark, Ann Nolan.
BLUE CANYON HORSE.
New York: Viking, 1954. (1–4)
This story of a young Indian boy (apparently Navajo, from the illustrations) and his horse that runs away and returns is one of Clark's better books. The writing is good, easy for primary students to read, and expressed in poetic language:
Night comes,
lonely and long,
For the Indian boy
    whose horse has gone.
Sleep does not come
    to heal his heart.
Dreams do not come
    to kindle hope.
His horse has gone. [p.16]
The illustrations are by Allan Hauser, who uses a style reminiscent of Beatien Yazz. It is hoped that the book will be reissued in a more modern format someday, one that does more justice to the author, the illus-

trations, and the book's message about freedom to grow. Good.

156. Clark, Ann Nolan.
CIRCLE OF SEASONS.
New York: Farrar, 1970. (3–6)

This book, a description of old and new ceremonies and rituals that mark the Pueblo year, including ceremonial shinny and the cleaning of irrigation ditches, features a beautiful layout and poetic writing. A well-written, concise description of Pueblo past and present is given in the foreword. The book notes that not all Pueblo Indians live in their ancestral pueblos and mentions the importance of maternal descent. Ceremonies are described as part of a way of life; age is seen as important. Indian ambivalence about school celebrations of white Thanksgiving is described: "White ways may be good, but they are difficult to comprehend and to accept" (p.39). Watch for occasional stereotyping: "Pueblo Indians are gentle, kindly, laughter-loving people" (p.41). The book concentrates on "man-work" (p.18), and only deals in a perfunctory way with women. Good.

157. Clark, Ann Nolan.
THE DESERT PEOPLE.
New York: Viking, 1962. (1–3)

The team of Ann Nolan Clark, writer, and Allan Hauser, illustrator, has produced a reflective book. Hauser's illustrations are better than his usual (as, for example, in *Blue Canyon Horse*); the picture of the whirlwind is different from the way he usually illustrates a book. Clark's writing is poetic, in simplified language easily read by young children, and gives an authentic picture of old ways of the Papago. While neither a nonfiction book nor a story, the book interprets the year of the Papago. It needs to be revised to include recent material, or to be supplemented with more current books. The introduction section is simplified, but good. Good.

158. Clark, Ann Nolan.
IN MY MOTHER'S HOUSE.
New York: Viking, 1969. (3–5)

The Tewa Indian children of the Tesuque Pueblo in New Mexico helped the author write this book, and it emphasizes things of importance to them. It tells of Tesuque, where much of life centers around the fireplace in the mother's house. Exceptional illustrations by an Indian artist, Velino Herrera, grace this beautiful book. A classic, it was one cf the first books written for children from the viewpoint of the Indian. It is highly recommended, not only for content and language patterns, but also for its importance in children's literature. The picture presented is of an older day. Good.

159. Clark, Ann Nolan.
JOURNEY TO THE PEOPLE.
New York: Viking, 1969. (6 and up)

Ann Nolan Clark shares in this book a collection of personal reminiscences of her life as a teacher of Southwestern Indians, some of her findings about Indian culture, and some of her speeches at her book award presentations. Do not dismiss the book as just another about a white who set out to "save the Indians." That would be an injustice to Indians and to Ms. Clark, alike. Some conscientious moderns will wince at her use of *racial* as a substitute for *cultural;* as in "racial characteristics differ" (p.19), but it is hard to quarrel with some of her explanations of Indian life. There are many different levels of understanding about Indians; Ms. Clark offers us a deeper view. A sampling of the type of writing the reader will find in this book can help buyers judge its suitability for their needs:

A child can carry a lasting scar without knowing what caused the wound. Many of our Southwestern children stand in two worlds of conflicting concepts. [p.19]

He did not work for pay of any kind. An Indian worked because the work in itself was important to his own, his family's, or his community's welfare. If he did not consider the work important, he did not do it. [p.22]

At last I learned. If I praised a child's accomplishments, a drawing, a poem, an examination paper, he threw it in the wastebasket, not in defiance, but in shame—shame to be singled out, either for praise or failure. [pp.33–34]

This book would be especially useful for non-Indians and non-Southwestern Indian adults who are interested in learning more about this culture. Teen-agers can profit from the example of a woman who lived a different life from most in her culture and time. Good discussions about stereotyping could come from student exploration of stereotype versus cultural traits, with this book providing material for the debate. Adequate.

160. Clark, Ann Nolan.
LITTLE BOY WITH THREE NAMES: STORIES OF TAOS PUEBLO.
Washington, D.C.: U.S. Dept. of the Interior, Bureau of Indian Affairs, Div. of Education, 1940. (4–7)

Written for use primarily in Indian schools, this is a story of a Taos Pueblo boy and his three names—school, home, and church names, all different—and how he got them. The illustrations by Tonita Lujon are good, but suffer from being reproduced in black-and-white instead of color. Actually, the book format is not as good as the writing and the illustrations warrant. The book contains material that is of historical interest but is now dated: "During the summer all Taos men wear the white sheet, either around their shoulders and over their heads or at least tied around the waist" (foreword); today there is not such distinction in costume, either for men or school children. In addition, modern Taos children would probably be more insistent on choosing a name they wish to be known by, and Taos children now usually live at home and go to school through secondary school. The book is of interest today primarily for its historical content. Writing: Good. Format: Poor. Facts: Dated.

161. Clark, Ann Nolan.
LITTLE HERDER IN SPRING.
Lawrence, Kans.: Haskell Pr. for U.S. Dept. of the Interior, Bureau of Indian Affairs, (no date). (4–7)

162. Clark, Ann Nolan.
LITTLE HERDER IN SUMMER.
Lawrence, Kans.: Haskell Pr. for U.S. Dept. of the Interior, Bureau of Indian Affairs, (no date). (4–7)

163. Clark, Ann Nolan.
LITTLE HERDER IN AUTUMN.
Lawrence, Kans.: Haskell Pr. for U.S. Dept. of the Interior, Bureau of Indian Affairs, (no date). (4–7)

164. Clark, Ann Nolan.
LITTLE HERDER IN WINTER.
Lawrence, Kans.: Haskell Pr. for U.S. Dept. of the Interior, Bureau of Indian Affairs, (no date). (4–7)

These texts, intended for use with Indian children, are beautifully written in a traditional style of phrasing. The story of a young Navajo girl's life for a year is written in graceful, poetic form. Hoke Denetsosie's illustrations are superb. The format and the reproductions of the drawings are cramped and small; it is too bad the budget did not allow for a more appropriate layout. Good.

165. Clark, Ann Nolan.
THE LITTLE INDIAN POTTERY MAKER.
Eau Claire, Wisc.: Hale, 1955. (1–3)

This book, in flowing, authentic-sounding language, tells the thoughts and reactions of a Pueblo Indian girl as she watches her mother and other women make pottery and as she begins to work with them herself. The vocabulary is controlled for easy reading by primary children, but this factor does not limit its poetic impact. Although the book speaks of pottery making as primarily women's work (not as true now as in 1953), this occurs in a matter-of-fact, reportorial fashion, rather than in a sexist one: "I have worked with earth and water doing woman's work" (p.31) Don Percival's illustrations are soft, good, and apt. The implications of the title are unfortunate; the book is not at all trite. Good.

166. Clark, Ann Nolan.
LITTLE NAVAJO BLUEBIRD.
New York: Viking, 1943. (2–5)
This story deals with the conflict within Doli, a young Navajo girl, over whether to go to school or stay home. Her relationships with her brothers and sisters are explored. The young reader can readily empathize with the story. The early publication date does not necessarily affect the story, but does suggest that the book needs to be supplemented by more recent material. The black-and-white illustrations by Paul Lantz are few, but good. Good.

167. Clark, Ann Nolan.
MEDICINE MAN'S DAUGHTER.
New York: Farrar, 1963. (7 and up)
In this story about Tall-Girl, the daughter of a Navajo Medicine Man, the young reader sees something of present-day (1963) life on the Indian reservation, as well as the relationship between Catholic missionaries and the Navajos. The author, who has had long experience in service with the Bureau of Indian Affairs as well as an equally long career as an author of children's books, has infused depth as well as individuality into her characters. In addition, she has managed to include, in a visionary yet sensitive way, the subtle similarities that exist among all religions as well as among medical practices in different cultures. She describes the strengths and weaknesses of each, although she is somewhat more self-righteous insofar as Christianity and Western medicine are concerned. The black-and-white illustrations by Donald Bolognese seem consistent with the theme of the story. The general advocacy of Christianity may make this book objectionable to some groups. Adequate.

168. Clark, Ann Nolan.
SUN JOURNEY.
Washington, D.C.: U.S. Dept. of the Interior, Bureau of Indian Affairs, Div. of Education, 1945. (3–6)
Written to be used by Indian children in government schools, this book tells the story of a Zuñi boy and his conflict over white versus Zuñi learning. He is taken out of school by his family to spend a year with his grandfather learning Zuñi traditions. He leaves reluctantly; and then, after the year, he is equally reluctant to leave his grandfather, but decides he can learn from both. The grandfather voices many feelings to the boy; for instance, he says about whites: "He [the white man] wraps his feelings up in words and puts them with marks on paper for you to see. Here we keep our feelings in our hearts. To know them you must live them" (p.2). The black-and-white illustrations by Percy Tsisete Sandry are great, but, as is often the case with BIA publications, the format and printing are not as good as the writing and the illustrations. In one of the sections, the artist explains his work. This is a long book, yet can be easily read by elementary school children. Although the customs described reflect the publication date (1945), this book still offers much information to non-Zuñi readers. Good.

169. Clark, Ann Nolan.
THIS FOR THAT.
San Carlos, Calif.: Golden Gate Junior Books, 1965. (K–3)
A story about a young Papago boy, this book tells about his troubles remembering where he puts things after he takes them. The format, the story, and the illustrations are charming; and the book imparts a sense of wonder at all the things there are to do and learn. The leading character is portrayed as a mixture of good and bad behavior in a kind of "Indians are just like the boy next door" style. This offers the non-Indian reader a feeling of commonality with the character but may not do justice to the uniqueness of growing up Papago. The wording of the book is in a poetic format:

Mother said, "Put-it, Pick-it,
I don't know
what to do
with you."
Mother said that
and she meant
every word
that she said. [p. 27]
Good.

170. Clark, Ann Nolan.
WHO WANTS TO BE A PRAIRIE DOG?
Washington, D.C.: U.S. Dept. of the
Interior, Bureau of Indian Affairs, Div.
of Education, 1940. (1–3)
Although written for Indian children in
Bureau of Indian Affairs schools, this book
offers much to non-Indian children. The
story of a small Navajo boy who is learning responsibility, the book is still a delight
after thirty-six years, in spite of some
dated material. Clark, as she so often does,
writes the story as a series of connected
poems:

> This little boy is Mr.
> Many-Goat's son.
> If you do not believe his
> story it is because
> you are not short,
> Nor fat,
> Nor slow,
> And never, never have you
> been down a prairie dog hole.

The sheep dipping episode is different
from adventures usually included in children's story. It is unfortunate that Clark
used the word *hurry* to mean responsibility (as she does in describing a person
who hasn't learned to hurry); current
usage of the word often implies that a person who *hurries* is a person too busy to see
the finer things (to *Stop, and Smell the
Roses*). Van Tsihnahjinnie's black-and-
white illustrations are good, but the book
format does not display them to advantage. The section in which the artist tells
of his work in his own words is a good
addition. Good.

171. Clark, Electa.
CHEROKEE CHIEF: THE LIFE OF
JOHN ROSS.
New York: Macmillan, 1970. (5–8)
The author links together various stories about Cherokee relationships with
white men, anecdotes of conversations
between white men and Cherokees, and
selected aspects of John Ross's life in this
book. Although extremely interesting and
often humorous, the author's style of listing one anecdote after another may pre-
vent the reader from gaining any sense of

chronology. However, the section describing the roundup of Cherokees after their
land had been taken from them in the
lottery and the account of "The Trail of
Tears" are written simply, but with great
clarity. The chapter describing the devastating result of the Cherokee alliance with
the South during the Civil War is also
done well. The author adequately conveys
the contribution of John Ross who, although only one-eighth Cherokee, managed to be accepted by both the white and
Indian peoples as a major spokesman for
the Cherokee Nation. John Wagner's illustrations are beautiful. Good.

172. Clark, Electa.
OSCEOLA, YOUNG SEMINOLE INDIAN.
New York: Bobbs-Merrill, 1965. (3–6)
This is a fictionalized account of Osceola's boyhood years, but generally consistent with facts known about Seminole
customs and practices. The story begins
with Asi-Yahola's (Black Drink) boyhood
and centers around the tribe's relationship
with white plantation owners and Osceola's (probably fabricated) friendship with
one of the white families. The author correctly points out the runaway black slaves'
position and acceptance into the tribe, as
well as some of the more salient features
of daily life. Basically, the author deals
with Osceola's youth and compresses his
adult years into the last three chapters.
She includes an annotated time line of
contemporaneous people and events, a
helpful innovation. The questions, glossary, and other suggested activities may
discourage some young readers and stimulate others. The tinted illustrations by
Robert Doremus are consistent with the
text. Adequate.

173. Clark, Ella E.
INDIAN LEGENDS FROM THE
NORTHERN ROCKIES.
Norman: Univ. of Oklahoma Pr.,
1966. (8 and up)
This is an outstanding book. Arranged
into six sections by language patterns, it
contains legends different from the usual
"culture-hero-transformer-trickster" (in-

troduction) formats of most collections. More than half of these stories appear in print for the first time, a result of careful author research. The introduction contains fascinating bits of information: for example, the author tells of the difficulties ethnologists and Indians, alike, had with time —there were often tribal prohibitions against storytelling in the summer when most students and researchers were free; and she quotes college-educated Indians as being shocked at the caliber and the unrepresentativeness of most collections. This book includes not only traditional stories, but stories that have evolved since the immigration of non-Indians: for instance, "The Story of Sacajawea" (p.207) and "How the Piegans Got Their First Horses" (p.276). Another unusual feature of the collection is that it offers tales from the Indians of Idaho, Montana, and Wyoming, often ignored by other writers. The book has an adult level format, but many of the legends could be read by junior high and elementary school children, although the small print is enough to discourage anyone. This would be a rich source for children's book writers looking for new legends to put into an elementary format. The book contains a chapter on how these Indians lived, an overall introductory section, introductions to each legend, source notes, bibliography, and index. Good.

174. Clark, Ella E.
INDIAN LEGENDS OF THE
PACIFIC NORTHWEST.
Berkeley: Univ. of California Pr., 1953. (9–12)
More than 100 tribal tales, recounted in the oral tradition of the Indians of Washington and Oregon, are included in this book. The prevailing theme is the Indian's belief that everything in nature has life and spirit—the trees, rocks, water, wind, birds, and animals. Two maps, one of geographical features and one of tribal locations, are included, as well as a bibliography, a glossary, and a few illustrations, all of which provide an excellent resource for the teacher. The tales are grouped into the following sections: myths

of mountains; legends of lakes; tales of rivers, rocks, and waterfalls; myths of creation, sky, storms; and other myths and legends. Suitable for mature readers, this is a good source for classroom discussions on oral literature. Good.

175. Clarke, Thelma.
FABLES OF INDIAN DANCES.
Albuquerque, N. Mex.: Chaparral Pr., 1970. (1 and up)
Regina Albarado De Cata is a lady of eighty-nine years, of Spanish descent, known for her dolls and pottery making, and married to a Pueblo Indian man. She told these tales of Pueblo dances (Deer dances, etc.) to Thelma Clarke for a pamphlet benefiting the San Gabriel Historical Society. An impressive list of Indian artists donated illustrations for the pamphlet, including Pablita Velarde, Henry Suazo, Mary Agnes Bradley, Peter Povijna, and Helen Harding. Researchers, historians, visitors to the Rio Grande Pueblos, and others interested in Indian dance may find the pamphlet worthwhile. The format and the level of the writing reflects its purpose, and the purchaser will want to select accordingly. Good.

176. Clarke, Thelma.
RUNAWAY BOY (RATON JEMEZ).
(no place): Clarke Industries, 1969. (2–6)
This is an old Pueblo legend about a boy—Raton Jemez—or Mouse Person—who is transformed into a mouse because he is lazy. The author gives two endings: in one Raton Jemez is boiled alive for trying to pilfer food from the ants; in the other he wakes from a bad dream, and changes his ways to become a working, contributing member of the tribe. The legend, like most, has an obvious moral similar to one found in tales from other cultures, such as the Greeks, Egyptians, or Hebrews; that is, if you do not work or contribute your part, you no longer can belong to the group or society. The message is quite clear, especially in the accumulative, repetitive "this is the house that Jack built" narrative style of the book. While the moral is presented

in a rather heavy, pedantic manner, the story has interesting illustrations by Tsa-sah-wee-ah and a nine-year-old named Sheree. The book also includes an introduction and pictures of Regina Albarado De Cata, the Spanish-Indian woman who told the story to the author, and Tsa-sah-wee-ah, or Helen Harding, the illustrator. The format and style of printing are rather young for fifth and sixth graders, but the content is appropriate for these grade levels. This combination of primary layout and upper elementary reading level suits the book for advanced readers in the lower grades. Adequate.

177. Clements, Bruce.
FACE OF ABRAHAM CANDLE.
New York: Farrar, 1969. (6–9)
The plot in this book is an involved one. A young man goes to a Mesa Verde-type ruin to explore abandoned caves and search for Indian artifacts. His face changes from a young, open face to a stronger, more adult face as he decides whether he and the people he digs with should take away the artifacts. A side plot involves his proposed marriage to a young widow, who needs someone to help her with her children. She eventually marries someone else, but he decides to stay anyway. The book suffers from occasional striving on the author's part for hidden significance and meaningful dialogue. The author has a feel for digging, and captures the sense of working alone in an Indian ruin. This book may give young readers the feeling they, too, would like to dig artifacts to sell, especially since the prices the author lists are so enticing. It is a respectable work of fiction, not particularly about Indians but about their artifacts. Adequate.

178. Cleven, Cathrine S.
BLACK HAWK: YOUNG SAUK WARRIOR.
New York: Bobbs-Merrill, 1966. (3–7)
This is an interesting, well written story of an Indian boy who became war chief of the Sauk Nation when his father was killed. Beginning with Black Hawk's birth and his early childhood as "Little Hawk," the author presents a series of adventures, both humorous and serious, which include Black Hawk, his family, and friends. Roughly three-fourths of the book is devoted to Black Hawk's growing-up years. Like many stories of Indian leaders during the wars with whites, the joy and fun of their childhood is transformed into terror, sadness, and feelings of futility or inability to have any control over their own lives as they reach adulthood. Similarly, few Indian women are prominent in the story. The illustrations by Gray Morrow include some full-page and numerous smaller pictures. An interesting but somewhat confusing time line is included at the conclusion of the story. There is a brief glossary; however, most of the words and definitions are of English origin. A series of questions and exercises following the time line gives the book a textbook quality. Adequate.

179. Clifford, Eth.
SEARCH FOR THE CRESCENT MOON.
Boston: Houghton, 1973. (6–9)
This book's story was suggested by the life of Frances Slocum. Captured at the age of five by Delaware Indians, she told a trader sixty years later that she was white. She had lived as an Indian all that time. In the book, the author takes some historical liberties, rearranging geographical facts and making shifts in time to suit the story. The crescent moon of the story is a birthmark on the palm that the woman and her twin brother both have. The search took sixty years. The author presents some vivid scenes: he reminds us of the harshness of the frontier for women as he tells of the pioneer mother losing father, husband, son, and daughter in one hour; he gives a moving account of the brother first finding the wrong woman. However the story does strain belief at times, as when the woman tells her brother that not even her children knew she was white. This is especially hard to accept since she had red hair. The bad treatment she reports at the hands of her first Delaware husband seems contrived; Delaware women did not us-

ually accept such treatment, as they had other alternatives. An interesting touch pictures a kind and understanding man as a thief, while a mean and ugly character turns out to be innocent—a good reversal that helps young people learn not to judge hastily on superficial appearances. The black-and-white drawings by Bea Holmes are good. Good.

180. Clifford, Eth.
THE YEAR OF THE THREE-LEGGED DEER.
Boston: Houghton, 1972. (7–9)
In an involved and well-written book, the author succeeds in giving the reader a good story, characters with considerable depth, and some feel for the Indian/non-Indian marriages of the time. The plot is an intricate one. A part-Indian man comes to visit the white second family of his white father. They reminisce about the past and solve some old problems that existed between them. As a boy, the son had brought home a wounded, three-legged deer. His sister nursed it to health, and was killed during a massacre by whites as she tried to rescue the deer. The boy had neglected to repair a fence, and the deer had wandered away, causing the girl to fall into the whites' hands. The killers are convicted; some hang, but some are pardoned by the governor in a melodramatic gallows scene. The Delawares flee. The Indian mother, the boy, and a black friend go with the tribe; the white father stays. A fine piece of writing, it is further enhanced by Richard Cuffari's sympathetic and congruent black-and-white illustrations. Good.

181. Clutesi, George.
SON OF RAVEN, SON OF DEER.
Sidney, B.C., Canada: Gray's Publishing Ltd., 1967. (4 and up)
A collection of American Indian legends by an Indian author, this book is well written, and the black-and-white illustrations by the author are charming. He presents an analysis of white fairy tales from an Indian point of view in the introduc-

tion: "The Indian child feels bewilderment with this type of nursery rhyme [Jack and Jill] because there seems to be no concern or regard for a very apparent injury inflicted upon a little child—which, in his own world, may very well be himself. He may reason also, why go to the top of the hill to get water when in his world all water is found at the bottom of hills" (p.12). The reading level of the legends is considerably less than that of the introductory section. Some of the language may be too Canadian in tone for young American children: "All throughout the great struggle for the possession of the fire Ah-tush-mit had been gambolling about the beach" (p.19). Good.

182. Clymer, Eleanor.
CHIPMUNK IN THE FOREST.
New York: Atheneum, 1966. (2–5)
This is a slightly more sophisticated Indian Two Feet and His Eagle Feather (see the review of Margaret Friskey's book, #306) type of book. The story is charming; the book is less than accurate in its portrayal of Indians. The Indian boy in the story, apparently from some Eastern tribe, judging by the illustrations, is afraid of the dark. He saves his little sister after failing other coming-of-age tasks. No one familiar with the hard work Indian women performed would say, "The other boys made fun of Chipmunk. 'You have an easy life,' they said. 'You are doing girls' work'" (p.22), especially since Indian women in Eastern Indian tribes generally were held in such high esteem. The black-and-white line drawings by Ingrid Fetz show style and talent, especially the illustration of trees opposite the frontispiece; her depiction of Indians is not especially good. Story: Adequate. Portrayal of Indians: Poor.

183. Clymer, Eleanor.
THE SPIDER, THE CAVE, AND THE POTTERY BOWL.
New York: Atheneum, 1971. (4–7)
Illness, the gradual loss of strength in old age, and the approach of death are

scnsitively handled by the author as she tells of a Hopi girl who comes home to the reservation to visit her grandmother, only to find her slowly weakening. Character motivation is convincingly handled: for instance, the girl's feelings about her grandmother: "I wished my mother were there. I didn't know what to do. Grandmother did not seem to be sick. She just seemed far away" (p.19); her feelings toward her grandmother's house: "Grandmother is still living in her house. It was her mother's mother's, and some day it will be mine. I'll go away, but I'll always come back, I think" (p.66); and her explanation of why some Hopis leave the reservation: "It is hard work. That is why some people moved away. My father doesn't mind hard work, but he needed to earn money for us. So we had to go away to town" (pp.4–5). Another realistic touch is the elder man's reprimanding of the misbehaving brother. Why a traditionally minded grandmother would keep a prehistoric bowl in her house is not clear. Some Hopis would, and many would not. Ingrid Fetz's black-and-white drawings are good and mirror the transition stage now taking place for some Hopis. Good.

184. Clymer, Theodore.
FOUR CORNERS OF THE SKY; POEMS,
CHANTS AND ORATORY.
Boston: Little, 1975. (K and up)
This collection of short poems, chants, and speeches from a wide divergence of tribal sources is the type of book that grows up with the reader. It can be read at many ages. The author includes a one or two line explanation under each entry. The illustrations are in blue, orange, black, white, and olive tones, demonstrating how a few colors can make a large visual impact. Art students could learn much about overall design, Indian motifs, and techniques that use a sparsity of color from this volume. The introduction helps the reader put these examples of oral literature in perspective: "For many of these poems and chants we have clear information about their use and meaning; for others we can only guess." A bibliography is included. Good.

185. Clymer, Theodore.
THE TRAVELS OF ATUNGA.
Boston: Little, 1973. (1–3)
Easy to read, biblical in tone ("Even in the days before grandfathers, hunger was with the people" [p.7]), well written, these Eskimo legends describe attempts to please and seek help from Sedna, the old woman of the sea, and Tungarsug, the lord of the land animals. The author's introductory statements are good, but brief. Although the book's wording and language patterns are adult, the pictures and the format are designed for primary-age readers. John Schoenherr's illustrations are excellent, imparting a feeling of cold and space through the use of simple colors, including blue, brown, black, and white. The people are authentically drawn. Good.

186. Coalson, Glo.
THREE STONE WOMAN.
New York: Atheneum, 1971. (5–8)
The author recorded these stories as they were told to her by an Eskimo woman. The book's overall layout is pleasing; the pictures, mainly bold strokes of black paint, are admirable, and the format is good. The ending may seem too harsh to some readers (the woman is left to eat stones because she did not share), but it shows the importance of food to these people. Younger advanced readers would find this book interesting. Good.

187. Coatsworth, Elizabeth.
THE CAVE.
New York: Viking, 1958. (4–8)
This is a fictional account of a young Navajo boy hired by his brother's boss, a sheep rancher, to help a young Basque sheepherder take 1,000 ewes and lambs to summer pasture. The author focuses on the strained relationship between Fernando, the Basque, and Jim Boy-Who-Loves-Sheep, as well as on Jim's fears that something about the trip is not quite right. The story moves quickly and is written in a manner that will hold the interest of most young readers. Its value as a reflection of a present-day young Navajo is adequate for its time (1958), if somewhat

oversimplified. The illustrations by the Apache artist, Alan Houser, add to the story and accurately picture the high desert regions of Arizona. Good.

188. Coatsworth, Elizabeth.
INDIAN ENCOUNTERS.
New York: Macmillan, 1960. (7–9)
In this book the author offers the reader fifteen short stories and includes an equal number of short poems. Beginning with a story about a Viking boy's adventure in what is now Minnesota, the stories feature adventures experienced by Indian and non-Indian boys and girls, including kidnapped white children adopted by Indians, and Indians adopted by whites. Although few tribes are named specifically, the stories represent encounters which take place throughout North America, judging by geographical references and other contextual clues. Like most of the author's books about children, the characters seem real and have distinctly different personalities; however, some characterizations may be based more upon historical fancy than fact. Black-and-white illustrations by Frederick T. Chapman appear at the beginning of each story. The poems reinforce the theme of each preceding story. Adequate.

189. Coatsworth, Elizabeth.
SWORD OF THE WILDERNESS.
New York: Macmillan, 1966. (7–9)
The story for this book parallels that of many captive tales. The Abenaki Indians attack the village of Pemaquoit in Northeast Maine in 1769 and capture Seth, a young white boy, and others. Seth finally finds satisfying relationships with John Hammond, another captive, and Keoka, an English girl who has been reared by the Indians. Many harrowing experiences, some of which are quite inhumane, are recounted. Eventually Seth returns to his people with Keoka. There are a few black-and-white illustrations by Harve Stein. This book may appear cruel and inhumane to some readers, although the story is believable and probably best suited for older readers. Adequate.

190. Coblentz, Catherine Cate.
SEQUOYAH.
New York: Longman, 1946. (5–9)
One of the earliest biographies for young people about Sequoyah, this story is well written and seems free of stereotypes. The author combines the factual and conjectural in an interesting, plausible manner; her characters are fully developed. Beginning with Sequoyah's youth, shortly before a combined tribal battle against St. Clair and 1,500 white soldiers, the author works backward into Sequoyah's early childhood and explains some of the history of the tribe. She relates Sequoyah's experiences with other tribe members, as well as his development of the "talking leaves," his Cherokee syllabary. Without question Sequoyah, like most Indian leaders, was an exceptional individual. The author explains Sequoyah's development into an unusual, gifted man in a sound, believable manner, once again combining the factual with the inferential. There is no superhero in the book. Unfortunately, few women are described, but those included are fully developed and not the shadowy silhouettes the young reader usually meets in biographies about men. Each chapter is introduced by black-and-white "decorations" by Ralph Ray, Jr. Good.

191. Cody, Iron Eyes.
INDIAN TALK: HAND SIGNALS OF THE AMERICAN INDIAN.
Healdsburg, Calif.: Naturegraph, 1970. (1 and up)
Iron Eyes Cody, an actor familiar to most children from his film and television roles, has produced a dictionary of sign language. Listed in alphabetical order, each word or phrase is accompanied by a photograph of a person, usually the actor, making the appropriate sign. It is interesting to watch the actor age and the costumes change from photograph to photograph. The black-and-white illustrations by Ken Mansker, a Flathead Indian artist, add considerably to the overall design and layout of the book. The introduction gives the reader some feel for the history and

diversity of sign language, and points out some modern uses of nonverbal language. The book is poorly printed, making it hard to read. It is hoped it will be reissued in a better format. Good.

192. Coen, Rena Neumann.
THE RED MAN IN ART.
Minneapolis, Minn.: Lerner, 1972.
(5–8)
An explanation of American Indian cultures through an analysis of famous paintings of Indian subjects, this book is primarily filled with pictures of Eastern and Plains Indians. Most of the art reviewed was painted by white men who drew the Indians they encountered; the author explains that this selection process evolved because Indians, until recently, painted unrealistic art and drew pictures of the group, not individuals, a conclusion with which many experts would disagree. The reproductions of paintings are well done, and the author evaluates the painters he chooses for inclusion in a personal and interesting fashion. A sample:

> Catlin's painting [of Black Hawk] is quick and sketchy, but it too gives us a vivid picture of the Indian chief who led his people against the white man. However, Catlin's chief interest in his portrait of Black Hawk was in the Indian's costume and tribal ornaments. Jarvis' portrait, on the other hand, probes much deeper into the human personality of the proud Sauk chief. It shows him not as an Indian but as a man. [p.37]

The title is inappropriate, both for its sexist tones and because the contents of the book are not as universal as might be assumed from its name; few California, Southwest, or Northwest Coast Indians are included. It is fascinating to see the differences in appearance between the costumes of Indians of various tribes as contemporary painters drew them and the costumes of those same tribes as portrayed in many modern films and television programs. Good.

193. Cohoe.
A CHEYENNE SKETCHBOOK.
Norman: Univ. of Oklahoma Pr., 1964. (7 and up)
One of seventy-two captive Cheyenne taken to Fort Marion, Florida, in 1875 after the surrender at the end of the Wars on the Plains, Cohoe kept a sketchbook-diary of what he saw. Each painting from that sketchbook is reproduced in this volume, followed by an exhaustive analyzation and commentary. At times, the reader may well wish a chance to look at the pictures without access to this simultaneous commentary, no matter how well done. The paintings are superb—full of movement, color, and pattern (see especially "War Dance at Fort Marion" on page 83). They show glimpses of life of a time many Americans would like to forget. Photographs of Cohoe, the prison, and the other Cheyenne are featured throughout the text. They add immeasurably to the reader's understanding. The author apparently misidentifies Wovoka as Comanche when he is usually identified as a Paiute: "In 1874 many of the Southern Cheyennes placed their trust in a Comanche messiah who claimed to have been given the power to endow himself and any who would follow him with immunity to bullets" (p.3). The book includes a catalog of the art of other Indian prisoners at Fort Marion and an index. The entire volume is exquisitely done; the reader is left with a feeling of incomprehension of how the man was able to see and express such beauty in such a desperate situation and time. A classic. Good.

194. Colby, C. B.
CLIFF DWELLINGS: ANCIENT RUINS OF AMERICA'S PAST.
New York: Coward-McCann, 1965.
(5–7)
A travelogue-style book, this volume is filled with black-and-white photographs of various cliff dwellings. A page or two of text is devoted to each. The author emphasizes safety as a problem in exploring remote dwellings where the walls are not reinforced. This is a vital point, as the re-

viewer has seen the walls of a ruin collapse at a dig supervised by one of the top archaeologists in the country after a New Mexico cloudburst, a danger even to experienced excavators. This book could be used with slow readers up to high school level, since it has a low reading level and an older format. Adequate.

195. Collier, Peter.
WHEN SHALL THEY REST?
THE CHEROKEE'S LONG STRUGGLE
WITH AMERICA.
New York: Holt, 1973. (7 and up)
Peter Collier has written a book of opposites and extremes. It consists of scholarly research, including a well-written review of the history of the Cherokee with an analysis of the Scot-Irish and Cherokee backgrounds of many tribal members, the process of acculturation, and how Tennessee's Davy Crockett ruined his congressional career by championing the Cherokee cause. This research contrasts sharply with his wholesale condemnation of non-Cherokees:

> There is something defective in the white culture that has not only taken almost everything these people once possessed, but also seeks to destroy finally the world mirrored in this dance. Is it just obsessive greed? Or is it the dangerous jealousy of people who suspect that their way of relating to their fellow men is drastically limited in comparison with the Indians'—that they have lived only for themselves for so long that they are now in the words of a current Indian leader named Earl Old Person, a series of "one-man reservations." [p.146]

He champions the right of one man to a fair trial:

> At another time perhaps Chewie would have received the usual justice meted out to Cherokees: a patronizing reprimand and a few days in jail to teach a "lesson." But on the day he came to trial, the usually shy Cherokee full bloods . . . armed with shotguns and rifles . . . stood in silent vigil, not threat-

ening anyone but sending shivers of fear through the town. When it became clear that John Chewie would not be convicted, they went home as quietly as they had come. [p.142]

while questioning the motivations of W. W. Keeler, Cherokee Tribal Chairman: "While W. W. Keeler sits in the boardroom of his oil company, speaking for a people he doesn't know or understand, the problems facing the Indians fester and grow worse" (p.141). The book asks for understanding, while setting up categories of its own for defining Cherokees (a "good" Cherokee, as the author apparently defines one in this book, is a full blood belonging to one Indian organization and not to another). The overall feeling the author gives the reader is that controversies consist of obvious bad guys versus obvious good guys, and that his demand for acceptance and tolerance from the reader does not obligate him to a similar stance. He is offering a point of view to the reader; the book should be purchased accordingly. The book includes a center section of interesting black-and-white photographs, a bibliography, author's notes, a section on leading figures in Cherokee history, and an index. It is, perhaps, one of the finer examples of current partisan authorship. Good.

196. Colton, Harold S.
HOPI KACHINA DOLLS; WITH A KEY TO
THEIR IDENTIFICATION.
Albuquerque: Univ. of New Mexico
Pr., 1949. (9–12)
This is a good resource book that tells how to identify over 266 different varieties of kachina dolls. All the dolls are beautifully illustrated, some in color photographs, and some in simple drawings used as a key for identification. The book tells what a kachina is, how they are made, their principal features and descriptions, Hopi deities, and provides an index. Readers interested in Indian art as well as Indian religion will find this a useful book, although there are more recent books available. Good.

197. Culver, Anne.
BREAD AND BUTTER JOURNEY.
New York: Holt, 1968. (3–5)
This is not primarily a book about American Indians, but a story about the trials of two white pioneer families as they move to a new home beyond the Alleghanies. The two teenage sons make friends with Flying Cloud, chief of an unspecified group of Indians, who warns about unfriendly Indians (also unspecified) further west and helps them reach their destination. Indians don't fare too well in this book. Not only are they not identified as to tribe, but they are easily routed by the young pioneer girl:

"I remembered that Indians were afraid of owls and I made a sound like this—," she pursed her lips but only a small squeaky "whoo" came from her dry throat. "An Indian was afraid of *that*?" Tess giggled. "Anyway he *ran*." [p.93]

Useful primarily for its picture of pioneer life, the story is based on the life of the author's great-grandmother. Story and development: Good. Portrayal of Indians: Poor.

198. Compton, Margaret.
AMERICAN INDIAN FAIRY TALES.
New York: Dodd, 1971. (3–7)
This collection of seventeen legends has not been edited or altered to any extent in form, maintaining authenticity and oral patterning. Lorence Bjorklund provides vivid illustrations and an interesting introduction for the tales. These stories appeal to the reader's imagination with their giants, ghosts, and magical feats. Type style and content are appropriate for the intermediate grades. Originally told by Indian storytellers, from tribes on the Pacific coast to those in the New England hills, these tales coincide with historical records. Adults will enjoy the stories, too. Good.

199. Cone, Molly.
NUMBER FOUR.
Boston: Houghton, 1972. (5–9)
This is a fictionalized version of an episode involving a young Indian boy who drowns himself and is, judging from author's remarks, based on a true episode: "For dramatic structure, some details were omitted, some combined or adapted, and others added" (introduction). In the book, a high school Indian boy, popular and successful in school, reevaluates his life, takes on the high school principal, and dies tragically. The author writes well but, except for the character of the Indian boy, peoples her book with stock, one-dimensional figures, such as the villainous principal and the "good" high school teacher who pushes the students to action with his admonitions: "'There are no dirty words,' Mr. Otis said to his class . . . 'unless you want to make them that way'" (p.32). Adequate.

200. Conklin, Paul.
CHOCTAW BOY.
New York: Dodd, 1975. (4 and up)
The author's prose and photographs give readers a clear picture of a contemporary Choctaw boy: natural, unposed, having fun. The writer does not intrude himself into this balanced account of boys and girls, men and women (whom he treats with equal respect) who live a prideful life in Mississippi today. He is neither overly optimistic nor overly pessimistic; he doesn't gloss over hard facts, nor does he see a hard life as being devoid of fun. Factual but readable, this book would be appropriate for pleasure reading as well as for reference work. Good.

201. Cooke, David C.
FIGHTING INDIANS OF AMERICA.
New York: Dodd, 1954. (5–9)
This is a collection of biographies of ten Western and ten Eastern Indian leaders, who were born and/or lived primarily in the nineteenth century. Separating the sections about Western and Eastern leaders is an interior chapter devoted to Captain Jack and the Modoc War. There are no female leaders included. Although sympathetic to the Indians' plight and position, the author nevertheless concentrates on these leaders in regard to the Indian wars, hence the title of the book. Several

lesser-known leaders included are Mangus Colorado, Victorio, and Nana, all Apaches, and Roman Nose, the Cheyenne. In the sections about the East, biographies of figures not often found in print include Opechancanough, the Pamunkey; Logan, the Cayuga; Weatherford, the Creek; and Wildcat, the Seminole. This is a "blood and guts" type of adventure book, full of superhero characterization and frequent oversimplifications. The author has included photographs of some of the leaders and reproductions of some of the more famous paintings on display at the Smithsonian Institution, the National Archives, and the New York Public Library. Adequate.

202. Cooke, David C.
FIGHTING INDIANS OF THE WEST.
New York: Dodd, 1954. (5–9)

This book is exactly the same (even to the identical photographs) as the second half of *Fighting Indians of America,* and published in the same year. Although specifically addressed to wars, the book suffers from the same oversimplification and superhero characterization as the other. It includes ten biographies of Western Indian leaders, half of whom are Apaches. The first leader, Mangus Colorado, is described as follows:

[Mangus] stood six feet, five inches in his moccasins, and he had the strength of two ordinary men. His head was huge, his eyes small and deep and very bright, his chin as hard as the stone from which arrowheads were made.... He was more than seventy years old when white soldiers finally stopped him, but even then no man, Indian or white, would have dared attack "Red Sleeves" single-handed.

The rest of the leaders are described as equally formidable. Adequate.

203. Cooke, David C.
INDIANS ON THE WARPATH.
New York: Dodd, 1957. (5–9)

This book is identical to the first half of his earlier book, *Fighting Indians of America,* and the counterpart of his *Fight-ing Indians of the West* (the second half of *Fighting Indians of America*). The ten leaders described in this book were members of Eastern American tribes. Consistent with his series, these biographies cover the Indian war years, include no women (except by oblique reference), and provide details about battles, but not much about people. The young reader interested in wars, per se, will find the book appealing, but will get more mileage from *Fighting Indians of America,* which also includes ten Western Indian warriors. The photographs and reproductions of paintings on display at the Smithsonian Institution and New York Public Library are the same as in the author's previous book. Adequate.

204. Cooke, David C.
TECUMSEH: DESTINY'S WARRIOR.
New York: Messner, 1959. (6 and up)

Similar to many books about Indian leaders who faced the changes confronting their culture and civilization, Tecumseh's story is told with poignancy, but with a sense of futility. There is no laughter, little joy, and a great deal of terror in Tecumseh's life as depicted by this author. Although free of such stereotypes as the "Indian as happy child of nature" or "cunning but ignorant and foolish savage," the author may have become so preoccupied with historical fact and detail as to have drawn his characters, both Indian and white, as rather shadowy figures moved about like chessmen by some mysterious and malevolent being. Certainly Tecumseh and his contemporaries frequently moved throughout the Northeastern states and Ohio River valley; however, except for reasons attributed solely to broken treaties, the author does not elaborate on the other reasons precipitating these moves, such as to follow game, or on descriptions of what was involved when some or all of the tribe packed up and moved to a new location. While readers will acquire much information about what happened when, to whom, by whom, they may be left with a rather unsatisfied feeling about both the Indians and the white men described in the book. Few women are mentioned with the exception of Tecumseh's mother, Methoataske, who is pictured as abandoning Tecumseh and her younger children; Manete, a "half-breed Shawnee woman considerably older than Tecumseh" who had "crude ways" and a "generally shiftless nature"; and Rebecca, the young white woman who taught Tecumseh to read and write English and with whom he fell in love but left because she wished him to give up his Indian way of life. Female readers may be disappointed and angered by the author's treatment of women. Adequate.

205. Cooper, James F.
DEERSLAYER.
New York: Scribner, 1925. (7–12)
This adventure story, written in 1844 but set in 1760, is about a young Indian in his twenties named the Deerslayer. The characterization of the Indian is a positive one. The story presents a fine delineation of non-Indian life of that time, stressing, as it does, the moral seriousness of Deerslayer, the feminine wiles of Hetty and Judith Hutton, and the romanticized aspects of Indian culture. The legend recounted is pure fiction, but many of the descriptions of scenery are accurate. It is a long story for younger readers, nearly 500 pages. N. C. Wyeth has provided some beautiful illustrations in rich detail and color. A classic. Good.

206. Copeland, Donald McKillop.
THE TRUE BOOK OF LITTLE ESKIMOS.
Chicago: Childrens Pr., 1953. (K–2)
Copeland uses the story of two children to picture Eskimo life for his young readers. The writing style is simplistic and stereotyping: "This is the story of Amak and Toota. And it is the story of every little Eskimo boy and girl, wherever you go in the far, far Northland" (p.44). The author includes charts on birds, plants, and animals of the North. Mary Gehr's illustrations are typical of most textbook drawings: straightforward pictures sketched for quick understanding on the part of the reader and not particularly for style. Poor.

207. Cottrell, Leonard.
DIGS AND DIGGERS: A BOOK OF WORLD ARCHAEOLOGY.
Cleveland, Ohio: World, 1964.
(5 and up)
A good beginning book for young readers interested in archaeology, this is a simplified introduction to archaeological practices and digs all over the world. The wording employs scientific method and thought on an easy level that does not condescend to young people; thus, archaeology is "the study of the past through the tangible objects people left behind" (p.11). The archaeologist's interest in pottery is explained well. The part of the book dealing with the Americas, pages 149–98, provides a link with world practices. Young readers learn archaeological methods as the author speculates on theories, then gives reasons for the speculations, leaving room for further thought. The book is illustrated with photographs. Good.

208. Courlander, Harold.
PEOPLE OF THE SHORT BLUE CORN: TALES AND LEGENDS OF THE HOPI INDIANS.
New York: Harcourt, 1970. (6–9)
Eighteen Hopi myths and legends on subjects ranging from explanations for the origins of life, the existence of good and evil, and how clans were named are included in this collection. The author provides comments on Hopi oral literature, giving a short history of the Hopis, an explanation regarding variations of some of their myths and legends, and an analysis of recurring themes. Author's notes on each of the myths and legends provide additional information and background to help the young reader understand Hopi culture and history. The highly stylized line and point drawings by Enrico Arno are effective, if small, and the pronunciation guide and glossary add interest as well as stimulation to read other Indian myths and legends. Good.

210. Coy, Harold.
MAN COMES TO AMERICA.
Boston: Little, 1973. (5 and up)

This well-paced narrative follows early human progress from the Eurasian continent through the Americas and gives attention to the influence of geography, geology, and meteorology on the development of cultures. Homo sapien is the protagonist in this lively book, written as if it were a novel. Archaeological discoveries are the backbone of the commentary and are presented similarly to the unfolding of a mystery. The student is left with many unanswered questions, but with a panoramic concept of what is now known about Paleo-Indians and their descendants. This book motivates the reader to seek additional sources, and to respect the meticulous methods of the discipline of archaeology. Good.

211. Craig, John.
NO WORD FOR GOODBYE.
New York: Coward-McCann, 1971.
(6 and up)
Average writing, no matter how earnestly done, about real injustices and good causes is not usually enough to make a great book, as is illustrated in this story. For example:

"Once they get their hands on a little money, you can kiss them goodbye." "Are you talking about the Indians?" Ken asked. "Of course" said his Aunt Marion. "They're all the same. Work until they get some money for liquor, and then disappear. And I wouldn't leave anything around that they can steal, either." "Oh, I think you're a little prejudiced," Ken's mother put in. "I think it's wrong to generalize about any people. Some of them may be dishonest and lazy, but not all." [p.13]

The plot concerns an Ojibwa boy and a white boy who become friends, fight fires and Empirico, a giant Eastern conglomerate, and lose to the company. The Ojibwas go away quietly, leaving the white boy "no word for goodbye." There are many scenes that will appeal to the young reader, such as the fight against the company, and the feelings the boy has when his friends leave without a word. Adequate.

212. Crary, Margaret.
SUSETTE LaFLESCHE: VOICE OF THE OMAHA INDIANS.
New York: Hawthorn, 1973. (6–9)
In a remarkable book that considers all members of LaFlesche's family (her sisters, Susan, Rosalie, and Marguerite; her mother, Mary Gale; father, Joseph; and her brother, Francis) instead of focusing upon a single individual with little or no attention to other influential but less known family members and friends, the author traces Susette's career as a public speaker or self-styled politician from her childhood through her marriage to a journalist, Thomas Tibbles. There are few stereotypes. LaFlesche and her contemporaries, Helen Hunt Jackson (author of Ramona) and Louisa May Alcott, as well as other men and women, are described in the context of their histories as writers, journalists, and intellectuals accepted into literary and political circles that included Oliver Wendell Holmes and James Russell Lowell. The book provides an interesting contrast between her and Indian leaders who, scarcely a generation before, had fought and lost battles, unable to accomplish with fighting what LaFlesche was able to do as an accomplished journalist and painter, although, in fairness, some of her gains were temporary. The book contains photographs of the LaFlesche family, "Tibs" (LaFlesche's husband), and the Tibbles' home. Occasionally Crary's writing style proves tedious. Good.

213. Creighton, Luella Bruce.
TECUMSEH: THE STORY OF THE SHAWNEE CHIEF.
New York: St. Martin's Pr., 1965.
(6–9)
This is a well-written biography covering Tecumseh's life from boyhood through death. The author makes the reader well aware of the distinction between those facts known about Tecumseh's life, the events that might be attributed to legend and therefore probably possess a portion of the truth, and what clearly is fancy. Beginning with Tecumseh's boyhood, the author develops her characters in a way

that retains reader interest, but without either glamorizing or stereotyping them. She describes well the peculiar position in which the Shawnees were placed when both wars between the British and the "Americans" were fought. She clarifies Indian relationships between the Shawnee and some whites as opposed to their relationships with other whites, illustrating that these relationships were more complex than history books concerned with the battles between them suggest. Several maps are included, as well as many black-and-white sketches by William Lytle. Good.

214. Crompton, Anne Eliot.
THE WINTER WIFE: AN ABENAKI FOLKTALE.
Boston: Atlantic Monthly Pr., 1975. (3–5))
An explanation of the plot can give a false impression of the worth of this truly fine book. In the story an Indian man finds and lives with a wife only in the winter time. Babies and happiness come, but the man succumbs to pressure, marries a chief's daughter, and brings her to his winter wife's home. The winter wife and her children then transform themselves back into moose in sorrow. This may be the kind of book that an adult wants very much to share with a favorite child and then is surprised when the child does not share the adult's enthusiasm for it. The story, itself, is written in such a manner that only intermediate and higher-grade students can understand all the nuances; unfortunately, the format and recommended grade placement are primary. Robert Andrew Parker's color and black-and-white illustrations are excellent. Good.

215. Crowder, Jack L.
STEPHANNIE AND THE COYOTE.
Bernalillo, N. Mex.: Jack L. Crowder, 1969. (1–3)
Written in Navajo and English as a reading text for Navajo children, this is a charming story about a seven-year-old Navajo girl and her adventures tending a flock of sheep, exploring, and so on. Although written simply, using a basic vocabulary and style, the book nevertheless manages to convey more complex meanings and concepts. For example, in Stephannie's good-night message to other children who must stand in the cold: "If you're not Navajos, you may not know the trails, and if you hear a coyote howl, perhaps you are afraid" (p.123), the author combines the fear of being alone and cold, which most young children have experienced, in an uncomplicated yet meaningful manner. Excellent color photographs taken by the author provide a good identity model for the young Navajo reader, as well as information and examples for the non-Indian reader. Of special interest are the photographs of Stephannie living with her grandparents in their hogan. The life and clothing depicted in the photographs are rather traditional, but many Navajos continue to follow this pattern. Good.

216. Crowell, Ann.
A HOGAN FOR THE BLUEBIRD.
New York: Scribner, 1969. (5–8)
Utilizing a theme common to works of fiction concerned with Indians, that of a boy who longs for a horse, and a simple format, the author describes the relationships among a "modern" Navajo family in an interesting but somewhat contrived manner. Included and described in depth are a "grandfather," or old one, who goes to the hospital because he likes it, a sister, who comes home from boarding school, and a brother, who gives up his horse so his sister can have a piano. The ending is somewhat romanticized—the boy gets the horse back, yet the girl keeps her piano—but there is a theme of good family feeling throughout which compensates for the rather contrived plot. The black-and-white illustrations by Harrison Begay are well done and enhance the book. Good.

217. Crowell, Ann.
SHADOW ON THE PUEBLO.
Champaign, Ill.: Garrard, 1972. (3–6)
A Yaqui legend similar to the Phoenix myth, this is the story of a young boy who kills a man-eating bird. The bird's feathers

and flesh then become birds and animals, providing a legendary explanation for the creation of animal life. The black-, white-, and-red illustrations by Philip Smith are given enough space and emphasis that they enhance the text greatly. Good.

218. Curry, Jane Louise.
DOWN FROM THE LONELY MOUNTAIN: CALIFORNIA INDIAN TALES.
New York: Harcourt, 1965. (3–7)
In this series of legends and tales originating among the California Indians, the author provides examples of stories of creation, of animals, and, in general, of how things came to be. The stories are well written but would be most effective if read aloud. The book's greatest strength lies in its potential. It needs a new format as well as an introduction or some other information section to let the reader know which tales belong to which tribes. A list of sources would also be helpful. The black-and-white illustrations by Enrico Arno are small, typical of textbooks. The material needs to be republished with a new design that gives the illustrator a chance. Adequate.

219. Curtis, Edward S.
IN A SACRED MANNER WE LIVE.
Barre, Mass.: Barre, 1972. (K and up)
Composed of a collection of sepia-colored photographs taken by Edward Curtis, a photographer and ethnologist, during the early 1900s, this book records the Indians he encountered. Pictures such as an old Arapaho warrior (p.48), an Assiniboin placating the spirit of a slain eagle (p.40), a bridal group of Northwest Indians (p.138), as well as views of dwellings and cultural accoutrements such as "Sacred Bags of the Horn Society" (p.46), speak eloquently for themselves. The book includes an introduction and brief commentaries introducing some eight regional groups of Indians. Good.

220. Curtis, Natalie, ed.
THE INDIANS' BOOK: SONGS AND LEGENDS OF THE AMERICAN INDIAN.
New York: Dover, 1950. (K and up)

This book contains a carefully researched and documented selection of songs and legends of the American Indians. The author discusses some of the problems and dangers involved in finding and recording secret songs as an explanation or apology for not obtaining more information about Indian culture or practice. The foreword describes the editor's task, begun in 1921: "When Miss Curtis first began . . . recording Indian music, native songs were absolutely forbidden in the government schools. On one reservation she was warned by a friendly scientist that if she wished to record the Indian songs, she must do so secretly" (p.vi). It is no wonder that so few songs and legends have been preserved, since some tribes forbade passing them on to non-Indians while the U.S. government prohibited their inclusion in Indian schools and sometimes even their performance on the reservations. This book is lacking in representativeness. For example, it contains no examples of the songs and legends of the California Indians. An appendix and notes on the songs are included. The author's writing style is rather old-fashioned and reflects the "Indian as noble savage" thinking of many writers of her time: "This book reflects the soul of one of the noblest types of primitive man—the North American Indian" (p.xxi); or "The child race of a bygone age has left no written records of his thoughts. Silent through the ages has passed barbaric man" (p.xxix). Adequate.

221. Cushing, Frank H.
MY ADVENTURES IN ZUÑI.
Palmer Lake, Colo.: Filter Pr., 1967.
(9 and up)
This is a rather quaint first-person account of Cushing's experiences with the Zuñi during the late 1870s. The introduction by Oakah L. Jones, Jr., gives a brief history of Cushing's career as an ethnologist, as well as his controversial impact upon the field. (Senator Logan said he would smash the Bureau of Ethnology if Cushing were not recalled when Cushing helped keep Zuñi lands from going to the

Anglos in New Mexico.) A "first facsimile reprint" of Cushing's articles, which appeared in *Century Magazine*, this book contains all the original illustrations reproduced in their proper locations in the text. Most readers will enjoy the writing style, which is typical of the slightly romanticized type of articles that were current—and avidly read—during Cushing's time. For the rest, Cushing's studies of Pueblo culture are noteworthy for their accuracy and groundbreaking stance. Good.

222. Cushing, Frank H.
THE NATION OF THE WILLOWS.
Flagstaff, Ariz.: Northland Pr., 1965.
(7 and up)
Reprinted from two 1882 issues of the *Atlantic Monthly*, this is an account of Cushing's journey to the Southwest and his descriptions of the Indians he observed and their way of life. Written in the style of the late 1800s, the account is somewhat flowery; the younger reader may find it quaint. There are no illustrations to help describe some of the things Cushing saw and some of the Indian practices he describes. The uninformed reader may need supplementary or introductory material regarding the history of the Southwest, as well as more information describing the Indians Cushing met. The introduction by Robert C. Euler will provide background regarding Cushing's life and times. This book is of special interest because of its historical nature and because of Cushing's contributions. Students with a bent for history will doubtlessly find the book of more value than those more concerned with current relevancy. Good.

223. Cushman, Dan.
STAY AWAY, JOE.
New York: Viking, 1953. (7 and up)
This story of a Korean veteran in 1953 is not much different from one that could be written about a Vietnam veteran today. The book tells the story of a Cree family chosen for an experimental land program, part of a federal program. The father is given twenty head of cattle, and they grad-

ually are used up: the bull for a "whoop-up," cows to pay for a wedding, and so on, until he has nothing. The author writes beautifully; his story is funny, exasperating, infuriating, but above all true. The motives of the federal agents are mixed:

In the Cadillac rolling back across the clearing, Wilcox said, "Well, don't you think he'll make a go of it?" "Mr. Wilcox," said Morrisey, "I want every man and woman whose name appears on that petition to be notified that I alone am responsible for this, but aside from them, I'd rest just as easily if no living soul in this great state of Montana knew about it." [p.14]

If the reader doesn't believe this story reports actual conditions, let him or her stand outside the bar just off the San Carlos Reservation, or one just outside White River, Arizona, or one in Fort Washakie, Wyoming, for a night. A classic. Good.

224. D'Amato, Janet, and D'Amato, Alex.
INDIAN CRAFTS.
New York: Sayre, 1968. (1–4)
Designed for scout-type groups, classroom social studies activities, parent-child projects, or for the young child who is good at working on crafts alone, this book is a comprehensive guide to making such Indian craft items as household goods, transportation equipment, ceremonial and ritual paraphernalia, and lodgings. The illustrated instructions are clear and easy to follow, and the authors intersperse information about the items among the directions: "There are at least 200 Hopi Kachinas" (p.55). Materials, supply sources, and a bibliography are given. The average reading level of the book is third grade. "Cute" pictures of children working on crafts are superimposed over often very good drawings of Indians. At times, the instructions may be too directive: for example, "Use of all materials and supplies should be strictly supervised when handled by children" (footnote, table of contents). This suggestion is usually valid, but too rigid an adherence to this policy would sometimes discourage experimentation on the part of the child. Good.

225. D'Aulaire, Ingri, and Parin, Edgar.
POCAHONTAS.
New York: Doubleday, 1946. (3–5)
This is a fictionalized account of Pocahontas, who is depicted, rather conde-
scendingly, as having tatoos on her arms
and legs. The illustrations, lithographed
directly on stone in four colors, apparently
were done by the authors and seem consistent with the fairy-tale tone of the book.
The character of Pocahontas as presented
by these authors seems quaint, if not somewhat misleading:
> One day Pocahontas sat in the garden,
> playing with a doll she had made of a
> corncob. Suddenly she laughed right
> out loud! The palefaces looked just like
> her corncob doll. Then she was certain
> their magic could not be evil, for corn
> was the Indian's best friend.
Adequate.

226. Damjan, Mischa.
ATUK.
New York: Pantheon, 1964. (2–3)
An effective, colorful, easy-to-read format, including childlike illustrations by
Gian Casty, boosts the impact of this book.
The plot involves an Eskimo boy who becomes a feared hunter and learns about
love from a flower. The writing is good,
although the flower episode seems deter-
minedly "literary." Good.

227. David, Jay, ed.
THE AMERICAN INDIAN: THE FIRST
VICTIM.
New York: Morrow, 1972. (7–9)
The American Indian is a collection of
stories from Indians representing various
American Indian tribes, such as the Sioux,
Odawa, Cherokee, Choctaw, Chippewa,
and others. The purpose of the book is to
pinpoint causes of white-Indian conflict,
and to emphasize the worthy aspects of
the Indian culture. The theme of the book
is not that the Indian cannot be American-
ized, but that this is possible without for-
saking their own culture. The authors
want whites to know and appreciate the
Indian culture, and through this knowledge understand why the Indians insist
on being treated as a separate people. The
Indians and whites are both somewhat
stereotyped in this treatment, but this book
is an excellent addition to a library on
Indians if other information on the conflicts cited in the book is available for
balance. Good.

228. Davis, Russell, and
Ashabranner, Brent.
CHIEF JOSEPH: WAR CHIEF OF THE
NEZ PERCÉ.
New York: McGraw-Hill, 1962. (7–12)
Beginning with a list of Indian leaders
in the Nez Percé War (which started in
1877) and a historical note regarding the
causes of the war, this extremely well written book details Chief Joseph's leadership
and strategy. Few, if any, stereotyped Indians are described in this book; both men
and women are presented with dignity as
real people. Except for a route map of Nez
Percé marches and battles on the front
and back covers, a picture of an Indian
leading his warriors, and drawings of four
leaders, two Indian and two white men
prominent in the Nez Percé War, no other
illustrations are included. The clash between whites and Indians, as well as the
treacheries and misunderstandings, are
presented by the author in an unbiased
fashion. Also included are the more well-
known recorded speeches by Chief Joseph,
particularly the famous lines, "From
where the sun now stands, I will fight no
more—forever." With little background regarding Chief Joseph's childhood and
events leading up to his leadership, the
reader is plunged into the first of the Nez
Percé battles and may wish for more introductory information. Good.

229. Day, A. Grove.
THE SKY CLEARS: POETRY OF THE
AMERICAN INDIANS.
New York: Macmillan, 1951.
(8 and up)
In this excellent collection of selected
poetry of North American Indians, the au-
thor provides the reader with more than
200 translations of poems from forty
North American tribes. The poems are

grouped into chapters representing cultural areas, as the author believes that the most important poetic motivation for Indians was cultural and that, unlike European poetry, most American Indian poetry had a utilitarian purpose. In addition, where appropriate, the author points out other distinctions of Indian poetry, such as the absence in this collection of love songs or "Indian love calls," which he labels as pure fantasies on the part of whites. For the most part the poems are brief, and many are followed by interpretations or explanations. Appended to one chapter, dealing with the poetry of the horse nations of the plains, is a description of the songs of the Ghost Dance religion. A useful bibliography of North American Indian poetry provides additional sources. Good.

230. DeAngulo, Jaime.
INDIAN TALES.
New York: Wyn, 1953. (5 and up)
The author, who lived among Pit River Indian groups for forty years, uses the basic structure of a fictionalized journey on which to string poetry and tall tales, some of which he invented in the storytelling style of California Indians. Well written, it contains the author's frequent personal asides:

> Then you discover a lot of very interesting things about primitive thinking. Living among them, sprawling under the oak trees, watching the clouds or a procession of ants, or a hawk perching on a dead pine, you gossip, you argue, you talk about so-and-so and what a liar he is, or two old men start arguing about who made the world, and a young fellow tries to reconcile his knowledge of motors and the electric spark with Indian ideas of medicine and religion. [p.4]

The customs and life styles he observed and reports in this book are, for the most part, accurate and pictured in authentic detail. However, he does give the reader the erroneous impression that the house he helped build is the only style of dwelling built by the California Indians. This is not so; a variety of shelter types were used. The author's black-and-white line drawings and the appendixes add to the book's effectiveness. Good.

231. Dedera, Don.
NAVAJO RUGS: HOW TO FIND,
EVALUATE, BUY, AND CARE FOR THEM.
Flagstaff, Ariz.: Northland Pr.,
(no date). (6 and up)
In addition to providing a guide for those interested in purchasing a Navajo rug, the author describes some of the history of the Navajo Indians, such as where they have lived and from whom they presumably acquired their skills in rug weaving (the Pueblo Indians and the Spanish). The book has many color and black-and-white photographs of old and new rugs, pictures of tools, a labeled sketch of a loom, and a map of the Navajo Reservation designating the origins and locations of regional styles. The book includes background information on yarns, dyes, and rug designs, providing an excellent source book for the reader interested in Indian arts and crafts. The author adds rather interesting personal asides to the text: "Before long I had, though not easily, learned an awful lot about rugs, and damned if I didn't begin thinking about writing a book on Navajo rugs" (p.xi). The book has an index and a bibliography. Good.

232. Deer, Ada, with Simon, R. E., Jr.
SPEAKING OUT.
Chicago: Childrens Pr., 1970. (5-8)
This is an unusual book—a feminist and activist story written in appropriate language for eleven- through fourteen-year-olds. The reading level of the book is about fifth grade, making it a good book for slow junior high and high school readers. The author is half Menominee, and this book details some of her history as she learned how to be successful in "speaking out." Some fascinating vignettes of her development are given, such as the scene where her mother's white twin sister comes to take her home, the Hollywood

starlet episode, and the time a hotel refused her a room:

> I know that what happened that night wasn't earthshaking. It's happened too often to minority-group people. But to me it was important to fight unfair treatment because of my color and my heritage.
>
> I've always been that way. When people tell me, "No, you can't." I am determined to show them that "I most certainly can." That includes speaking up and speaking out. [p.9]

Judging from her writing, she does not always appear too understanding herself with those who disagree with her. There is an excellent description of the career of a group social worker which career guidance people will appreciate, and the book's photographs provide the readers added information. Good.

233. Deloria, Vine, Jr.
CUSTER DIED FOR YOUR SINS.
New York: Macmillan, 1969.
(7 and up)
Deloria is witty, articulate, and knowledgeable, an effective combination for looking, as he does in this book, at the past and present of the American Indian. He turns his scholar's background and the celebrated wit on such subjects as anthropologists and missionaries, and the results are as funny as they are precise. The rhetoric is angry, the facts presented are appalling; yet Deloria is wise enough, too much a scholar, and has enough empathy not to indulge himself in wholesale accusations or the branding of whites as a homogeneous group (no doubt he has seen this happen too often to Indians). His style is most effective—nothing convinces like humor solidly backed up with facts. Although the book was written for adult readers, many junior high and high school readers will find it invaluable. A classic. Good.

234. Dennis, Henry C., ed.
THE AMERICAN INDIAN 1492–1970:
A CHRONOLOGY AND FACT BOOK.

Dobbs Ferry, N.Y.: Oceana, 1971.
(6 and up)
Dennis presents a detailed book divided into several sections: a chronology of important events in American Indian history; lists of brief biographies of prominent Indians of the past and present; appendixes concerned with such data as Indian population, wars, museums, newspapers, and the like; a reading and research bibliography; and an index. The text reminds us, "As much as there is a desire to do so, Indian history cannot be changed. Its writing can, however" (p.vii); and that the Indian in the past was "fighting for his very life, his liberty, his property, and the pursuit of his happiness" (p.ix). Previous works about Indians he characterizes as a "portrayal of the American Indian as benefactor to savage, to pawn, to recipient, and finally to property owner and citizen" (p.vii). This is a remarkable piece of scholarship. Arguments will doubtless emerge over his choice of events to include or leave out, over his opinionated writing style, and over some of his conclusions. Nevertheless, he has made an excellent beginning which will undoubtedly be followed up by other researchers in the future. The reading level is approximately sixth grade in difficulty, but the format and the small print will probably discourage most elementary age scholars. A sample (p.45):

> 1890 Unarmed Sioux men, women and children were massacred by federal troops at the infamous Battle of Wounded Knee.
>
> Old Comanche War Chief Quanah Parker, having surrendered in 1875 to become a virtual collaborator in white government policies, had been appointed a judge, but was relieved of his duties for having broken white man's laws by possessing too many wives, which violated the codes of the Courts of Indian Offenses.
>
> Congress enacted laws to cover the costs of tuition of Indians attending public school.

Good.

235. Deur, Lynne.
INDIAN CHIEFS.
Minneapolis, Minn.: Lerner, 1972.
(3–5)
This book contains fourteen brief Indian biographies from the war years. It places these Indians into a context of defense and emphasizes the chiefs' repeated attempts to reconcile differences between Indians and whites, as well as their roles as mediators between Indian tribes and within their own groups. A little pedantic in the preface, "Indian Patriots and White Savages," the author nevertheless has prepared concise, interesting biographies that point out several misconceptions, such as the fact that Indian chiefs are viewed correctly not as chiefs but as heads of tribes. The primary weakness of the book is the small number of Western Indian leaders (except for Chief Joseph, Geronimo and Cochise), which, as represented on the two maps, gives the impression that no Indian leaders emerged from other parts of North America. The author includes many photographs, reproductions, and several maps. Good.

236. Dewdney, Selvyn, and
Kidd, Kenneth E.
INDIAN ROCK PAINTING OF THE
GREAT LAKES.
Toronto: Univ. of Toronto Pr., 1963.
(6 and up)
A thorough, scholarly book by authors clearly enthralled with their subject matter, this volume includes complete listings of sites, techniques for finding and recording rock paintings how to interpret these paintings, and other facts useful to the study of this art and communication form. An interesting account of the authors' search for these paintings, it includes many of their personal reactions:

What the psychologists call projection is a real problem in recording these sites. For instance, on my brief visit to the Jorgensens the previous year, they had mentioned a man with a bow and arrow and I was sure I recognized one at the time. Yet on my return neither Peter nor I could find even a hint of one. [p.68]

The authors give examples of Schoolcraft's sketches, often including some showing European content. There are plenty of illustrations in the book, both photographs and sketches, often rather small, and a complete bibliography and index. Good.

237. Dines, Glen.
CRAZY HORSE.
New York: Putnam, 1966. (K–2)
Illustrated by the author, this book traces Crazy Horse from his boyhood as "His Horse Looking" until his death. Except for his wife, Black Shawl, and a white man, Casper Collins, no other person is mentioned by name. This may leave the young reader with many questions concerning the identity of other Indians and of the soldiers Crazy Horse fought, and to whom he eventually surrendered. The author, at times, focuses on some events in Crazy Horse's life that appear unrelated to the rest of the story, and which tend to be disruptive as well. For instance, soon after he had "been in many battles" as a warrior and earned his new name, Crazy Horse visited a very pretty girl who would not marry him. From this experience he then is shown in the mountains, where he sees snow, thunder, and lightning, which he calls "magic," as well as telegraph poles with humming wires, which he also says are "magic." From the way these scenes are presented, it seems apparent that the young reader may have a great deal of trouble in placing Crazy Horse and his experiences in any sort of context. Poor.

238. Dines, Glen.
INDIAN PONY.
New York: Macmillan, 1965. (2–5)
A thorough look at the effect horses had on American Indian life and history, this book gives the young reader many interesting facts about Indian ponies. For instance, the Pueblo uprising provided the Indians many horses; the army respected them ("Saddle-weary U.S. Cavalry troopers called them 'hang-dog' with legs like a

churn . . . and head and neck joined like a hammer . . . but rarely outran one" [p.10]); and a Plains family of eight needed at least twelve pack and saddle animals, two buffalo runners, plus four or five extra mounts. The author also illustrated the book, and he is a better illustrator than writer: "Their blood ran hot with the strains of fleet and hardy ponies of the eight-century Moorish invaders who came to Spain from Africa" (p.5). Occasionally the author gives the young reader the impression that every horse was a thoroughbred, and every Spaniard an hidalgo. There is an account of a horse raid, a glossary, a bibliography and many diagrams. Good.

239. Distad, Audree.
DAKOTA SONS.
New York: Harper, 1972. (3–7)
This is the story of a white boy and a Sioux boy who become close friends. Ronnie lives at the Indian school three miles away from Tad's home. His father is a sometime rodeo rider and has left Ronnie at the school to get an education. Tad and Ronnie do all the things eleven-year-old boys do—ride bikes, go on picnics, form secret clubs, and so on. Ronnie is very aware that he is an Indian and that, because of this, he is looked down on by some children and adults. He feigns lack of interest in his heritage and rejects the opportunity to learn the traditional Indian dances until the crisis at the end of the story convinces him that he should be proud to be an Indian. The book tells of Ronnie's struggle to come to terms with his Indian identity and Tad's growing awareness and appreciation for Indian customs and values through his association with Ronnie. Adequate.

240. Dobrin, Norma.
DELAWARES.
Chicago: Melmont, 1965. (2–3)
Black-, white-, and-blue drawings featuring Indian figures that look amazingly like "Mr. Clean" illustrate this account of the Delawares. The author interjects fictional excerpts to describe Delaware life

before the whites. The writing is simplistic and poorly done: " 'We have buried this hatchet,' said Red Fox. 'It is our hope it will never again be dug up. May there be peace among our nations' " (p.31). Poor.

241. Dobyns, Henry F.
THE APACHE PEOPLE.
Phoenix, Ariz.: Indian Tribal Series, 1971. (7 and up)
In this history of the Apache, the author begins with the development of the Western Apache tribes, then concentrates on a century (1871–1971) of reservation life at the White Mountain Reservation, located in eastern Arizona. In his history, the author traces the positive and negative effects of the land losses, the problems created by forced relocation, economic integration, and the influence of Christianity. The book includes some impressive black-and-white and color photographs as well as several maps prepared by Debbie Westlake. The book is well written; an excellent overview. Good.

242. Dobyns, Henry F.
THE MESCALERO APACHE PEOPLE.
Phoenix, Ariz.: Indian Tribal Series, 1973. (7 and up)
A scholarly history of the Mescalero Apache, this is another of the series of books sponsored by the Indian Tribal groups. It is authentic, written in readable, but not easy reading, fashion. The type is easy to see, and the pictures complement the text. A small, annotated bibliography is included, as well as a section on the author. Good.

243. Dobyns, Henry F.
THE PAPAGO PEOPLE.
Phoenix, Ariz.: Indian Tribal Series, 1972. (7 and up)
Beautifully conceived and executed, this is one of the Indian Tribal Series books sponsored by various tribal councils. It is complex and authoritative, yet written in a readable fashion. Illustrated by color and black-and-white photographs, the book contains an annotated bibliography. A scholarly tome, not particularly de-

signed for pleasure reading, the book is as valuable for adults as for young adolescents. Good.

244. Dodge, Nanabah Chee.
MORNING ARROW.
New York: Lothrop, 1973. (3 and up)
This is an unusually well-written story about a Navajo boy who lives with his grandmother. Characters, whether male or female, are fully developed. The story includes true-to-life touches, such as a tablecloth made from flour sacks, dishes from cereal boxes, lamb jerky and mint tea, running in the morning, gathering and roasting piñon nuts, the tribal fair, the trading post, and the use of Navajo words. Good black-and-white drawings by Jeffery Lungé illustrate the story. The book would be equally effective with Indian and non-Indian children. Good.

245. Dolch, Edward W., and
Dolch, Marguerite P.
NAVAHO STORIES IN BASIC
VOCABULARY.
Champaign, Ill.: Garrard, 1957. (2–5)
Utilizing the Dolch list of 220 basic sight words, the authors have written an easily read collection of the more widely known Navajo myths and legends. Included are stories dealing with Changing Woman, the first medicine man, the medical and religious importance of "the Sing," as well as several representative chants as they relate to each story. Although stated in simple language, the stories seem relatively free of white cultural influences and interpretation. Billy M. Jackson's black-, white-, and-brown illustrations provide interesting, although not literal, representations of animals and early Indians. Since the stories are legends and myths, the young reader may need additional references or help to understand how these are linked with Indian life and culture. Good.

246. Dorian, Edith, and Wilson, W. N.
HOKAKEY: AMERICAN INDIANS THEN
AND NOW.
New York: McGraw-Hill, 1957. (5–8)

Even, thorough writing and research characterize this history of the American Indian. A fair book, it does not gloss over hard issues: "There is another memory, though, in which no one could take pride—the memory of the white man's greed, arrogance, ruthlessness, and broken treaties" (p.9). It treats women fairly; for example, in the section on the Iroquois, it tells of their power of inheritance and of making and breaking chiefs. The "Today and Tomorrow" chapter is good as far as it goes (1957) but is severely dated. It would be worth the publisher's time to bring the text up to date, redoing banal chapter headings such as "The Tower of Babel," or "Wigwam and Longhouse." Occasionally the authors intrude with unnecessary value judgments:

> Pueblo Indians were far more artistic craftsmen than the Iroquois; Navajo and Pawnee ceremonies were more richly poetic than theirs. But in outright genius for political organization and for transforming simple culture tracts into vital forces in their lives, the Iroquois towered over every other Indian group in the United States. [p.25]

The authors include a bibliography and an index. Dated. Adequate.

247. Duncan, Lois.
SEASON OF THE TWO-HEART.
New York: Dodd, 1964. (7–8)
Natachu Weekoty, a Pueblo girl of high school age, makes the decision to leave the reservation and go to Albuquerque to attend school. To do so she must live with a prosperous white family, taking care of their two young sons. Natachu finds life among the whites difficult and confusing. The two worlds are described by her mother as "a two-hearted season, neither summer nor autumn." Problems of living among the whites and obtaining an education are resolved as Natachu finds good friends who are white, and who help her discover her talents, singing and music. A good beginning for discussions of problems Indian students face, this book is helpful as well for teaching the use of fig-

urative language in literature. Realists may find the happy ending somewhat pat. Good.

248. Dunn, Dorothy.
AMERICAN INDIAN PAINTING OF THE SOUTHWEST AND PLAINS AREAS.
Albuquerque: Univ. of New Mexico Pr., 1968. (7 and up)
Exquisite color and black-and-white reproductions of the art of Southwestern and Plains Indians are featured in this thorough, complete treatment of past and modern Indian art of those regions. Although elementary school children would probably enjoy looking at the pictures, the text, which analyzes traditional and modern Indian art, is written at an adult level: "A consideration for convention in the attitude of different creatures is apparent" (p.62). The book includes references and an index. Good.

249. Dunn, Marion Herndon.
TENASE BRAVE.
Nashville, Tenn.: Aurora, 1971. (5–7)
The writing is strained and jerky in this story of a pre-Columbian eleven-year-old Cherokee boy. In the story, the boy hasn't received a "real name." Much of his adventures have to do with seeking "a good name." He finally saves a girl from a buffalo and gets his manhood name. The black-and-white illustrations by June Moore, although average in execution, are the best part of the book, including the interesting one of the boy and rattlesnakes on page 77. There is a word list explaining Indian words used in the text. Poor.

250. Dutton, Bertha P., ed.
THE INDIANS OF THE SOUTHWEST.
Santa Fe, N. Mex.: Southern Assn. on Indian Affairs, 1963. (5 and up)
Prepared for tourists or visitors with little or no knowledge about Southwest Indians, this book provides some historical, religious, cultural, and current background information about five Southwestern tribes: the Pueblos, the Navajos, the Apaches, the Utes, and the Pimas. It includes a discussion on Indian arts and crafts (mainly Navajo blankets, pottery,

and jewelry); maps of Arizona, New Mexico, and parts of Utah and Colorado; "Katsina figures"; a calendar of Indian ceremonies; and a suggested reading list. Intended as a "pocket handbook," the book contains many black-and-white photographs, as well as numerous advertisements of local merchants in and around the Albuquerque and Santa Fe areas, which the young reader will probably find either distracting or amusing. Adequate.

251. Dutton, Bertha P.
INDIANS OF THE SOUTHWEST.
New York: Prentice-Hall, 1975.
(9 and up)
A textbook extension and update of her previous book, just reviewed, this edition is complete with table of contents, list of illustrations, a foreword, a preface, acknowledgments, and linguistic notes. The author concentrates on five major Indian peoples, including several tribes within such groups who live on reservations located in Arizona and New Mexico: the Pueblos, Atabascans (i.e., the Navajos and Apaches), the Utes, the Southern Paiutes, and a lesser known group of tribes she has labeled "the ranchería peoples" (i.e., Mojave, Yuma, Havasupai, Papago, Yaqui). She provides a brief overview of the origins of the Southwestern Indians, their physical characteristics, as well as the development of socioreligious patterns. Next, treating each tribe separately, the author describes the basic characteristics or similarities each grouping shares, and then describes each individual tribe. About forty photographs are included, grouped at the center of the book, as well as a map illustrating the geographical location of each group of tribes. Except for seven "chapter-opening drawings" there are no other illustrations. Although each section is brief, due to the number of tribes discussed, the book provides an excellent overview or beginning reference. Good.

252. Dutton, Bertha P.
NAVAJO WEAVING TODAY.
Santa Fe: Museum of New Mexico Pr., 1975. (5 and up)

This little paperback book includes a short history of Navajo Indians and weaving. Numerous black-and-white photographs of Navajo rugs illustrate the book, intended primarily as a guide for the uninformed person interested in purchasing a Navajo rug. The book includes a description of how the yarn is dyed and woven, selection and types of designs, and regional distinctions between rug designs. A suggested reading list is provided. The reader interested in Indian arts and crafts will find this book a good resource. Good.

253. Earle, Edwin.
HOPI KACHINAS.
New York: Museum of the American Indian, Heye Foundation, 1971.
(6 and up)
Earle's drawings, in color and black-and-white, are exquisite in this book about Hopi kachinas. The history and meaning of kachinas and kachina dances; the changes in customs "There has been an amazing increase in the number, duration, and frequency of Kachina dances" (pp.ix–x), and the financial and economic burdens of sponsoring such a dance are carefully detailed. Also included is a calendar listing the scheduled dances. Good.

254. Eastman, Charles A. (Ohiyesa.)
INDIAN BOYHOOD.
Boston: Little, 1924. (5–9)
Somewhat dated in language usage but almost poetic in style, with long, compound sentences alternating with short, this story is remarkably free of some of the stereotypes and weaknesses of more recent works. Beginning with his earliest recollections, the author describes the culture of his tribe, the Sioux, and impressions he received in his childhood up until his father took him to live among the whites to attend school. The descriptions of battles with other tribes suggest that the author grew up in the late 1800s. He refers to his father's involvement, capture, and imprisonment following the "Minnesota Massacre." Surprisingly enough, there is no anger or bitterness in this book. There is sadness, but it is expressed in a

context of everyday life, along with laughter and other emotions. The author describes in great detail the size, composition, and daily life of his tribe. He includes a few legends and adventures. The illustrations by E. L. Blumenschein are characteristic of black-and-white sketches done in the 1920s. Good.

255. Eastman, Charles A., and
Goodale, Elaine.
WIGWAM EVENING.
Eau Claire, Wisc.: Hale, 1937. (2–5)
The author's phrasing gives a coherent flow to this collection of Indian legends and tales, some of which appeared earlier in such magazines as *Ladies' Home Journal, Good Housekeeping,* and *Woman's Home Companion.* In this adaptation for non-Indian children "we have chosen from a mass of material the shorter and simpler stories and parts of stories, and have not always insisted upon a literal rendering, but taken such occasional liberties with the originals as seemed necessary to fit them to the exigencies of an unlike tongue and to the sympathies of an alien race" (p.vii). In the process they omitted much detail and repetition characteristic of the original oral storytelling style. Designed for daily reading "beside an open fire" (p.xii), the stories often have a moral, like an Aesop fable. The black-and-white drawings by Edwin Willard Deming are charming and old-fashioned. Good.

256. Eckert, Allan W.
BLUE JACKET: WAR CHIEF OF
THE SHAWNEES.
Boston: Little, 1969. (7–9)
This is a highly romanticized version of how Blue Jacket, a white boy born Marmaduke Van Swearingen, was kidnapped and adopted into the Kispokotha sept or clan of the Shawnee tribe. Although the writing is not lacking in interest and features many adventures, the author nevertheless tends to stereotype his characters and to infuse some Anglo-Christian pedantry into Shawnee religious beliefs and cultural practices. For example, the "chief's word was absolute law and any persistent

refusal to obey him . . . was punishable by severe flogging, or even death. . . . The most dreadful crime of which any woman could be convicted was . . . gossip about people" (p.36). For the rest, it is a good swashbuckling adventure. The author seems not to have strayed from historical information available about relationships between the Indians and whites in the Northwest Territory during the post-Revolutionary War years. Adequate.

257. Edmonds, Walter D.
IN THE HANDS OF THE SENECAS.
Boston: Little, 1947. (7–10)
In 1778, the Seneca Indians surrounded a fifteen-family community of homesteaders. They killed most of the men and took several women captives. These are the stories of those captives. One story, for example, involves the only male captive, who escapes with the help of two women captives, Delia Borst and Mrs. Staats. Mrs. Staats is killed, but Delia's assistance remains undetected. She eventually becomes the wife of the chief and bears his child. The author points out that she did not realize a marriage ceremony was taking place at the time. If she had known, he states, she would have had an opportunity to refuse. When the war ends, Delia returns to her husband, who rejects her when he finds out that she had been the wife of the chief. Later he realizes he still loves her and returns to save her from an Indian renegade. The stories of other captives are also related in the book, in a similar fashion. In general, the Indians are pictured as good people by their standards and, generally, by white standards. There is a renegade Indian and a sadistic woman in the story, but a more valid criticism involves the author's use of terms such as *squaw* and his supplying of white cultural motives to the Senecas. Adequate.

258. Edwards, Cecile Pepin.
KING PHILLIP: LOYAL INDIAN.
New York: Houghton, 1962. (3–5)
The story of King Philip, Massasoit's son, is written in novel format in this version of his life. The author reports that

King Philip's childhood was normal and happy, and he provides a good description of the tests of manhood Philip underwent as he came of age in his tribe. Philip led the fight against the whites when the Wampanoag first realized the meaning of the Pilgrims' arrival. The author includes such details as the fact that Pilgrims sold into slavery all the Indians they captured at the end of this war, including King Philip's family, while Philip's head was exhibited for years on a stake. Women are left out of the book almost completely; when they are included, they are referred to as "squaws" in a rather derogatory fashion. The black-, white-, and-red illustrations by Forrest Orr are of the "tomahawk, war, and scalping" variety, and show more ferocity than the text warrants. The author includes notes on the lack of facts about Philip, a section on the weapons of the Indians and the Pilgrims, and a pronunciation guide. Adequate.

259. Eisenberg, Phillip, and
Eisenberg, Miriam.
THE BRAVE GIVES BLOOD.
New York: Messner, 1954. (2–4)
This book, really designed as a science story about ways to categorize animals, rather than a social studies text, makes a plea for not judging a person by his or her exterior. Two boys at camp have an Indian counselor. They gradually move from a stereotype view of him to an increased understanding of modern day (1954) Indians. The counselor donates blood when one boy is injured, and they decide that people are alike, underneath. The Indian in the story is portrayed as a science student, and he teaches the boys to observe and catalog what they see. An adventure story, the book provides an interesting and different setting for a science text. Adequate.

260. Ellis, Melvin R.
SIDEWALK INDIAN.
New York: Holt, 1974. (6–8)
Ellis' plot line involves Charley Nightwind, an Indian who has never been out of the city, fleeing to the reservation after

being accused of murder. Here he "finds" himself and helps dynamite a new dam threatening the reservation. The ending of this romantic tale has him either dying in the blast or fleeing; the reader must determine the ending. This simplistic tale of cardboard figures does touch on the city/reservation dilemma of many young Indians, and for that reason may serve as a focus for classroom discussions for Indian and non-Indian students. The choice of a deserving and true theme, however, is not enough to absolve a writer from the necessity for developing fuller characterizations and a plot where good versus bad is more convincingly discussed. Adequate.

261. Ellis, Melvin R.
THE WILD RUNNERS.
New York: Holt, 1970. (7 and up)
This book features two parallel plots, one about a half-breed Ojibwa boy, the result of a rape of an Ojibwa woman by a white man, and the other about "coy-dog," the result of a mating between a coyote mother and a hound dog father. There are vivid, detailed descriptions of the mating of the animals, the birth of the pups, the coyote mother eating all but the one little dog, and the hound's impotence (if this were a film, it would carry a PG rating). Decidedly downbeat, the story tells of the Indian woman drowning herself and trying, at the same time, to drown her baby; of the boy's white father attempting to kill him; of the old Indian who raised him shooting the white man with an arrow; and of the death of the old man—all this written in a jarringly beautiful fashion. The wild runners of the title are those who don't belong in the wild or with man. Good.

262. Elting, Mary.
THE HOPI WAY.
New York: M. Evans, 1969. (4–6)
This is a good story, simply told, about a Hopi boy who lived in New York City. Summer finds his family travelling west to the Hopi village, his father's boyhood home. During the summer he learns about the customs of his people. Of help to stu-

dents who may think all Indians wear feathers and live on a reservation, this book is illustrated by Louis Mofsie, the leading character. The author presents some interesting pictures, including men weaving, the kiva clubhouse, a fascinating description of cultural difference: "This strangeness, which invites amazement and surprise, is anthropology's first delight" (introduction). A glossary defines the Hopi words used by the author. Good.

263. Elting, Mary, and Folson, Michael.
THE SECRET STORY OF PUEBLO BONITO.
Irvington-on-Hudson, N.Y.: Harvey House, 1963. (2–5)
A read-aloud book for younger children and an account that will interest upper elementary readers as well, this book dramatizes the clues and mysteries of Pueblo Bonito National Monument in New Mexico. The careful work of archaeologists, the questions, and some of the interpretations are told with an aura of suspense. The book has been checked for scientific accuracy by Neill Judd, leader of the National Geographic Society Pueblo Bonito expeditions. The vivid writing and beautiful illustrations will motivate children to learn more about the ancient people who built the pueblos in the Southwestern part of the United States. Good.

264. Elwood, Ann.
LEGENDS FOR EVERYONE.
New York: Globe, 1973. (6)
Included in this collection of legends from all over the United States are two dealing with Indians, "Crazy Horse" and "Pine Leaf and Medicine Calf." Both stories are followed by vocabulary aids and study questions in a basal-reader format. "Crazy Horse" is a story of a Sioux who met with Grouard, Sitting Bull, and General Cook in an attempt to save Indian lands for the Indians. As usual, the Indians kept their word, but the white man did not. "Pine Leaf and Medicine Calf" is the story of a girl who becomes a brave and of a black woodsman, adopted by the Crow Indians, who becomes an Indian

chief. The story is an excerpt from the book written by Chief Medicine Calf, and tells of many battles as well as his marriage to Pine Leaf. Both stories are interesting, but do not add much to the store of knowledge about Indians. Children will enjoy reading them and discussing the reasons for the incidents described in the legends, however. Good.

265. Embry, Margaret.
MY NAME IS LION.
New York: Holiday House, 1970.
(4–6)
Readers will find this book especially helpful in broadening their perceptions about the difficulties young Navajos have reconciling conflicting value systems and, whether Indian or non-Indian, will be able to find elements that match their own conflicts of family as opposed to school culture. The author frequently overstates her case. For example, a great amount of drunkenness is depicted on the part of Navajo men. It is true that this is a problem for many Navajos; still, the amount the book describes seems excessive. The ending also seems contrived. The book also has many strengths: the author writes well, the book helps do away with many stereotypes of Navajo life, and the struggles the boy undergoes are pictured to be as agonizing as they would be in real life. The black-and-white illustrations by Ned Glattauer are good and in keeping with the story. An especially fine example is the illustration of the pickup truck scene. The language of the book and the plot are designed for older readers than format might indicate. Adequate.

266. Embry, Margaret.
SHÁDÍ.
New York: Holiday House, 1971.
(7 and up)
This book faces realistically the great amount of family and personal responsibility many Indian children have. It tells of Shádí (My Older Sister) who has seven younger brothers and sisters to help care for after her mother's death. The book

talks plainly about sex, birth, and maturation. In fact, the first few lines of the story take the reader into a realistic Navajo girl's world:

> It seemed to Emma that most of her bad times had started that spring at school when she became a woman. *Kinaasdá*, the Navajos called it. The other girls in the dorm told her not to mention that first bleeding, or her family would hear about it at home and send for her to come and have a *kinaaldá*. [p.9]

The writing is good: the scenes of the coming-of-age ceremony, the birth of her sister, and the mourners at her mother's funeral are examples of the author's ability to picture reality, although the view of the white missionaries is unnecessarily one-sided. A classic. Good.

267. Emmons, Della Gould.
SACAJAWEA OF THE SHOSHONES.
Portland, Ore.: Binford and Mort, 1943. (6–9)
This is a story written with great sensitivity. In her foreword, the author correctly notes that Indians, like other people, express emotions, but that "after the Indian dealt with the white man he masked his emotions," a not uncommon practice among any people who are or have been conquered or subjugated. With this in mind, the author developed her characters, utilizing the original journals of Lewis and Clark and enough other early sources to satisfy the most critical historian. At the end of most chapters the author includes direct quotations from her sources, which lend credence to her interpretations. The characters seem relatively free of stereotyping. The author's female characters, Sacajawea and her female contemporaries, are more fully developed than the men in the story (Sacajawea's brother, Cameahwait; Charbonneau; and Captain Clark). This author takes the position that after guiding the Lewis and Clark expedition, Sacajawea lived a long life with many adventures and rejoined her sons after a long separation. Unfortunately, she has relied more upon legend

here than in her chapters about Sacajawea's earlier years. Good.

268. Engel, Lor.
AMONG THE PLAINS INDIANS.
Minneapolis, Minn.: Lerner, 1970.
(5–12)
This book was first printed in Germany,
and the English translation was made by
Susan W. Dickinson. The paintings in the
book are from George Catlin's *North
American Indian Portfolio*, published in
1884, and from a volume of Bodmer's en-
gravings. The text following each picture
was taken from Prince Maximillian's account of his travels with George Catlin
among the Indians of North America and
Canada. The writing is interesting, and
the pictures, alone, are worth the price of
the book. For example, Catlin's picture of
the Snowshoe Dance (p.42) is more modern than many contemporary paintings.
Good.

269. Erdoes, Richard.
THE PUEBLO INDIANS.
New York: Funk & Wagnalls, 1968.
(5 and up)
This book contains factual information
about the Pueblo Indians of the Southwest.
Customs, religions, and attitudes are discussed. Values such as responsibility to
the tribe as a whole, generosity, the sense
of sharing, and the importance of the extended family are explored. The history of
the Pueblo people is presented from a description of life before the Spaniards, to
life under the Spanish, Mexicans, and
Americans, up to present-day living. The
book is well written, and good photographs
are used as illustrative examples. Good.

270. Erdoes, Richard.
THE RAIN DANCE PEOPLE: THE
PUEBLO INDIANS, THEIR PAST AND
PRESENT.
New York: Knopf, 1976. (6 and up)
A comprehensive history of various
Pueblo Indian groups, this book is not a
standard history text. The author writes
well in a smoothly flowing prose that in-
cludes interesting, personal discussions
about such little known cultures as that of

the Mogollon and about various Pueblo
governmental, child-rearing, and social
practices. He includes an accurate account
of women's rights in Pueblo life, he carefully differentiates among the various Pueblo cultures, and he provides the reader
with a fine account of archaeological practices. Erdoes has a distinctive, activist
point of view, but he is careful to inform
the reader of this: "The view presented on
the following pages is one-sided. It represents the view of the Indian-conservative
and activist, traditionalist and progressive" (p.259). Although he does wait until
nearly the end of the book to state his bias,
many groups would not endorse his views
as representative of "the view of the Indian." However, this book as a whole
amounts to much more than any criticism
of its separate parts. Erdoes is a romantic
writer:
> Archaeologists tell us that this particu-
> lar hunt had its happy ending twelve
> thousand years ago. Was it happy?
> Seemingly, yes. [pp.16–17]
who occasionally indulges in popular stereotyping about whites,
> White Americans are essentially with-
> out roots. [p.12]
about prehistoric groups,
> Cochise men were not particular. If
> they could get nothing better, they ate
> snakes, lizards, or insects—and loved it.
> [p.22]
about mountain men,
> The shiftless, the wild ones, men who
> boasted that they were half timber wolf
> and half alligator, went West. [p.134]
about white pioneers,
> Behind the mountain men was the
> great mass of land-hungry, silver-hun-
> gry, grasping, industrial *Norte Ameri-
> canos*. They were like rambunctious
> children. [p.135]
and about Protestant missionaries,
> They were puritan killjoys, forever
> shocked at the things Indians did.
> [p.144]
He scatters throughout the book personal
phrases that reflect his point of view, such
as: "We must feel sorry for the people who
so carefully and lovingly built this town"

(p.66), and "Lo, the poor hunter! Archaeologists have given him names that would
have astounded him" (p.16). However,
the smoothness of Erdoes' writing, the
thoroughness of his research, and the in-
clusiveness of his presentations of present-
day Pueblo life styles, among other attributes, make the book well worth purchasing. The numerous black-and-white photographs add immensely to the reader's view
of Pueblo life. A bibliography and an index
are included. Good.

270a. Erdoes, Richard.
THE SUN DANCE PEOPLE: THE PLAINS
INDIANS, THEIR PAST AND PRESENT.
New York: Knopf, 1972. (5–8)
Erdoes, a writer and photographer, has
compiled a thorough work exploring the
culture of the Plains Indian. He is ambivalent about woman's place in the culture:
Experts say that there are six things
that make up the true Plains Indian;
the horse, the buffalo, the tepee, the
warrior's society, the sun dance, and
the absence of agriculture. [p.13]
he nonetheless tries to picture their work:
The prairie was very much a man's
world because a tribe survived by hunting and warfare. Still, women had
many rights and were respected members of the tribe. A man was conscious
of the fact that even the proudest warrior could not exist without the help of
a woman. A woman ruled in the tepee.
She had a right to her own property.
[p.76]
The book covers the history of the Sioux
from prehistoric days to the present. He
talks with much feeling of the land the
Indians lived in: "Curiously enough, the
same [white] men also agreed on one other
thing: the prairie gave them a feeling of
freedom and happiness such as they had
never experienced before" (pp.1–2). His
photographs show today's Sioux Indians
as they carry on traditional work—the pictures are largely of men. His feelings
about their life today are summed up in
the following quote: "It is hard to exag-
gerate the power of the BIA" (p.193).
Adequate.

271. Erickson, Phoebe.
WILDWING.
New York: Harper, 1959. (3–6)
The setting of this romanticized story
is the Wyoming desert. The story involves
Bronze Feather, a young Arapahoe, and
his little sister, who gain the confidence
and affection of a colt orphaned when
white men drove the colt's mother and
many other horses into a feverish stam-
pede in an airplane roundup. The story
focuses upon love of nature, the horse,
and the friendship which grew between
the Indians and some of the whites. It is
written with compassion and empathy
and, although it is not a great story, it is
the type to hold a child's interest. The detailed black-and-white illustrations by the
author add to the total effect. Adequate.

272. Estep, Irene.
IROQUOIS.
Chicago: Melmont, 1961. (2–4)
This is a simple, illustrated, factual
account of Iroquois customs and lifestyles.
Food, clothing, shelter, festivals, men's
and women's work, recreation, family and
community organization, and the high position of women are all mentioned. This
book is a good free reading or enrichment
choice for the classroom, but its lack of
detail does not make it a good reference
for an in-depth paper or report. Dated.
Adequate.

273. Euler, Robert C., and
Dobyns, Henry F.
THE HOPI PEOPLE.
Phoenix, Ariz.: Indian Tribal Series,
1971. (7 and up)
An overview of the Hopi people from
prehistoric times to the present, this is an
excellent resource for a student or reservation traveler. The section devoted to
modern-day Hopi life is as complete as
any available at this time. The authors are
anthropologists, and their writing style
shows it. They give complete data, even to
climate, as if they were preparing for a
dig: "The mean annual temperature, as
recorded at the Keams Canyon agency, is
51° F." Budding archaeologists and an-

thropologists can get some idea of what such work entails from this book. It includes a bibliography and a section on the two authors. Good.

274. Falk, Elsa.
THE BORROWED CANOE.
Los Angeles: Ritchie, 1969. (3 and up)
This story of a California Indian boy gives a picture of Hupa life styles and values before Europeans came to California. Beautifully told in accurate detail, the story involves the ethics of "borrowing" without permission and the chain of events that follows. The ceremony of becoming a man climaxes the story. Patterns of Hupa life are woven throughout the narrative. Good.

275. Falk, Elsa.
FIRE CANOE.
New York: Follett, 1956. (6 and up)
Basically the story of a white boy of the 1850s who gets a job on a Mississippi steam boat taking food to the Indians, this book deals with Indians only incidentally, as background objects. The story details the boy's discovery of the worth of the values of his own home and parents. The book is illustrated by Robert Frankenberg. Story: Adequate. Portrayal of Indian life: Incidental; Poor.

276. Falk, Elsa.
FOG ISLAND.
New York: Wilcox & Follett, 1953. (4 and up)
A story that includes authentic facts about Chumash life and an interesting plot makes this book worthwhile for elementary children as a read-aloud book or, for the better readers, as a book to read silently. Recreating the life of the Chumash before exposure to European culture, Falk tells the story of a fatherless teen-age boy gaining acceptance from his peers and developing responsibility. The author has incorporated a great many facts about the Chumash culture. Falk evidently was under the impression that early California coastal Indians made pottery before the missionaries arrived, and

one strand of the story involves a pottery jar. Aside from that error, most elements of the book are accurate and the story is well told. Good.

277. Fall, Thomas.
EDGE OF MANHOOD.
New York: Dial, 1964. (6 and up)
Thomas Fall, a Cherokee himself, writes a story about a young Shawnee coming to manhood as whites moved into Oklahoma Territory. The dissension as several Indian tribes (Shawnee, Osage, Cherokee, and others) were moved onto the same land is described. The author writes movingly of the Shawnee coming of age rites. He also strives to present a fair picture of the various tribes and of the whites; in fact, he perhaps is overly generous: "The boy was comforted. He had learned, as his father had told him he must learn, that some white men, if not all of them, could understand the stain in the heart of a young boy who was not white" (p.88). The black-and-white drawings by Henry C. Pitz are good and add to the story. Good.

278. Fall, Thomas.
JIM THORPE.
New York: Crowell, 1970. (K–2)
In this story, Jim Thorpe is described as the child his father, Hiram, had hoped for, one who would "wrestle at an early age," "run fast," and "jump," unlike his older brother George, who was not very athletic. His mother Charlotte, on the other hand, insisted that "he must go to school" and that, when he and his twin brother were born "they could keep each other company" (virtually the only words attributed to her in the entire book). The author tells about Thorpe's early years at the reservation school and later at Carlisle, where he played for Pop Warner against West Point. The author mentions Thorpe's athletic prowess at the Olympics, where he won the decathlon event, and later his shame when he had to give up his medal after the officials discovered he had played baseball one summer for fifteen dollars a week. The book seems directed toward an

audience interested no only in male physical prowess, but in stamina and perseverance as well. From the beginning, the reader is told that Thorpe's family was different from other Indian families, that Thorpe's father was "independent and did not like reservation life," and that he built a house that was "warm and dry," instead of "grass huts," as the Indians' "ancestors had done." The brownish-red illustrations by John Gretzer suggest a subtle Freudian slip. If a book could be said to contain pervasive stereotypes, this one is it. Poor.

279. Fall, Thomas.
WILD BOY.
New York: Dial, 1965 (6–9)
This story is concerned with the plight of the person in the middle of events. In an effort to capture the wild horse, Diablo Blanco, a young Mexican boy, Roberto, joins the Comanches to learn riding and mustang-catching. He hopes eventually to become a horse dealer. He quickly learns the bitter feelings of hatred and contempt held by white and red men for each other in the 1870s and experiences the harsh realities of both worlds. The author portrays Roberto as someone caught in the middle in the somewhat precarious position of being able to see the follies and the brilliance of Indians and whites alike. Although the story is directed toward young male readers with no female characters in the book, the more sophisticated readers of both sexes will understand the uncomfortable position of a young person alone, caught in the middle of two opposing groups. The author includes some cultural information, particularly regarding the use of peyote and the purification procedures required of white or half-white initiates in the Comanche art of warfare. The black-and-white illustrations by Henry C. Pitz are highly stylized and well done, somewhat reminiscent of Remington's art depicting the same historical period. Good.

280. Farnsworth, Frances Joyce.
WINGED MOCCASINS: THE STORY OF SACAJAWEA.
New York: Messner, 1954. (7–8)

In this story, as with many other stories written by women about Indian women who lived during the white settlement of North Carolina (see #545, Pocahontas, by Patricia M. Martin and #694, Bird Girl: Sacajawea, by Flora W. Seymour), the Indian heroine is apparently so restless that she imposes herself upon the male world, and is constantly apologetic for the intrusion. For example, in this book Sacajawea kills a deer with a stone but hides her prowess by saying that Cameahwait, her brother, should take credit for the kill. Throughout the book she is described as "different" in a negative sense, not in the same way as, say, Sitting Bull or Black Hawk are usually described. Although always depicted as brave and ingenious, she is also described as faithful, able to endure severe hardship, and accommodating to Indian and white men. The author presents interesting theories regarding Sacajawea's later years. Recent biographers concur that Sacajawea probably lived on into her nineties quietly on a reservation, and that her grave is located in the Wind River Reservation in Wyoming. In this story, however, Sacajawea remarries after her first husband's death, has five more children and, after many years, is reunited with her son, Baptiste, to whom she gave birth shortly before her experiences as guide for Lewis and Clark. Although the story is highly romanticized and often as sugary as the title suggests, some young readers may find redeeming qualities, such as the descriptions of her intelligence and ingenuity, perhaps the person most responsible for the success of the expedition. The black-and-white sketches by Lorence F. Bjorklund are consistent with most illustrations of books written for youngsters in junior high during the 1950s. Adequate.

281. Farquhar, Margaret C.
INDIAN CHILDREN OF AMERICA: A BOOK TO BEGIN ON.
New York: Holt, 1964. (1–3)
The customs and child-rearing practices of Eastern Woodlands, Great Plains, Pueblo, and Northwest Coast tribes are

rather indiscriminately thrown together in this book about Indian children written for primary age readers. The book uses extensive stereotypes: "Many of these American Indians were cruel warriors. But they were all kind to their women and to their children" (unpaged), and belabors the obvious: "There were no schools for the Indian children before the colonists came to America" (unpaged). Brinton Turkle's color and black-and-white illustrations of children do not look particularly Indian. Poor.

282. Faulknor, Cliff.
THE WHITE CALF.
Boston: Little, 1965. (5–7)
This story about a young Piegan boy who finds a white buffalo calf, keeps it in his camp, and eventually lets it go, details Piegan life in adventure form and presents the coming of the whites. A good adventure story for young readers, it concentrates on a boy's life among the Piegan. The book does contain several questionable incidents, such as the incongruity of keeping such a big pet in a nomadic camp, the implausibility of a horse suckling a buffalo calf, and the unlikelihood that a buffalo calf that has lost its own mother will be accepted by another cow. Still, fiction sometimes demands the suspension of belief, and as long as young readers have access to books presenting more scientific findings, such a good, rousing adventure may be fun. Supplement with books about Indian girls having fun and doing important things; otherwise youthful readers may conclude that "boys really do have more fun." Adequate.

283. Feber, Doris.
THE LIFE OF POCAHONTAS.
Englewood Cliffs, N.J.: Prentice-Hall, 1963. (4–6)
This is a rather modernized version of Pocahontas's life, her introduction to whites, and her first meeting with Captain John Smith. The author describes Pocahontas's relationship with her dog and her family, particularly with her father, in such a way as to suggest more of a nuclear

family structure and relationship than existed among Indian kinship groups at that time. The author provides great reader interest, however, in her descriptions of Pocahontas's adventures. In terms of what little is known regarding Pocahontas as a captive, her meeting and ultimate marriage to John Rolfe, and her trip to London, the author seems less prone to literary license than in her descriptions of the feelings and attitudes of the characters in this biography. The black-and-white sketches by Elinor Jaeger provide an adequate supplement except in the Indian women's hairstyle and clothing—these seem most definitely modernized. Adequate.

284. Federal Writers' Project, South Dakota.
LEGENDS OF THE MIGHTY SIOUX.
Chicago: Albert Whitman, 1941. (3–6)
Primarily of historical interest, this book was a result of the U.S. Federal Writers' Project of the 1930s. The writing style and the facts presented are severely dated now, but many of the legends are well written and still of interest. The writing is simplified and fosters the concept of the "mighty" Sioux in the title of the book; for example, "The Sioux Indians were great hunters and warriors. Buffalo meat, wild fruit, and vegetables made them strong. Hunting made them brave and adventurous" (p.17). Various Indian artists drew the black-and-white illustrations, reproduced here in a cramped, small fashion. There is a key to Sioux symbols or pictographs. Dated. Adequate.

285. Felton, Harold W.
ELY S. PARKER: SPOKESMAN FOR THE SENECAS.
New York: Dodd, 1973. (4–7)
This story emphasizes Parker's prowess in intellectual, as well as physical, activities. The author begins with Parker's return to school at fourteen after an unsatisfying experience as a mule driver; takes the reader through his legal education (which he never used, because Indians were not allowed to be lawyers at that

time); and finally ends with his work as an engineer. Parker's career as Ulysses S. Grant's military secretary during the Civil War and his subsequent appointment by President Grant as Commissioner of Indian Affairs are described, as well as his eventual resignation after political pressure and false charges drove him out of office. Despite the weaknesses of the book, the author's feeling for his hero as well as for other American leaders, white and Indian, of Parker's time contribute to reader interest and involvement. Lorence F. Bjorklund's black-and-white illustrations show equal involvement. Written almost exclusively about men, only one woman, Parker's mother, is described early in the book. Adequate.

286. Felton, Harold W.
NANCY WARD, CHEROKEE.
New York: Dodd, 1975. (4)
Written almost as an epic poem, this is the true story of a Cherokee heroine during the American Revolution. Women are portrayed throughout as important individuals; the book clearly shows the Cherokee position regarding women in the issue of peace or war: "Among the Cherokees, women voted in the councils that met to consider war. Who had a better right to take part in such a question? It was their sons, husbands, and fathers who faced the danger of war" (p.29). Courtship and marriage customs are explained in detail. The author also gives still another version of how Kentucky came to be labeled "The Dark and Bloody Land." This book could easily be included in a feminist bibliography. The black-and-white illustrations by Carolyn Bertrand are well done. Good.

287. Fenner, Phyllis R.
INDIANS, INDIANS, INDIANS: STORIES OF TEPEES AND TOMAHAWKS, WAMPUM BELTS AND WAR BONNETS, PEACE PIPES AND PAPOOSES.
New York: Watts, 1970. (4-6)
The title says it all—this is a hodgepodge of ideas, legends, and short stories about "Indians," a group of people indiscriminately lumped together:

Later, some of the Indians became foes of the settlers. I guess you would have been angry too, if someone had killed off your animals, cut down your forests, and driven you far away from where you had always lived. Many Indians became cruel and revengeful; they scalped and burned and broke their agreements. . . . you will find that white men were not always persons of honor. [introduction, p.14]

The stories fare better; the selection is good, and the stories vary in interest and depth. In one, a white girl warns the Indians of danger—usually it is the reverse in stories of this kind. Manning de V. Lee's illustrations are adequate. Stories: Adequate. Portrayal of Indians: Poor.

288. Fergusson, Erna.
DANCING GODS: INDIAN CEREMONIALS OF NEW MEXICO AND ARIZONA.
Albuquerque: Univ. of New Mexico Pr., 1966. (6 and up)
No finer or more scholarly explanation of Indian dance and ceremonials is available today. The author provides a thorough description of the dances of many Southwestern Indian tribes, and the black-and-white reproductions of the work of various artists are excellent. The book's main problem is its intrusion of the author's attitudes, ranging from condescending statements about Indians and artists:

Southwestern Indians have no better friends than artists, who recognize that the Indian is essentially an artist. They value his art in all its forms, they help him without condescension, and they respect his integrity too much to make him over into something foreign. [introductory statement]

to stereotyped statements about whites:

Every year more white visitors crowd the villages, threatening the frail roofs, making crude and loud comments, squirming in agony of pleasant horror to see men handle venomous snakes. [p.148]

and Indians:

Apaches are defeated. Pueblos move smoothly between an outward conciliatory conformity to American ways and an inner adherence to their customs; Navajos yield nothing of their own integrity as they slowly adopt certain mechanical aspects of white civilization, but the Apache seems completely conquered. Even the casual observer gets the impression that his capitulation is deeper than any military surrender. His savage spirit is broken. Now he is sullen and uncommunicative, often drunken and lazy. [p.249]

Coverage of Indian dances: Good. Portrayal of Indians: Poor.

289. Field, Edward, tr.
ESKIMO SONGS AND STORIES.
Cambridge, Mass.: Delacorte
Pr./Seymour Lawrence, 1975.
(2 and up)

The poems included in this volume are based upon songs and stories collected by the Danish explorer Knud Rasmussen, who was part Eskimo. Many of the selections deal with the bleak Arctic and natural phenomena; most deal with hunger, famine, and sharing, illustrating the severe and demanding environment of the Eskimo. The illustrations by two Eskimo artists, Kiakshuk and Pudlo, are consistent with the theme of the poetry, and add immensely to the effectiveness of the book. Good.

290. Fife, Dale.
RIDE THE CROOKED WIND.
New York: Coward-McCann, 1973.
(5–8)

The language is a little flamboyant in this story of Po Three Feathers, a twelve-year-old boy who lives with his grandmother on a Paiute reservation in Nevada after the death of his parents. The story is basically one of reconciliation of Indian and non-Indian values. The old Indian grandmother is a wise and capable woman, well skilled in the Paiute lifestyle, who distrusts the white man's schools. Po loves and respects his grandmother and never questions her attitudes or decisions. Although Po is also fond of his uncle, he avoids him because the uncle had attended the "white man's school." The grandmother becomes ill, and the uncle places her in a hospital for better care. Po does not agree with his uncle's decision. When he is enrolled in an Indian boarding school against his wishes, he nearly rebels. At school Po meets Indians from fifty different tribes and gradually learns to reexamine his own attitudes and those of his grandmother, to understand her protectiveness, and accept this as a demonstration of her love for him. He also comes to respect his uncle's opinions and attitudes. Po benefits from his schooling and becomes a responsible adult. The book shows that the author has done considerable research about Paiutes. Richard Cuffari's black-and-white line drawings are good. Adequate.

291. Fink, Augusta.
TO TOUCH THE SKY.
San Carlos, Calif.: Golden Gate Junior
Books, 1971. (5–7)

This highly romanticized story perpetuates the myth that the settlers of Southern California were all Spanish Conquistadores instead of the mulatto-mestizo-black-Indian-Spanish mix they actually were. The story will appeal to the idealism in young people, and with its extensive action, they are apt to overlook some of the book's deficiencies. In the story a fourteen-year-old Spanish boy journeys with his family to take possession of a ranch. Among other adventures, he saves an Indian boy, runs away to live with Indians, decides to turn the ranch into a refuge for Indians, changes his mind, and at the end goes to live with the Indians permanently. The writing style is flamboyant: "With its proud tower and many pillars, to me it [Mission San Luis Rey] looked like some splendid palace" (pp.5–6). The characterizations are stereotyped and weakly drawn, particularly the women. The book does, however, deal with a subject few authors have attempted—the vanquished people of Santa Catalina Island—and the description of the ceremonies for the boys' coming-of-age rites is well done. The author gives the reader a feeling of what it's like to be conquered:

There a large number of Indians were congregated. Both men and women were clothed in shapeless shifts made of coarse cloth. All were ragged and dirty. A few of the men were engaged in some kind of gambling game, but most sat about listlessly on the refuse-strewn ground. [p.12]

This kind of book carries the young reader along with an elaborate plot and a series of adventures that can be enjoyed without too much introspection or thought. There is a map of the Mission area and a glossary of Spanish words. Adequate.

292. Fisher, Anne B.
STORIES CALIFORNIA INDIANS TOLD.
Sacramento: California State Dept.
of Education, 1957. (3–7)

These twelve tales about the Shasta, Pomo, Maidu, Miwok, Yokuts, Chumash, Gabrieliño, Yurok, Karok, Hupa, Yuma, Mojave, Diegueño, Cahuilla and other California tribes are authentic, providing the reader with pictures of the Indians of Northern California engaged in fishing, basket making, and carving; the Central California Indians growing grain and preparing food; and the Southern California Indians involved in pottery making and weaving. In all the tales, however, Coyote provided the humans with necessities of life. The three-tone illustrations by Ruth Robbins and a map add significant visual dimensions. Well written, these stories will be appreciated by upper primary and intermediate grade students. Good.

293. Fleischmann, Glen.
THE CHEROKEE REMOVAL, 1838: AN ENTIRE NATION IS FORCED OUT OF ITS HOMELAND.
New York: Watts, 1971. (8 and up)

This is an account of the Cherokee removal to lands west of the Mississippi River in 1838 by the U.S. Militia. The book cites parallels between Cherokee and white standards of living and points out the unfairness of the removal. A selected bibliography and black-and-white photo-

graphs, sketches, and maps contribute to the effectiveness of a well-written book. Good.

294. Floethe, Louise, and Floethe, Richard.
HOUSES AROUND THE WORLD.
New York: Scribner, 1975. (1–3)

Richard Floethe's color illustrations—clear, good, and childlike—spark this well written book on shelters from around the world. The authors use cautious language for the most part, seldom overgeneralizing, although a quick reading could give children the impression that all Eskimos live in igloos. This is a good example of the use of simple language in a literate way; for instance, "This is the story of houses around the world. Not big houses. Not rich houses. But the houses of farmers and workers and hunters and herders; town people and country people" (p.5). The book needs a table of contents. Good.

295. Floethe, Louise, and Floethe, Richard.
THE INDIAN AND HIS PUEBLO.
New York: Scribner, 1960. (4–5)

An everyday account of Pueblo life is provided in this book. The various tasks and duties of men and women are explained, and a little information is given on some ceremonies. There are many illustrations; the type is easily read; and the sentences are simple. The text is informative for the period it was published, but is dated now. Adequate.

296. Folsom, Franklin.
RED POWER ON THE RIO GRANDE: THE NATIVE AMERICAN REVOLUTION OF 1680.
Chicago: Follett, 1973. (7–9)

One of the best parts of this well-written book is an introduction by Pueblo Indian Alfonso Ortiz, Assistant Professor of Anthropology, Princeton University. He suggests that the Pueblo uprising was another successful revolution, that the Little Bighorn was not the only Indian victory. Professor Ortiz feels this book to be especially valuable for Native Americans who want to know more of their own history.

This is a different story of the Pueblo revolt, and the author suggests that Spanish records of the event are biased. A clear description is given of repartimiento (forced Indian labor) and the Inquisition in the pueblos. This is a social studies type of book but, nevertheless, is good reading. Young readers will probably be motivated to do more research after reading it, especially on the Spanish records question raised by the author; adults will do well to have supplementary material available or to help students locate this material. This type of writing can spark a young historian into research. Although recommended for grades seven through nine, this book would also be useful for many advanced readers in grades four through six. Good.

297. Folsom-Dickerson, W. E. S.
CLIFF DWELLERS.
San Antonio, Tex.: Naylor, 1968.
(4–6)
The setting for this discussion of Cliff Dwellers is the Four Corners area of the Southwest. Written in a "what do we know" type of format, the book would be useful as a travel guide for vacationers to this part of the country or for a beginning reference. Adequate.

298. Forbes, Jack D.
NATIVE AMERICANS OF CALIFORNIA AND NEVADA.
Healdsburg, Calif.: Naturegraph, 1969. (8 and up)
This scholarly, exhaustive, comprehensive study by Jack D. Forbes will be invaluable for students from accelerated junior high school age through adult level. The book gives a history of the native peoples of this geographic region; includes an extensive section on Indian education, and his suggestions for improvement; and provides a bibliography, linguistic classification chart and map, and an index. The black-and-white photographs are good, but too few in number. A reading of this book and Theodora Kroeber's *Almost Ancesters* (see review #493) would give young researchers a thorough beginning

for a study of California history. The author makes no pretense of providing readers with a neutral piece of scholarship, but he is too competent a researcher to present a diatribe. His introductory statement sets the tone:

The Indian experience in California since 1769 has been an especially ugly one. The author has made no effort in the pages which follow to "tone-down" or soften the harsh realities of native history in the region being dealt with. . . . Finally, the author wishes to state that he does not assign any kind of collective guilt to the white population as regards what has happened in the past. The future, though, is a different matter, for we all have a responsibility which cannot be brushed aside. The kind of society which is now being brought into existence is *our* collective challenge. [p.iv]

Even so, he may not reveal to the reader the true horror of some periods; for example, the shooting of Central Valley Indians for sport by Spaniards, Mexicans, and Americans (California was a part of Mexico for much of this time, hence the use of the word "Americans"), although he does detail their capture in slave raids. The section on identity problems for California Indians, whose tribes have been forgotten or annihilated and whose ancestral grounds now belong to others, is good. Good.

299. Forest, Earle R.
THE SNAKE DANCE OF THE HOPI INDIANS.
Los Angeles: Westernlore Pr., 1961. (5–8)
This is a comprehensive discussion of the Hopi Snake Dance, in which the author comments on its origin and compares it to the snake legends of Mexico. The author is an anthropologist, and he includes more background information than most authors would. The black-and-white illustrations by Don Louis Perceval and the author's photographs are in keeping with the tone of the text, and there is an index and bibliography. Good.

300. Forman, James.
THE LIFE AND DEATH OF
YELLOW BIRD.
New York: Farrar, 1973. (7 and up)
This is the fictionalized story of a part-Sioux, part-white boy at the time of the Little Bighorn fight, who takes up the Ghost Dance religion and dies at Wounded Knee. In the historical note at the end of the story, the author comments that this might be the story of Custer's son—he and a Cheyenne girl at the Washita did have a boy of this name. The writing is stylistically different from most children's books, more descriptive without striving for arty effects, as many highly descriptive books do; for example, "The thunder beings had danced all that night in the northwest, beating their terrible drums, throwing spears of fire, and Yellow Bird, tossing in restless sleep, had heard them" (p.3). The sections on the death of Crazy Horse, Wounded Knee, and of Cody's Wild West Show are convincingly done. But the most impressive parts of the book deal with Yellow Bird's inner thoughts and growth. In short, this is a superb book encompassing a whole philosophy and style of life. A classic. Good.

301. Foster, Elizabeth C., and
Williams, Slim.
THE FRIEND OF THE SINGING ONE.
New York: Atheneum, 1967. (3–5)
This is the type of book most young readers find fascinating. The story appeals to their sense of adventure and desire to lose themselves in the strange and far away. In the story an Eskimo boy quarrels with his family, runs away, and becomes trapped on an ice flow with a wolf. The wolf and boy become friends. At the end of the story, the boy returns to his people and the wolf goes free. The book's format is appealing—the type is easy to read, and Fermin Rocker's illustrations are large and colorful, even if the people he draws don't look particularly Eskimo. The authors write well, holding the reader's interest. Some of the premises used in the plot are shaky; would an Eskimo boy share his last bite of fish with a wolf? Would the

boy live more than a few seconds after falling into the freezing waters surrounding the ice flow? Would the wolf jump into the water to save him? Adequate.

302. Foster, Elizabeth C., and
Williams, Slim.
THE LONG HUNGRY NIGHT.
New York: Atheneum, 1973. (3–5)
The format of this book is impressive. The black-and-white illustrations by Glo Coalson reveal a fine technique, even if the people look more like Christmas card figures than Eskimos. The authors write well of the old style of Eskimo life. The plot concerns an Eskimo boy who befriends a wolf when he goes out to find meat for his starving village. The story does ask the reader to accept some illogical occurrences, such as the idea that an Eskimo and a wolf would be friends (the wolf would be too similar to Eskimo dogs, which are not usually treated as pets, but as a working asset), and the Eskimo villagers taking time to cook the meat the boy finds—they would be more likely to eat it raw. Still and all, it is a captivating adventure story. This is a sequel to the authors' book, *The Friend of the Singing One*. Adequate.

303. Frazier, Neta Lohnes.
SACAJAWEA, THE GIRL
NOBODY KNOWS.
New York: McKay, 1967. (10–12)
Based almost entirely upon documents, this book traces the Lewis and Clark Expedition from its inception. Details are provided about Thomas Jefferson's presidency, Napoleon's empire, and the backgrounds of Lewis, Clark, and Sacajawea. Sacajawea first meets the expedition accompanied by her husband, Charbonneau, described by Captain Lewis as a "man of no peculiar merit," and Charbonneau's other two Indian wives. Only Sacajawea, her son, Baptiste or Pomp, and her husband join the expedition. The story then follows Sacajawea throughout the journey, up until her mysterious and speculative disappearance shortly after the travelers returned to the Mandan villages in

Missouri. Although the author exercises quite a lot of literary license based upon the many documents she quotes, she infuses a sense of reality into her characters and into the story of the expedition. Both Indian and non-Indian historians will appreciate the thoroughness of the author's documentation, but may take issue with her interpretation. Good.

304. Fredericksen, Hazel.
HE WHO RUNS FAR.
New York: Young Scott Books, 1970.
(4 and up)
This story pictures the Papagos as unyielding and opposed to change. Pablo Red Deer lives in a tiny village on the Papago reservation in Arizona with his parents, his brother and sister, and Little Dog. When he is about ten years old, his grandfather, governor and Keeper of the Smoke of a much larger village, arrives to take Pablo back to the big village to learn the ancient legends, "white man's magic," and eventually to become governor and Keeper of the Smoke himself. He struggles with many new adjustments in the village of his grandfather and later at the Indian school. After five years of school and work at various jobs, Pablo returns to his grandfather's village with the knowledge of how to find water for the arid land, but is rejected by his grandfather and the other members of his family. The ending implies that Pablo may eventually return to be accepted for what he can contribute to his people, but the book's descriptions of the traditions and character of the people of his village suggest that this will probably not happen in Pablo's lifetime. The author's detailing of the tribal heritage and religion, carefully preserved in his village by the elders and effectively isolating the village and its people from the influence of non-Indian America, gives the reader a feeling of helplessness. The story provides an interesting account of life in a BIA school and can serve as a good point of contrast with white public school education. The "English only" rule at the school is shown to be a very lonely and isolating experience for Pablo and the others;

once English is learned, however, it becomes a viable means of communication for the students, whose native languages differ so markedly from each other. Incidents of prejudice and exploitation of Indians are presented in the story, along with positive and helping contacts with whites. This is a moving story about the Papago Indians, in particular. The reader's sympathy is aroused for the young Indian man caught in the clash of values between young and old. Whether or not all Papagos are this rigid in resisting change is debatable; still, this is a situation many Indian youngsters face. Adequate.

305. Freuchen, Pipaluk.
ESKIMO BOY.
New York: Lothrop, 1951. (see comment for grade level)
This tiny book is packed with the realities of Eskimo life, though it is written as fiction. Translated from the Danish, it is a vivid story and should be read by every teacher planning an Eskimo unit. Care should be exercised if children are to read it, however. The stark realities of Eskimo life are shown through the struggles of a very young boy to become the provider for his family after he sees his father killed by a walrus. This episode is described in detail, and so are other occurrences which Eskimos could understand, but young children in other cultures might consider fearsome. The illustrations are line drawings, much too small for children. Though the boy hero in the pictures appears to be six or seven years old, this book is not especially suitable for children. Use with appropriate precautions. Good.

306. Friskey, Margaret.
INDIAN TWO FEET AND HIS
EAGLE FEATHER.
Chicago: Childrens Pr., 1967. (K–3)
This story is filled with simplistic writing: "I'm an IN-di-an, IN-di-an, IN-di-an. Proud-of-it. Proud-of-it. Proud-of-it, too" (unpaged); stereotypes of the "feathers, tepee, and moccasin" format; and inaccurate information, such as the reasons

given for awarding an eagle feather. The story is about a young boy who saves his village from the danger of a beaver dam bursting and flooding the country. John and Lucy Hawkinson's illustrations are of "cute" Indians in "cute" activities, and suffer from the same faults as the text. The book does show a charming, imaginary world where charming, imaginary people live charming, imaginary lives–hardly the world of the American Indian. Poor.

307. Friskey, Margaret.
INDIAN TWO FEET AND HIS HORSE.
Chicago: Childrens Pr., 1959. (K–2)
This book suffers from the same drawbacks as Friskey's other works: the tribe is not identified, the book tends to promote a view of stereotyped Indians, and the whole effect suffers from a "cute" syndrome. The plot has an Indian boy wanting a horse, finding an injured one, and helping it get well. The vocabulary is controlled so that primary-grade children can easily read the text. Katherine Evans' illustrations are better than those for most of the "Two Feet" series. Poor.

308. Friskey, Margaret.
INDIAN TWO FEET AND THE
WOLF CUBS.
Chicago: Childrens Pr., 1971. (K–3)
In this story, Margaret Friskey tells of a young Indian (tribe unspecified, but with the usual eagle feathers in his hair) who is adopted by wolves, takes the cubs home to his tepee, and eventually finds they belong in the wild. The problem here is not the author's ability to write, not John Hawkinson's fine watercolor technique, and not the delineation of the family patterns of wolves, but the stereotyping effect of an unidentified "Indian" boy and the overgeneralized "feather, tepee, and horse" syndrome. Story development: Good. Portrayal of Indians: Poor.

309. Gardner, Jeanne Le Monnier.
MARY JEMISON, SENECA CAPTIVE.
New York: Harcourt, 1966. (5–7)
Based on a true incident, this book tells the story of Mary Jemison, who was cap-

tured by the Seneca at age fifteen and never returned to her former life, even when free to do so. The illustrations by Robert Parker are warlike, show good technique, and, for the most part, feature Indians wearing feathers and using a tomahawk on whites. The plot moves along well and will keep most young readers interested. In a few instances the author compares Indians unfavorably with whites, as in her description of Mary's hair: "One or two reached out to touch her hair–so pale and silken in contrast to the black coarseness of their own" (p.65). The book includes a map of Mary Jemison's journeys, notes on Mary Jemison, and a bibliography. Adequate.

310. Garst, Shannon.
CRAZY HORSE: GREAT WARRIOR
OF THE SIOUX.
Boston: Houghton, 1950. (7–9)
This story begins with "Has-ka" or "Light-Complexioned One," which this author claims was Crazy Horse's boyhood name. Other biographers have referred to his boyhood name as "Curly" or "His Horse Looking," but most seem to agree that his skin and hair were considerably lighter than that of other members of the tribe. According to Sioux custom, he could have been known by all these names, in addition to many others. Has-ka's experiences may remind some readers of similar descriptions of the youth of other Indian leaders (as in Black Hawk: Young Sauk Warrior by Catherine Cleven; see review #178). One of the better books about Crazy Horse, illustrating his love for his people, his hatred of the whites, and his determination despite overwhelming odds, this book provides a reasonable chronology of Crazy Horse's life and some of the other events that occurred during his lifetime. The black-and-white sketches by William Moyers seem accurately done. Adequate.

311. Garst, Shannon.
THE PICTURE STORY AND BIOGRAPHY
OF RED CLOUD.
Chicago: Follett, and Toronto:
Kyerson Pr., 1965. (4–7)

This story is divided into two parts: a color-illustrated "Picture Story," which highlights events of Red Cloud's life from his boyhood until his death, and an un-illustrated biography, which describes in greater detail those events featured in the first part. Although somewhat romanti-cized and oversimplified, the story is writ-ten in an interesting manner and moves sufficiently well to hold most young read-ers' interest. The feelings and attitudes attributed to Indians, as well as language presumably used by Indians to describe white men and their ways, are somewhat overly dramatic, such as "thundersticks" and "Blue Coats." The book's major weak-ness seems to be the rather condescending manner in which the author has her char-acters speak to one another: "We are braves. Let us move back to our hunting grounds. Let us drive the whites from the Holy Land. . . . Braves, let us be men." Adequate.

312. Garst, Shannon.
SITTING BULL: CHAMPION OF
HIS PEOPLE.
New York: Simon & Schuster, 1946.
(6 and up)
This biography traces the life of Sitting Bull in a compassionate manner, detailing the events leading up to the end of his par-ticular way of life and the ultimate de-struction of many Sioux cultural practices. Beginning with Sitting Bull's youth and the personal achievements that led to his becoming a chief, the author presents Sit-ting Bull as a somewhat superhuman in-dividual, able to control his life in a very directive manner. As a young boy, in the space of a few years, Sitting Bull rides a wild buffalo calf, hence his name, kills a bear single-handedly, and "takes coup first" in a counter-raid against a maraud-ing tribe of Crows to become the leader that his father had predicted. In his later years, on the other hand, long after a series of battles and many attempted re-conciliations with the whites, the author depicts Sitting Bull as a rather pathetic, ineffectual, but gentle old man who is neither able to control his own destiny nor the fate of his people. Sensitive readers

may respond to this contrast and, in turn, make comparisons with the modern shifts and changes that influence the direction of an individual's life today. The author describes Sioux practices and attitudes in a detailed manner, inserting Indian words and definitions appropriately and unob-trusively. In various sections, she provides descriptions of games and Indian role models such as shamans, clowns (Heyo-kas), and chiefs, which could lend them-selves to illustration or dramatization pos-sibilities. Both male and female roles are objectively defined, providing a balanced view of Sitting Bull's Indian contempo-raries and times. In addition, the author presents both "good" and "bad" Indians and their counterparts among whites. The book includes shaded black-and-white il-lustrations by Elton Fox, which are con-sistent with the tone of the biography. A brief chronology of events inserted at the end of the book provides a context through which the reader can place Sitting Bull and other Indians with other notable peo-ple and events. The author also includes a bibliography and an index. Good.

313. Geary, Clifford N.
TICONDEROGA: A PICTURE STORY.
New York: McKay, 1953. (2–4)
The story of Fort Ticonderoga from its inception to the recent restoration by Wil-liam Pell, this book is beautifully illus-trated by Geary's color sketches and draw-ings. These supplement his writing so well that art and journalism teachers might wish to use the book as an example of book illustration for their classes. This is a "dates and war" kind of book, but well done, with an appropriate level of lan-guage for young readers. A good, authen-tic, beginning history book, it does not delve deeply into motives and at times is oversimplified. Good.

314. Georgakas, Dan.
THE BROKEN HOOP: THE HISTORY OF
NATIVE AMERICANS FROM 1600 TO
1890, FROM THE ATLANTIC COAST TO
THE PLAINS.
Garden City, N.Y.: Doubleday, 1973.
(6–8)

The first in a two part series on the history of Native Americans (*Red Shadows* is the second), Georgakas here describes the tribes of the Northeast, Southeast, and Great Plains. He writes of complex issues in simple terms, and whites do not come off well. Occasionally the quality of the writing lapses: "During times of peace, the Iroquois tended to be mild-mannered and polite individuals who were very kind to their children" (p.4); but, for the most part, the author organizes his presentation well. At times his interpretations of cause and effect are unique, and the reader may not agree with him:

> Some of the ferocity of their warfare may have stemmed from the frustration of living in houses with only small slits in the ceiling to bring relief from the smoke, dogs, cooking odors, and noises of so many people. Taboos such as not being able to speak to one's mother-in-law made life somewhat easier, but if a couple quarreled the whole family would sit in judgment. [p.4]

This is an interesting, selective, personal vision of Native American history. Good.

315. Georgakas, Dan.
RED SHADOWS: THE HISTORY OF NATIVE AMERICANS FROM 1600 TO 1900, FROM THE DESERT TO THE PACIFIC COAST.
New York: Zenith Books/Doubleday, 1973. (6–8)
In the relatively short space of 128 pages, the author manages to convey a great deal of information. He discusses the history of the Southwestern, California, and Northwestern Indian tribes from 1600 to 1900. He writes from the Indians' point of view, as much as possible using direct quotes and tribal poetry to tell the story. Occasionally he stereotypes his subjects: "The Native Americans greeted the first Europeans with friendship and hospitality. . . . The white tribes wanted to destroy Indian religion and to make Indians work as slaves" (p.10); and,

> Like the Pima they [the Papago] withdrew into apathy as they grew poorer while watching the whites grow richer. Like the Pima they drank too much. Like the Pima, they withdrew into a world of daydreams and memories. Like the Pima, they became listless.

Often he turns a phrase in an unusual way, as in the use of "white tribe" or terms such as "Rain Lovers" for Southwestern Indians, and in descriptive passages such as the following:

> Their [Pima and Papago] suffering was less dramatic but no less intense than that of the regal warrior societies of the plains. The world of the buffalo hunters ended with a bang, the world of the rain lovers with a sigh. (p.22)

He often manages to convey great horror in a few sentences, as when he describes the Yana's life under whites in California. There is an index. Good.

316. George, Jean Craighead.
JULIE OF THE WOLVES.
New York: Harper, 1972. (7 and up)
This account of a young Eskimo girl who learned to communicate with a pack of wolves is excellent fiction. Destined to become a classic, this winner of the John Newbery Medal portrays the thirteen-year-old Eskimo heroine as a resourceful, courageous, perceptive girl who meets the many challenges of her environment successfully. The author's interest in animal behavior, particularly the behavior of wolves, has caused her to base much of this book on the actions of wolves the author has known personally. The plot: Miyax, whose English name is July Edwards, in her thirteen years has lived the old Eskimo way with her father, the American way at school, and the transitional life at Barrow. The theme is problem solving, from interpreting the language of the wolves, to finding her way across unfamiliar Arctic terrain, to resolving a conflict of values with modern, tourist-oriented Eskimo practices. Readers interested in women's liberation issues will enjoy the nonsexist characterization. Good.

317. Gessner, Lynne.
NAVAJO SLAVE.
Irvington-on-Hudson, N.Y.: Harvey
House, 1976. (5–7)
Set at the time of the capture of the
Navajos at Canyon de Chelly, this book
tells the story of a young Navajo boy who
escapes the Long Walk, only to be sold
into slavery by the Utes to a New Mexico
ranch owner. His four years of slavery are
lightened by a friendship with the owner's
son and the white foreman, Jake. When
the boy returns to his homeland, he finds
he has lost some of his Navajo spirit. It
is interesting to note the customs he has
adopted that are not considered Navajo:
for instance, he is jealous when his
brother is praised; he thinks himself better than others; he believes that his family's turquoise is his to trade; he wants to
be a hero; he sulks. He asks for a healing
ceremony, the Enemy Way. He has a
choice at this point, and decides to stay
with his family instead of going to live
with Jake. This is a sensitive, plausible
story. The author's writing style is awkward and often trite: "Although to his
family he was a man of gentleness and
understanding, to his enemies Red Band
was a merciless foe" (p.8). Good.

318. Gibson, Michael.
THE AMERICAN INDIAN: FROM
COLONIAL TIMES TO THE PRESENT.
London: Wayland, 1974. (4–6)
The British wording and tone of this
text may not appeal to many American
students. An overview of the American Indian, the book is fair and does not sugar-
coat the issues. Perhaps the best part of
the book is the summary of modern-day
conditions. The book's tone may be
judged from a picture caption on page
111: "The exploitation of the Indian—
many reservation-dwellers only survive by
dressing up and selling their photographs
to white tourists." The John Smith legend
is repeated as fact; adults may wish to
discuss the controversy over the accuracy
of this story. Black-and-white prints, illustrations, and drawings are found throughout the text. Adequate.

319. Gillham, Charles E.
BEYOND THE CLAPPING MOUNTAINS:
ESKIMO STORIES FROM ALASKA.
New York: Macmillan, 1964. (3–6)
This book presents a message to the
creative spirit by its very format: do it,
begin, go ahead, use what you have. The
examples of the illustrator, Chanimum, a
young Eskimo girl who drew her sketches
with an old, broken steel pen and a frozen
bottle of India ink, are a powerful argument for action. The book itself contains a
series of Eskimo tales explaining how various animals in the Arctic got their characteristic features. The author spent eight
summers among the Eskimo as a biologist
for the U.S. government, and the stories
reflect the English patterns of speech used
by the Eskimos who told him the stories.
He describes the feelings he encountered:
"They not only think they have a tale too
poor to tell but, often, wonder what business it is of the white man" (p.ix). Occasionally his own prejudices creep in: "The
missions have done much to discourage
the influence of the medicine men because
of their superstitions and primitive methods of healing" (p.xii). He provides the
reader with a good introduction to the
book, named for the mythical mountains
which may clap together unexpectedly
and trap the birds as they fly through on
their way north. Almost all the tales, true
to Eskimo tradition, have a moral. Good.

320. Gillham, Charles E.
MEDICINE MEN OF HOOPER BAY:
MORE TALES FROM THE CLAPPING
MOUNTAINS OF ALASKA.
New York: Macmillan, 1955. (4–7)
A sequel to *Beyond the Clapping Mountains*, this volume is also illustrated by
Chanimun, who uses black-and-white line
drawings to form childlike sketches. The
stories themselves are relatively pure, little influenced by white culture. They tell
of the importance of medicine men, or
shamans, to the Eskimo of Hooper Bay,
and present the legendary reasons for
place names and how things got to be the
way they are. The author is noticeably
sincere and earnest as he tries to convey

something of his feeling for these people: "I marveled at the endurance of these people. Blue with cold, they stuck to the business of hunting. Little ones in the igloos must be fed. I stayed with them (as they hunted), I would have felt guilty not to" (p.x); and "Food is all important to the Eskimos. They must have fish, seals, or birds or they starve" (p.vii). Good.

321. Gilpin, Laura.
THE ENDURING NAVAJO.
Austin: Univ. of Texas Pr., 1968.
(6 and up)
Unusual and exquisite photographs by the author illustrate this presentation of Navajo life. Such pictures as those of Navajos irrigating melons, riding the ferris wheel, and the like are not often seen. The text is written for adults, but can be read by advanced upper elementary grade readers. The writing gives a good feel for what life is like on the reservation (as of 1968), and the current Navajo clamor for more and better education is stressed. Maps, legends, tools, crafts, tribal government, ceremonies, and so on are among the topics covered in the book. There is a pronunciation guide to Navajo words, a bibliography, and an index. Good.

322. Ginsburg, Mirra.
THE PROUD MAIDEN, TUNGAK,
AND THE SUN.
New York: Macmillan, 1974. (K–2)
Igor Galanin's unusual blue-and-white illustrations, in which the focus of attention is often formed by the lightest shade of blue, highlight this book of Eskimo legends. The book is short, which may cause some purchasers to believe that it is only for primary-age children. Actually, many third through sixth graders will also enjoy the stories. The author presents Eskimo legends in an Eskimo style on such subjects as why there is a moon, why nights are long in the Arctic, and the defeating of evil spirits. Good.

323. Glass, Paul.
SONGS AND STORIES OF THE
NORTH AMERICAN INDIANS.
New York: Grosset, 1968. (2–5)

Songs from five tribes, Yuma, Mandan, Teton Sioux, Pawnee, and Papago, are presented in simplified notation with rhythm indications for drum accompaniment in this book. A brief overview of Indian music and its purposes—sacred or religious, stories and songs from dreams, old legends, games and fun—is included. There are short histories and comments on the customs of each tribe, with just enough information to set the stage for the music, and not intended as an in-depth sociological or anthropological analysis. Brief introductions and explanations for each song are given. H. B. Vestal's line drawings are good, and the black-and-white photographs are helpful in establishing a background for each song. Good.

324. Glubok, Shirley.
ART OF THE ESKIMO.
New York: Harper, 1964. (2–6)
A handy reference, this book is profusely illustrated with art objects made by Eskimos. Museums and private owners have cooperated by permitting photographs of realia in their collections to be included. The arrangement of the book is designed to show the interests and the lives of these people who call themselves the Innuit. The Innuit consider their art objects magical, and when readers of any age come to the last page of this book, they can sense the magic. Elementary school children will enjoy it for browsing and reference. Good.

325. Glubok, Shirley.
ART OF THE NORTH AMERICAN INDIAN.
New York: Harper, 1964. (2–6)
Photographs of miscellaneous art objects from many geographical areas on the North American continent are crowded together with little apparent organization, and the text that accompanies them leaves much to be desired in this presentation of Indian art. The explanations are so simplified that they leave a confused impression. For instance, the single entry in the text about baskets mentions cooking baskets, but the only two baskets photographed, one a Tlingit and

the other an Apache basket, are neither of the type used for cooking. If a map had been included, showing the juxtaposition of the Indian nations the author mentions, it would have helped young readers understand why the author ends the book by saying, "North American Indian Art is many arts of many tribes." The book could have been improved by organizing it in sections for each tribe or nation. Poor.

326. Glubok, Shirley.
THE ART OF THE NORTHWEST COAST INDIANS.
New York: Macmillan, 1975. (4–6)
The illustrations and writing do not match in this book about designs, totems, and buildings of the Northwest Coast Indians. The designs are often inappropriate for younger children, while the writing style would impress adolescents as being too juvenile. The author stresses the beauty of everyday objects from these tribes, although many of the examples are circa 1914. This does not imply that there is anything wrong with 1914 design, but the artistic development of these tribes did not stop at that point. More complete coverage of modern design would have been helpful, as would the rewriting of this book for seventh grade and older students. Adequate.

327. Glubok, Shirley.
ART OF THE SOUTHWEST INDIANS.
New York: Macmillan, 1971.
(4 and up)
A great variety of Southwest Indian art objects is shown in photographs accompanied by a text geared to elementary school children. Careful distinction is made between the art of each tribe of the Southwest. The book is organized by craft, showing dance wands, rock art, architecture, sculpture, baskets, sand painting, kachinas, ceremonial robes, jewelry, weaving, ritual dance costumes, and pottery. Photographs of art objects from cooperating museums are explained in language not too difficult for upper elementary school children. Well organized, this book is filled with valuable informa-

tion for the teacher and children who are studying original American cultures in the Southwestern United States. Good.

328. Goble, Paul, and Goble, Dorothy.
BRAVE EAGLE'S ACCOUNT OF THE FETTERMAN FIGHT.
New York: Pantheon, 1972. (5–7)
Whites called it the Fetterman Massacre, but to the Indians, it was a battle. In this book, Brave Eagle recites his account of it. The introduction by the Gobles sets the stage for the reader, and Paul Goble's black-and-white and color illustrations, while they may be too antiseptic at times for battle scenes, are crisp and clean and use perspective in such an unusual way that he obtains an interesting patterning effect that looks authentic (see the picture of the fort and the Indians on pages 20–21). The format is admirable; it looks as if the book would be good to read. It may, however, be too youthful for the reading level of the text. In addition to the accounts of the battle, Brave Eagle comments on the world he saw; his evaluation of white women on page 20 is especially interesting. Good.

329. Goble, Paul, and Goble, Dorothy.
LONE BULL'S HORSE RAID.
New York: Bradbury Pr., 1973. (4–6)
In this story, a young Oglala Sioux boy becomes both a man and a warrior with much honor because he is successful in capturing horses during a raid on a Crow village. The plot is exciting, but the book is not. The style is stilted, and British expressions such as "What a fright they had given me" coming out of the mouth of a fourteen-year-old Sioux Indian boy startle the reader. The Gobles do not restrict themselves to "Lone Bull's Raid," but talk of Plains Indian warfare in a cultural context: "Children grew up in a society which held the warrior as its highest ideal, and at every step in life were encouraged to follow the example of the bravest men" (unpaged). (This statement is not entirely accurate, since hunters, medicine men, and the aged, among others, were equally or more highly honored.) The

Gobles detail the Indian wars among tribal groups, and discuss horses as a measure of wealth—hence, Lone Bull's raid. Paul Goble's color and black-and-white illustrations are fitting, colorful, and full of pattern. The authors include a bibliography. Good.

330. Goldwater, Barry M., and
Harvey, Bryan.
THE GOLDWATER KACHINA DOLL
COLLECTION.
Tempe: Arizona Historical Soc. for the Heard Museum, 1969. (6–9)
Goldwater and Harvey provide the reader with a thorough review of the history, function, and evaluation of kachina dolls. Goldwater writes well, and his description of his kachina collection is a source of information for other collectors. He explains the "who" and "what" of kachinas, showing the gradual growth of elaboration of detail in recent years. The color pictures and James Varner Parker's decorative panels make an effective format, although there is occasionally too much promotion of the Museum. Good.

331. Gonzales, Clara.
THE SHALAKOS ARE COMING.
Santa Fe: Museum of New Mexico, 1966. (5 and up)
The writing in this account of the Zuñi Shalako ceremonial is strained, at times almost breathless:

As fall moves into winter, and the ceremonial year is drawing to a close, village activities at Zuñi, one of the fabled Cities of Cibola, increase in tempo. All must be in readiness for the most important religious celebration of the year. The Shalakos are coming. [p.1]

The book would be of special interest to visitors attending the Shalako ceremonial. It presents the reader with a full account of Shalako participants, masks, pre-Shalako ceremonies, and Shalako day. Adequate.

332. Graff, Stewart, and Polly, Anne.
SQUANTO: INDIAN ADVENTURER.
Champaign, Ill.: Garrard, 1965. (2–5)

The usual Garrard series introduction, which provides general background information about the Algonquins and specific information about Squanto's tribe, the Wampanoag, is included in this book, as well as a map of the Massachusetts/Connecticut/Rhode Island area, where the Algonquins and Pilgrims lived. Squanto's adventures, his trip to London, his capture and enslavement, as well as his relationship with the Pilgrims, are told in an interesting manner. The author includes very little about the Indian culture and practices of this tribe, but deals mainly with the relationship of one Indian, Squanto, and the whites he knew. Some historians may quarrel with the author's chronology of major events in Squanto's life. As is usual with the Garrard series, the illustrations by Robert Doremus support the text. Adequate.

333. Grant, Campbell.
ROCK ART OF THE AMERICAN INDIANS.
New York: Crowell, 1967. (8 and up)
This paperback condenses and rewrites portions of Grant's classic, *The Rock Paintings of the Chumash,* and gives a simplified overview of rock art in many areas. The book is a handy introduction to the rock art of Native Americans, and to Campbell Grant, who has contributed so much to improving the understanding of the Chumash of California. His main thrust in this book is the scope and diversity of rock art in America. This volume will serve to motivate readers to learn more about the subject, although it leaves a great deal unsaid. The illustrations are black-and-white photographs and brightly colored sketches of original rock art. Adequate.

334. Grant, Matthew G.
CHIEF JOSEPH OF THE NEZ PERCÉ.
Chicago: Childrens Pr., 1974. (2–4)
Simply written and free of the more obvious romantic (and misleading) notions about Indians and Indian leaders, the author highlights widely known facts about Chief Joseph and his relationships

with white leaders. Unlike many books about Chief Joseph, in this text the author reminds the reader that Joseph's Indian name was Thunder-Rolling-in-the-Mountain; white leaders named him Chief Joseph. The author includes historical facts and dates without making his characters seem any less real. The book includes colorful illustrations by John Keely. Good.

335. Grant, Matthew G.
GERONIMO.
Chicago: Childrens Pr., 1974. (K–2)
Beautifully illustrated in color and black-and-white by John Kelly and Dick Brude, this story is simply written in an easy-to-read style and will appeal to most young readers. Consistent with the majority of books written about Indian leaders who lived during the Indian wars, little mention of Indian women and everyday affairs of tribal life is given. An abundance of historical facts is provided, including dates and the names of some of the better known white leaders who fought Geronimo. Except for reasons of revenge, little background information as to why the Apaches fought the Mexicans and later the American settlers is cited. Adequate.

336. Grant, Matthew G.
OSCEOLA AND THE SEMINOLE WAR.
Chicago: Childrens Pr., 1974. (1–3)
This war history of the Seminoles from the time of Tecumseh's visit to Osceola's death in prison is illustrated by fine black-and-white drawings. An oversimplified view of Seminole history and customs and repeatedly marred by editorial comment, the book does, however, show that Indians also won battles. A superficial reading could give children the impression that blacks and Seminoles lived separately in the same village, while, in fact, intermarriage was common. The book should be supplemented with books on Seminoles that stress other aspects of social, economic, family patterns and that show that some of the Seminoles were, in fact, women. Adequate.

337. Grant, Matthew G.
PONTIAC: INDIAN GENERAL AND STATESMAN.
Chicago: Childrens Pr., 1974. (5–7)
This biography of Pontiac, the Ottawa war chief who tried to unite the tribes of the old Northwest frontier against the whites, is marred by many weaknesses. It presents unusually selective information: for example, "Their [the Ottawas] customary way of making war was very cruel. The warriors killed not only the soldiers, but also unarmed settlers, women, and children" (p.12). (It is doubtful that many of the settlers were unarmed.) The book presents the Ottawas in an unfavorable light: "Of the three tribes, the Ottawa were least friendly to the whites. They refused to become Christians, and they mistrusted the strangers" (p.8). It presents simplistic cause-and-effect relationships: "His war had started a fire of hatred between white men and red that would burn for more than 100 years—until the last western Indian surrendered to the white invaders" (p.31). However, there is an unusually good map of the area under discussion, and the book is an attempt to fill the scarcity of historical material for primary-age readers. Harold Henriksen's illustrations, while demonstrating good technique and unusual color selection, present idealized Indian men, largely engaged in war activities. Poor.

338. Grant, Matthew G.
SQUANTO, THE INDIAN WHO SAVED THE PILGRIMS.
Mankato, Minn.: Creative Educational Soc., 1974. (2–4)
This book documents Squanto's incredible life—captured and taken to England, returned to America by Captain John Smith, captured and taken to Spain to be sold as a slave, taken back to England, sailed for Newfoundland with Captain Thomas Dermer, taken to Maine where he found all his village dead of disease, discovering the Pilgrims at Plymouth, and finally dying on a trading voyage with the Pilgrims. It tries to present a fair picture of a complex subject in primary language,

a hard task that results in a "fairy tale" story that gives no hint of the subtleties of the issues involved, such as "Bad" Captain Hunt, "good" monks, and the like. It is factual, but does not put enough stress on the fact that without the Indians, perhaps none of the Plymouth Colony would have survived. Squanto was a complex man; perhaps another author can make that complexity clearer in a more interesting fashion. John Nelson and Harold Henriksen's illustrations are good. Adequate.

339. Gravelle, Kim.
INUK: THE ESKIMO WHO HATED
THE SNOW.
Chicago: Childrens Pr., 1975. (2–4)
That the author knows his subject in most other ways is apparent, but his basic assumption–that an Eskimo would hate snow so intensely that he would stow away on a steamer to Hawaii–is hard to accept. He writes well, but his tone seems more white than Eskimo: "It was always the same. Clean the fish. Cut the meat for the dogs. Set traps for the white fox and hare. Ice the runners for the sled" (p.10). The pictures are good; the author's stencil prints follow Eskimo tradition closely, and his message on stenciling directed to the child reader is interesting. The section on the life of the author is well done, written in language children can easily read. Adequate.

340. Grey, Herman.
TALES FROM THE MOHAVES.
Norman: Univ. of Oklahoma Pr.,
1970. (6 and up)
This book successfully departs from the usual legend book format. Herman Grey, a Mojave himself, provides the reader with the type of writing that flows smoothly, is simple and clear, yet poetic, and seldom found in collections of legends. His description of dreaming as a basis for Mojave culture, unity, and legends is masterful:

The Mohave clings to his belief in dreams as a basis for everyday life. Not only all shamanistic power, but all myths, songs, bravery, fortune in bat-

tle, and good fortune in gambling derive from dreams. Every special event is dreamed. Knowledge is not a thing to be learned, a Mohave will say, but something to be acquired by each person through his dreaming. [p.xi]
He discusses Mojave history, religion, clan structure, and similar items in the introduction. The foreword by Alice Marriott gives an understandable and highly readable history of research into legends, a good introduction to ethnological methodology for young readers. The book includes a bibliography and a list of University of Oklahoma Press publications. Good.

341. Gridley, Marion E.
AMERICAN INDIAN TRIBES.
New York: Dodd, 1974. (6–8)
A simplistic book, featuring factual but not particularly inspired writing, this volume presents a picture of past and current Native American cultures. The language used suffers from much overgeneralization: "A principal chief of the Catawbas was King Hagler, a man of sterling character who was respected by the whites and loved by his people" (p.53). The book does give a good description of some reservation industries. Use it for basic, overall coverage, but supplement with other, more interesting, less judgmental books. The publisher's recommended grade placement for this book is grades six through ten, but it may not appeal to many students above eighth grade. Adequate.

342. Gridley, Marion E.
AMERICAN INDIAN WOMEN.
New York: Hawthorn, 1974. (9–adult)
Any teacher who introduces Indians and Indian leaders to his or her classroom should read this book first. Even if no more than the eight-page introduction, "The Indian Woman," is read, the reader will obtain information that not only dispels myths about Indian women, but about Indians in general. According to the author, Indian women, unlike most early white women, had "considerable power and in a number of groups they were supreme." They also "voted long before any

other women of the world did so." Included in this anthology are nineteen rather complete biographies about Indian women leaders, as well as an additional six biographical sketches of equally impressive, but lesser known, women. Some of the more widely known women include Pocahontas, Sacajawea, Susan LaFlesche Picotte, Maria Montoya Martinez, Maria and Marjorie Tallchief. The author includes photographs of most of the Indian women in the book. Good.

343. Gridley, Marion E.
CONTEMPORARY AMERICAN INDIAN
LEADERS.
New York: Dodd, 1972. (7 and up)
This book includes twenty-six biographies of current Indian leaders, four of which are women. Representing a number of tribes, vocations (dentist, artist, teacher, author, congressman) and viewpoints (liberal, militant, conservative), each biographical sketch acquaints the reader with the leader's beginnings, tribal links, and whether or not each chose to join the mainstream of white American life or to work within the Indian community. The author writes in a straightforward, documentary style with few, if any, editorializations. She presents the reader with historical and background information about each of the tribes from which the Indian leaders came. Each Indian leader seems to have a defined purpose and direction, as well as suggestions as to which aspects of Indian life and culture should be preserved and offered as solutions for some of the problems of contemporary civilization in general. The author includes photographs of each Indian leader. She gives information about several historical antecedents and about other contemporary Indian leaders not included in the biographies. Good.

344. Gridley, Marion E.
INDIAN LEGENDS OF AMERICAN
SCENES.
Northbrook, Ill.: Hubbard Pr., 1939.
(7–9)

In this collection, the author includes Indian legends that explain various natural geological formations throughout the United States, including the Grand Canyon, Mt. Shasta, Niagara Falls, and the Badlands, as well as phenomena such as Spanish moss and Hot Sulphur Springs. Organized by state in alphabetical order, the book provides descriptions of the historical backgrounds of the Indians who inhabit or inhabited each of the twenty-six states represented. She follows this with a legend or series of legends about each state. Several legends set in Canada are included as well. Of greatest interest to the young reader already familiar with Indian legends, these tales are not widely known. The illustrated initial letters and black-and-white drawings by Chief Whirling Thunder add to the effectiveness of the layout. Good.

345. Gridley, Marion E.
INDIAN NATIONS: THE STORY OF THE
IROQUOIS.
New York: Putnam in association with Country Beautiful Foundation, 1969.
(3–5)
This is an interesting and authentic account of the Iroquois League, its founding and its end. The author tells of Iroquois village life, food, clothing, shelter, legends, games, crafts, hunting and fishings, and the life of boys and girls. She describes how the Iroquois shaped the course of American history and the richness of their contributions to the American heritage. Their abuse by whites who took their land, gave them whiskey, and abandoned them after the Revolutionary War is painfully recorded. The illustrations are powerful and beautiful; they suggest the strength and bravery of a great people struggling against the forces of nature and human venality. Good.

346. Gridley, Marion E., ed.
INDIANS OF TODAY.
Chicago: Indian Council Fire, 1960.
(6–9)
This is one of Gridley's earlier editions

of *Contemporary American Indian Leaders* (see review #343), and includes biographies of some 100 individuals who are one-quarter or more Indian. Most of the biographies are brief, covering one-half to one full page, and include, in addition to background information, such items as education, organization and civic activities, marital status, children, and honors. Most of the biographies are accompanied by photographs. The interested reader might wish to compare Gridley's 1936 and 1946 editions of *Indians of Today*, as well as the later 1970 edition, and *Contemporary American Indian Leaders* (1972). Adequate.

347. Gridley, Marion E.
INDIAN TRIBES OF AMERICA.
Northbrook, Ill.: Hubbard Pr., 1973.
(4–6)
A typical social studies type of book, accurate, with pedestrian writing, this text is illustrated and features such subtitles as "Dwellers Along the Sea Coast." Useful as a basic reference, it needs to be supplemented with more interesting and thorough material. Adequate.

348. Gridley, Marion E.
INDIANS OF YESTERDAY.
Chicago: Donahue, 1940. (3–5)
This very large book (about 10 inches by 11 inches) contains brief histories of some eight tribes in six geographic regions of the United States: for example "Dwellers Among the Leaves" features an area composed of the New England states, lower Canada westward to Minnesota, and the region north of the Ohio River. Before each of the geographic regional histories the author lists some of the principal tribes of the regions, where they lived, where they are now, and also provides notations of those tribes no longer together as a tribal group. She describes the religion, habits, clothing, food, and dwellings of each, emphasizing how the geography, climate, flora, and fauna shaped their behavior. She details differences between and within regional tribes. Illustrated by

Lone Wolf, the book is endorsed by the Indian Council Tribe, and is a revision of her 1940 book of the same title. The book would be worth another update. Dated. Good.

349. Gridley, Marion E.
MARIA TALLCHIEF: THE STORY OF
AN AMERICAN INDIAN.
Minneapolis, Minn.: Dillon Pr., 1973.
(5–9)
As in most stories about Maria Tallchief, this book is more concerned with ballet than with anything that can be specifically characterized as Indian. The author does provide an informative first chapter, however, in which she describes the origin and history of the Osages. She describes the discovery of oil in Oklahoma on Osage land, as well as Maria's and her sister, Marjorie's, introduction to Indian dances. In one of the closing chapters, the author again refers to the Osage tribe, this time in connection with Maria's honor name "Wa-Xthe-Thonda" (Woman of Two Standards), awarded to her by the tribe, and her first experience in taking "part in an Indian feast," eating Indian food. The book is well written, moves at a fast enough pace to sustain the interest of an older reader, and is not so confusing in its descriptions of the various ballet companies as to discourage the younger reader. It is illustrated by photographs and a map of Osage County, Oklahoma. Some critics may feel that the first chapter and a few subsequent references to Osage Indians are artificial and condescending. Adequate.

350. Gridley, Marion E.
OSCEOLA.
New York: Putnam, 1972. (2–3)
This story of Osceola's life is written in simple language for primary grade readers. The author states that Osceola's father was an Englishman; other authorities believe he was a Creek Indian. The issue is actually not as clear as stated in this book. Lloyd E. Oxendine's black-, white-, and-orange illustrations are the best part

of the book. A key words and phrases guide is included. Poor.

351. Gridley, Marion E.
PONTIAC.
New York: Putnam, 1970. (1–3)
Consistent with most biographies of Indian leaders written for this age group, the major portion of this book deals with Pontiac's boyhood, how he perceived Ottawa life and the tribe's relationships with the French. The mood of the book is similar to that of most stories about Indians and white settlers, in which an Indian allies himself with an important white person but is betrayed for his efforts, either by his own people (Pontiac presumably was killed by an Indian hired by the English) or by the whites (earlier the French, too, had disappointed him when they signed a treaty with the English guaranteeing all Indian lands for English settlers). The illustrations by Unada are alternating black-and-white and black, white, and turquoise, reminiscent of the Dr. Seuss stories. The expressions on the faces of the people illustrated initially are those of happy people (white and Indian); they grow progressively more somber and, finally, extremely agitated or angry as the book closes with Pontiac dying from a blow from a large, vicious-looking Indian. Adequate.

352. Gridley, Marion E.
THE STORY OF THE HAIDA.
New York: Putnam, 1972. (4–6)
In social studies textbook language, this book tells of Haida life, art, totems, ceremonies, and some famous Haida of today. The format is good; Robert Glaubke's gold-toned illustrations are appropriate; but the main weakness of the book is its pedestrian and simplistic language. The book presents a multitude of facts; for example, pointing out that the Russians were the first whites the Haida saw, living as they did on the coast of Canada and the northwestern United States. The section on present-day Haida needs to be expanded or continued in greater depth in

another book. There is also a section about the author and an index. Adequate.

353. Gridley, Marion E.
STORY OF THE NAVAJO.
New York: Putnam, 1971. (2–5)
This book chronicles Navajo life from prehistoric times, tells of some famous Navajo men and women, and depicts Navajo life styles, including descriptions of planting, harvesting, and weaving wild cotton; raising sheep; culture; dress; shelter; and legends. The color illustrations by Robert Glaubke are well done and the people look Navajo. There is a good account of the Long Walk written in language young children can read and understand. The author does oversimplify at times: "At last, matters were so bad that Kit Carson was sent in 1864 to remove the Navajo to Fort Sumner, three hundred miles away" (p.17). Adequate.

354. Gridley, Marion E.
THE STORY OF THE SEMINOLE.
New York: Putnam, 1973. (3–5)
Robert Glaubke's unusual and beautiful illustrations are a highlight of this volume relating the history of the Seminole Indians. The writing is less inspired, but thorough, as village and chickee life, battles, manner of dress, and child-rearing practices are described in detail. Descriptions of the stick ball game known as Little Brother War, because differences between tribes were often settled by means of the game, and the green corn dance are examples of the author's careful attention to the listing of unusual detail. The book is packed with information about the past and modern times. Young readers should find this an interesting reference book about an admirable and proud people. Adequate.

355. Gridley, Marion E..
THE STORY OF THE SIOUX.
New York: Putnam, 1972. (5–8)
This short book of sixty-two pages provides a good overview of the culture of one of the most representative of Plains tribes. The text moves rapidly from descriptions

of the time when the tribes eventually known as the Sioux flowed into the Great Plains, which they were to dominate, to descriptions of their final forced removal onto the reservation. Throughout the book, the life and customs of this hunter-warrior people are depicted: tribal organization, housekeeping, education of the young, coming-of-age rites, and ceremonies of a religious and social nature are all described. Good.

356. Griese, Arnold A.
AT THE MOUTH OF THE
LUCKIEST RIVER.
New York: Crowell, 1973. (4–6)
A book that gives the feeling of authenticity through the author's language, its format, and the appropriateness of its illustrations, this book tells of a lame Athabascan boy who lived approximately 100 years ago. The conflict in the story deals with the boy's training dogs to carry him on a sled and the disapproval of the medicine man. Eskimos and Athabascans are depicted here as sometimes friendly and sometimes not. Glo Coalson's black-and-white illustrations are well done. There are sections introducing the author and the illustrator at the end of the book. Good.

357. Griese, Arnold A.
THE WAY OF OUR PEOPLE.
New York: Crowell, 1975. (3–6)
The white men in this story of Alaskan Indians over 100 years ago are Russians, a surprise to many readers who may forget that the threat of Russian colonization along the Pacific coast motivated much of the foreign and internal policies of Spain, Mexico, England, and the United States at that time. The story is good, but perhaps overambitious, as a boy learns to master his fears and becomes a peacemaker between his tribe and the Eskimos. It does serve as a framework for describing Alaskan Indian customs. The introduction is informative and well written:

> Today there is still a village called Anvik at the place where the Anvik River runs into the Yukon River, and the In-

dians still live there. These Indians still love their rivers, hills, and forests because it is the way of their people.

The color and black-and-white illustrations by Haru Wells are well done, and a map of the area of Alaska featured in the story is included. Good.

358. Grimm, William C.
INDIAN HARVESTS.
New York: McGraw-Hill, 1973.
(7 and up)
The author, a botanist, lists native plants used by the Indians in different parts of the North American continent and comments on their use. The illustrations are botanically correct, and include some drawings of gathering and preparing plant foods. Forty different plant "families" are illustrated. These families do not necessarily conform to botanical terminology. The author is much more interested in the eastern part of the continent, but occasionally mentions western or southwestern plants. He also occasionally mentions particular groups: Seminole, Chippewa, Dakotas, Menominee, Leni-Lenape, Nez Percé, Adirondack, Cherokee, Pomo, Blackfoot, and Kiowa, which indicates that he does know of individual cultures. For the most part, however, he refers to "the Indians" and generalizes a great deal. He includes patronizing remarks such as:

> Pine bark bread would be most unpleasant to our taste, . . . but to the Indians, it was food. . . . Unless we were extremely hungry, the Indian's acorn bread would not be very tempting . . . but the Indians seemed to relish it; most boys, like the Indians of yesteryear, seem to be quite fond of the ripened mayapple fruits . . . [which] have a peculiar flavor . . . sweet.

Older children can best use this as a reference. Adequate.

359. Grinnell, George Bird.
BY CHEYENNE CAMPFIRES.
New Haven: Yale Univ. Pr., 1926.
(7 and up)
George Bird Grinnell was one of the most famous early amateur anthropolo-

gists. In the foreword of this book, he is described as follows:

> Equally at home in the drawing rooms of intellectual Boston and New York and in the tepees of the Cheyenne, he maintained practical business activities concurrently with scientific exploration and, at the same time, kept a dedicated sportsman's enthusiasm for hunting and fishing. [p.v]

A scholarly man, he gives a lengthy and thorough general introduction to this collection of Cheyenne tales about war, mystery, heroes, creation, culture heroes, and Wihio, and comments on a diversity of facts; for instance, the Cheyenne were of the Algonquin linguistic stock, they often farmed as well as hunted, and the training of children began in infancy, "the first lessons being that they should always be good-natured and never quarrel with their fellows" (p.xx). The stories, themselves, reflect the fact that most of them were written for adult listeners. The black-and-white photographs by Elizabeth C. Grinnell were some of the few taken of the old ways of the Cheyenne. Good.

360. Grinnell, George Bird.
WHEN BUFFALO RUN.
Norman: Univ. of Oklahoma Pr., 1966. (5–7)

A chronicle of Cheyenne life of 1850 before the coming of large numbers of settlers, this is a classic, written in first person format by a boy growing up in that culture. Cheyenne life is realistically drawn:

> The people that he knew well were those of his own camp. Once a year perhaps, for a few weeks, he saw the larger population of a great camp, but for the most part half a dozen families of the tribe, with the buffalo, the deer, the wolves, and the smaller animals and birds, were the companions with whom he lived and from whom he learned life's lessons. [p.10]

The author's description of marriage customs is especially interesting. This book, with all due respect to the University of Oklahoma Press, deserves a more popular and colorful format. Written in gentlemanly, old-fashioned language, the book is one of the basics on old Cheyenne life. Good.

361. Gurko, Miriam.
INDIAN AMERICA: THE BLACK HAWK WAR.
New York: Crowell, 1970. (7–9)

The following quotation will give the reader some feel for the enlightened scope, the careful writing, the scholarly presentation, and the even-handed treatment the author provides in this book:

> Their [Sac and Fox] struggle against the United States lasted only fifteen weeks and could hardly be called a war. But on its own small scale it was typical of all the sad little wars fought on the frontier. It contained all the elements that illustrate the whole tragic story of Indian-white relationships. There were the usual misunderstandings between Indians and whites, the badly executed treaties, the broken promises, the betrayals, the split between hawks and doves—both white and Indian—the sufferings of the innocent, the useless heroism, the unquenchable land greed which lay at the bottom of it all, and the agony of being uprooted from long-established homes. There was the whole rhythm of Indian-frontier movement: two steps forward, one step back, with the whites always winning the extra step forward to the West. [pp.xi–xii]

She tells of how many Indians felt toward whites:

> It never occurred to the white man that the Indian might regard white civilization as inferior to his own. [p.11]

> The white man, in Indian eyes, would do disgraceful things for money. He would lie, cheat, demean himself, even risk his life. [pp.11–12]

She details tribal history from the first European contacts through Black Hawk's life, and presents a compassionate picture of Black Hawk's blaming of Keokuk for what happened. There is a thorough bibliography and an index. Good.

362. Hafer, Flora.
CAPTIVE INDIAN BOY.
New York: McKay, 1963. (4–6)
This story is about Chukai, a youthful Cliff-Dweller who lived in the Mesa Verde village in Colorado in the thirteenth century. Because he is young, Chukai must remain with the women, aged, and very young when the hunters leave to seek food. The Painted Faces attack the village, and Chukai is struck by a poisoned arrow, taken captive, and eventually escapes. When he returns to his village, he finds it deserted due to a drought, which he believes he created because of his prayers that the Painted Faces be destroyed. He finds a friendly tribe of Cliff-Dwellers who reassure him and teach him another way of life before he moves on to his own tribe, where he shares all the lore he learned from his captors, the Painted Faces, and from the other friendly Cliff-Dwellers. Eventually he is named chief of his tribe. Black-and-white illustrations by Don Lambo add interest, and a pronunciation key is useful. Adequate.

363. Haig-Brown, Roderick.
THE WHALE PEOPLE.
New York: Morrow, 1963. (7–9)
This tale revolves around a teenage Nootka Indian boy whose ambition is to be a "whale chief." The author transmits an understanding of the danger and excitement of the whale hunt, the beauty of the sea, and the spiritual beliefs of these pre-Columbian Indians. Written in a believable style, each chapter has symbolic black-and-white illustrations by Mary Weiler which enrich the detail the author puts into the story. There is a map showing the Tsitikat and Hashute villages and other significant spots alluded to in the book. The book provides a deeper understanding of the structure and complexity of the life of these Indians. Good.

364. Haines, Francis.
INDIANS OF THE GREAT BASIN AND PLATEAUS.
New York: Putnam, 1970. (6–9)
This is an unusually good social studies type of book featuring better than average writing: "Primitive man, like most recent pioneers, usually tried to find a home for himself where he had the best chance of survival" (p.9). It details the geology, history, social life, horses, treaties, and so on, of the Great Basin and Plateau area of the Nez Percé, Flatheads, and Shoshone. The section on contemporary events includes items such as the way tribal funds are spent and the success of the Nez Percé youth programs. The black-and-white photographs are typical of social studies texts, designed more for information than for artistic value, and there is a bibliography and an index. Good.

365. Hale, Janet Campbell.
OWL'S SONG.
Garden City, N.Y.: Doubleday, 1974. (7–9)
This story of fourteen-year-old Billy White Hawk, as he moves from the Idaho reservation to a California city and back, tells of the curious mixture that is present day reservation life and describes in rather explicit detail problems that usually arise from relocation of Indians in a city. It deals in a straightforward way with areas that a non-Indian writer might gloss over and covers the traditional teen problems of our culture that often intensify for Indian youth (sex, virginity, teen-age suicide, running away, prostitution, inept counselors), as well as special Indian concerns (loss of old values and beliefs, relocation, passing as white, BIA education, blacks versus Indians, half-forgotten tribal rituals). Well written, the book tells what happened with little editorial comment from the author. Young readers will also need access to books that present black/Indian relations more favorably and that describe Indians who made a better adjustment to city life. Good.

366. Hall, Geraldine.
KEE'S HOME: A BEGINNING NAVAJO/ENGLISH READER.
Translated into Navajo by Irvy Goosen.
Flagstaff, Ariz.: Northland Pr., 1971. (K–2)

This is an English/Navajo text designed for Navajo beginning readers, but non-Navajo readers will also find it of value as a presentation of Navajo life and as a reminder of the special educational needs of many Indian children for bilingual reading materials. The foreword explains that the book's purpose is helping Navajo children learn that English and Navajo, alike, can be written down and read. The writing is highly reminiscent of the old Dick and Jane readers:

"My name is Kee." [p.2]
"I am Navajo." [p.4]
"This is my dog." [p.6]
"My dog's name is Shep. My dog eats frybread." [p.48]

but the expression on the face of the Navajo boy in the illustration on page 4 as he says "I am Navajo" is good to see. Vera Louise Drysdale's illustrations in tans, white, and black are very good. The people pictured are happy, look Navajo, and the parents are suitably young for the age of their children. There is a glossary, a pronunciation guide, and a word list. Good.

367. Hall, Gordon Langley.
OSCEOLA.
New York: Holt, 1964. (5–9)
This is a historical chronology of Osceola's life, concomitant events surrounding his and his tribe's circumstances, as well as selected historical events with respect to the United States government and the political situation of the time. The book includes documentation, selected correspondence between Indians and the American government and government officials. There is an extensive bibliography. The chronology is factual; the author makes few, if any, generalizations. The book is a good source of information, but not especially designed for readers interested in depth of character or the Seminole Indian culture or habits. It clearly illustrates mistakes, mistreatments, and mistrust between Indians and whites. A map of Florida, South Carolina, Georgia, and Alabama is given. No further illustrations are included. Good.

368. Hall, Moss.
GO, INDIANS! STORIES OF THE GREAT INDIAN ATHLETES OF THE CARLISLE SCHOOL.
Los Angeles: Ritchie, 1971. (6–10)
This is a book for sports fans, especially those interested in the early days of college football, baseball, and in the Olympics. Included as well are Pop Warner, Jim Thorpe, Charles Bender, "The Elegant Arm," and all the other Carlisle athletes. Carlisle was intended as a sort of military school, but the Indian boys and the coaches nevertheless managed to put the school on the sports map for about twenty of the fifty years it existed. The author describes ten outstanding athletes, focusing mainly on their sports prowess, rather than providing much background information about any of the young men. Since the school was founded to "make" an Indian into a white man, it is probably just as well that it was closed in 1918, ostensibly due to lack of government funds. The book is illustrated with photographs of the Indian athletes. Good.

369. Hall-Quest, Olga W.
CONQUISTADORS AND PUEBLOS.
New York: Dutton, 1969. (7 and up)
A history of the Southwest from Cortez's capture of Mexico to the Gadsden purchase (with a few notes on latter-day events in a short epilogue), this is a scholarly, well-researched work. It concentrates primarily on the history of New Mexico, with special emphasis on Santa Fe. Hall-Quest occasionally intrudes herself into the narrative through the use of descriptive words that reveal some of her attitudes toward Indians: for example, "None battled the savage foe [Indians] more valiantly than Juan de Zaldivar (p.79); "It was clear to him that the Acomas should be punished for their dastardly treachery" (p.80); and "The Indians—Pawnees, Comanches, Kiowas—unleashed their fury by making murderous attacks upon the wagon trains" (pp.237–238); although she does describe fairly such events as the horror the Acoma people faced at the hands of the Spanish. She has a tendency

to stereotype various groups: "Santa Fe still has a large Spanish-speaking population. As a people who have always loved song and dance, they stage many picturesque celebrations during the year" (p.242). The author includes an index and a bibliography. Adequate.

370. Hannum, Alberta.
PAINT THE WIND.
New York: Viking, 1958. (7 and up)

Although probably intended as light, humorous reading, this book tends to make fun of reservation Indians in terms of what happens when two cultures meet on one or the other's home ground. This is the continuation of an account regarding the friendship between the Navajo artist, Jimmy Toddy, and the Lippincotts, a husband and wife archaeologist team. The story begins with the renewal of friendship when Jimmy, who joins the Marines at the outbreak of World War II, meets the Lippincotts (Mr. Lippincott is a lieutenant commander) at the Marine base in San Diego. From this point on, the author documents a series of Jimmy Toddy's misadventures, his philandering father, and his friends. The book is extremely well written. Certainly the author knows how to write in a humorous manner. Unfortunately, the self-righteous attitudes she conveys by placing the Indians as the butt of the misadventures is a sad way to use her talents. Consistent with the rather condescending treatment regarding the Indian and his art, the author includes several color reproductions of Jimmy Toddy's works at the beginning of the book. It is true that funny things happen to Indians; it is not true that they should be the butt of every joke. Poor.

371. Hannum, Alberta.
SPIN A SILVER DOLLAR.
New York: Viking, 1956. (7 and up)

This book is a surprising contrast to its sequel, *Paint the Wind*. Here the Navajos are pictured as cagey and proud, and whites are pictured as the beginners, the ones who make mistakes, the ones who have to learn. Yet, except for occasional stereotyping, such as "clumping along behind them in the heavy yellow shoes all Navajos love" (p.1), neither whites nor Navajos are made to look stupid. The story describes the lives of a young white couple who learn to run a trading post and who help a Navajo boy become an artist. The Navajos are pictured as the couple sees them, and the book is well written. There are some errors. The author states that all Navajos have two names. Actually, they may have two or a dozen; there is no set number. However, she does attempt to describe things usually not included in books of this sort, such as wildness in a girl, sex, witchcraft, werewolves, rocks and sand in bags of wool for sale. Although the book at times has a flavor of "benevolent whites help needy natives," it presents one in-depth view of Navajo life. Good.

372. Harnishfeger, Lloyd C.
THE COLLECTOR'S GUIDE TO
AMERICAN INDIAN ARTIFACTS.
Minneapolis, Minn.: Lerner, 1976.
(4–7)

In this book Harnishfeger helps students develop good methods of scientific inquiry. Statements throughout the book urge the reader to be tentative in generalizing from scarce data:

Readers will notice that in this book, frequent use is made of phrases such as "it is believed . . ." or "most scholars think. . . ." This has been necessary since much of the material is based on opinion; factual information about the Indians and prehistoric peoples of North America is still quite scarce. [pp.7–8]

The reviewer, who has done some exploration of prehistoric ruins and has a small collection, found the section on hunting arrowheads and other artifacts especially good, dealing as it does in a thorough way with pertinent laws and with recording, classifying, mounting, and displaying finds. Adults will do well to help children understand the controversial nature of the author's suggestions for restoring prehistoric items, and the feeling against digging that many Indian groups hold. The book has a good index and is illustrated in black-and-white. Good.

373. Harrington, Isis H.
TOLD IN THE TWILIGHT:
A COLLECTION OF PUEBLO AND NAVAJO STORIES AND NAVAJO MOTHER GOOSE RHYMES.
New York: Dutton, 1938. (2–5)
Without any explanations, introduction, or setting of the scene, this book proceeds right into its group of stories, largely of personal or family experiences of Pueblos and Navajos. The rhymes the author scatters throughout the book (in an attempt at a Navajo Mother Goose) are strained in language, content, and context:

I'm Navajo Pesh-la-kai,
And these, my boys.
We make pretty ornaments
Set with turquoise.
Belts, rings, bracelets,
We make for you
From Mexican pesos
And turquoise blue. [p.111]

The stories themselves are handled more competently. Black-and-white illustrations by Glen O. Ream and a glossary of Indian words are also included. Poor.

374. Harris, Christie.
MOUSE WOMAN AND THE VANISHED PRINCESSES.
New York: Atheneum, 1976. (4–6)
Based on Swanton's, Teit's, and Boas's early works for the Bureau of American Ethnology, this book is a retelling of myths about Mouse Woman, a legendary figure of the Northwest Coastal Indian groups. In the stories, some princesses are lured away by supernatural creatures. Since the girls are needed by the tribe for their bloodlines, Mouse Woman is asked to rescue them—and does, using clever strategies. Douglas Tait's drawing are good, incorporating as they do the text as part of the design, and Harris's writing and introduction are scholarly and literate. A sample: "At the other end of awesomeness, there was Mouse Woman, the Tiny One" (p.3). Good.

375. Harris, Christie.
ONCE UPON A TOTEM.
New York: Atheneum, 1963.
(4 and up)
This book contains five stories of Indians of the Pacific Coast. One is a tale of the killing of the one-horned mountain goat and the calamity which ensues; another is a story of the terror of the sea caused by the wrath of the "Storm Spirits," and of the efforts to appease that wrath by scattering white eagle down. All five tales reinforce the belief that calamities are caused by human interference with the laws of nature. The totems, telling of the achievements of the tribe and family and suggesting qualities of courage, strength of purpose and/or gentleness of spirit, are used both symbolically and literally. The format of the book is excellent, the type is large, and the woodcuts by John Frazier Mills are striking and add much to the tales. Good.

376. Harris, Christie.
RAVEN'S CRY.
New York: Atheneum, 1966.
(7 and up)
Not literal in style, plot design, or orientation, it is obvious that this book and its subjects have a great deal of emotional meaning for the author. She writes in a mystical style, and her plots or purposes are not easily apparent. Such literary devices, while handing the readers an abundance of material for thought, avoid the crushing, heavy-handed morality many authors use to try to bring home to the readers the author's involvement in the horror of the subject matter. Harris writes beautifully, and achieves her purposes without browbeating the reader with accusations of guilt or with writer condescension. The story is difficult and involved. Haida history is traced from the time of the Russians; through Captain Cook's men making so much money in China from the sea otter pelts they bought from the Haida that they almost mutiny in China; through the explanation of the Haida side of the killing of all Haida aboard the *Lady Washington* by Captain

Kendrick; ending with the story of Bill Reid, the illustrator, descendant of the Haida chiefs detailed in the book, and his decision to explore and continue Haida art. Harris works Haida customs into the plot in a natural way, and her use of the old New England ballad of the ship, the *Lady Washington,* is effective. The constant detailing of the beauty, sophistication, and intricacy of Haida arts makes the reader wish for the inclusion of even more examples and illustrations than are given. Good.

377. Harris, Christie.
SKY MAN ON THE TOTEM POLE.
New York: Atheneum, 1975. (6–9)
Based in large part on Marius Barbeau's 1928 book *The Downfall of Temlaham,* this book is an attempt to link the Man-in-the-Sky legends of the Pacific Northwest Indians to ancient astronauts, as in Von Daniken's *Chariots of the Gods,* and to ancient cosmic disasters, as in Velikovski's *Worlds in Collision.* The story design alternates vignettes of ancient Indians, astronauts from a different planet, and a modern Indian boy. It is the author's intention to show that each of the two older cultures had much to offer the other and the modern boy. Although she may very well be right in her conjectures about ancient astronauts, her premises are based on incomplete data in several instances; for example, the blue-eyed, fair Indians that were born into the tribe from time to time could as well be from ancient intermarriages in Asia before migration to North America as from intermarriage with astronauts. The author's presentation is so compelling that it would be well to remind young readers that she is writing about theories, not facts. Douglas Tait's dramatic black-and-white line illustrations are effective, and a brief bibliography is given. Good.

378. Harris, Marilyn.
HATTER FOX.
New York: Random House, 1973.
(8 and up)
The plot of this book is concerned with Hatter Fox, a beautiful young Navajo Indian girl, one of those tragic figures who seems determined to destroy herself despite special attention and help from a young white doctor, Teague Summer. This romantic story is replete with sadness and despair that, despite an element of truth, seems to appeal to the emotions rather than to the intellect. It also seems very much like other stories about young poor whites (or ghetto blacks or barrio Chicanos) who become involved with drugs, prostitution, and rebellion against society, in which the allusions to race seem forced and an attempt to cash in on current societal interests. For the young reader, stories regarding more positive adjustments of young Indian girls are strongly recommended to provide a better balance with respect to Indian teenagers, if this book is chosen. Adequate.

379. Hausman, Gerald.
SITTING ON THE BLUE-EYED BEAR:
NAVAJO MYTHS AND LEGENDS.
Westport, Conn.: Lawrence Hill, 1975.
(8 and up)
Good illustrations by Sidney Hausman, a gracious acknowledgement section, and a helpful introduction contribute to this interesting volume of Navajo poetry. The descriptive sections give the reader insights into Navajo art, religion, and history: for instance, "The presence of evil spirits still affects the lives of many modern Navajos, who may have given up all outward trappings of the old style of living" (p.17). The inclusion of examples of contemporary Navajo poetry serves to differentiate this book from other anthologies. This is a good text for literature appreciation as well as for general pleasure reading. Although the recommended grade level is eight and up, many students in grades four through six will be able to read the book. Good.

380. Haverstock, Mary Sayre.
INDIAN GALLERY: THE STORY OF
GEORGE CATLIN.
New York: Four Winds Pr., 1973.
(5 and up)

112

A book that uses George Catlin's paintings and drawings as illustrations and Catlin's own letters and notes as part of the text, this volume tells of Catlin's life and times. Written in a popular, if slightly overblown, style ("The air was thick with the fumes of turpentine and varnish in George Catlin's little workshop" [p.18]), it details his history, from his mother escaping the Wilkes-Barre fight alive to his going to California during the Gold Rush. Catlin tried to show Indians as real people whose old culture was doomed. In this book, Haverstock has fixed on a good format—pictures for slower readers and her text for faster ones. There is a bibliography and an index. Good.

381. Hayes, Florence.
THE GOOD-LUCK FEATHER.
Boston: Houghton, 1958. (2–4)
This is a story of a young Indian boy and his understanding parents. Cheedah herded sheep while his father made jewelry and his mother wove rugs which were traded for food at the local store. One day, the little boy was given an opportunity to attend school for four weeks. He wanted to go because he could only count to three, and he wanted to be able to count big numbers. If he does go to school, no one would herd the sheep. Cheedah's mother agrees to rise early, weave late, and herd the sheep so that Cheedah can go. The father agrees to assist with the household chores. Cheedah is an apt pupil, and thoroughly enjoys his thirty days in school. He learns to count, to work with hammer and nails, and he learns many things about his state of Arizona and the nation's capital in Washington, D.C. It is a wonderful experience for the boy, who returns happily to his proud parents, grateful to them for their understanding and careful planning so that he could go. Cheedah attributes his good luck to an eagle's feather which he had found one day while herding sheep. Adequate.

382. Hays, William D.
INDIAN TALES OF THE DESERT PEOPLE.
New York: McKay, 1957. (4–7)

The author chose stories for the young reader, omitting those with no logical motive or in which the symbolism was not clear, and adding descriptions of the desert and the mountains in this retelling of legends from Pima and Papago peoples. He describes storytelling customs: for example, the Pimas had a storyteller to keep traditions and tell the stories once a year in a ceremony lasting four nights. These are creation, animal, and custom stories, often making clear to the reader some aspect of Pima or Papago life: "and as the custom [if a girl refused marriage] was among the Desert People, her refusal was final" (p.103). The book is illustrated by black-and-white drawings by the author. Good.

383. Hays, Wilma, and Hays, R. Vernon.
FOODS THE INDIANS GAVE US: HOW TO PLANT, HARVEST AND COOK THE NATURAL INDIAN WAY.
New York: Washburn, 1973.
(4 and up)
Foods from the Americas introduced to Europe after Columbus's voyages are identified, described, and discussed in this book; especially since the authors regard food as the real treasure the Europeans took home from the New World. These native American plants today provide over eighty percent of our present food. The history of familiar native American foods, methods of preparation, and recipes adapted from the Indians all make this book a necessity for any class studying Indian cultures. Corn, peanuts, potatoes, and wild rice are only a few of the plants whose ancestry began on the American continents. Facts are presented in a style appealing to children. Good.

384. Hays, Wilma Pitchford.
LITTLE YELLOW FUR.
New York: Coward-McCann, 1973.
(2–4)
This story is basically about a white girl, Susanna, and her family who moved from the East in 1913 to homestead on free public land near the Rosebud Indian Reservation in South Dakota. It tells of her

mother's fear of the Indians who often rode by, her father's understanding and compassion for them, and Susanna's adventures in their village when she wanders off and is taken there by Red Cloud, the village chief. She learns about their food, clothing, and games, and develops appreciation for the Indian way of life. The story ends happily with the Indians presenting Susanna, Little Yellow Fur, with gifts of moccasins and a soft doeskin dress. The characters are idealized and seem, sometimes, much too good to be true. The information about the Sioux village life seems accurate enough, but there is a sense of a lack of real depth throughout. The story is based on the author's childhood. Richard Cuffari's color and black-and-white illustrations are good, if somewhat romanticized, and there is a section on both the artist and the writer. Adequate.

385. Heady, Eleanor.
SAGE SMOKE: TALES OF THE
SHOSHONE-BANNOCK INDIANS.
Chicago: Follett, 1973. (2–5)
The setting of this collection of twenty legends is Idaho, Utah, Nevada, Montana, and Wyoming, where the Shoshone and Bannock Indians lived. The legends center about the worship of Aps, the Creator, who had three sons on earth—the beaver, the otter, and the muskrat. Many other animals are introduced in the legends. The old storyteller described in the book always concludes his tale with the phrase, "The rat's tail is off." There are seven imaginative black-and-white illustrations by Arvis Stewart. A well-written book of less than 100 pages, this book reiterates an old Shoshone proverb which undergirds these tales: "The birds in the sky and the wind in the grass told us the earth was our gift from the Father and it belongs to all." Good.

386. Heady, Eleanor.
TALES OF THE MINIPOO: FROM THE
LAND OF THE NEZ PERCÉ INDIANS.
Cleveland, Ohio: World, 1970. (4–6)
This is a collection of legends from the Nez Percé Indians dealing with the animal kingdom on earth before people came, the creation, and natural phenomena. For example, one tale is about how light was brought to a dark world by a young boy who ran from East to West with a cedar bow fastened to his head. There are eleven tales in all, and Coyote is a central character. Eric Carle's black-and-white linocuts are not particularly Indian in appearance, but are good. The book is well written and would read aloud well. Heady reminds us that these tales, as is true for most Indian legends, "have, of course, changed in the telling, so that no one version can be called exactly correct" (p.10). There is a descriptive paragraph about both the author and the illustrator. Good.

387. Heard, J. Norman.
THE BLACK FRONTIERSMEN:
ADVENTURES OF NEGROES AMONG
AMERICAN INDIANS, 1528–1918.
New York: Day, 1969. (6 and up)
Many blacks have Indian ancestors. The author cites a 1928 study by an anthropologist that found one-fourth of the students in a black college were partially of Indian ancestry. This book is an attempt to trace this tie between the two peoples, and tells the story of ten blacks in Indian history (Estevánico, Briton Hammon, John Marrant, Pompey, Ed Rose, John Stewart, Jim Beckwouth, Luis Pacheco, Henry Ossian Flipper, and York). The idea behind this book is interesting, and other books need to deal with black women, the Buffalo Soldiers, slavery, and Indians to complete the picture. There is a bibliography and an index. Good.

388. Heiderstadt, Dorothy.
INDIAN FRIENDS AND FOES.
New York: Van Rees Pr., 1958. (4–7)
This book includes thirteen biographies of the more well-known Indian leaders of the war years, beginning with Pocahontas and continuing chronologically to Geronimo. The only other woman included is, predictably, Sacajawea. Although the author professes objectivity and implies absence of stereotypes, each biography

subtitle suggests that stereotypes may have prevailed in her sources, which include such early works as C. T. Brady's *Indian Fights and Fighters,* 1904, and F. Starr's *American Indians,* 1899. Some of the subtitles: "Who dreamed of an Indian State?" (Tecumseh); "Who taught his people to read and write?" (Sequoyah); and "The Last Barbarian" (Geronimo). The author includes lists of sources and other books. The black-and-white sketches by David Humphrey Miller are informative. The author's organization includes a half-page introduction to each biography. Adequate.

389. Heiderstadt, Dorothy.
STOLEN BY THE INDIANS.
New York: McKay, 1968. (4–6)
This is a series of stories about whites kidnapped or captured by Indians. The author is fair to all sides in her story treatment, describes old dungeons and torture weapons common to Europe as proof of the universality of captive abuse, and details the hold that captive stories had on the American frontier:

It was as thrilling to know an Indian captive in pioneer days as it would be to know a space hero today. In both cases the person would be someone apart from ordinary people, someone who had had a terrific adventure and lived to tell about it. [p.ix]

The author writes well, setting forth the stories of Esther Wheelright, Eunice Williams, Tom Brown, Regina Leining, Mary Jemison, Fanny Slocum, Horatio Jones, Joseph Brown, John Tanner, Oliver Spencer, Matthew Brayton, and Cynthia Ann Parker. She includes little known facts along the way, such as: "In 1957, their [Quanah Parker and Cynthia Ann Parker] bodies were moved when the United States Army took over the area for an atomic cannon range" (p.109). There is an epilogue, a bibliography, and an index. Carl Kidwell's black-and-white illustrations often feature Indians holding tomahawks or war clubs, a jarring note in an otherwise temperate treatment. This book, with

its captivity theme, is sure to cause disagreement as to whether its purpose is worthwhile. It is, however, effective and well done. Good.

390. Henderson, LeGrand.
CATS FOR KANSAS.
Nashville, Tenn.: Abingdon Pr., 1948. (1–3)
Not basically a book about Indians at all, this is a fanciful tale of an old man who journeys East to get cats for catless, pioneer Kansas, and of his adventures and misadventures along the way. There are only five pages of the story devoted to Indians. The first page mentions that there were Indians in Kansas at that time and shows a man in a warbonnet chasing buffalo with a bow and arrow. The other four pages deal with other warbonneted Indians, unspecified as to tribe, trying unsuccessfully to stop the train he rides on with a rope. One picture shows a plethora of chiefs and the other details Indians with feathers flying. The author's black, white, and orange illustrations are fanciful, not designed for authenticity. Story development: Adequate. Portrayal of Indians: Poor.

391. Henderson, Nancy Wallace, and Dewey, Jane.
CIRCLE OF LIFE: THE MICCOSUKEE INDIAN WAY.
New York: Messner, 1974. (3–5)
The photographs by David Pickens and the text by Henderson and Dewey both show old and new Miccosukee life styles and variations of integrations of the two. A good, factual, social studies type of book, the volume gives interesting, unusual glimpses of the tribe, such as that children are members of the mother's clan, that couples build their houses near the girl's family, and that some Miccosukee do not want to become part of the new tribal structure. A good evaluation of the roles of so-called chiefs is contained in this statement from the book: "The tribe finally decided to accept the BIA offer. The Medicine Men asked Mr. Tiger to be their spokesman" (p.40). Good.

392. Henry, Thomas.
WILDERNESS MESSIAH: THE STORY OF
HIAWATHA AND THE IROQUOIS.
New York: Bonanza Books, 1955.
(7–9)
An anthropological treatment largely
based on the work of J. N. B. Hewitt, a
Tuscarora from the Smithsonian Institution, this book details a vast arena of
Iroquois life and Iroquois/white interac-
tion, including material on their prehistoric life, variations in Indian culture,
matriarchal structure, society and government, daily life, religious belief, federation, dealings with France and England,
myths, their effects on the young United
States, and so on. The author gives the
reader a myriad of facts and comments on
Iroquois life; for example, "Within the
rules of their own society, they were a
generous and friendly people" (p.24); and
"Among the Iroquois, men never achieved
the right to vote" (p.70). The Hiawatha
described in this book is vastly different
from Longfellow's. He is a statesman and
a missionary for the Long House religion.
There is extensive coverage of the roles
women played in Iroquois life. This would
be a good reference source for junior high
school students and teachers, particularly
in the Northeastern and Midwestern sections of the country. Good.

393. Heuck, Sigrid.
BUFFALO MAN AND GOLDEN EAGLE.
New York: McCall, 1970. (K–3)
Most of this book is spent driving home
the moral that cooperation is better than
selfishness. A Plains Indian and a mountain man are friends. Both dream of owning a horse. They each fail to capture it
separately, and so cooperate to catch and
train it. Adults will need to explain to
young readers that not all Plains Indians
had such elaborate warbonnets as pictured in the illustrations, nor were they
worn night and day. The author's illustrations are good, childlike, and colorful, and
could easily spark children's own art projects. Story development and book format:
Good. Portrayal of Indians: Adequate (see
caution above).

394. Hickman, Janet.
THE VALLEY OF THE SHADOW.
New York: Macmillan, 1974. (6–8)
This is a well researched, well-written
fictional story about an Indian Christian
boy who escaped the Moravian Massacre
in 1781 during the American Revolutionary War. Readers unacquainted with the
killing of the Moravian Christian Indians
by a ragtag of American colonial forces or
with the importance of the battles on the
western frontier during the Revolutionary
War may have trouble believing these
things actually happened, but they did.
Good.

395. Highsmith, Bonnie.
KODI'S MARE.
New York: Abelard-Schuman, 1973.
(4–6)
This story tells of two young Navajo
boys, Kodi and his brother Sanasuk, who
are orphaned. After numerous events in
which the author utilizes the plot as a
means of describing Navajo customs and
of the difficulties and loneliness of boarding school life, the two brothers are reunited. A school is built on the reservation,
and the brother Sanasuk, becomes the
school's teacher. Adequate.

396. Hill, Kay.
MORE GLOOSCAP STORIES.
New York: Dodd, 1970. (4 and up)
These eighteen tales of the Watanaki
Indians of North America were initially
adapted for television. They tell of great
Chief Glooscap, of enormous size and
magical powers, successfully engaging in
battles with giants and wizards. He succeeds in teaching the "incorrigible" badger,
the otter, the caribou, and other animals
(even the Wind Giant and a few wayward
Indians) how to live wisely and well. Well
illustrated by John Hamberger, these tales
emphasize the hopes and fears and the life
and lore of these Indians. The glossary is
useful, and the 178 pages are written in
words intermediate grade readers will understand and appreciate. Good.

397. Hiller, Carl E.
FROM TEEPEES TO TOWERS: A
PHOTOGRAPHIC HISTORY OF
AMERICAN ARCHITECTURE.
Boston: Little, 1967. (7 and up)
This 98-page collection of photographs
includes four pictures of original American dwellings: the Iroquois long house,
the Cheyenne tepee, the Navajo hogan,
and the pueblo of Taos. The rest of the
book pertains only to European influences.
The writing is for adults, but the average
junior high student could read it successfully, if motivated. For information about
American Indians, this book must be rated
poor, although it does place Indian architecture within a certain framework. General interest: Adequate. Portrayal of Indians: Poor.

398. Hillerman, Tony.
THE BLESSING WAY.
New York: Harper, 1970. (7 and up)
Following the lines of a good detective
story, the author provides suspense and
interest in the story of Joe Leaphorn of the
Law and Order Division of the Navajo
Reservation. In this story superstition is
exploited to cover a real crime, the murder
of a young Navajo who goes to Many
Ruins Canyon to chant to Talking God.
For most young mysteries aficionados,
the story will hold great appeal. The plot
moves quickly, the characters are interesting. The story may be somewhat lacking,
as the author admits, with respect to
"scholarly and scientific standards" in
dealing with "ethnological material." Nevertheless, the author's treatment of Navajo
Indians, their culture and practices is quite
good. The villains are white and Navajo,
resolving an interesting dilemma for a
writer who chooses an Indian setting for
a detective story. Along the way, Hillerman helps the reader to see the diversity
among Navajos:

"California Navajo. That's what had
me hung up. I was expecting him to act
like The People and all he knew about
The People he must have got out of a
book."
"Case Studies in Navajo Ethnic

Aberrations, for one," McKee said, "by
John Greersen." [p.198]
Good.

399. Hillerman, Tony.
THE BOY WHO MADE DRAGONFLY:
A ZUÑI MYTH.
New York: Harper, 1972. (5–8)
Adapted from material in the Bureau
of American Ethnology files collected by
Frank Hamilton Cushing, who adopted
Zuñi ways and lived as a Zuñi, this book
presents a Zuñi myth about a young boy
and girl. Left behind when their village
is abandoned due to drought, the boy
makes a dragonfly for the girl to help her
loneliness. The dragonfly comes to life
and helps to overcome the drought. Years
later, the children become leaders, and the
dragonfly becomes a symbol for rain. The
feel of the story is good, and the author
sets the stage well in his author's note.
Laszlo Kubinyi's black-and-white illustrations are fine; there could be more of them
and they could be reproduced in a larger
format. As with many myths, this book
would even be more interesting read aloud.
Good.

400. Hillyer, William Hurd.
THE BOX OF DAYLIGHT.
New York: Knopf, Junior Literary
Guild, (no date). (4–6)
Emphasizing the universality of cos-
mology and the story of creation, this collection of legends and myths from Pacific
Northwest Coastal tribes is similar to
many Asian and European stories: for example, "In the very time of night lived
only Anvik, the Oversky Chief, with his
wife and three children" (p.3); and "At
that time there were no people on Earth—
only, as we have said lumps and shadows" (p.4). Based on Franz Boas's research for the Bureau of American Ethnology of the Smithsonian Institution, this
book is a collection of tales of Raven, described as follows by the author: "Here
also was a real hero, Indian style, Tscham-
sim—brave, strong, boastful, crafty, devoted, greedy, treacherous, successful"
(p.xiv). The author has adapted the lan-

117

guage and pattern of the stories to fit into a written format, avoiding redundancies, inconsistencies, and contradictions. The description of Haida, Tlingit, and Tsemishian life is accurate, detailing customs, dress, housing, villages, slaves, the use of copper coins as a medium of exchange, and so forth. The red-, white-, and black drawings are by Erick Berry. Good.

401. Hirsh, S. Carl.
FAMOUS AMERICAN INDIANS OF
THE PLAINS.
Skokie, Ill.: Rand McNally, 1973.
(3–6)
With great color and black-and-white illustrations by Lorence Bjorklund, an interesting foreword by N. Scott Momaday, and Hirsh's competent writing, this book would make an impressive gift or a reference for travelers or vacationers. The title really doesn't give the reader any indication that this book is written with such flare and interest: for example, "He [the Plains Indian] was a free-hearted wayfarer" (p.13); or "He made for himself a style of living such as the world has never seen, full of daring and brilliance" (p.13). Hirsh also states:

Defeated, the Plains Indian of old has become the most famous af all Indians. Feared and hated by the whites in his heyday, the mounted tribesman of the prairies can now be hallowed. [p.93]
Good.

402. Hodges, Margaret.
THE FIRE BRINGER: A PAIUTE
INDIAN LEGEND.
Boston: Little, 1972. (2 and up)
The setting of this story is the land of the Paiutes, who lived in California, Utah, Oregon, and Arizona. The hero is a little Paiute boy who was helped by the Coyote to bring fire to the tribe. In the center of each small wickiup, a round hut, the Paiute "kept the fire," which was one of Coyote's best gifts to the Indians. A well-written and thought-provoking story, ably illustrated by Peter Parnall, it is appropriate for upper primary and intermediate grade readers. Good.

403. Hoffman, Virginia.
LUCY LEARNS TO WEAVE: GATHERING
PLANTS.
Rough Rock, Ariz.: Board of Education, Rough Rock Demonstration School, Navajo Curriculum Center, 1969.
(K–2)
Designed as a basic reader for Navajo children, this text features fine black-and-white illustrations by Hoke Denetsosie. The book gives a good feeling about women and girls, a plus for groups interested in feminist consciousness-raising. The feeling for the worth of girls and the joyous feelings about nature, birds in particular, more than offset the limited vocabulary of a beginning reading text. The use of an ambiguous dwelling that could be a house or a hogan as part of the illustrations is interesting. Buttes seen through the windows of the house give the book a reservation or Southwestern setting. Navajo children, particularly, should be able to identify with this representation of a life that reflects old and new ways. The book can also be useful for showing teachers who work with Indian students the possibilities of developing good curriculum material, and showing primary children who are non-Indian how other American subcultures live. But, and perhaps of most importance, this book is a fine example to use in showing the difference that illustrations can make in furthering story plot and mood. Although recommended for primary grades for reading purposes, junior high art students could profit from this example of the illustrator's relationship to story design. Good.

404. Hoffman, Virginia, and
Johnson, Broderick H.
NAVAJO BIOGRAPHIES.
Rough Rock, Ariz.: D.I.N.E., 1970.
(5–7)
A series of biographies of current and historical Navajo leaders, this book is designed for use by Navajo students. The writing is not as smooth as some of the Rough Rock Curriculum material; it is more earnest and admonishing. Still, it is effective: "When we are young we often

do not understand why it is important for us to study and learn about our forefathers" ("Message to Navajo Students from the Rough Rock Board of Education," p.13). The illustrations by Hoke Denetsosie, Andy Tsinajinnie, and Clifford Beck, Jr., are good, and the book contains a pronunciation guide to Navajo words and a bibliography. The leaders discussed are largely male (Narbona, Antonio Cebolla Sandoval, Zarcillos Largos, Mañuelito, Barboncito, Ganado Mucho, Jesus Arviso, Henry Chee Dodge, Sam Ahkeah, Albert George [Chic] Sandoval, Paul Jones, Chabah Davis Watson, Annie Dodge Wauneka, Dr. Taylor McKenzie, and Raymond Nakai). Good.

405. Hofman, Charles.
AMERICAN INDIANS SING.
New York: Day, 1967. (3–6)
This collection of Indian music and poetry includes information on instruments and dance steps from seven Indian nations. The importance of music in many Indian cultures is described. A record is included, containing music from Kiowa, Hopi, Iroquois, Chippewa, Sioux, Zuñi, and Yaqui peoples. Photographs of instruments, music, diagrams of dance steps and song-poetry in English versions are all useful for children and instructors. Descriptions of ceremonies, with music, photographs, and sketches, help to preserve this aspect of Indian life. Valuable also are the reading lists—one for students, another for teachers and parents. This book is a fine addition to any library. Good.

406. Hofsinde, Robert (Grey Wolf).
THE INDIAN AND HIS HORSE.
New York: Morrow, 1960. (4–6)
A fascinating account of how horses changed the Indian way of life, told in a style appropriate for elementary pupils. This book traces the history of horses in North America from 1519 A.D., when Cortez brought them into Mexico. Hofsinde, who received his Indian name when he saved the life of a Chippewa Indian boy, has written an account that will appeal to every child who has owned (or

dreamed of owning) a horse. How Indians caught wild horses and trained them is described with appealing detail. The style and vocabulary make this book a good reading experience for children who have recently become independent readers. Good.

407. Hofsinde, Robert.
INDIAN ARTS.
New York: Morrow, 1971. (4–6)
Divided in sections by medium (clay, copper and silver, and the like), this book is a reference on Indian arts, limited in scope by the poor reproductions and lack of details in the photographs of the objects described, and the incompleteness of the sampling offered the reader, particularly in modern Indian art. The black-and-white drawings illustrating the book are the author's, and there is an index. The author's explanations of the art he features in the book are written in social studies text style: "The Indian's desire to record events taking place around him resulted in artistic expression" (p.13). Adequate.

408. Hofsinde, Robert.
INDIAN BEADWORK.
New York: Morrow, 1958. (5–9)
The what, why, and how of American Indian bead art is explained simply and logically by Hofsinde, whose black-and-white drawings illustrate the book. Most of the book consists of specific instructions for making such things as a bead loom, or designing and creating belts, necklaces, headbands, bracelets, coin purses, bags, sheaths, book covers, and moccasins. A "how to do it" book with helpful illustrations and easy-to-read instructions, it is an excellent book for teachers, youth leaders, and people who wish to work on a project in bead art. Good.

409. Hofsinde, Robert.
INDIAN COSTUMES.
New York: Morrow, 1968. (4–6)
The author describes in detail selected examples of Indian dress from ten representative tribes—Apache, Blackfoot, Crow,

Iroquois, Navajo, Northwest Coast Indians, Ojibwa, Pueblo, Seminole, and Sioux. This book is a refreshing antidote to the stereotyped picture of the Indian resplendent in warbonnet, breechclout, and moccasins, though these subjects are treated in detail where appropriate. What comes through strongly is style; each tribe had a distinctive dress for a number of occasions and for reasons relating to geographic location, availability of materials, customs and beliefs, climate, and seasons. This book is an excellent reference for anyone interested in accurate descriptions and illustrations of Indian costumes. The author's illustrations are black-and-white line drawings which parallel the detail of the text. Good.

410. Hofsinde, Robert.
INDIAN FISHING AND CAMPING.
New York: Morrow, 1963. (4–6)
In this book, Hofsinde explains the different methods used by various Indian groups for making fishing equipment, capturing fish, preparing the catch, and cooking it. He is not teaching survival techniques but a way of life, and his attitude toward fishing is that of a woodsman rather than a sportsman. The variety of Indian cultures is emphasized as sketches and text contrast fishing gear made by Northwest tribes, the Ojibwa, the Pacific Coast tribes, the Iroquois, and the Eskimo. Good.

411. Hofsinde, Robert.
INDIAN GAMES AND CRAFTS.
New York: Morrow, 1957. (3 and up)
Written and illustrated by the author, this book is an interesting collection of games and crafts representing about ten North American Indian tribes. Detailed instructions, with diagrams and measurements provided for the more complex tasks, will enable the reader to reproduce most of the selections. Of particular interest is the chapter dealing with the construction of Hopi kachinas—even color suggestions are included. The black-and-white illustrations provide excellent guides. Good.

412. Hofsinde, Robert.
INDIAN HUNTING.
New York: Morrow, 1962. (3 and up)
Starting with evidence that prehistoric man in North America hunted wild game, and sketching some of man's earliest weapons for hunting, Hofsinde describes the development of more sophisticated techniques for hunting food. The deer was hunted more than any other animal throughout North America, and Hofsinde, with great attention to detail, recreates the drama of the hunt by different tribes, emphasizing the diversity of Indian cultures; for instance, the Ojibwa used one procedure, while the Zuñi employed totally different skills to capture deer. He describes the characteristics of each type of game and the devices various tribes invented for hunting it. Good.

413. Hofsinde, Robert.
THE INDIAN MEDICINE MAN.
New York: Morrow, 1966. (3–6)
Illustrated by black-and-white drawings by the author, this book describes the functions of and the differences between Indian healers and seers, past and present. A good idea and well executed, the book describes such diverse items as sleight-of-hand tricks, Iroquois mask medicine, medicine men of today, and women's role in Indian medicine. His section on the cooperation between medicine men and medical doctors in hospitals is interesting but may give the impression that such joint ventures are more common than they in fact are. Many tribal practices are discussed, Apache through Iroquois. Good.

414. Hofsinde, Robert.
INDIAN MUSIC MAKERS.
New York: Morrow, 1969. (3–6)
This is a thorough coverage of different types of Indian music and instruments, concentrated especially on Ojibwa customs. The author discusses a variety of types of songs (prayers, medicine songs, ceremonial songs, children's songs, etc.) and instruments (drums, rattles, flutes, and the like). His explanations of the im-

portance of music in tribal life are fascinating: "To the American Indian, singing was a serious matter. It was a part of his whole being from birth until the last moments of his life" (p.9); and "When a man came home from a visit with another tribe, one of the first questions he was asked was what new song he had learned" (p.11). His detailing of song characteristics is thorough:

Indian songs may sound a little discordant to a white man who hears them for the first time. The Indian sings certain notes not found in our scale, and he can sing a little above or below a note. Furthermore, an Indian song may begin in three-four time, only to change to two-four time, and after a few measures, change back again to three-four. Our songs rarely if ever change beat in this way. [p.73]

He bases much of the older content of his book on the work of the Bureau of Ethnology, and includes a section on modern Indian music. The book, although well done, would have been strengthened even more by additional examples of actual songs and/or a record to accompany the text. Good.

415. Hofsinde, Robert.
INDIANS AT HOME.
New York: Morrow, 1964. (4–6)
This book corrects stereotyped ideas about Indian dwellings by describing in detail the variety of native American homes appropriate to different environments and lifestyles. The diversity is described vividly in this book. In the first paragraph, Hofsinde destroys the common assumption that all Indians lived in tepees. He describes the wigwam of the Algonquins, the plank house of the Indians of the Northwest coast, and the Pueblo adobes. This book is recommended reading for any teacher planning to teach a unit on Indians, as well as for pupils doing research. Good.

416. Hofsinde, Robert.
INDIANS ON THE MOVE.
New York: Morrow, 1970. (4 and up)

A detailed discussion of Indian migrations is presented in this text, illustrated by the author. Starting with the migration across the Bering Strait some thirty to forty thousand years ago, Hofsinde suggests some of the pressures that caused various tribes to change their locations during the ensuing centuries. With his customary attention to detail, he contrasts the gait of the whites with that of the Indians, and the care taken by Indians to conceal their route. These details make the account come alive for children. He has included sketches of types of moccasins of varied patterns from four tribes. When horses arrived with the Spaniards, Indians discovered a new dimension to travel. Hofsinde's talent for sketching provides accurate details of saddles invented by Indians to meet this new demand. His chapter on water travel includes water craft built by many tribes, but he has omitted one of the most seaworthy Indian boats in all of North and South America: the tomol of the Chumash. The sections on winter travel, portable lodgings, and modern Indian travel are all excellent. Good.

417. Hofsinde, Robert.
THE INDIANS' SECRET WORLD.
New York: Morrow, 1955. (3 and up)
The meaning of Indian customs and ceremonies and the legends that explain why each is important are beautifully described in this book, illustrated by the author. The making of artifacts, the storytelling purposes of design, the deep religious motives in whatever the Indian accomplished are all included in language which the young readers who select this book will appreciate. Hofsinde differentiates between tribes and emphasizes the diversity of Indian cultures. Good.

418. Hofsinde, Robert.
INDIAN WARRIORS AND THEIR WEAPONS.
New York: Morrow, 1965. (3–5)
This book describes the weapons, costumes, and war-making techniques of the Ojibwa, Iroquois, Sioux, Blackfoot, Crow, Apache, and Navajo. The materials and

construction of shields, bows, war clubs, quiver designs, body painting and head gear are presented together with scattered illustrations. The Indian is depicted as a brave and fierce warrior who raided enemy tribes and white settlers for horses, goods, and captives to add to the population of the tribe. The author interprets Indian customs; for instance, any Indian suspected of being a coward was challenged to prove himself. If he did not accept the challenge, he was exiled from the tribe. Not everyone will agree with his interpretations, either the one above or others, such as "In early times there was little fighting among the American Indians. The hunters did not go far afield, and therefore they did not know that other tribes existed" (p.7). The book is full of oversimplifications, such as his statement that the Indian warrior now fights for his country. Adequate in execution of the basic idea in back of the book, the author's characterization of Indians is stereotyped, although he does give Indians credit for being good fighters. Book Organization: Adequate. Portrayal of Indians: Poor.

419. Holberg, Ruth L.
LUKE AND THE INDIANS.
New York: Hastings House, 1969.
(4–6)
Full of the fantasy that an Indian's life is wild, free, undisciplined, and with no responsibilities, this book is full of stereotypes of the Indian as a "noble savage," impossibly idealized. For example, at first glance the following quote seems acceptable: "From our study of his history, we have come to know that the Indian of early America was a perceptive, understanding, proud individual" (p.5). Upon reflection, the impossible burden such an idea puts on any group of people becomes apparent. Which Indian? Which group? In short, such all-inclusive positive statements are as surely stereotypes as if they were negative in tone. The plot involves a boy from the Massachusetts Bay Colony who runs off to join the Indians. The book is concerned with his adventures and reactions: for example, "He was happy, he was free,

he was living with the Indians . . . and he had a dog" (p.47). The black-and-white illustrations by Joshua Tolford are unobtrusive, and there is a short bibliography. The writing is adequate. Poor.

420. Holden, Glenn.
TALKING TOTEM POLES.
New York: Dodd, 1973. (3 and up)
The linguistic aspect of totem poles is examined by a professor of English in this well-written book. Illustrated with beautiful photographs and a map, this is a must for teachers, as well as for children interested in this art form. Holden has carefully researched the historic background, the geographic areas, the customs, ceremonies, songs, secrets, skills, material (red cedar), tools and artisans of the totem pole. The book is full of fascinating information: for example, a skilled carver was carefully selected and often went long distances to carve a pole, for which he was well paid. The names of some of the great carvers are included in this account. Unfortunately, the life of a totem pole is about sixty years, so the story it tells lives about as long as the person who designed it. The problems of preservation for older poles has not yet been solved. Good.

421. Holling, Holling C.
THE BOOK OF INDIANS.
New York: Platt & Munk, 1962. (2–5)
This history book has both pluses and minuses. Among the pluses: there are cautionary statements for scholars, such as "No writer can tell all about the North American Indians in one book, and no artist can draw all the pictures there are to draw" (p.11), and customs are often clearly delineated, such as the role of the mother's brother in child rearing. Among the minuses: the book is dated, limiting the effectiveness of the presentation, and feminists will not appreciate some of the author's sentiments, for instance: "remember this about the old-time Indians . . . they were men. They were honest. They faced life unafraid. Be a good Indian" (dedication). Each section of the book includes fictional accounts of the life of boys

and girls in the tribes the book describes. The illustrations, by H. C. and Lucille Holling, include some color reproductions. There is a glossary. Adequate.

422. Hood, Flora.
LIVING IN NAVAJOLAND.
New York: Putnam, 1970. (K–2)
After a brief introduction of what she calls Navajoland ("Navajoland is a picture book land where Dezbah and her brother live under a sky that is high and wide and blue"), the author describes a year in the life of a Navajo family of five: mother, father, two teenage children (a boy and a girl), and a baby. Other characters, including a trader, Tall Man, a singer, and a medicine man, appear from time to time. In terms of seasonal aspects, such as lambing season and various celebrations, the text seems accurate, if unstimulating. The Navajo family appears to be somewhat unreal, with a rather stereotyped "father as silversmith, mother as weaver" pattern. The black, white, and red illustrations by Mamoru Funai depict happy, smiling faces throughout the book, and clothing, hairstyles, living accommodations, and so on seem appropriate. Adequate.

423. Hood, Flora.
PINK PUPPY.
New York: Putnam, 1966. (3–5)
This is the story of a little Cherokee girl, Cindy Standingdeer, whose mother has just died and who, lonely and afraid, is sent off to a boarding school. The story is interesting, and the illustrations are excellent. Many of the old and new customs and ways of the Cherokees are mentioned. Although the story is fictitious, many authentic Cherokee names and places are used. Some adult readers may wish that the author had not had the teacher encourage the girl to give up her imaginary toy in favor of real friends, but instead encouraged her to see the importance of both. The account of her invention of an imaginary toy dog could spark discussions of similar happenings in the reader's life. Good.

424. Hood, Flora.
THE TURQUOISE HORSE.
New York: Putnam, 1972. (2–5)
Highly stylized in format, this collection of short poems can be quickly and easily read by most young readers. The book seems too brief to sustain interest and too general either to provide information or to stimulate further reading, despite the colorful illustrations. The few poems included are excellent for reading aloud, but probably would be better appreciated if the author had provided additional supplementary material. The illustrations by Marylou Reifsnyder are interesting, although so romanticized as to be misleading. There seems to be a discrepancy between the text and the illustrations; both, separately, are good, but together they clash. Adequate.

425. Hooker, Forrestine C.
STAR: THE STORY OF AN INDIAN PONY.
Garden City, N.Y.: Doubleday, 1964. (4–7)
A romanticized account of Cynthia Ann and Quanah Parker from the viewpoint of one of their horses, this is a well written fantasy with a fine foreword by Lieutenant General Nelson A. Miles. The novel is based on the lives of actual historical characters, and young readers may need help to understand that these people really lived. The story may make the surrender of the Quahadi Comanche more hopeful than it actually was. Good.

426. Hopkins, Marjorie.
THE THREE VISITORS.
New York: Parent's Magazine Pr., 1967. (1–3)
The fantasy tale of a young Eskimo girl who helps three visitors to her igloo (a pelican, a seal, a baby bear) and is rewarded in magical ways for her kindness, this story stresses the unexpected outcomes of assisting others. For instance, the girl's grandmother would never have found her way home through a storm if the girl hadn't helped the visitors. The book will provide the spark for many human relations discussions with young chil-

dren. Anne Rockwell's illustrations are good and colorful, although the people in them do not look particularly like Eskimos, which can be both good and bad. As a story focusing on people, the nondelineated faces serve to encourage easy child projection into the characters. As a story about Eskimos, the nondifferentiated faces serve to throw the emphasis on the girl's act of giving, and not on Eskimo life. Good.

427. Houston, James.
AKAVAK: AN ESKIMO JOURNEY.
New York: Harcourt, 1968. (3–5)
Reviewers differed so greatly on this book that both reviews are presented:

A. The author is primarily an illustrator who tells adventure tales with far north window dressing. Fiction writers have this privilege, but the reader must look elsewhere for Eskimo values, Eskimo ingenuity, Eskimo themes, and Eskimo culture. The writing is beautiful, the illustrations are charming, the story is easy to read, and the setting might have been anywhere, but Houston has chosen the Far North. Do not include this volume for a social studies unit on Eskimos. As a volume of fiction, it is satisfactory. Adequate.

B. This story of a young Eskimo boy who goes to the North on a journey with his grandfather and grows up in the process emphasizes the old pattern of Eskimo life. The language flows well, the book is beautifully illustrated, the story is well told. Good.

428. Houston, James.
EAGLE MASK: A WEST COAST INDIAN TALE.
New York: Harcourt, 1966. (4–6)
Powerful black-and-white illustrations by the author are the most effective part of this book about a young boy of the Pacific Northwest Coast tribes before the coming of the Europeans. The story itself is mediocre: a boy seeks a vision and sees the ships of the whites, and at times highly anglicized in form. The author has obviously done his research on tribal life and customs. An introduction to orient the reader more precisely would be helpful. Adequate.

429. Houston, James.
GHOST PADDLE.
New York: Harcourt, 1972. (4–6)
The principal character in this very readable book is fifteen-year-old Hooits of the Ravens clan. The setting is along the Northwest Coast. Hooits's father, weary of continual war with the Island chiefs, has decided to work for peace between the tribes. With the aid of a "ghost paddle," canoes of unarmed Ravens make the journey into the territory of the Island people safely. As a result, peace is restored, and trading resumes. The author's black-and-white illustrations add dramatic interest to the story through their suggestions of strength, persistence, and action. The story is well written and well researched. Good.

430. Houston, James.
KIVIOK'S MAGIC JOURNEY: AN ESKIMO LEGEND.
New York: Atheneum, 1973. (1–4)
James Houston wrote *White Dawn*, one of the best adult books about Eskimos, and the same meticulous attention to detail and research is present in this book. His color illustrations are well done, accurate, and show a great deal of motion in their composition, but the people he draws are "cuter" than his usual style, with big eyes like those drawn by the artists Keen. The language in the book is easy to read and childlike, but the flow of the writing itself is not as good as most of his work; for example "Suddenly Kiviok saw a wicked raven swoop out of the sky and snatch up one of the white feather coats that the girls left on the shore" (unpaged). The plot is similar to the fairy tale of the girl with the seven swan brothers: Kiviok, an Eskimo man, marries a bird-girl. Raven steals her feather coat and she cannot fly. Kiviok wins back the coat, the girl, and the family. This is a good read-aloud story. Adequate.

431. Houston, James.
SONGS OF THE DREAM PEOPLE.
New York: Atheneum, 1972.
(4 and up)

This book provides an interesting look at the use of songs, speeches, and words by various Native American groups. The author has taken on an area that even those writers interested in American Indian literature often overlook and does it with insight and thoroughness:

> Within the Eastern Woodland tribes, chiefs were sometimes chosen because of their ability to deliver orations with great gestures and eloquence. These sachems had the strongest feeling for the use of similies and metaphors. [foreword]

Grouped by geographic areas, various tribal songs are presented and analyzed. Many of the selections are suitable for reading aloud to younger children, and others for adult reading. His black-white-brown and black-white-green illustrations are well done and faithful to old design patterns. There is an acknowledgment section and suggestions for further reading. Good.

432. Houston, James A.
TIKTA' LIKLAK: AN ESKIMO LEGEND.
New York: Harcourt, 1965. (2–4)
An Eskimo legend about Arctic hazards and Eskimo ingenuity is beautifully illustrated and retold in this book that stresses the values by which Eskimos live. The plot: confronted by serious hazards, Tikta' Liklak has the choice of giving up, or of using his intelligence, ingenuity, and skills for solving his problems. Houston's prose and illustrations complement the theme, which emphasizes the Eskimo philosophy of perseverance. Good.

433. Houston, James A.
WHITE ARCHER: AN ESKIMO LEGEND.
New York: Harcourt, 1971. (3–5)
This story is a showcase for Houston's illustrations, which in this case happen to have an Eskimo theme. The author has an appealing style of writing and is a talented artist. However, this story is not necessarily based on Eskimo values, even though the title claims it is an Eskimo legend. It begins with a bloodbath and pursues a theme of revenge. The last chapter

has a happy ending. This is another of Houston's adventure stories, and some parts may be too gory to use with some children. Illustrations and format: Good. Story design: Poor.

434. Houston, James.
WOLF RUN: A CARIBOU ESKIMO TALE.
New York: Harcourt, 1971. (3–5)
This book is adventure fiction using the Far North as background, illustrated with lithographs by the author. Pure fiction, it has almost a Walter Mitty flavor, as it climaxes with two wolves killing a caribou and delivering it to the boy hero. The illustration then shows the boy carrying the caribou over one shoulder and trudging toward home, which was several "sleeps" away. The vocabulary might be suitable for gifted third grade pupils, but it is more appropriate for fourth grade and up. It should probably not be used for a social studies unit about Eskimos, but has some appeal as adventure fiction. Adequate.

435. Hoyt, Olga.
AMERICAN INDIANS TODAY.
New York: Abelard-Schuman, 1972. (6 and up)
In this description of the lives of various modern Native American groups, the writing is caustic: "The exploits of famed Indian fighters, such as Sitting Bull and Geronimo, are so well known as to be parodies of the Indian people" (p.13); honest; and unsparing:

> Various tribes throughout the country have been—and are—faced by vicious problems: they are poor, they are sick, they haven't enough land, or good land, they get inferior education, they are isolated, they are discriminated against, they suffer rashes of juvenile delinquency and alcoholism. [p.15]

The book is organized by geographical areas, and the author describes modern conditions for Indian groups in each section. She presents interesting pictures of the lives of the remaining twenty-four Cabazon Indians of California, for example. The section on urban Indians is well done, and the numbers of Indians in big cities may surprise some readers (e.g., San Francisco: 10,000; Oakland: 10,000; Los Angeles: 45,000; as of 1972). The author writes in a winning style, and her speculations about possible futures for Native American groups are plausible and sensible. The black-and-white photographs used for illustration are fascinating, and the reader can only wish there were more. There is a bibliography and an index. Good.

436. Huffaker, Clair.
NOBODY LOVES A DRUNKEN INDIAN
New York: McKay, 1967. (7 and up)
This is probably as good a picture of what reservation life is like for some Indians today as any book available. The witticism, sophistication, and unsparing knowledge of reality of some of the characters is a delight. Huffaker's delineation of characterization, always one of his strong points, is thorough and caring. He is as good at sketching women characters as he is at detailing his men, and his dialogue, especially in the opening sequence, is fine. He makes an improbable plot seem life-like, and he in no way spares the reader from some rather harsh truths about some conditions to be found today. His ending is abrupt, sorrowful, and heart-breaking. This is a controversial book. Some people react violently against it; others consider it a classic. One could scarcely consider oneself to be knowledgeable about the field of children's literature on today's American Indians without reading it. A classic. Good.

437. Hulpach, Vladimir A.
AMERICAN INDIAN TALES
AND LEGENDS.
New York: P. Hamlyn, 1965.
(7 and up)
This book could serve as an object lesson for both readers and publishers on the way great illustrations, good printing and color reproduction process, and a suitable format positively affect the quality and the readability of a book. Printed in Czechoslovakia, Miloslav Troup's illustrations are beautifully reproduced. Hul-pach makes a good representative selection of Indian tales and legends and presents a thoughtful summary of American Indian oral literature in the final section. Good.

438. Hunt, Ben.
THE BIG INDIANCRAFT BOOK.
Milwaukee: Bruce, 1969. (5 and up)
The sort of book that librarians constantly have to reorder because their readers simply read the book to shreds, this is a book of directions for projects based largely, but not entirely, on Indian crafts and objects. For example, there is an interesting section on rustic furniture that has little to do with traditional Indian design. Hunt reproduces some of the same diagrams he has used in his other books here, but most projects are new and vary all the way from birch-bark baskets to love-flutes. The lists of materials and the directions are clear and easy to follow (as in *Popular Mechanics*), and there is an interesting section on the author's workshop and life. The book is directed to boys; for instance, "Boys often ask, 'Where can we work?' " (p.13), somewhat limiting its usefulness. There is a glossary of Sioux names for the craft articles featured in the book and an index. While this book is not the greatest or most accurate account ever written about Indian life, it does provide a way for less verbal learners to gain some feeling for the intricacies of Indian life, crafts, and design and for more verbal learners to approach concepts in a more physical way. Good.

439. Hunt, W. Ben.
THE COMPLETE BOOK OF INDIAN
CRAFTS AND LORE.
New York: Golden Pr., 1954.
(6 and up)
This "how to do it" book is a classic used by youth leaders for more than twenty years for craft projects. Its success is due to the precise instructions and careful, full color illustrations. Ben Hunt first met Indians in a circus when he was twelve years old, beginning what evolved into a lifelong study. He has been able to

incorporate his knowledge of the Indian ways of life with his involvement in Boy Scouting. Hunt has generated widespread interest in Indians. In this book, he carefully differentiates between Native American cultures. Since his Indian friends were Wanblee Sioux, most of the artifacts illustrated in this book are typical of the Plains Indians. Hunt is careful to make this distinction. Teachers will find many ideas that can be used in the classroom. Details of several Indian dances are included. Good.

440. Hunt, W. Ben.
THE COMPLETE HOW-TO BOOK OF INDIANCRAFT.
New York: Collier Book, 1973. (6–10)
This is a book designed for older children and young adolescents, but adult purchasers, particularly if they are persons who enjoy working with their hands, will enjoy browsing through the fascinating directions for making necklaces, rawhide, beadwork, silver conchas, kachinas, leather clothing, pack saddles, and the like. The book has the same sort of magnetism as seed catalogs and mail order books. The directions are complete and easy to follow, but the projects described for the most part are not simple, one-day affairs. These are real items that the maker can use; consequently, the book is a rich source of ideas for parent-child, teacher-class, and a lone, self-reliant young person's projects. Good.

441. Hunt, W. Ben.
THE GOLDEN BOOK OF INDIAN CRAFTS AND LORE.
New York: Golden Pr., 1961. (2–5)
This book features Hunt's fine attention to detail and easy-to-follow directions for making everything from beadwork to parfleches, offering youngsters who learn better through perceptual-motor styles an avenue for appreciating the painstaking processes involved in Native American crafts. A special tie is often created between people working with crafts that those who never work with their hands miss, such as the feel of the hours involved

in putting beads on leather or the time spent polishing silver, and the pride of using the finished object. Hunt's books offer this avenue to all children and, for once, he remembers that girls are as often involved in crafts as are boys. There is a section on Ben Hunt, himself, a feature not often found in primary books; an index; and a section on how to pronounce Indian words. He writes fairly fluently, and, while he tends to concentrate on Plains Indian crafts, he has organized a book that will appeal to a variety of readers, including the often-neglected slow readers. Good.

442. Hurdy, John Major.
AMERICAN INDIAN RELIGIONS.
Los Angeles: Sherbourne Pr., 1970.
(8 and up)
This is a heavy-handed book; a personal account of personal belief, written, for the most part, in a mixture of the language current at the time of its publication, 1970: "How much you dig these records depends in large part on how ear-conscious you are. One things is certain—sound must be experienced; words don't make it happen" (p.192), and sociological terms:

> But every checkpoint demonstrated that what we called religious freedom was the right to worship within the confines of a slightly relaxed Puritan ethic. Ask the Mormons. Ask the Lakotas. Ask the Navajos. But the list becomes embarrassing. [p.7]

The author is opposed to most white traditional church practices. He operates from some basic stances. For example, he talks of white religious infighting:

> . . . but she [his grandmother] found the [Christian] Scientists' consternation over a party cocktail and cigarette untenable. Eventually she died unshriven, unsatisfied, but honest [p.8]

without understanding that infighting is not confined to whites or Christianity (e.g., some of the Pueblo fights over ceremonial form). He asks for perfection before action, and the gives the reader the impression that organization, particularly of religious ritual, is something white, without mentioning that some Indian rituals are so precise that one word or mistake can often undo the total effect. Hurdy calls condemnation of the ancient Iroquois fire torture "quibbling about details" after Hiroshima, Korea, Biafra, and Vietnam (p.109). He is self-righteous about the correctness of his views. But the largest flaw in the book is an overall feeling of rigidity—Indians are this way, whites are that way; he neglects to delineate for the reader the nuances of his chosen field of religion. The content of the book is selective in nature, dealing primarily with Hopis, Lakotas, Iroquois, Kwakuitl, Navajos, and the Native American church. There is a listing of campgrounds in or near Indian reservations, Indian newspapers, recommended books, and records. Adequate.

443. Icenhower, Joseph B.
TECUMSEH AND THE INDIAN FEDERATION 1811–1813.
New York: Watts, 1975. (6–10)
The devastating Mississippi and Ohio River area earthquake of 1811, predicted by Tecumseh to the exact day, was taken as a sign for a general Indian uprising in the Northwest Territory in protest of the moving of the Proclamation Line of 1763, the line beyond which non-Indians were not to settle. This account, well written in an inconspicuous and nonjudgmental fashion, tells in an episodic format the interrelationships among the men involved, Indian and non-Indian alike. Illustrated in black-and-white with maps, old portraits, and the like, this book provides excellent background for an important part of the Revolutionary War. The author may treat the Prophet, Tecumseh's brother, both too lightly and too respectfully. An introductory, but not a thorough, view of this controversial figure is included. This is basically a reference text, much better written than most. Good.

444. Irving, Washington.
A TOUR ON THE PRAIRIES.
New York: Pantheon, 1967. (6–8)

An excellent picture of prevailing white American intellectual feeling about the Indians in the mid-nineteenth century, this book is adapted from Irving's revised edition of *The Crayon Miscellany*, a story of his 1832 trip with Charles Joseph Latrobe, later governor of Australia, and Count Albert Pourtales through the Indian camps of the Plains. The writing is excellent; the book would be a good choice to read aloud. Irving talks about the white settlers he meets: "He had the frontier propensity to charge everything to the Indians" (p.24), and pictures the Indians as "noble savages," a not uncommon attitude held by many white easterners of the time. His writing is funny (read the account of the horse "stealing" episode) and thorough (prices of commodities are given on page 237; for example, whiskey, 25¢ a gallon in St. Louis—sold at $16 a gallon to Indians on the Plains). The book is illustrated by the etchings of Charles Bodner and other artists. The appendix contains Henry Ellsworth's report to the secretary of war on this trip, in which he recommends that whites be prohibited from using Indian pasture land, that laws against trapping on Indian land be enforced, that the government and Indians meet annually in council, and that the Indians be given medical assistance; an ironical note in view of the actual fate of these Plains people. Good.

445. Israel, Marion.
APACHES.
Chicago: Melmont, 1959. (3–5)
In this story, the author describes how the Apaches lived; how they gathered and prepared food, built shelters, and made clothing. Included are some examples of tools and a step-by-step series of illustrations of the preparation of a doeskin hide to be made into a dress. Although the tinted illustrations by Harry Timmins are quite good, the story is too simplified and over-romanticized. Many young readers may conclude that the "One-From-Whom-All-Things-Come" (p.5) left little of interest for these Apache Indians except "slim young trees for poles to frame huts," "reeds

and grasses for baskets," and "fruits and seeds and roots, good to eat." Perhaps life would have been much easier for the Apaches had they lived as simply (and as dully) as do the "Apaches" described in this book. Poor.

446. Israel, Marion.
CHEROKEE.
Chicago: Melmont, 1961. (2–6)
This book describes the Cherokee Indians before the arrival of the whites. It details a one-year period from fall to fall, and tells about the different activities of the tribe, emphasizing Indian ritual and respect for other beings. Adequate.

447. Israel, Marion.
DAKOTAS.
Chicago: Melmont, 1959. (1–3)
A cute, coy account of the history and customs of the Sioux: "Sometimes a little warrior came to a tipi" (p.17), this book is designed for primary-age children. Full of inaccuracies, such as "There are no buffaloes on the prairie now. One small herd is kept in Montana. No one is allowed to hunt these buffalo" (p.6) (these buffalo are hunted on a limited basis as part of herd upgrading); or "All the tipis in the village looked alike" (p.8) (each tipi was decorated in an individual style); the best part of the book is Paul Souza's black-brown-white illustrations. There is a section describing the author and the illustrator. Poor.

448. Jacka, Jerry, and Gill, Spencer.
TURQUOISE TREASURES: THE SPLENDOR OF SOUTHWESTERN INDIAN ART.
Portland, Ore.: Graphic Arts Center, 1975. (6 and up)
Jerry Jacka's noteworthy color photographs show the reader some of the finest Indian jewelry and turquoise objects made by the best known Southwest Indian artists. The pieces pictured here are predominantly traditional, although some contemporary pieces are also present. Spencer Gill's text details the history of the use of turquoise all over the world, includes quotes about turquoise from numerous

places and eras, and tells some of the meanings turquoise has for various Arizona and New Mexico Indian groups. This is a pretty, enjoyable book, designed to give pleasure; and although the text is well written and researched, the reader's first attention will probably be directed to the photography. Occasionally, Jacka includes pictures of scenery which, while certainly attractive, could just as easily have been replaced by more pictures of turquoise designs. Jacka is a straightforward photographer. For the most part his pictures simply set forth the objects in the best light and background to display them well for the reader, but occasionally he adds something unusual, such as the snow in the picture of Leroy Hill's squash blossom, and the tiny ore cars in the picture of the Morenci mine. Good.

449. Jacobson, Daniel.
THE HUNTERS.
New York: Watts, 1974. (6–8)
Excellent black-and-white drawings by Richard Cuffari illustrate this book on hunting Indians. Fictional accounts are interspersed into factual materials. Hunts from mammoth days to the last of the buffalo hunts are described in detail, including customs, tools, and horses. Facts are quickly and skillfully given, and women's lives as well as men's are detailed—the author makes both sound interesting. On the minus side, the book is not easy reading and suffers from labored prose. There is a glossary and an index. Good.

450. Jagendorf, Moritz A.
KWI-NA THE EAGLE, AND OTHER INDIAN TALES.
Morristown, N.J.: Silver Burdett, 1967. (4–6)
This is a valuable collection of seventeen tales from various tribes. Each tale is written in a brief fashion; consequently, the seventeen are told in less than 100 pages. The stories represent the oral literature from several Indian groups: for instance, the story of Kuena comes from the Utes; a buffalo story comes from the Comanches; the legend of the rabbit and the

coyote from the Zia; the creation of the world from the Zuñis. Jack Endewelt has provided interesting illustrations, which are both symbolic and literal. There is a pronunciation key which should prove helpful for intermediate grade readers. Good.

451. Jakes, John.
MOHAWK: THE LIFE OF
JOSEPH BRANT.
New York: Crowell-Collier, 1969.
(7–9)
This story details Joseph Brant's life from his childhood to his death; however, the major portion of the story deals with his relationship with the British, primarily with Sir William Johnson, the man often linked to Brant's parentage by historians. The orientation of the story is British in point of view, but the author deals as objectively with them as he does with the French and Americans, almost to the extent that they seem alike. Joseph Brant is described in his youth as someone who was "free to do whatever he wished" (p.4) and who had "a raging temper [that] indicated the approach of manhood" (p.5). For the rest, although skillfully written, this is yet another story depicting a happy, carefree people who were tricked, cajoled, and mistreated by all but a few whites. Here, too, is the great Indian leader, Joseph Brant, who tries in vain to unite all of the Indians into one group to stand and fight. The illustrations by Roger Hane are consistent with the "Yellow Submarine" cartoon style which had become popular the year before this book was published. Adequate.

452. James, H. L.
ÁCOMA: THE PEOPLE OF THE
WHITE ROCK.
Glorieta, N. Mex.: Rio Grande Pr.,
1970. (6 and up)
This book features H. L. James's color photographs illustrating various historical writings about the Ácoma Pueblo, with excerpts from Lummis, Alvarado, and Sedgwick, to name a few. Frank Waters provided the introduction which, more than anything else, serves to orient the reader. James's photography in this book is not always of the best. For the most part, he simply takes a picture of what he wants to talk about. His pictures, therefore, tend to run to tiny figures perched on giant cliffs, as on page 32. Sometimes, however, these cliff-figure pictures are exceptional (see lower right hand picture, page 33). The photographic work is always on a good journeyman level, but occasionally rises far above mere competency, as in the three-dimensional look to the photograph on pages 28–29. Occasionally the pictures are not sharply in focus (see page 20), or the negative or slide used for reproduction is scratched and/or dirty (see pages 82–83). For the most part, the prose selections used as captions for the author's photographs are involved passages, extravagantly worded, written in a flamboyant, almost "purple" prose style: "The Pueblo people have always dwelt in a land of canyons and high plateaus, rising from great stretches of sand that touch at last the far blue horizon" (p.74). James's own prose, as seen on pages 84–86, is spare, blunt, straightforward—much better than he seems to be aware of. Good.

453. James, H. L.
POSTS AND RUGS: THE STORY OF
NAVAJO RUGS AND THEIR HOMES.
Globe, Ariz.: Southwest Parks and
Monuments Assoc., 1976. (6 and up)
An outstanding, definitive study of Navajo rug-making, this book is encyclopedic in scope, detailing the history, definitions, and locations of Navajo rug-making. The author's color and black-and-white photographs are excellent and informative. For example, the photographs of the actual plants used for making dye are easier to use for identifying these plants than drawings would be (see pages 20–21). The book includes a time-cost chart, maps of areas where different types of rugs are woven, rules for rug-making, instructions for care of rugs, lists of awards for rug-makers, a bibliography and an index, all uniformly well done. Good.

454. James, Harry C.
A DAY IN ORAIBI: A HOPI
INDIAN VILLAGE.
New York: Melmont, 1959. (2–5)
In this story, two Hopi children from
Oraibi show a white boy how they live,
including gardening, hunting, weaving,
pottery, jewelry-making, and the kiva.
John meets the chief and, with his class-
mates, plans to make a model of a Hopi
village. Readers familiar with Hopi culture may entertain doubts as to the proba-
bility of two Hopi children showing two
white children the ceremonial kiva. Dated.
Adequate.

455. James, Harry C.
A DAY WITH HONAU–A HOPI
INDIAN BOY.
New York: Melmont, 1957. (2–5)
This is a story about the daily life of
Honau, a Hopi Indian boy from Oraibi.
The book, although written in the format
generally used for social studies texts of
the fifties, sometimes offers surprising
insights: for instance, "The men weave
blankets, which they sell" (introduction).
The author does not introduce the concept
of the variability of lifestyles among the
Hopi, and much of the material in the
book is now dated. Don Perceval's black-
white-gold illustrations are good. Dated.
Adequate.

456. James, Harry C.
THE FIRST AMERICANS.
Los Angeles: Elk Grove Pr., 1971.
(2–4)
A good introductory book for giving
young readers an overview about prehistoric groups in America, this work is written in simple, easy-to-read language. The
book is well researched; for instance, there
is an especially good section on projectile
points. However, the author is often un-
duly positive in dealing with some of the
theoretical portions of his text; for example, "Across this isthmus men and animals
wandered into and out of North America"
(p.6); and "Man had been living in Asia
long before there was a man, woman, or
child anywhere in America" (p.13). The

author includes sections on vocabulary
and new words. Good.

457. James, Harry C.
THE HOPI INDIAN BUTTERFLY DANCE.
Los Angeles: Melmont, 1959. (3–6)
In this story, which depicts prepara-
tions leading to the Hopi Butterfly Dance,
the author provides young readers with a
description of these events through the
eyes of two Hopi children who are to be
part of the dance. Although the descriptions of the costumes seem accurate, the
importance and sense of the dance is left
out. Unfortunately, the characters are romanticized and anglicized in personality,
which is misleading and distracts from
the meaning of the ceremony. An oversimplified introduction is equally uninform-
ing. Don Perceval's illustrations provide
more information than the story. Poor.

458. James, Harry C.
OVADA: AN INDIAN BOY OF THE
GRAND CANYON.
Los Angeles: Ritchie, 1969. (2–5)
It is hard to find children's books on the
Havasupais, and this book is an attempt
to give middle level elementary-age readers a book that describes the life of a young
Havasupai boy. In general, the author depicts their life in an adequate manner,
although he occasionally makes stereotyping comments: "They are pleasant friendly
people who smile a great deal" (p.8); and
"The Havasu women all make baskets"
(p.22). Don Perceval's red-white-black
illustrations are good. Adequate.

459. Johnson, Broderick H., ed.
GRANDFATHER STORIES OF THE
NAVAHOS.
Rough Rock, Ariz.: Board of Education,
Rough Rock Demonstration School,
Navajo Curriculum Center, 1958.
(3–6)
The Rough Rock, Arizona, Demonstration School is performing a truly incredible
task, preserving the Navajo heritage for
its students. This book is another example
of the curriculum materials the district
uses. A book designed to promote the posi-

tive self-image of Navajo school children, it presents eleven traditional stories dealing with Navajo culture, history, and mythology. There is a picture history of the Navajos (page 12) and photographs of herbs and plants and their uses, including ceremonial rites. An eloquent "Talk with Navajo Students" is written by board member John Deck, who is described as having no formal education;

> The Navahos of Rough Rock and elsewhere are happy about what is going on at the Demonstration School. They say it is a good thing to improve our lives and living conditions through more jobs and better education, but we do not want to lose the real strength and power of our people. [p.10]

There are few groups who would start an account of their history by reciting legends and passages from ceremonials, as this book does. Even though the book was designed for Navajo students, it will give non-Navajo young readers much information, and it would be helpful to use in training teachers. The black-and-white drawings by Hoke Denetsosie and Clifford Beck, Jr., although small, are excellent. Good.

460. Johnson, Broderick H., ed.;
Callaway, Sydney M.; and others.
DENETSOSIE.
Rough Rock, Ariz.: Board of Education,
Rough Rock Demonstration School,
Navajo Curriculum Center, 1969.
(5–8)

The story of a Navajo man who was important in recent Navajo history (he died in 1969), this book is another of the curriculum materials designed by the Rough Rock Demonstration School for use by Navajo students, and as such is vastly different from most curriculum materials designed for use with non-Indian readers of the same age. It discusses life matter-of-factly:

> Some of the Navajos thought they recognized a Navajo woman among the Mexicans. They were sure of who she was when one of the men who had known her as a child remembered that

Naakai' Asdzáá had a finger nail missing when she was captured. Her bosom seemed full, as though she might be nursing a baby. That turned out to be true. The baby girl was brought. [pp.7–8]

and tells of important historical events, such as the reduction of grazing stock to relieve overgrazing problems:

> Denetsosie had suffered great personal abuse throughout the enforcement of the reduction program and for some time afterward. Even his present wife, when he first asked her to marry him, had exclaimed, "You're not going to marry me. You took all of my livestock away." [p.31]

This book gives more of the flavor of Navajo belief and attitudes than do many books designed for this purpose, as in the description of the ritual of selling a rug, on pages 38–40. Andy Tsinajinnie's black-and-white illustrations are masterful, even though they are reproduced in a very small size. Good.

461. Johnson, Dorothy M.
WARRIOR FOR A LOST NATION.
Philadelphia: Westminster, 1969.
(6–8)

Sitting Bull's own pictographs illustrate this story of his life. His pictures are charming; he draws similar designs in almost every scene: he is on the right on an Appaloosa horse that even has its legs in identical positions in each drawing, and he is vanquishing an enemy pictured to the left. The book characterizes Sitting Bull as a warrior as well as a medicine man, and cites instances of his exploits. It describes his friendship with Catherine Weldon, a white woman, and the mistakes and tragedy of his death. Sioux customs are worked naturally into the biography:

> A Sioux girl had no doubt whatever about what she was going to do when she grew up. She would marry and have a family. There were no spinsters among the Sioux, and no career girls. Every woman got married and kept house. [p.13]

Such little-known facts as the stealing of

his thigh bone after his death are documented. Good.

462. Johnson, Elizabeth B.
ANIMAL STORIES THE INDIANS TOLD.
New York: Knopf, 1927. (3–5)
This book may prove to be hard reading for modern youngsters because of its old-fashioned wording. Animal tales from several tribes are included. The appendix gives a series of brief paragraph summaries of the histories of various Indian groups. The black-and-white photographs that illustrate the book are small and dated. Adequate.

463. Johnson, Enid.
COCHISE: GREAT APACHE CHIEF.
New York: Messner, 1953. (6 and up)
This biography of Cochise is characterized by stereotyping: "Savage and barbarous as he may have been, Cochise was one of the great characters of American history" (p.x); extravagant phraseology:
> In the annals of the Southwest this stronghold has ever been surrounded with mystery and fame. This is the home of the most warlike Indians in Arizona history, the Chiricahua Apaches. And here their chief reigned supreme. [p.ix];
condescending wordings: "like every good Apache squaw" (p.80); and no real understanding of the Apache culture: "This boy, called Naretena, though a weak and sickly child, was soon to show himself as possessing qualities rare in an Apache—pity and deep sensitivity" (p.8). Written as if it were a novel, it has an index and a bibliography. Poor.

464. Johnson, Johanna.
THE INDIANS AND THE STRANGERS.
New York: Dodd, 1972. (2 and up)
Truly fine black-and-white woodcuts by Rocco Negri illustrate a story written in poetic form of encounters between Indian and white as the frontier moved West. Both sides are presented, perhaps in oversimplified fashion. Indian historians may be taken aback by the incompleteness of some of the accounts: "Soon Crazy Horse

was captured. Later, by accident, he was killed at the prison" (p.105). Adequate.

465. Jones, Charles, ed.
LOOK TO THE MOUNTAIN TOP.
San Jose, Calif.: Gousha, 1972.
(7 and up)
A comprehensive compilation of articles about Native Americans, this volume contains a variety of writers and topics. Alfonso Ortiz, a Tewa and Associate Professor of Anthropology at Princeton, wrote the introduction; Stewart L. Udall contributed an article on Indians as ecologists; Vincent Price one on Indian art; Theodora Kroeber Quinn one on Indian literature; and so on. Other features in the book include articles on Indian women, warriors, religions, healing, farming, foods, wealth, law, and politics; a chronology of Indian history; maps; Indian writing systems; speeches; crafts; recipes; arts and crafts dealers; a bibliography; and an index. The book is good looking, has a fine format, and is set in easy-to-read type. More than a coffee table-type book, however, it contains good writing and many seldom-discussed ideas, such as the following:
> Implanted in our history is the erroneous idea that most American Indians belonged to nomadic bands that did not develop permanent ties with particular land areas. This is a misconception (rooted in the white man's preconceived idea of land ownership), for even the tribes who were not village dwellers had land areas they regarded as their own. (There is evidence, for example, that the primary cause of conflicts among Indian tribes was the invasion of "territory": "rights" were closely tied to the regular use of land, and Indians went to war when raiding parties crossed invisible but vital boundaries.)
> The Indian was emotionally attached to his mountains, valleys or prairies by religious feelings that went to the very essence of existence. Tribes had no "title" to their homeland, and sometimes its boundaries were not pre-

cisely defined, but the land was the center of the universe for each tribe or clan. [p.2]

Nancy Oestreich Lurie's article on "Indian Women: A Legacy of Freedom" is another example of the outstanding writing to be found in this book. Good.

466. Jones, Gene.
WHERE THE WIND BLOWS FREE.
New York: Norton, 1967. (6–9)

Adults and teen-agers alike will enjoy the author's evenhanded and easy-reading collection of ten stories about boys and girls, men and women (Indian, white and Mexican) of the American West. There is a haunting quality to the stories: Mo-Keen, a Mexican boy, who begs the Kiowa to take him away from the poverty of his village; John Osage Ross caught in the horror of the Cherokee-Osage clash in eastern Oklahoma; Cynthia Ann Parker starving herself to death in her brother's house when her attempts to run away from the whites, whose language she no longer could or wanted to understand, back to the Comanches were thwarted; Mary Cook, freed after years as a captive, trying to persuade her younger sister, who could no longer remember her white childhood or language, to leave her adopted Indian life, and Mary's turning away in tears as she fails. The book gives excellent coverage to the motivations of both Indians and non-Indians. The author writes well, with feeling and compassion:

The young westerners in this book did not know they were part of a great movement in history. They thought of their lives as sometimes adventurous, sometimes fun, occasionally dull. Some were trying to make a new country into a home, others trying to keep their old homes from being destroyed. [p.ix]

He uses analogy, metaphor, and similes:
After the Civil War, when surveyors arrived on the Great Plains, the Indians were puzzled to see them measuring the land. It was like some exotic ritual. The Indians used pegs for their tepees. But these men were not putting up tents. They were setting their "stick-stucks" all over the prairie. It was as if they staked some huge, invisible tent to cover all the land.

This is an excellent book, suitable either for reading aloud or for reading for pleasure. Chances for teen-agers to identify with historical characters their own age are abundant. Good.

467. Jones, Hettie.
COYOTE TALES.
New York: Holt, 1974. (6)

These are adult Indian tales edited, combined, and summarized for children and young adolescents. The four stories in the text are about Coyote, important in Indian mythology as trickster, enigma, transforming and creative spirit, and winner and loser combined. Well written with a feeling akin to the Uncle Remus stories in form and wording, this work is illustrated with black-and-white drawings by Louis Mofosie. In addition to pleasure reading, this book would be useful for several instructional processes; for instance, English teachers can use it to demonstrate similarities to myths from various cultures, the importance of authentic dialogue in a story, and the writer's unusual use of word patterning; drama and speech teachers can have their students try their interpretations of this dialogue pattern; social studies teachers can have their students examine the differing value patterns illustrated here. Good.

468. Jones, Hettie.
LONGHOUSE WINTER: IROQUOIS TRANSFORMATION TALES.
New York: Holt, 1972. (3–7)

These four tales come from the Iroquois nation. Each tale is different, yet each involves a human transformed into an animal. The methods of transformation are interesting: (1) a young chieftain becomes a robin; (2) a beautiful princess becomes a fish; (3) an evil dancer is transformed into a rattlesnake, and (4) a dead hunter is revived by wood animals. Fine, colorful geometric watercolor drawings by Nicholas Gaetano, reminiscent of art deco, add artistic dimensions to the brief stories. He uses muddied colors for details and clearer colors for accent and focus. Suitable for readers of all ages, the book may have greatest appeal for older readers who need visual stimulation. Good.

469. Jones, Hettie.
THE TREES STAND SHINING: POETRY OF THE NORTH AMERICAN INDIANS.
New York: Dial, 1971. (1 and up)
This book contains thirty-two brief American Indian songs, prayers, stories, and chants about nature. Written at approximately a second grade readability level, the contents would be good for reading aloud to children of all ages. Robert Andrew Parker's illustrations are good and his use of highlighting is interesting. Each drawing is different, and each is separate in content from the others (see his renditions of pain, the cricket, wind, and wounded men). Good.

470. Jones, Jane Clark.
AMERICAN INDIAN IN AMERICA: VOLS. 1 AND 2, EARLY 19TH CENTURY TO THE PRESENT.
Minneapolis, Minn.: Lerner, 1973. (5–11)
A description of Indian-white relations divided into three parts (Part I, "The Conquest of America in the 19th Century"; Part II, "The 20th Century Indian Awakening"; and Part III, "Amerindian Contributions") this is an excellent history book. It offers no easy solutions and deals, for the most part, in a balanced way with an incredibly varied subject area: genocide, white ambivalence, railroads, public lands, the buffalo, reservations, the Dawes Severalty Act of 1877, reservation scandals, squatters, World Wars I and II, Wovoka, relocation, termination, Indian unity, urban Indians, and prominent Indians (in sports, crafts, art, entertainment, professions, and community work). The book may be too optimistic about pan-Indian movements and may make gains seem more solid than they actually are. It does not present an in-depth study of Indian women, but describes well the controversy over who is an Indian. In attempting to counterbalance the traditional history as presented by whites, this book may err in forgetting white dreams and motivations. However, it *is* a book about Indians; adults will do well to offer young readers access to other books that present white diversity on these questions. The contents are illustrated by black-and-white drawings and photographs. Good.

471. Jones, Kenneth M.
WAR WITH THE SEMINOLES: 1835–1842.
New York: Watts, 1975. (4 and up)
Well written in an unobtrusive way, this book emphasizes the need for land as the basic source of Indian/non-Indian confrontation. It discusses the complex ingredients of the Seminole War: Spain; disagreeing factions among the Seminoles; blacks as slaves of the Seminoles; and the ambivalent relationships among black, Seminoles, and whites. The book presents unusually complete views of issues in a fair, evenhanded way. The language patterns found in the book are not limited by the fact that children are its designated audience; adults can also benefit from reading the author's skillful treatment. The child reader is seen as a partner, and the author writes to him or her as an equal, never as an inferior. Use for reference and background for both adults and children, grades four and up. Good.

472. Jones, Louis Thomas.
HIGHLIGHTS OF PUEBLOLAND.
San Antonio, Tex.: Naylor, 1968. (6–9)
The writer details his concept of life on the Pueblo and Navajo reservations of New Mexico, Arizona, Colorado, and Utah. An account of the personal beliefs about Indians of an apparently good, earnest, and worthy man, this book is not so much selective in what it includes as incomplete in what it leaves out. And it neglects, among other things, depth of coverage and scholarship, to name two. The writer's style can be seen in the following sample: "Upon my arrival from

the East my footsteps quickly found their way to this treasure-house of information" (preface). The book contains a section of author's notes and references, a bibliography, and an index. Poor.

473. Jones, Louis Thomas.
INDIAN CULTURES OF THE SOUTHWEST.
San Antonio, Tex.: Naylor, 1967.
(6 and up)

An excerpt from the preface gives a sample of the author's style of writing, largely composed of personal reaction:

> Childhood's schoolrooms had told me next to nothing about these Red Men. All seemed centered on the White Man's achievements. The Indian was spurned as a savage—fit only to be destroyed. My textbooks confirmed the adage that the "only good Indian was the dead Indian," a doctrine against which my innermost soul revolted. [p.vii]

Florid, courtly, old-fashioned writing gives the reader the feeling that he or she is having a personal chat during which Jones reminisces about his experiences. This book is like a travelogue about the Zuñi, Hopi, and Pueblo cultures: "Old Santa Fe lies at the base of the beautiful Sangre de Cristo Mountains, overlooking the rich lands of the Upper Rio Grande Valley" (p.4) and:

> As travellers we might like to linger in Old Santa Fe. Its spacious Cathedral of St. Francis of Assisi, its Fine Arts Museum, its new state capital building, its Laboratory of Anthropology, and many other institutions have their lure. [p.7]

He describes each pueblo he visits along the way, often stereotyping the Indians:

> True to ancient custom, the women of Taos still carry their household water from Taos Creek nearby, gracefully balanced on their heads, as did the maidens of Biblical times. Even today the women of Taos have no craving for running water or modern bathtubs, much less for our innumerable deter-

gents—thought to be essential to our modern life. [p.8]

However, in fairness, there are interesting delineations of games, ceremonies, Zuñi Salt Lake, the future, and an informative diagram of a Zuñi home, among other features. The book concentrates more on the Zuñi than any of the other Southwestern Indian cultures. There is a map of pueblos along the Rio Grande, a reading list, author's explanatory notes and references, and an index. Adequate.

474. Jones, Louis Thomas.
RED MAN'S TRAIL.
San Antonio, Tex.: Naylor, 1967.
(8 and up)

As usual, Jones includes many personal references and anecdotes in this book about Indian trails: "Those who have bolstered my slim gleanings in this quest are far too numerous to mention here" (p.ix). There is little sequence to or little easily discernable reason for selections of content other than the author's personal background, and the chapter headings reflect this confusion: "Highways and Byways," "A Visit to the Pueblos," "To the Apaches We Go." Jones leaves Asian-Americans and Afro-Americans out in the cold as he describes American history:

> Before we undertake to map the main travel lanes used by America's natives prior to the coming of Europeans, it might be helpful to explore some of the main characteristics of these trails, together with the items of trade which were related to their usage. [p.3]

There are, however, some interesting parts to the book. For example, Jones describes fifty-seven prehistoric shrines near Palm Springs, California, and gives a thought-provoking definition of an archaeologist's work, "to make the past live" (p.vii). The book is illustrated with black-and-white photographs, and there is a bibliography. Poor.

475. Jones, Louis Thomas.
SO SAY THE INDIANS.
San Antonio, Tex.: Naylor, 1970.
(7 and up)

Jones looks for Indian origins and histories in the folk tales he chooses for this book as he compares Indian folklore with that of other peoples. This book is autobiographical in places; in other parts the author intrudes his personal opinions, values, and feelings into the narrative. Some of his comparisons and analogies work fairly well, as, for example, his comparisons between Neil Armstrong and Columbus. But often his descriptions are inaccurate as well as condescending; for instance, in the following excerpt he has apparently forgotten about the Indian crops of beans, corn, squash, and peanuts: "These native sons then lived a simple life, close to the heart of nature. They seemed almost unaware of the wonder working fertility of the soil which lay under their unshod feet" (pp.174–75). He presents comments on Indian ethics, behavior, and culture patterns, all highly spiced with his personal opinions. He includes a background statement for each tale. Poor.

476. Jones, Weyman.
EDGE OF TWO WORLDS.
New York: Dial, 1968. (5–8)
This book, selected by the *New York Times* as one of the outstanding books for 1968, combines great writing and a wild plot. Calvin Harper, a young white survivor of a wagon train massacred by Comanches, meets Sequoyah, who is looking for the origins of his people. He takes Calvin along to make his trip safer from dangerous whites. In reality, Sequoyah did journey, probably into Mexico, to look for a band of Cherokees, and the book uses this as a point of departure. The work shows the controversy that surrounded Sequoyah: a silversmith who learned to read at age thirty-six, he was blamed by some tribal members for the loss of the eastern Cherokee lands. The author includes a vivid description of Oklahoma grasshoppers; anyone who has been plagued by them will readily understand it. J. C. Kocsis is a fine illustrator, and his black-and-white line drawings reflect his unusual talent. Whether the reader will appreciate his portrayal of Sequoyah in his

drawings as old, fragile, and ugly is a matter of taste. Good.

477. Jones, Weyman.
THE TALKING LEAF.
New York: Dial, 1965. (5–7)
This is a story about the Cherokees in the early part of the nineteenth century. The main character is Atsee, a wild Cherokee boy who determines to learn to read both Sequoyah's Cherokee syllabary and English. The book tells of Atsee's early life in the woods with his father, his days as a student, and his desire to teach other Cherokees to read. The author has obviously done a great deal of research, obvious in his mention of such aspects of Cherokee culture as the strings of beads that prompted Cherokee storytellers as they recounted old legends. The story reflects a feeling of the inevitability of white customs and culture as prevailing while the Cherokee culture is lost, and maintains a curiously hopeless stance for a book concerned with education. E. Harper Johnson's black-and-white line drawings are outstanding, particularly the closeups of faces (see pages 12 and 13), although occasionally the terrain looks more like Monument Valley than the East (see pages 84–85). Adequate.

478. Josephy, Alvin M.
THE AMERICAN HERITAGE BOOK OF INDIANS.
New York: American Heritage, 1961. (4–6)
Profusely illustrated with pictures, maps, and photographs and opening with President John F. Kennedy's fine introductory section, this book presents a survey of American Indian history, brief sketches of the life of some of the more widely known tribes, such as the Navajos, and some comments on American Indians of today. Kennedy reminds the reader that "American Indians defy any single description. They were and are far too individualistic" (p.7), a view adhered to throughout the book. The tone of the book is scholarly without being pedantic, the orientation of the writing is toward fairness and steadi-

ness, and the feel of the wording is surprisingly poetic for a textbook: "Time is the tonic chord in the story of the Indian" (p.10), although occasionally it is overly romantic, as in the section headed "People of the Dawn." The book is highly tied to dates and artifacts in its organization, and consequently, there is little detailing of social customs and mores. It correctly describes the types of settlers that England sent as "felons, toughs, and whores . . . swept over from London streets to fill colonist quotas" (p.166), and includes such explanatory details as the following, typical of white-Indian confrontations in California in 1871:

> Some ranchers in the Sacramento Valley found a steer wounded by Indians, trailed the Indians with dogs, cornered them in a cave, and killed "about thirty." . . . in the cave . . . were some Indian children. Kingsley could not bear to kill these children with his 56-calibre Spencer rifle. "It tore them up so bad." So he did it with his 38-calibre Smith and Wesson revolver. [p.305]

There is a thorough index. Good.

479. Josephy, Alvin M.
THE PATRIOT CHIEFS: A CHRONICLE OF AMERICAN INDIAN LEADERSHIP.
New York: Viking, 1969. (7–9)
This well-written historical review of Indian leadership begins with the legendary Iroquois, Hiawatha, before the coming of the whites, and ends with the surrender of Joseph's Nez Percés in 1877. Both the tragedy and heroism of the Indian is told through the lives of these men. The stories are well balanced, and would add valuable information on Indians for an educational component in the classroom. There are several portraits in black and white at the beginning of the chronicle, and maps are scattered throughout the book as needed. Good.

480. Katz, Jane B., ed.
WE RODE THE WIND: RECOLLECTIONS OF NINETEENTH-CENTURY TRIBAL LIFE.
Minneapolis: Lerner, 1975. (5–7)

Legends, traditions, autobiographies, and historical events are told by both Indian men and women in this fine collection of Indian recollections. The difficulties of translating from Indian languages to English are discussed. A good introduction presents a picture of the contrasts to be seen in various Indian lifestyles. Although the volume has more stories about boys than girls, there are good discussions of the role of women: "A woman had to be neither a wife nor a mother in order to maintain a place of respect with her people" (p.62). Good.

481. Keegan, Marcia.
THE TAOS INDIANS AND THEIR SACRED BLUE LAKE.
New York: Messner, 1972. (2–4)
The Taos Indians in 1916 had their sacred Blue Lake taken from them by the United States government. This is the story of how the Taos struggled to get it back again. The book details the sophisticated legal fight the tribe waged and provides readers, both Indian and non-Indian, with a picture of a successful Indian activity produced by concerted action. This is an unusual concept to present to such young readers, and the author does it well through the use of easy-to-read (but not simplistic) language utilizing quotes from people actively involved in the fight, including young children. The book presents Taoseño history up to the present (1972). It is illustrated by effective black-and-white photographs that present realistic views of present-day life, such as a picture of the family seated around a table on which can be seen a milk carton and a kerosine lamp. The author could easily revise her material to write another book for older children or junior high and high school readers on the same subject. A rarity—this book is an outstanding, literate example of a presentation of meaningful current issues to very young children. Good.

482. Keith, Harold.
KOMANTCIA.
New York: Crowell, 1965. (7 and up)

In the story of Pedro, a young Spanish boy captured and adopted into the Comanche tribe, the author emphasizes the stark reality of the survival of a group of Indians who lived in one of the bleakest, most demanding sections of North America. Separated from his brother, who was captured along with him, Pedro vows to bide his time until he can escape, find his brother, and rejoin his father, whom he feels will leave Spain to find his sons when he learns of their capture. The book seems to follow what is known of rancho life in 1867, and includes the migration of the Spanish to Mexico, and the relationships between the Spanish emigres, the Mexicans, the Americanos and the Comanches. In addition, the descriptions of the culture and practices of the Comanches appear to be quite accurate. Unlike most stories about captive whites (or vice versa), no situation or character is romanticized. If anything, each is depicted in a completely realistic context. This is not a book for the squeamish. Some of the cultural practices described may upset very young readers. The writing is exceptionally well done and shows the effects of thorough research on the author's part, although his use of the term *squaw* seems unnecessary and out of place. Notwithstanding, the story is a fascinating series of adventures, which seem both plausible and possible. Good.

483. Key, Alexander.
CHEROKEE BOY.
Philadelphia: Westminster, (no date). (4–6)
This story has its setting in the Cherokee Nation, presently Georgia and the Carolinas, in the year 1838. The hero is Tsi-ya, who is fifteen. When it becomes apparent that the Army will act upon orders to remove the Cherokee Nation, Tsi-ya's father leaves for Washington to appeal the decision, telling Tsi-ya to find the "Secret Place" where the Nation could be safe from the whites in case the Army comes. The lad succeeds, but before he can return with the information, the Army has moved in. Following the youthful Tsi-ya, the men of the tribe march the "Trail of

Tears" from the Carolinas to Indian Territory. They suffer many trials and dangers —weather, animals, illness, and death. Finally he and a few survivors of the tribe arrive at their destination. Adequate.

484. Kilpatrick, Jack Frederick, and Kilpatrick, Anna Gritts.
RUN TOWARD THE NIGHTLAND: MAGIC OF THE OKLAHOMA CHEROKEES.
Dallas, Tex.: Southern Methodist Univ. Pr., 1967. (7 and up)
Jack Frederick Kilpatrick has been called America's greatest composer by no less a musician than Leopold Stokowski, and Kilpatrick received the second citation ever given by the Cherokee Nation (the first went to Sequoyah). In a demonstration of remarkable versatility, this same man has written a book about the place of magic in Cherokee life. This is, in effect, a recipe book for Cherokee spells, medicines, and magic—the reader can look up any life situation, such as hunting, weather, plants, traveling, love, law courts, law enforcement problems, and so on, and find a cure, a chant, or an action to take. The author comments that during his research for writing the book, he often came across Cherokee journals written in Sequoyah's syllabary where, "side by side with an incantation to discomfort a demon may be a set of figures that attest to the comforting fact that the Lord's work is prospering in the Baptist Church nearby" (p.4). The book is fascinating, and will open up a new world to many readers. There is a section of author notes and a bibliography. Good.

485. Kimble, George H. T.
HUNTERS AND COLLECTORS.
New York: McGraw-Hill, 1970. (2–3)
This is a social studies type of book that details the hunting and collecting of food in several cultures throughout the world, including the African Bushmen and BaMbuti, modern-day Americans, Australian Aborigines, and the Eskimo. The writing is similar to that often found in social studies texts: "These are very cold places most of the year" (p.12), as is the style of the

black-white-green illustrations by Jean Zallinger. There is an index. Adequate.

486. Kirk, Ruth.
DAVID, YOUNG CHIEF OF THE QUILEUTES.
New York: Harcourt, 1967. (3–4)
This is a perceptively written and photographed account of the daily life and activities of an eleven year-old Quileute Indian boy, David, picked by his grandfather to be chief when he was three years old. He is being prepared to lead his people when he is grown. The photographs and the narrative tell a heartwarming and authentic story of the past, the present, and the closeness of the Indians to the rivers and forests. The book describes traditions which are slowly being lost because many of the young no longer learn them or pass them on. The author suggests that living in two worlds is difficult, and that the Indians hope the young chief will grow wise and guide them through troubled times. The photographs, while not exceptional technically, successfully picture David's life as he studies spelling, washes a school bus, and watches his grandfather shape a canoe. There is an interesting description of a modern-day potlatch. Good.

487. Kirk, Ruth, with
Daugherty, Richard D.
HUNTERS OF THE WHALE: THE ADVENTURES OF NORTHWEST COAST ARCHAEOLOGY.
New York: Morrow, 1974. (5 and up)
This story of the excavation of an archaeological site on the Makah Reservation in the Pacific Northwest is written in such an interesting fashion that it could be mistaken for a novel, and makes archaeology fascinating. It is illustrated by large, plentiful black-and-white photographs by Ruth and Louis Kirk. The details of the Makahs' participation in the designing of the project, the actual excavation, and the establishing of the Makah Museum are encouraging signs of effective tribal decisions. The whole organization of the book indicates the fine reportorial skills of the authors. This book represents a great journalistic idea well executed, and would make a good idea text for journalism and photography students at high school and college levels, as well as a good reference on Indian initiative for all students. Good.

488. Knudson, R. R.
FOX RUNNING.
New York: Harper, 1975. (7 and up)
This is an excellent story incorporating the idea of the bravery and skill of a young Apache girl, Fox Running, with the attitudes essential for all accomplished professional and nonprofessional athletes. The story concerns a young Apache girl who is recruited to run for the Uinta University track team. She effectively combines the techniques learned from the coach and her teammates with the teachings of her grandfather. The book is written in a style that will appeal to most junior high school readers. Because it is written almost exclusively in dialogue, it is suitable for reading aloud to children younger than the designated age group. The way in which the author has captured the "spirit" of the Apache may satisfy the more demanding reader but may confuse the less sophisticated. For this reason it is suggested that supplementary readings or explanations accompany the book. The story and the prose is romanticized to a certain extent, but manages to overcome this handicap through a believable execution of an unusual idea. Good.

489. Kohn, Bernice.
TALKING LEAVES: THE STORY OF SEQUOYAH.
New York: Hawthorn, 1969. (1–4)
This is an uneven biography of Sequoyah. On the positive side, the book certainly impresses the reader with its beautiful format, simple language, thought-provoking concepts, interesting details (for example, his wife burned Sequoyah's first efforts at a syllabary), and, of course, the book is about a superb man. On the negative side, the plot skips from the South to Mexico to Oklahoma, with little motivation provided for the moves;

there is no mention of the Trail of Tears at all, leaving out one of the most important events in Cherokee history occurring during Sequoyah's lifetime; and the writing is often too simple: "Even the president of the United States heard of what Sequoyah had done. To show how proud he was of Sequoyah, he gave him a gift" [unpaged], or "They [Indians] did not keep records of when people were born or when they died" (unpaged). Valli's color illustrations are pretty, but the subjects often don't look particularly like Indians. Poor.

490. Koob, Theodora.
HEAR A DIFFERENT DRUMMER.
Philadelphia: Lippincott, 1968. (7–9)
The plot of this story is more concerned with white colonial life than with Indians. Obadiah Douglass is apprenticed to Ezra Wickhart, sadistic master leathercraftsman. Mistreatment causes Obad to run away as often as he can. He is discovered in his latest hiding place by Feste Tennent, a soldier and spy for the English army. Feste takes pity on him and makes him his servant until Obad decides to return to Ezra, because his mother is ill and needs him. When they part, Obad promises to join Feste, his hero, someday at Fort Cumberland. When his mother dies, Obad sets out to find Feste, whom he now believes is his father. He is helped on his long journey by a trapper, his daughter, and an Indian named Chaugegau. Chaugegau is the inscrutable, silent type of Indian who appears and disappears from the depths of the forest at intervals to help Obad. The treatment of Indians in the story is rather sketchy. As individuals, with the exception of Chaugegau, they are incidental to the trials and tribulations of the main characters. As a group they cause great suffering by their attacks on the English. Indians on both sides are shown to take scalps, including Chaugegau. Story: Good. Resource for Indians: Poor.

491. Kopit, Arthur L.
INDIANS: A PLAY.
New York: Hill & Wang, 1969.
(9 and up)

In this play, it is difficult to separate fact from fiction regarding Buffalo Bill, Wild Bill Hickok, and the Indians—Geronimo, Chief Joseph, Sitting Bull, and others. Farce and fraud reign throughout the plot and the characterizations, especially in the cases of Buffalo Bill, Hickok, Buntline, and the politicians who were sent to "deal fairly" with the Indians. The Indians are clearly the victims, and Buffalo Bill, deluded by his own "super hero" publicity, cannot quite figure out why things are not as Ned Buntline wrote them. This is an excellent and sophisticated play about a period of American history that could stand as a monument to white greed and stupidity. Good.

492. Kroeber, Theodora Krob.
ISHI, LAST OF HIS TRIBE.
Berkeley, Calif.: Parnassus, 1964.
(6 and up)
The story of Ishi describes the life of the last known living Yahi of the Yana tribe, both in the western foothills of Mount Lassen and at the anthropological museum at the University of California at Berkeley, after his rescue from loneliness by Alfred Kroeber, the curator of the Indian Museum, who was also chairman of the Department of Anthropology and Ethnology. An incredible story, movingly written, the book details Yana customs and beliefs and presents a fine portrait of Ishi and his lives. A classic, the book is a must for every library. Good.

493. Kroeber, Theodora, and
Heizer, Robert F.
ALMOST ANCESTORS: THE FIRST CALIFORNIANS.
San Francisco: Sierra Club, 1968.
(4 and up)
A tremendous book, this volume combines poetic text with fine black-and-white pictures of California Indians taken from 1850 to the present. The faces in the photographs are beautifully reproduced, even those in the earlier photographs. Explanations of the process used would have been of interest to photographers. Historical and cultural comments and asides, in the

typically effective Sierra Club prose, are interspersed among the photographs. Younger children can enjoy the photographs, but the readability level of the text is around seventh grade. A great gift book for anyone interested in California, this is a classic. Good.

494. Kubie, Nora Benjamin.
THE FIRST BOOK OF ARCHAEOLOGY.
New York: Watts, 1957. (3–7)
An overview of archaeology, this book briefly comments on Greece, Ninevah, Stonehenge, Egypt, Rome, Europe, Mesopotamia, Troy, the Americas, stratigraphy, and the discipline of archaeology. In this very brief, simplified introduction, four pages are given to archaeology in the Americas: one page to North America, two pages to Central America, and one page to the Inca empire. The vocabulary is fairly simple. The book should not be used alone, but could be helpful in exposing children to the vocabulary of the archaeologist, and could be an initial reading experience. Adequate.

495. LaFarge, Oliver.
A PICTORIAL HISTORY OF THE AMERICAN INDIAN.
New York: Crown, 1956. (6 and up)
An incredible range of black-and-white photographs from pictures of shanties in Pinoleville, California, to Tlingit blanket designs highlight this pictorial history of the American Indians. LaFarge writes well, and he does not talk down to young readers in this comprehensive coverage. The content is not restricted to history; there are sections on art, the "Non-Vanishing American" (Indian), and customs and social organization, such as the description of berdaches. The book should be reissued in a more modern, more exciting format: it still has much to say. There is an index. Dated. Good.

496. Ladd, Elizabeth.
THE INDIANS ON THE BONNET.
New York: Morrow, 1971. (3–6)
This is a surprisingly well-written book.

"The Bonnet" is a forty-acre estate along the coast of Maine belonging to Mr. Barnes, who now resides in Florida. Although Mr. Barnes professes to be honest and honorable, he is really a designing cheat. Jess, a young white boy, meets a little Indian girl who lives with her father, a caretaker for Mr. Barnes. The two discover Mr. Barnes's plan; upon his return to the estate, he repairs the skiff poorly (and cheaply), insures it for a large amount of money, and attempts to sink it for the insurance money. He is apprehended. This story portrays a scheming, contriving white man and honest, trustworthy Indians in stereotyped terms. Although the plot is exaggerated and juvenile, some of the dialogue rings true. The sentiments expressed are often pious and prissy: "The Ravens were not only Indians, they were Catholics as well, the first Catholics he had ever known" (p.41). Richard Cuffari's black-and-white illustrations reflect his usual satisfactory work. Adequate.

497. Lampman, Evelyn Sibley.
CAYUSE COURAGE.
New York: Harcourt, 1970. (7–9)
A fictionalized account of the Whitman "massacre," this book tells the Cayuse Indian side through the story of a young Indian boy. Samuel Little-Pony had broken his arm in a white man's abandoned trap. Even though Dr. Whitman had cured the poison which affected the wound, the arm was shattered, as was Samuel's dream of being a Cayuse warrior. Samuel stayed with the whites after his recovery, learning their language and their lifestyle. But when more and more settlers arrived, Dr. Whitman sent Samuel back to the Indian village. This puzzled and angered Samuel, and he vacillated, one moment cursing the whites and urging the Cayuse to fight them, the next trying to warn them. Samuel was grieved when Dr. Whitman, his wife, and many others were killed by the Cayuse. The Cayuse had attacked because over half the tribe had died of measles, because Whitman hadn't paid for the land he used, and because Cayuse

ponies couldn't graze on their old pasture land, among other reasons. Lampman writes well, and does a great deal of research. Her description of the spirit vision episode is particularly good, and her characterization of the Whitmans as kindly, but prejudiced, is convincing: for example, Cayuse visitors were only allowed into the "Cayuse room." However, her portrayal of the Cayuse treatment of women shows them as more subservient than they probably were or are: "Woman, where is my hat? Find my hat or I will whip the skin from your back!" (p.9); or "Samuel was momentarily sorry about Helen, but there was no time to think of her then. After all, she was only a girl-child, and he had a man's responsibility of interpreting for his chief" (p.176). Samuel's final decision to go away with a Catholic priest to become a translator seems too convenient. Adequate.

498. Lampman, Evelyn Sibley.
HALF-BREED.
New York: Doubleday, 1967. (6–8)
Lampman adds new depth and insight to the dilemma of being a half-breed in this story. Hardy Hollingshead, a Crow half-breed, leaves the home of his Crow mother in search of his white father, Jesse. He eventually locates his father's cabin, but finds it empty. His father's sister, Rhoda, arrives unexpectedly from the East and takes over both cabin and Hardy. He resents bitterly the chores she gives him because they are "woman's work" in the Crow tradition, and resolves to return to the Crows as soon as she is able to manage on her own. Hardy's father eventually returns, and explains that white people, men and women, do what needs to be done on the land and at home without regard for whose work it is. The remainder of the story concerns the life Rhoda, Hardy, and the wandering Jesse create for themselves. The treatment of Crow customs is well done through the device of juxtaposing white and Crow ways in Hardy's mind as he constantly compares the two during his periods of adjustment and conflict: for instance, his aunt's fetish

for washing bothers him because Crows are clean, not dirty like the Indians he sees on the town streets; he resents having to dress the deer after he kills it because that is woman's work; and when his aunt burns his medicine bag, hatred and resentment almost cause him to bolt. The process of learning about each other's ways takes place slowly. Eventually Hardy comes to respect his aunt and she learns to understand him. The characters in the story are sharply delineated; the story moves along briskly; the sometimes painful process of one human being coming to know and understand another very different individual is artfully detailed; there is a good cadence to the talk of the mountain men; and the boy's gradual acceptance of his wandering father is movingly done. Lampman as an author is either liked or disliked by her readers. The black-and-white drawings by Ann Lampman are competently done. Good.

499. Lampman, Evelyn Sibley.
NAVAJO SISTER.
New York: Doubleday, 1956. (4–7)
This book presents the adjustment problems of a Navajo Indian girl attending school away from home for the first time. With so many books concerned with adjustments to boarding school, adults may wish to provide students with additional sources that will acquaint children with other possible lifestyles for Indian young people. This book is not quite as good as most of Lampman's work, either in story design or plot development. The speech patterns are not quite right for Navajos, and the ending is not quite convincing. Paul Lantz's illustrations are good, and his people look like Navajos. Adequate.

500. Lampman, Evelyn Sibley.
ONCE UPON THE LITTLE BIG HORN.
New York: Crowell, 1971. (5–8)
Flashing back and forth between whites and Indians, spotlighting main characters and lesser known participants, Lampman has written a readable account of the battle of the Little Big Horn for

young readers. Factual and unromanticized, the book tells the story from many points of view. Lampman ends the story at the point where Captain Benteen learns of the deaths of Custer and his men and rides back to camp; she does not include the aftermath of trials, accusations, and the pursuit of the Indians. Usually fair in her treatment, occasionally she uses questionable words such as *buck* and *squaw*. She deals rather gently with all her characters, Custer, Sitting Bull, Gall, Benteen, and the rest, leaving the assessing of rights and wrongs to others. This very evenhanded treatment, while admirable in some respects, casts a dullness over the book that keeps it from igniting into excitement. Good.

501. Lampman, Evelyn Sibley.
THE POTLATCH FAMILY.
New York: Atheneum, 1975.
(7 and up)
Controversial as ever, in this book Lampman tells the story of a Chinook Indian girl who does not live on the reservation, but comes to cherish her Indian traditions. Controversial because of what she has her characters say:

And I found out that right now the Indian is very big. White people are interested in him, and it's paying off financially. Not from the government especially, but from the people themselves. . . . The whites come and shell out high prices to sleep in a luxury hotel just because it's run by Indians. Some of them pay to stay in a tepee and sleep on a cement floor. [p.67]

and do (the father has a tendency to alcoholism; the girl has adopted many white ways and attitudes). But the book is primarily controversial because it tackles difficult themes, because the characters choose actions that will offend some groups—non-Indian and Indian. Lampman tells a good story here, with an easy flow to the writing. The various episodes fit well into the plot, and she has a flair for teen-age conversation patterns: "Miss Miller always calls everybody by their last names. I don't know why" (p.4). Good.

502. Lampman, Evelyn Sibley.
RATTLESNAKE CAVE.
New York: Atheneum, 1974. (5)
Believable incidents and dialogue contribute to the effectiveness of this book, well illustrated by Pamela Johnson. In the story a sickly city boy comes to a Montana ranch where he meets Indian children and adults who influence him to become more natural, less spoiled. The author draws realistic pictures of a city home where the father travels too much and parents fight over the care of the children, as well as pictures of mischievous young Indians and non-Indians who delight in passing off a white boy as Indian to tourists and who aren't above tricking them into offering more money:

"Your name is Horse?" asked Jamie. "Just plain Horse?" "It's Horace, really," admitted the boy, making a face. "But Horse is better. Sometimes I tell the goofy tourists my name is Running Horse or Red Horse or something like that. It makes them feel good. If I make up a fancy enough name, they give me two bits extra to pose for a picture." [p.93]

Somehow, the idea of boys playing a typical prank on tourists makes them seem more real; the portrayal of constantly serious-minded boys would be more difficult to accept. The book contains a characterization of boys who read as odd, as the butt of jokes, and as amusing. Good readers deserve better than this sort of stereotype. Good.

503. Lampman, Evelyn Sibley.
WHITE CAPTIVES.
New York: Atheneum, 1975. (6–9)
In a fictionalized account of a true story about Olive and Mary Oatman, two white girls enslaved first by Tonto Apaches and later the Mojaves, the author presents a dispassionate view of life among the Southwest Indians during the mid-nineteenth century. While the plight of the two girls seems harsh as well as barbaric, the young reader is helped to understand the demands and often Pyrrhic victories of the Indians, who fought to survive in their en-

vironment. There is a bitter quality to the story, from both the white and Indian point of view. There is also wry humor when cultural practices clash; for example the older girl, Olive, who lived to be returned to the whites, is honored by the Mojave by having her face tatooed to make her beautiful. The young reader is helped to recognize that what brings joy to one culture can bring pain to another. An interesting story, written simply with clarity; though young readers may not necessarily be able to identify with the characters, they will certainly appreciate their circumstance. This book is based on the Reverend R. B. Stratton's *Captivity of the Oatman Girls, Being an Interesting Narrative of Life among the Apache and Mohave Indians*, written with the help of Olive and Lorenzo Oatman. (Stratton's book was a bestseller at the time, and was, perhaps, as influential in its way on Indian policy as *Uncle Tom's Cabin* was on the Civil War.) Many reviewers do not like this book, because they feel it puts Indians in a bad light. Others feel that Lampman's writing, evenhandedness, and careful research, plus the historical importance to the Indians of the capture and enslavement of these two girls is worth that price. Be prepared for controversy if you buy the book. Good.

504. Lampman, Evelyn Sibley.
THE YEAR OF SMALL SHADOW.
New York: Harcourt, 1971. (5–7)
This story revolves around Small Shadow, an eleven-year-old Indian boy whose father is sent to the penitentiary for one year for taking a white man's horse without permission. Small Shadow is placed in the custody of the attorney who defended his father. Renamed Shad (for Shadow), the boy learns to respect his foster father, a kind and loyal man. Many of the white villagers are skeptical about Shad and treat him with varying degrees of animosity and friendliness. However, Shad's good nature and gentleness eventually is appreciated by all. When his father is finally released from prison, Shad has problems deciding whether to stay with the whites or go back home. Set in the Pacific Northwest at the end of the nineteenth century, the book is well written and contains a number of convincing episodes, such as the scene in which the ladies make Shad some new clothes, and a funny episode where an Indian wants to trade thirty horses for a girl. Occasionally, Lampman lapses from her usual good writing, as in the pidgin English the boy talks at first: "I have eleven summers" (p.43). Good.

505. LaPointe, Frank.
THE SIOUX TODAY.
New York: Crowell-Collier, 1972. (6–9)
This is a collection of very short stories about young Sioux high school students and recent graduates. Approximately half of the stories are about boys and half about girls. An equal proportion of the stories end with the main character either dying or left in some bad situation. The stories are told in a documentary style, using brief sentences; few embellishments or literary devices are used by the author. He is a realist, in the classical sense of the term, and his stories, in style and content, are reminiscent of some of Stephen Crane's (such as *The Blue Hotel*). This is an excellent book in which the author presents the plight, struggles, and a few of the hard-wrought successes of many young Sioux at present. Photographs illustrating how reservation Sioux young people live (housing, clothing, entertainment, ceremonies) are scattered throughout the book. This book would be especially effective for, but not limited to, slow high school readers. The content and concepts presented are adult in scope, but the actual reading level of the text is about fifth grade —a happy circumstance for high school remedial reading teachers who are always searching for good books their students can read. Good.

506. Latham, Jean L., tr.
WA O'KA.
Indianapolis, Ind.: Bobbs-Merrill, (no date). (2–6)

This is a translation of a Spanish story. In it a young Dakota brave, Wa O'Ka, who holds enviable records for fleetness, archery, and riding but has no personal wealth, falls in love with the beautiful Starry Night. Her father will not approve the marriage until the brave demonstrates extraordinary bravery and cunning, and he demands that Wa O'Ka bring "five black horses with white manes, five white horses with black manes, the hide of Blue Bear, and a feather from Great Eagle." All these feats seem impossible, but with much effort and the help of an old woman (his godmother, and possibly a witch) Wa O'Ka accomplishes all and wins the hand of Starry Night. Upon the death of her father, Wa O'Ka rules the tribe and the land. Adequate.

507. Lauritzen, Jonreed.
THE ORDEAL OF THE YOUNG HUNTER.
Boston: Little, 1954. (5–7)
This is a story of a young Navajo boy maturing and growing in understanding of the values of his own culture and that of the whites. The central conflict revolves around his losing some of the sheep under his care to a cougar, the belief held by some Navajos that he is strangely influenced by bears, and his killing a cougar and becoming a hero at the Old Flagstaff Powwow. The plot at times is contrived, as at the ending, when everyone is impressed by his kill, and often pretentiously quaint in wording:

> "Do you know what she looks like, Antelope?" Jim went on. He saw how Jadih's eyes went to the goods on the shelves. "She is more beautiful than a can of pork and beans, a package of cornflakes, or even a bottle of cherry pop. Her eyes are the color of bright brown leather. Her hair is like the cloud ten minutes before sunup. Her skin glows like a ripe golden plum with the sunlight in it." [p.66]

The Navajo lifestyles described are more consistent with those of the 1954 publication date than the present and have a dated feel. Hoke Denetsosie's black-and-white illustrations are well done. Dated. Adequate.

508. Lavine, Sigmund A.
GAMES THE INDIANS PLAYED.
New York: Dodd, 1974. (5–8)
This book classifies the games played by various Indians as: (1) games of chance, such as stick and dice games; (2) games of dexterity, such as ball games and running games; and (3) children's games. Many facts and details about gaming are included: for instance, recognition of the Divine Twins, Spider Woman, and the Evil Spirit; the purposes of the games (entertainment, bringing rain, appeasing the gods, healing the sick, etc.); ceremonial supplications (prayers, gestures, fasting, and appeals for skill, speed, keen sight and fearlessness); wearing charms to assure success or ward off evil spirits; earning awards; physical punishment to combat evil spirits; burying gaming objects with dead athletes; trickery and gambling about a game; and sex-typed games (cornhusk dolls for girls, active games for boys). This book contains an interesting collection of stories about Indian games which should appeal to many middle school and junior high readers. Generally, this is a well written book; however, the author's use of the term *red men* is inappropriate. Interesting black-and-white photographs and old prints illustrate the book. There is a section describing the author and an index. Good.

509. Lavine, Sigmund A.
THE GHOSTS THE INDIANS FEARED.
New York: Dodd, 1975. (5–7)
A summary of the religious beliefs of past and present American Indians is given in this book. The author presents a definite view—valid no doubt, but in some instances overstated: "There was fear on every side"; and "However, many Indians have merely swapped the superstitions of yesteryear for those of the white man" (p.59). The book is well written and is illustrated by black-and-white drawings by Jane O'Regan, as well as by photographs and prints. The issues brought up in this book may not be what many people want to read, dealing as they do with fears, ghosts, and the like. This is not a presentation of Indian religious practices

as nice, safe "noble savage" rites, but of the religions of people who sometimes face awesome environmental realities. The vocabulary and readability level of the text is upper elementary; however, the content level is considerably older. This book presents a deep discussion of issues with which the superficial student of "Indians" may not be prepared to deal. Serious students will disagree on the accuracy of this book; such controversy should spark further study, and schoolteachers, in particular, should be prepared. An unusual book. Good.

510. Lavine, Sigmund A.
THE HORSES THE INDIANS RODE.
New York: Dodd, 1974. (4–6)
This story of the relationships between horses and Indians from their earliest encounters is illustrated with black-and-white photographs and old prints. The text is written at a level higher than the book format indicates. A good, factual social studies type of book, this one is unusual in that it would read aloud well. Good.

511. Lavine, Sigmund A.
THE HOUSES THE INDIANS BUILT.
New York: Dodd, 1975. (3–5)
Black-and-white prints and photographs illustrate a social studies type of text describing different Indian shelters. The content, writing, vocabulary, and concepts, is of a higher grade level than the format, making this book most useful to above average readers. By showing a variety of dwellings, this book certainly helps finish off the "tepee" legend. Adequate.

512. Lavine, Sigmund A.
INDIAN CORN AND OTHER GIFTS.
New York: Dodd, 1974. (3–5)
An instructional-style book of the kind often used for classroom social studies research, this is a thorough coverage about indigenous American plants and crops, extensively illustrated by black-and-white photographs and old prints showing such interesting processes as ancient ways of planting and the like. The author describes the histories and the uses of such plants as corn, sugar, beans, squashes, green

peppers, chili, tomatoes, peanuts, cacao, etc. He provides much detailed information, including the puzzle of the ancestry of the corn plant, which is complicated by the fact that corn does not reseed itself and will die out without human assistance. There is a section on the original territories of the tribes mentioned in the book, a bibliography, and an index. Good.

513. Lawson, Marion.
PROUD WARRIOR: THE STORY OF BLACK HAWK.
New York: Hawthorn, 1968. (5–9)
Based on Black Hawk's autobiography, this book tells the story of Black Hawk from the time he was thirteen until he died—old, bitter, and rejected. The author's writing style is pleasing but romanticized, as is apparent from the first three sentences of the book:
Paddles flashed over the flood-high waters. Horses, led or ridden by the strong young hunters and warriors, were trotting down the forest trails. Spring, Mannocumink, was calling the Sauk people home to Saukenuk from the winter hunting grounds. [p.11]
The book itself is accurate enough in its facts and dates, although Keokuk is portrayed as a villain with no redeeming qualities, which seems unlikely, since he was able to recruit so many followers. Adequate.

514. Leekley, Thomas B.
THE WORLD OF MANABOZHO: TALES OF THE CHIPPEWA INDIANS.
New York: Vanguard, 1965. (4–7)
These fifteen tales come from the Algonquin Indians, especially the Ojibwas and Ottawas. The hero of the stories is Manabozho, a wonder worker. Not quite a god because of his occasional selfishness or cruelty, he can turn himself into animal shapes, thus bewildering friend and foe. These legends were reedited, interpreted, and developed into a story for young readers, thereby deleting some of their authenticity. Yeffe Kimball, illustrator, uses the birch-bark picture writings of the Eastern Woodlands as an interesting visual accompaniment for the tales. This story has

appeal for older elementary children. Adequate.

515. Levenson, Dorothy.
HOMESTEADERS AND INDIANS.
New York: Watts, 1971. (3–5)
Primarily concerned with white homesteading and Indian wars on the Plains, this book is illustrated by black-and-white photographs and drawings from the era. There are brief discussions of other Indian wars, such as Chief Joseph and the Nez Percé. It is difficult from the book's design and organization to get an idea for the chronology and totality of the situation, and the writing is often so simplified as to be of little help to young scholars:

> After the Civil War, Custer was sent West to fight Indians. He had no high opinion of treaties or Indians or anyone who tried to stop him from doing what he wanted to do. [p.78]

The brief section on women of the West is confined to white women and is rather sexist: "Women out west had one advantage. There were more men than women" (p.31); and "A homesteader's wife had to work hard, but if her husband mistreated her there were other men ready to protect her" (p.32)—no doubt a great comfort to a woman in a soddy seventy miles from her nearest neighbor. The section does, however, mention that women's rights were often secured first in the West. The section on black settlers reminds the reader that blacks also played an important part in the settlement of the West. The major problem with the book is its stylistic jerkiness, its confused organization, and its lack of delineation between important and trivial facts. The major strengths of the book are the unusual photographs and drawings used as illustrations and the uniqueness of some of its subject matter. Adequate.

516. Levitas, Gloria; Vivelo, Frank R.; and Jacqueline, J., eds.
AMERICAN INDIAN PROSE AND POETRY: WE WAIT IN THE DARKNESS.
New York: Putnam, Capricorn Books, 1974. (8 and up)

This book includes literature from the Northwest Coast, Plateau, California, Great Basin, and Southwest Indians. There is a detailed introduction which discusses the tribal designation, culture area, and language of each Indian group. Many myths are included in the book; stories from both before and after the coming of the whites. Many of the early myths deal with animals and are allegorical. Good.

517. Lewis, Richard.
I BREATHE A NEW SONG: POEMS OF THE ESKIMO.
New York: Simon & Schuster, 1971. (3 and up)
Through this excellent collection of Eskimo poetry, the author has managed to convey the cruel beauty of the Arctic environment, and how the Eskimo people have learned to live and to deal with it. In addition to identifying the tribe with which each poem is associated, the author includes selections that explain the culture as well as the feelings and attitudes of the people the poems represent. The introduction by Edmund Carpenter provides background information essential to understanding the poetry. The illustrations by Jessie Oonark are consistent with the theme and beauty of the poetry. Good.

518. Libhart, Myles, and Amiote, Arthur.
PHOTOGRAPHS AND POEMS BY SIOUX CHILDREN FROM THE PORCUPINE DAY SCHOOL, PINE RIDGE INDIAN RESERVATION, SOUTH DAKOTA.
An exhibition organized by the Indian Arts and Crafts Board of the U.S. Dept. of the Interior.
Rapid City, S. Dak.: The Tipi Shop, Inc., 1971. (6 and up)
Each of the photographs and poems presented in this enchanting book was created by Oglala Sioux students of the Porcupine Day School, operated by the Bureau of Indian Affairs on the Pine Ridge Reservation in South Dakota. The book is one result of the innovative visual arts cultural program being conducted there. The poems and photographs are simple, yet remarkable in aesthetic expression,

and reflect dramatically a view of life close to nature, subtly affected by the inroads of modern technology. The predominant themes are winter, nature, places and people in the rural environment, sadness, the past, and hope for the future. A sample:

Open window
Greeting light and darkness
Cold, wind and heat
Waiting for nothing or anything.
Ethleen Iron Cloud
Age 14

Good.

519. Linderman, Frank B.
PRETTY-SHIELD: MEDICINE WOMAN OF THE CROWS.
New York: Day, 1972. (5–7)
A fascinating account of a Crow medicine woman who lived during the years that the old ways were vanishing, this book also tells a great deal about the author who researched the story, many times through the aid of a translator. The author knows his limits, for the most part: "I have found Indian women diffident, and so self-effacing that acquaintance with them is next to impossible" (p.9); but occasionally he misinterprets: "Nothing is more bewildering to me than recording the dreams of old Indians . . . to determine exactly where the dream begins and ends" (p.11). The writing is good; the story is convincing. Often the reader feels that the woman told only what she wanted the author to know, no doubt for good reasons; what she does permit him to glimpse is more than any of us could have seen. Good.

520. Lisitzsky, Genevieve H.
FOUR WAYS OF BEING HUMAN.
New York: Viking, 1965. (7 and up)
This anthropologist evaluates the cultures of people of the rain forest, the ice cap, the Pacific, and the desert. Devoting one section of this book to each culture, Lisitzsky examines the lifestyles of the Semang of the Malay Peninsula, who live in the rain forest; the Eskimos, in the Arctic; the Maoris, surrounded by the Pacific Ocean; and the Hopi, who dwell in the land of little rain. Their food, clothing, philosophies, values, and shelters, are all influenced by the geography and the meteorology of their homeland. The concepts developed in this volume will be thought-provoking for the youthful readers for whom it is designed, and for the adults who work with them. Good.

521. Lockett, Sharon.
NO MOCCASINS TODAY.
Nashville, Tenn.: Nelson, 1970. (5–8)
The portrayal of an Indian boy who learns to compete successfully in business as he sees the commercial possibilities of selling hand-hewn canoes and building up a resort on Indian land, this is an optimistic and romanticized book. It is good to read about Indians achieving success (in this case as a star basketball player, a businessman, and as a person able to combine two cultures). However, the writing is stiff, the characterizations poorly and superficially done, and the ending is contrived. Writing and organization: Uneven. Story: Adequate.

522. Loh, Jules.
LORDS OF THE EARTH.
New York: Crowell-Collier, 1971. (7 and up)
This is a short but complete history of the Navajo Nation and its customs, including historical, traditional, and spiritual perspectives. The book presents a good overview without being judgmental. The middle section contains interesting photographs. Good.

523. Loomis, Ruth.
VALLEY OF THE HAWK.
New York: Dial, 1969. (4–6)
This is a story about Jill, a white girl who is vacationing at the desert home of her uncle. Jill has been ill and is lonely until she meets Velvet Cruz, a little Indian girl. The two girls become friends and have several adventures in the story. Jill asks her mother to allow Velvet to come back home with her to go to school, and the story ends with the thought that this will probably happen. This routine book, pedestrian and dull, does not contain much new information about Indians. Poor.

524. Lourie, Dick, ed.
COME TO POWER: ELEVEN
CONTEMPORARY AMERICAN INDIAN
POETS.
Trumansburg, N.Y.: Crossing Pr.,
1974. (6–8)

This collection of prose and poetry by eleven modern Indian writers reflects a variety of feelings and moods, from traditional tribal upbringing to city sidewalks. There is an eloquent introduction by Joseph Bruchac. The comments the writers make about themselves are as interesting as their writing: for instance, Lew Blockcolski describes himself as "One of those fairly-well-educated mixed breeds who works for the government because [there is] no great demand for us anywhere else," and Leslie Silko, "I'm a mixed-breed Laguna Pueblo woman. If you know anything about Indian people, you'll know what this means." Adults need to be prepared for discussions on the writers' work as well as on what they say about themselves. English, literature, social science, and speech teachers will all find something here of interest for their classes. The book reads aloud well. Good.

525. Luger, Harriet.
THE LAST STRONGHOLD: A STORY OF
THE MODOC INDIAN WAR.
Reading, Mass.: Addison-Wesley,
1972. (6 and up)

This is a story of three teen-age boys (a Modoc; the son of a settler; and an immigrant Jewish soldier) and is set against the background of the Modoc War, which lasted from November, 1872, to May, 1873, when 50 Modocs tied up nearly 1,000 U.S. soldiers in the lava fields of Northeastern California. There is some rearrangement of the age and relationships of some historical characters, but the book gives young readers an introductory understanding of a part of history sometimes overlooked in classrooms. The foreword establishes the setting and the tone for the book. Oftentimes the author captures some understanding of the Modoc people, but occasionally she misses, as when she has a Modoc woman say,

"These dreams mean nothing. The spirits speak only in the dreams of the shaman, or the dreams a person dreams on a quest, or during the ghost dance" (p.21). The book contains a descriptive cast of characters, factual notes on the Modoc War, two maps, black-and-white photographs of the war, and a bibliography. Adequate.

526. Lyback, Johanna R. M.
INDIAN LEGENDS OF THE GREAT WEST.
Chicago: Lyons & Carnahan, 1963.
(2–4)

Short, brief stories, consisting of text covering a page or two of print, tell the legends of various tribes about creation, the origin of humanity and natural phenomena, and proper behavior. The coverage is extensive and includes tales from a representative selection of tribes. The author describes the role of older women as storytellers in certain groups. Much of the material could be read aloud successfully to even younger children than the ages recommended. The color and black-and-white paintings used as illustrations are very good and deserve a better display than this format allows. Good.

527. McCague, James.
TECUMSEH, SHAWNEE
WARRIOR-STATESMAN.
Champaign, Ill.: Garrard, 1970. (2–4)

McCague begins this biography when Tecumseh is six years old and his father dies and continues it through Tecumseh's death in battle. He delineates such facts as Tecumseh's hatred for the Shawnee practice of burning enemies at the stake and his attempt to do away with this torture as much as possible, and his joining with the British in the War of 1812. The book is accurate in details and chronology. The writing style is similar to that used in a historical novel in which the characters are provided with motivations and dialogue: " 'I will never forget you, Chiksika,' he whispered. 'And I will never stop hating the white men. Never!' " (p.30). The book is illustrated by David Dowd's black-, white-, blue-, and-brown drawings and a color map, and there is an introduction to orient the reader. Adequate.

528. McConkey, Lois.
SEA AND CEDAR: HOW THE
NORTHWEST COAST INDIANS LIVED.
Seattle: Madrona Pr., 1973. (3–5)

This book is built around the cedar tree and the sea. The author details the Northwest Coast Indians' dependence on the cedar tree for baskets, spoons, dishes, totems, and clothing, and on the sea for food. Some of the subjects described in the book include canoes, housing, food, clothing, tools, potlatches, beliefs, art, and the arrival of European and Asian explorers. Even though the book is designed largely for instructional purposes, its format, design, and illustrations are excellent. Douglas Tait's black-and-white illustrations are tremendous. This is a good introductory book for middle elementary school-age children featuring an appealing total book design and organizational pattern. There is an index. Good.

529. McDermott, Beverly Brodsky.
SEDNA: AN ESKIMO MYTH.
New York: Viking, 1975. (2 and up)

The layout of this book is directed toward very young children, but the illustrations and the legend are worth study by older art and creative writing students because of the overall effectiveness of the integration of story and book design. This Eskimo legend is adapted for children's reading tastes and contains the same strengths and weaknesses of most legend adaptations—the story is too old for primary school children to understand all the nuances, and the book's format is too young for many older children to feel comfortable choosing it to read. However, the author's use of words is fine, and her explanation of Eskimo art on the back of the book jacket is worth the reader's study. McDermott also illustrated the book, and her choice of cool colors becomes a part of the story itself. The illustrations are outstanding. There is a bibliography. Good.

530. McDermott, Gerald.
ARROW TO THE SUN.
New York: Viking, 1974. (2 and up)

A Caldecott Award Book in 1975, this book will be invaluable for art instruction purposes as well as for the teaching of literary appreciation. The color illustrations by the author are excellent, perhaps the best part of a fine book, and help carry the story forward. This use of design and color as part of the content is a talent few author-illustrators possess. The concepts discussed in this story, an adaptation of a Pueblo Indian creation myth, are difficult even for adults to understand, and the reader may wish for more explanations of "how" and "where." In one instance, the illustration shows a girl in a Hopi butterfly hair style, not a style usually affected by this group. However, with the mixtures of clothing and hair styles prevalent today, it may well be possible. Good.

531. Macfarlane, Allan.
THE BOY'S BOOK OF INDIAN SKILLS.
Harrisburg, Pa.: Stackpole, 1969.
(6–7)

A hodgepodge of a book, this volume contains all sorts of information in an unclear, disorganized format. Some items covered include Indian homes, trails, dress, gear and regalia, secrets of the red scouts, the wary brave, muscle, wit, coups, ceremonies, challenges, and the like. The book is designed for boys, effectively limiting its usefulness. The actual writing, itself is competent enough, but the directions for projects are not clear or easy to follow and the author frequently comes up with rather astonishing interpretations of customs and history: for instance,

If Indian scientists and wise men had known one-eighth as much about conservation as they knew about other sciences, these lands and their people would have flourished many hundreds of years longer than they did. [p.13]

It is hard to tell which tribes are being described, and the language and readability of the text are of a level considerably older than the age group the format aims for. Perhaps the best organized section is that on Indian games. The illustrations by Paulette Macfarlane are of the "how-to-do-it" variety, and the book would be improved by additional diagrams simplifying and clarifying the written directions. Writing and ideas: Adequate. Portrayal of Indians: Poor.

532. McGovern, Ann.
    ... IF YOU LIVED WITH THE
    SIOUX INDIANS.
    New York: Four Winds Pr., 1972.
    (3–5)
Using a question and answer format, McGovern discusses such issues as: What kind of house would you live in if you were Sioux? What were good manners? What would happen if you got sick? Such simple questions are of great interest to many children as they study an older culture and are not often answered in children's books. This book gives equal emphasis to men and women; provides a sense of the life lived by a Sioux child, which included the freedom to wander; gives a feel for the pleasures of having a large number of kin; honestly relates in children's terms the coming of the whites; and comments on the descendants of these Indians in today's world. It does suffer from a limited vocabulary, a textbook style, and a tendency to overgeneralize: for instance, "And there would be a kind word for anyone passing by" (p.23), and "Boys had the most fun" (p.21). The false idea that Sioux children had total freedom could be inferred from the book when, in reality, discipline was a part of the Sioux child-rearing process. The word *Sioux* (as well as the word *Indian*) is objectionable to some groups who prefer *Dakota* or *Lakota*. The book is beautifully illustrated in black-and-white by Bob Levering and includes a glossary. Adequate.

533. McGraw, Eloise Jarvis.
    MOCCASIN TRAIL.
    New York: Coward-McCann, 1952.
    (5–8)
This is a story of a white boy who is raised as a Crow, becomes a mountain man, fluctuates back and forth between Indian and white worlds, and finally returns to the whites. It is not basically about Indians, they are simply a part of the setting, and although the book is well written

and suspenseful, it offers little in the way of new information on the Indian way of life. Some of the passages show the author's cultural biases and feelings about Indians: "For Peter and Laurie–my own little wild Indians" (dedication); "One look at Sally, and all the bead-bedecked Crow girls in Absaroka seemed gawky and overgrown, homely as mud" (p.54); and "There was nothing of Jim Keath left at all in the painted face and glaring eyes of this naked savage" (p.227). Writing and story: Good. Portrayal of Indians: Poor.

534. Machetanz, Frederick.
    PANUCK: ESKIMO SLED DOG.
    New York: Scribner, 1967. (2–4)
Surprisingly modern, this book presents a good view of Eskimo life. Children who like dogs will appreciate this story, although Eskimos do not generally make such pets of their dogs as this book suggests in the sections devoted to training sled dogs. The book is written well and effectively takes care of the myth that all Eskimos live in igloos. Machetanz's black-and-white pictures are excellent. Good.

535. McKee, Louise, and
    Summers, Richard.
    DUSTY DESERT TALES.
    Caldwell, Idaho: Caxton, 1941. (3–5)
If some of the "heat" generated by American Indian groups about inaccurate and biased writing appears overdone, read this book. It will quickly illustrate, again and again, how infuriating it must be to read such comments about your people as the following, presented here without interpretation:
They [the Plains Apaches] would rather live idly and let the government support them. [p.81]

The original stories from which these tales have been adapted are many of them formless, for the Indians had no knowledge of the white man's story-telling art. The originals lack climaxes, proceed from one event to another, contain no descriptions and few explanations. [p.13]

For example, the Pima story of the flood must have had a partly Biblical origin. [p.13]

They [the authors] have also taken the liberty of using the word Pima to include both Pima and Papago Indians in order to avoid confusing the child reader. Pima and Papago cultures are almost identical, and many of the legends are similar. [p.14]

We'll ask this woman here, with the little brown baby, if she will let us look inside her house.
"May we look a moment inside, please? We are very much interested in what the inside of your house is like."
But she is only staring owl-like at us and not saying a word. Oh, yes, she probably understands English, but she thinks we're prying strangers and that it's none of our business what the inside of her house is like. We'll walk on to the next house. Perhaps we'll have better luck there. . . . But like the first woman, she simply stares at us. . . . Why, this woman, even though she has gone to American schools, still works as the Pima Indian women have worked for hundreds, perhaps thousands, of years. [pp.23–24]
Hurrah for the Pima women! J. Powell Scott's color and black-and-white illustrations are good, and the authors supply the photographs. This book is an object lesson on how not to write on the subject of Native Americans. Poor.

536. McLuhan, T. C.
TOUCH THE EARTH: A SELF-PORTRAIT OF INDIAN EXISTENCE.
New York: Outerbridge & Dienstfrey, 1971. (7 and up)
A beautiful book, its format consists of black-and-white photographs by Edward Curtis illustrating each of the American Indian historical speeches and modern writings included in the text. Curtis's skill as a photographer is well known, and his reputation is most deserved, as these pictures attest. The author selected a variety of speeches and writings. She in-

cludes a thorough note section, sources, and bibliography. An index and a more descriptive table of contents would have been helpful, as it is difficult to find individual entries; the reader must either go page by page or consult the notes section to find out who the contributors are. Good.

537. McNeer, May.
THE STORY OF THE SOUTHWEST.
New York: Harper, 1948. (3–5)
A rushed, brief history of the Southwest, this book also includes short segments on the American Indian tribes of that region: "After the most ancient known Indians, the so-called basket-makers, came the pueblo dwellers, who built community homes a little like our own modern apartment houses" (not paged). Fictional excerpts are interspersed among the book's more factual sections. C. H. Dewitt's lithographs are colorful and well composed, but the ones concerned with Indians are romanticized in the artistic style popular during the period of publication (1948). The reader is handicapped by the lack of a table of contents. Dated. Poor.

538. McNeer, May.
WAR CHIEF OF THE SEMINOLES.
Eau Claire, Wisc.: Hale, 1954.
(4 and up)
The author introduces Osceola with a detailed, but complex, explanation of the Seminoles' "runaway" origins as a tribe composed of remnants of Creeks, Cherokees, Choctaws, and Colusas. Although a lengthy book, this includes little about Seminole customs and culture except a five page sequence describing the palm-thatched hut, or chickee, that Seminole Indians built to protect themselves from rainy or cold weather, the origin of Osceola's name, and how the Seminoles made their canoes from a cypress tree that was "well seasoned in the mud" for two years. For the major portion of the book, the author concentrates on the battles between the white soldiers and Seminole warriors. Because the white leaders often knew little about either the Seminoles or Florida

swamps, the Indians were able to elude the U.S. troops. The author provides excellent descriptions illustrating how, only by piecemeal capture and imprisonment, were any of the Seminole leaders finally restrained. She points out that the Seminole Indians were the only tribe that never officially surrendered to the United States. By using the many illustrations (green-tinted sketches by Lynd Ward) as a guide, the reader can become familiar with the Florida terrain, clothing, and dwellings of either white or Indian people in the early 1800s. No mention is made of the relationship between the Seminoles and black slaves. However, in the foreword section of the book the author reports that her grandfather "planted one of the first big orange groves in Florida, and worked it with 350 slaves." Adequate.

539. McNickle, D'Arcy.
RUNNER IN THE SUN.
New York: Holt, 1954. (7–9)
A well-written story about a young Cliff Dweller boy in prehistoric times, this book gives readers a feel for the actual day-to-day life of the time. In the story, an intragroup dispute over customs and practices causes a break among the Cliff Dwellers, who are eventually united and move to a better location. Salt-Boy, the main character, brings corn from Mexico to enrich their lives. This author knows his facts and customs:

> As War Chief, or, as they sometimes said, Outside Chief, he was expected to see that men observed the fasts and purification rites required before they took part in important ceremonies. [p.17]

He occasionally lapses, however, when it comes to women: "'So, birdling. You charge like a buck deer! Do not the silly girls teach manners?'" (p.8). This book deserves to be reissued. It is excellent. Good.

540. Magee, Agnes Davis.
WHEN THE PINES GREW TALL.
San Antonio, Tex.: Naylor, 1968. (4–6)

Based on the life of the author's great-great-grandmother, this is the story of a white family that moved from Georgia to Texas and found and cared for a sick Choctaw boy along the way. The Choctaws were grateful for the help given the boy, and one part of the story deals with the Indians and whites celebrating Christmas together. The story is full of clichés: "Jim sat dreaming under the pear tree that was white with snowy blossoms of spring. The bubbling spring filled the creek with clear, cold, sparkling water" (p.1); and the dialogue passages are frequently of the pidgin English variety: "No, White Feather too small. White Feather had to stay with squaws. Me kill bear some day, though, just like my father" (p.31). Bruce Good's illustrations feature the ever-present Indian headfeather, but are otherwise satisfactory. Story: Adequate. Portrayal of Indians: Poor.

541. Maher, Ramona.
THE BLIND BOY AND THE LOON AND OTHER ESKIMO MYTHS.
New York: Day, 1969. (3 and up)
The stories featured in this book are the kind Eskimos use to entertain children and acquaint them with life. The preface gives a good overview of Eskimo myths and tales in the book, analyzing the elements they share with culture myths of other peoples: for example, there is a Pleiades story. The book is well written: "The stories draw on a thoroughly human reserve of emotions, and the emotions of the characters are frankly presented" (preface), and revolving around a theme of searching for food. Some excellent illustrations feature a variety of art techniques. The author includes a glossary. Good.

542. Marcus, Rebecca B.
THE FIRST BOOK OF THE CLIFF DWELLERS.
New York: Watts, 1968. (4–6)
The title of this book is well chosen; it is an introductory book for children on the Cliff Dwellers, rather than an in-depth presentation. The text is smoothly written,

but pedantic in tone, and the overall format is similar to most books designed for instructional purposes. The book concentrates on the ruins at Mesa Verde, although other cliff dwellings are briefly mentioned. Subjects such as geology and dating of structures are introduced. Some of the chapter headings reflect the author's attitudes: for example, "The Cliff Dwellers' Dreary Winters" (p.59). Black-and-white drawings by Julio Granda and photographs illustrate the volume. Adequate.

543. Marriott, Alice.
THE BLACK STONE KNIFE.
New York: Crowell, 1957. (4–6)
Adapted from a true story recorded by James Mooney in 1892, this is one of the few primary children's books available on the Kiowa. In it, a Kiowa boy looking for horses is captured by Apaches but manages to escape. There is a lot of involvement in wars, battles, revenge, and the like in this story: "Father was home from the war raid he had led against the Navahos" (p.9); one wonders when the Kiowa had time to sleep, find food, or have children. In one instance, the grandfather is too ready to disbelieve his grandson's vision: "'Your talking bird,' said Grandfather. 'You must have made that up'" (p.181). In actuality, much more attention would have been paid to the reporting of such a vision. The writing is mediocre, the characterizations superficial, and Harvey Weiss's black-and-white line drawings are undistinguished. There is a section on the author and the artist. Poor.

544. Marriott, Alice.
THE FIRST COMERS: INDIANS OF
AMERICA'S DAWN.
New York: Longman, 1960.
(7 and up)
Marriott presents the discipline of archaeology in a manner that will excite junior high and high school students. She cautions readers about using good manners in seeking archaeological sites on private property, and points out that, in the game of discovering the past, everyone can win—if the players follow the rules.

This discussion of archaeology is sure to motivate young people to seek relics of the past, so the author also motivates them to be aware, to interpret. She raises questions, hints at possible answers, and frankly leaves some unanswered. Through it all, the book reveals the deep love the archaeologist has for this work—exploring the beginnings. Good.

545. Marriott, Alice.
INDIANS ON HORSEBACK.
New York: Crowell, 1948. (3–5)
This is an older book reflecting the writing style, format, and illustrations popular in the 1940s. Starting with the standard theory about the migration from Siberia, the author traces the history of the Plains Indians. She presents a restricted view of the lives Indian girls and women lived. She also often interprets historical events in ways that few would agree with such as her statement that some Indians did not live on the Plains because they lacked in courage: "Not all of the Indian tribes dared to make the adventure of living out on the plains" (p.8). The material on Indians of today is, of course, limited by the publication date, but also by the author's style of writing. Margaret Lefranc's drawings are similar to those in most textbooks from this period. Poor.

546. Marriott, Alice.
SEQUOYAH: LEADER OF THE
CHEROKEES.
New York: Random House, 1956.
(4–6)
The author begins this book with a broad historical review of the various theories explaining the migrations (and the reasons for them) of the American Indian from Asia to the North American continent. Elaborating upon the Cherokee tribe's beginnings, she ascribes to them all of the characteristics of creativity and intelligence possessed by a thriving, successful civilization: brilliance and productivity in mathematics, science, religion, education, art, and history. Her broad, historical perspective encompasses Sequoyah's birth,

ancestry, marriage, and his later years. In this story, Sequoyah is portrayed as a creative man. Great attention is given to the events leading up to his development of a "syllabary" for the Cherokee language and his pursuit of the dream of discovering both the "Lost Indian Language" and the group of Indians who originated it. There is little anger or anguish, and a great deal of triumph for Sequoyah, in this book. Occasionally pedantic, the author intrudes now and then with rhetorical questions and some directive, summary reminders which may annoy the more mature reader. The book is illustrated by Bob Riger, whose pictures are authentic, accurately representing the clothing and other accouterments of the late eighteenth and early nineteenth century. The author includes some of the written characters of the Cherokee syllabary developed by Sequoyah. Adequate.

547. Marriott, Alice.
WINTER-TELLING STORIES.
New York: Crowell, 1969. (2–5)
Stories of Saynday, who "got things started" and who laid down the ground rules for storytelling (only at night, in the winter, and always begin, "Saynday was coming along . . ."), are featured in this collection of Kiowa tales. The author provides a good introduction to help the reader understand the stories. Marriott has included stories that can be read aloud with as much pleasure as they can be read silently. Richard Cuffari's fine black-and-white illustrations employ unusual perspective effects to add touches of fantasy. The format of the book would have been improved if these illustrations could have been reproduced on a larger scale, and if there had been more of them. Good.

548. Marriott, Alice, and
Rachlin, Carol K.
AMERICAN INDIAN MYTHOLOGY.
New York: Crowell, 1968. (7 and up)
This is a collection of myths from a diversity of tribal sources. The authors provide the reader with an excellent introductory section in which they relate his-

tory to oral literature. The writing tends to be flamboyant: "In the closely twined cord of any people's lore and religion and history, there must be ravelings as well as knots. Often it is difficult to tease out the end to which a frayed strand leads" (p.1), but is also properly cautious: "*Homo Sapiens*, so far as present knowledge stands, is the only humanoid species that has occupied the Americas" (p.2) and thought-provoking: "Whatever their nationalities, the first Europeans had a common language in Latin" (p.5). The book is divided into four sections: "The World Beyond Ours," "The World Around Us," "The World We Live in Now," "The World We Go To," and includes myths created since the coming of non-Indians, such as the Cheyenne and Arapaho stories about Yellow Hair Custer. The print used for the book is small, which limits readability, and is illustrated by black-and-white photographs. These stories could be the source for many other books using a more vital format. Good.

549. Martin, Fran.
NINE TALES OF COYOTE.
New York: Harper, 1950. (4–6)
This collection of tales about Coyote presents the Idaho Indians' oral traditions. The book is well done, but could use a more thorough introduction, and needs to say something more about the peoples represented than merely labeling them "Idaho Indians." Dorothy McEntee's color illustrations are effective. Good.

550. Martin, Fran.
NINE TALES OF THE RAVEN.
New York: Harper, 1951. (4–6)
Illustrated in color by Dorothy McEntee, this book has been reissued as *Raven-Who-Sets-Things-Right*, by the same author. See the review of the later edition, #551.

551. Martin, Fran.
RAVEN-WHO-SETS-THINGS-RIGHT.
INDIAN TALES OF THE NORTHWEST COAST.
New York: Harper, 1975. (4–6)

This is a revised edition of *Nine Tales of the Raven*, by the same author. It contains Indian tales of the Northwestern tribes, edited and combined to suit young readers' tastes. Illustrated in black-and-white by Dorothy McEntee, the book gives a good description of the importance of storytelling in the cultures of these tribes. These tales are different from non-Indian children's tales; they were intended originally for adults, and consequently the concepts presented in the stories are often at a far more advanced level than the book format would indicate. This may necessitate discussions with young readers about many ideas presented in this collection. Good.

552. Martin, Patricia Miles.
BE BRAVE, CHARLIE.
New York: Putnam, 1972. (2–4)
Bonnie Johnson's brown-, turquoise-, lavender-, and-white illustrations are superb, the best part of the book, and the layout is designed to display them to advantage. (It is true there are some minor errors in her scenes; for example, saguaro cactus is not usually found on the Navajo Reservation.) Martin's story deals with a young Navajo boy, reluctant to go to boarding school, who finds education to be better than he had expected, especially reading. The family relationship among the boy's relatives is well explained, and the author makes it easy to see the boy's reluctance to leave such a home. There are a few minor items that may cause debate; for instance, Charlie's aunt makes pottery. Although this is not usually thought of as a Navajo craft, it is possible that many Navajo have learned the skill today with so much mixing of tribal patterns at school and in social and crafts events. Good.

553. Martin, Patricia Miles.
ESKIMOS: PEOPLE OF ALASKA.
New York: Parent's Magazine Pr., 1970. (1–4)
Clarifying concepts and dispelling stereotypes, this book provides very young readers and listeners with a realistic understanding of the people of Alaska, including Eskimos. Up-to-date (1970) information on Eskimo life is written in a style and vocabulary appealing to these young readers. The author has taken pains to be authentic and to clarify stereotypes and incorrect ideas about Eskimos. For instance, all Eskimos live in igloos, because the word *igloo* means house. An igloo may be made of driftwood, earth, stone, furs, or other materials. The snow house, or snow igloo, was made in emergency situations in a storm when shelter was needed. Both teachers and children will learn much from this book. Good.

554. Martin, Patricia Miles.
INDIANS: THE FIRST AMERICANS.
New York: Parent's Magazine Pr., 1970. (1–4)
This is a survey-type book on American Indians for young children. Although the author is careful to stress the concept that tribes differ, she often treats Indians as a group and sometimes sets forward an impossibly idealistic view of Indian life, such as "Each man was loyal to his tribe. Each was loyal to his family. Each shared his food with those who had no food, and shared his shelter with those who had no shelter" (pp.5–6). The writing style is similar to a basal reader, and tends to be pedestrian. There is little coverage of American Indian women, and although she does write of Indians in the city, too little coverage of current happenings. Robert Frankenberg's black-, white-, and-tan illustrations are good, and there is an index. Adequate.

555. Martin, Patricia Miles.
NAVAJO PET.
New York: Putnam, 1971. (2–4)
The story of two school-age Navajo boys who are enemies, this book details the boys' gradual acceptance that they must cooperate with each other to find their lost pets, and in doing so they establish a real friendship. The story does not depend on the boys being Navajo; the same plot could apply equally well to two Fijians or two ghetto boys. In one sense,

this use of a standard plot is helpful; it demonstrates the commonality of experience across cultures. In another sense, it is objectionable; it can reduce real cultural differences to the level of banality. Joe Hamberger's illustrations carry forward the same cultural blurring, and the faces do not look particularly Navajo. Adequate.

556. Martin, Patricia Miles.
POCAHONTAS.
New York: Putnam, 1964. (2–4)
This biography of Pocahontas and her relationship with early white settlers follows most histories, both in chronology and events. The author presents few stereotypes of either Indian women or tribal life in general. Pocahontas remains in the village to help the women while hunters are out after bear, deer, rabbit, and wild turkey, but she also is shown as joining in games with all the children. Both men and women are featured in the illustrations of tribal dances by the artist, Portia Takakjian. This is a simply written story in which the author shows the reader folly and bravery as well as the consequences of poor communication and rigidity on the part of both whites and Indians. The young reader may need more background in early English manners and customs to understand the book. Adequate.

557. Martini, Teri.
THE LUCKY GHOST SHIRT.
Philadelphia: Westminster, 1971. (3–6)
This is the story of a young Indian boy in rebellion and in trouble. The boy is accused of stealing a horse from a rancher, and is defended by the principal girl character. Great-grandfather makes the boy's rebellion worse by giving him a lucky ghost shirt and telling him about the good old days. The story eventually ends with all conflict resolved satisfactorily. The book stresses the importance of everyone's finding his or her own solutions and ways of life, but is marred by stereotyped characterizations and a too facile ending. John Gretzer uses his fine technical skills to advantage in the illustrations. There is a

brief section about the author; the book also needs a section on the illustrator. Good.

558. Mason, Bernard S.
BOOK OF INDIAN CRAFTS AND COSTUMES.
New York: Ronald, 1946. (4–6)
This is a fairly complete manual on how to make and decorate articles of clothing worn by the Indians of the Woodlands and Plains. Step-by-step directions are accompanied by line drawings and black-and-white photographs. Just about everything from warbonnets to moccasins is treated in detail. Good.

559. Mason, Miriam E.
HOMINY AND HIS BLUNT-NOSED ARROW.
New York: Macmillan, 1959. (2–4)
It is difficult to determine the tribe under consideration in this book: the dwellings in the illustrations look like Iroquois long houses, the gathering of wild rice in the story suggests the Ojibwas, and the full Plains warbonnet on the cover adds to the confusion. This is the story of a young Indian boy (named Hominy by his older brother, who likes hominy) and his effective use of the blunt-nosed arrow of childhood. Women are treated with respect; there is a wise grandmother and a respected mother. The writing is simplified, clear, concise—and sometimes lacking in rhythm: "In the middle of summer came the green corn dance. Everyone had a good time then" (p.41). The black-and-white illustrations are by George and Doris Hauman. Adequate.

560. Matson, Emerson N.
LEGENDS OF THE GREAT CHIEFS.
Nashville, Tenn.: Nelson, 1972. (5–8)
This book contains stories from seven different American Indian tribes, each recounted by a descendant of the chief involved, such as Sitting Bull, Crazy Horse, Chief Red Cloud, and others. The stories touch on the Great Spirit, the peace pipe, the wind-cave, and other similar themes. Two maps showing the location of major

Indian reservations in the Dakotas, Nebraska, Wyoming, and Montana are given. Only one other element adds graphic interest: a picture of Chief Red Cloud. This book is suitable for intermediate grade students. Good.

561. Matson, Emerson N.
LONGHOUSE LEGENDS.
Nashville, Tenn.: Nelson, 1968. (3–7)
An easy-to-read collection of legends of the Swinomish, a Northwest Coast tribe, each story has a brief introduction by the author that effectively sets the stage for that particular selection. With so much explanatory material running through the stories, the reader gains a lot of information about these people: (1) stories were often told to children by parents as a way to keep family secrets and pass along family history, as stories and totems were often the only records; (2) a floor plan of a Tulalip dwelling is included; (3) Puget Sound longhouses are described in detail as part of the legends; and (4) in 1938, the Swinomish carved a log measuring sixty-one feet into a modern story pole, including President Franklin Roosevelt's face in the carving. The reader will find many parallels in these stories to Greek and Roman tales, as in the story of the maiden released from underground captivity if she will come back often to visit. Lorence Bjorklund's black-and-white drawings are good; there is a color picture of Chief Martin J. Sampson, who translated the stories for the author from Swinomish to English; and there is a brief bibliography. Good.

562. Matthews, Washington.
THE MOUNTAIN CHANT.
Glorieta, N. Mex.: Rio Grande Pr., 1970. (8 and up)
A reissue in exact format of the *Fifth Annual Report of the Bureau of Ethnology to the Secretary of the Smithsonian Institution, 1883–1884* by J. W. Powell, this is a beautiful book detailing one of the important Navajo ceremonies. The book successfully interprets the purpose and ritual of the chant:

When the man (or the woman) who gives the entertainment concludes he is sick and that he can afford to call a shaman, it is not the latter who decides what particular rites are best suited to cure the malady. It is the patient and his friends who determine this. Then they send for a man who is known to be skilled in performing the desired rites, and it is his province merely to do the work required of him. [p.387]
A complete description of the entire ceremony, interpretations of songs used in the chant, a map, and examples of Navajo sand paintings are included in the book. Good.

563. Maxwell, Gilbert S.
NAVAJO RUGS.
Palm Desert, Calif.: Best-West, 1972. (8 and up)
In addition to describing over fourteen different types of Navajo rugs, each illustrated by color photographs, this brief book includes a short history of the Navajos and of Navajo rug-making, a relatively new Navajo craft, about 1700. Of equal interest are illustrated descriptions of how a rug is made, how to buy a rug, how to collect Navajo weaving, and other interesting but seldom-reported facts about this craft. The only flaw is that the rug prices quoted are 1963 prices, somewhat misleading, since the last (twelfth) printing date is 1972. The book is written in a fairly detailed style for readers interested in making a purchase. The brief history is well worth studying, provided that supplementary histories are available. Good.

564. May, Charles Paul.
THE EARLY INDIANS: THEIR NATURAL AND IMAGINARY WORLDS.
Nashville, Tenn.: Nelson, 1971. (6 and up)
This seems to be a highly personal book of subjects of interest to the author and, as such, makes uneven reading. The photographs used as illustrations appear to be tacked on, as if it were necessary to provide something for the reader to view, and they include an inordinate number of

pictures of snakes. The book itself consists of an unrelated series of descriptions of various tribal practices about nature and religion and includes many of the author's comments similar to the following: "Some Indians of North America preserved the animals and plants in their territories; others did not. But they all relied on nature for food, for clothing, and for shelter" (p.7); or

> In a ball game players bashed one another over the head, tripped one another, and displayed as much viciousness as cunning. Perhaps a man killed another on the playing field. No matter, even if he did it on purpose. As punishment, his tribesmen expected him to give the dead man's family some presents. He might marry the man's widow so she would have someone to look after her. [p.68]

In spite of all this, the book does contain interesting passages. The primary difficulty with the book is that the reader would have to be extremely well informed to separate the actual facts presented by the author from the erroneous ones. Poor.

565. May, Julian.
BEFORE THE INDIANS.
New York: Holiday House, 1969.
(1–4)
Simple text and plentiful illustrations make this book a good introduction for young children to the coming of human beings to the Americas, their distribution, and their variety of life styles. A great many facts about ancient American cultures are expressed simply, effectively, and briefly. This would be an important book to use in a unit about Indians, especially in the primary grades. Brevity is both its strength and its weakness, because significant ideas are given a sentence or two. However, young readers probably will ask questions, and a chain reaction of learning could result. Good.

566. May, Julian.
QUANAH, LEADER OF THE COMANCHES.
Mankato, Minn.: Creative Educational Soc., 1976. (3–6)

This biography of Quanah Parker begins with the capture of Cynthia Ann Parker by Comanches and describes her background and the history and customs of the Comanches: for example, "The Indian parents never punished their children. When a boy or girl misbehaved other members of the tribe made fun of them and shamed them into being good" (unpaged). The book is accurate in chronology but sometimes sugarcoats the events it records. For instance, the author comments that Cynthia Ann was to be taken back to the Comanches after the Civil War was over, a highly conjectural statement. It also overgeneralizes from incomplete data: "Little Quanah seldom got into mischief" (unpaged), and is more optimistic about white motivation than often proved to be the case: the babies and children killed at Sand Creek, Fort Lowell, and the Moravian settlements would have been surprised to read, "When it seemed certain she [Cynthia Ann Parker] would be shot, she pulled up her pony and held out the baby. She knew that white men did not often kill children" (unpaged). The book has a readable format, and Phero Thomas's informative black-and-white line drawings are competent. Few of the actual controversies of the time are explored, but the book does give young readers an introduction to this period in history. Adequate.

567. May, Julian.
SITTING BULL, CHIEF OF THE SIOUX.
Mankato, Minn.: Creative Educational Soc., 1973. (2–4)
This story of the life of Sitting Bull emphasizes the adventurous and glamorous events he lived through and his activities as a Sioux warrior, such as counting coups, his limp from a Crow wound, and another version of how he got his name. Many of May's interpretations are subject to controversy: "And when they made war they did it Indian-fashion—killing not only men, but also women and children. It was their custom" (unpaged); or "Sitting Bull replied, 'The Black Hills belong to me. If white people try to take them, I will fight'" (unpaged). The last statement is espe-

cially questionable, since Indians were not in the habit of claiming personal possession of a geographic territory. The book details such events as the fight at the Little Big Horn, the flight to Canada, the Ghost Dance, and Sitting Bull's death in language young readers can understand. The format is good, the writing is adequate, Phero Thomas's black-and-white line drawings are appropriate, and the book is easy to read. Sitting Bull, however, does not emerge as a real person in this interpretation of his life. Adequate.

568. Mead, Margaret.
PEOPLE AND PLACES.
Cleveland, Ohio: World, 1959. (3–6)
Margaret Mead, among her other remarkable talents, writes for children beautifully, clearly, and effectively: "Wherever we find human beings, we find that they wonder about other people. The people who live across the mountain, in the next valley, or on the other side of the island" (p.11). In this book, one obviously planned for informational and instructional purposes, she defines the work of anthropologists and describes for her young readers some different cultures around the world, including Eskimo, Kalahari Bushman, American Indian, and the like. She does not write down to her young audience; the use of a chapter heading such as "Man as a Being" uses simple words, but not simple concepts. She is more optimistic than most of us about the progress of humanity, as can be seen from the following excerpt from the book:

> When members of the other group wandered into your territory you might get angry and try to scare them away or even attack them if they did not go. But actually, this would not happen to you in twentieth-century America, because your group could talk to the others and make friends with them, and together you could make rules about living next to each other. [p.13]

The sections devoted to traditional Sioux women's lives and to Sioux child-rearing practices are accurately done; she tells of the careful training of children and the importance the Indian women's clubs had, two subjects most writers know little about. The materials on modern Indians are, of course, now dated. W. T. Mars's and Jan Fairservis's illustrations and photographs are excellent, even though designed for a social studies type of book (see the picture of the Bushman on page 22). There is a bibliography, writer's source section, an index, and a write-up about the author. Dated. Good.

569. Meadowcroft, Enid LaMonte.
CRAZY HORSE: SIOUX WARRIOR.
Champaign, Ill.: Garrard, 1965. (2–5)
A part of the Garrard series, this book begins with a brief description of the Oglala Sioux and a map showing major events during Crazy Horse's life. In this story, which begins with Crazy Horse's boyhood and ends with his death, the reader is informed that Crazy Horse was first called "Curly" and had lighter hair and skin than other Indians. Although well written and interesting, in this version of Crazy Horse's life there are no good white people and no bad Indians, which may provide the uninformed reader with a rather biased viewpoint. The illustrations by Cary are similar to others in the Garrard series, in that they aid the young reader by providing supportive information. Adequate.

570. Meadowcroft, Enid LaMonte.
THE STORY OF CRAZY HORSE.
New York: Grosset, 1954. (6–9)
An earlier version of *Crazy Horse: Sioux Warrior*, written for older readers, this story begins with Crazy Horse in his childhood and ends with his death, following the format of the Garrard series book written some ten years later by the same author for a younger group of readers. Unfortunately, the same weaknesses are present in this book; all Indians are good and all white men are bad. In addition, other stereotypes are present; for instance, Crazy Horse's supposed attitude about girls: "What girls know isn't worth any more than a wind in the treetops" (p.9); and Indian children's relationships

with their parents and other elders (authoritative parents, children conspiring in secret so they won't get into trouble). However, the buffalo hunt is well described, as is the potentially humorous incident involving a runaway cow, which unfortunately precipitates a reaction from white settlers with devastating consequences for the Indians. For the rest, the illustrations, black-and-white sketches by William Reusswig, give the Indians a cadaverous appearance while lending more credence to the expression "The only good Indian is a dead Indian," contrary to any feeling about Indians the text conveys. Poor.

571. Means, Florence.
OUR CUP IS BROKEN.
New York: Houghton, 1969.
(7 and up)
This book features a "soap opera" type of plot, in which Sarah, a young Hopi woman, returns to her village after living nine years with a white family. It is as difficult for Sarah to accept traditional ways and the ancient religion as it is for the villagers to accept her new ways. Making her position even harder, she is raped by a Hopi boy. After bearing her illegitimate child, she marries Bennin, a Hopi man, and they move from their village to a nearby white community. In spite of the plot, the book is well written, providing a dilemma for book selectors: to buy or not. If purchased, be prepared for controversy. Adequate.

572. Meltzer, Milton.
HUNTED LIKE A WOLF: THE STORY OF THE SEMINOLE WAR.
New York: Farrar, 1972. (7 and up)
Characterized by thoroughness of research and fairness of treatment, this book is an exhaustive study of the Seminole War. The author sees the Seminole War as an archetype of injustice that began with Columbus, who sent 500 Tainos back to Spain as slaves, half of whom died on the voyage, the remainder dying soon after in Spanish prisons or on galleys as slave rowers. This writer is blunt:

What rule of international law permitted General Jackson to order that a fort in foreign territory be blown up and its people, now free citizens of Spain, be turned into slaves?

No rule, only the desire of the slaveholders to enslave or destroy blacks who were enjoying their lives in peace and prosperity. And Jackson's knowledge that the Spanish were too weak to protect their citizens. [p.75]

Twenty-two years later Congress paid a bonus to the officers and crews of the gunboats who had taken part in this massacre and piracy.

Nobody protested. [p.59]

There is a bibliography and an index. This is an excellent treatment of a complex subject. Good.

573. Melzack, Ronald.
RAVEN: CREATOR OF THE WORLD.
Boston: Little, 1970. (3–7)
A fine job of writing, this book was designed to meet non-Eskimo literary tastes by a reworking of materials to eliminate much of the detail and repetition characteristic of Eskimo storytelling, a primarily oral literature. Much of the material is based on the work of Frank Boas and Knud Rasmussen, and tells of Raven—the creator, superhuman; creative, ingenious, yet human. The author's introduction helps the reader understand old Eskimo customs and life patterns, and Laszlo Gal's fine black-, white-, and-blue illustrations serve to move the story forward. Occasionally the writer tangles his words, as in the excerpt where he fails to remember that the word *igloo* means house: "The Eskimos near the North Pole, before they were taught to build houses, spent much of the year in igloos" (pp.12–13), although that is a very minor fault in an otherwise fine book. Good.

574. Meyer, William.
NATIVE AMERICANS: THE NEW INDIAN RESISTANCE.
New York: International, 1971.
(7 and up)

An angry book: "It is only fair that you hear the Indian side as you have already heard the government's or perhaps have heard nothing. In the spirit of increased understanding, this indictment is submitted to you" (p.9), this is a detailing of past and present injustices resulting from non-Indian treatment of Indians in everything from fishing rights to land disputes. The writer makes no pretense of objectivity, and, although the book is well researched, has weakened his case through use of statistics subject to controversy: "Over five million Americans [are] of Indian descent" (p.8) and by rhetorical language that will turn away many readers who hold political positions different from the author's, who might otherwise read the material if the writer's choice of words did not serve to alienate them:

> Since the alleged discovery of the Americas by Christopher Columbus in 1492, the native peoples of both North and South America have resisted the onslaught of colonialism. [p.7]

> The most recent form of colonialism has been the combined intrusion of federal agencies, missionaries, capitalists, industrialists, researchers, anthropologists, do-gooders, and tourists. [pp.7–8]

In spite of this, however, this is not a "holier than thou" treatment, as a superficial glance at the language might suggest, but a biased treatment, in the sense of being one-sided, and needs to be selected accordingly. There is an interesting section detailing explorations before Columbus's voyages, such as the 458 A.D. voyage of a Buddhist priest of Afghanistan to Alaska, California, and Mexico, and the visits from various Norse groups. Included is an excellent bibliography on current (1971) social conditions and a section about the author. Good.

575. Mian, Mary.
TAKE THREE WISHES.
Boston: Houghton, 1971. (7–12)
An attempted comedy-spoof of whites, Indians, Chicanos, television culinary programs, and the whole Southwest, and written in "teen-age" language, this book is never quite successful in wrapping it all together. Part of the trouble stems from the characterizations. For example, the villain is too stereotyped to support belief —a town mayor who runs a restaurant where he puts stray cats into his tamales, cheats Spanish-Americans of their land, and is so dense that he tries to make Indians obtain an entertainment license for their solemn ceremonial dances. The book also suffers from too intricate a plot, in which two Girl Scouts, a cooking expert, two witches, an Indian, and a cowboy ghost become entangled with the mayor, sorcery, prejudice, and Chicano/Indian/teen-age problems. There are inaccuracies, such as misplacing the Hopi Reservation with that of the Navajo.

> "You tell 'em," said Pablo. "There's a big dance up in Hopi land, and Soyoko's invited Miss Hartigan and you girls. Tell 'em we're sleeping at the lodge, where it's warm. Window Rock, they'll think." [p.241];

and the dialogue lacks authenticity, as in the exclamatory use of the word *kachina* in, "My Kachina! He bought it" (p.255). Story: Adequate. Portrayal of Indians: Poor.

576. Miles, Miska.
ANNIE AND THE OLD ONES.
Boston: Little, 1971. (1–3)
This is one of the finest and most sensitive treatments of death available in children's literature. That fact alone may lessen the effectiveness of this story with Indian groups, especially Navajo traditionalists who may have other feelings regarding literature about death as a result of their religious beliefs. In the story Annie's grandmother tells Annie that she is going to die as soon as the rug being woven is finished. Annie behaves badly to delay the weaving, even ripping out part each night. After beautifully sensitive discussions with her grandmother, she takes up the weaving herself, as she begins to understand her grandmother's wishes and she realizes that death is a natural thing.

The relationship between the grandmother and the girl is well developed and the discussions on death finely drawn in the non-Indian sense, although not necessarily the way many Navajos would handle the subject. Whether or not a Navajo grandmother would will different items, as in this story, is a matter of dispute; customs are changing rapidly. Peter Parnall's black-, white-, gold-, and-brown illustrations are magnificent, although the ocotillo featured so prominently in the scenes is out of place on the Navajo Reservation, and the faces in the drawings do not always look Navajo. He makes effective use of unusual angles and perspectives (see the picture of boards and feet, pages 34–35). It is too bad his interpretations of plant life and Navajos did not come off accurately. Good.

577. Miller, Marjorie.
INDIAN ARTS AND CRAFTS:
A COMPLETE GUIDE TO
SOUTHWESTERN INDIAN HANDCRAFTS.
Los Angeles: Nash, 1972. (7–9)
This book contains many interesting facts about Indian arts and crafts, such as the historical background of silversmithing, which first started with the Iroquois in the Northeast, spread to the Lakes region, west to the Prairie and Plains Indians, and then to the Navajos, who learned the art of silversmithing from Mexican smiths who roamed the Rio Grande Valley in the 1800s. The history of kachina doll-making is discussed, and the significance kachinas have for the Zuñis, Pueblo Indians, and particularly the Hopis, is presented. A discussion of Navajo rugs is given, detailing the Yei blanket, the Chinle weavers, the Ganado-type rug, and various other patterns. The pottery of the Basket Makers, the Hohokam, the Pueblos, the Zuñis, and the Hopi is briefly mentioned. Each chapter not only includes the history of the art medium under discussion, but also a detailed explanation of how to make the object as well. The text is illustrated. This is an excellent book for those interested in Indian art as well as in obtaining authentic information on Indians. Good.

578. Mitchell, Emerson Blackhorse, and Allen, T. D.
MIRACLE HILL.
Norman: Univ. of Oklahoma Pr., 1976. (6 and up)
The Navajo coauthor relates his own story in his own words in this book. An extensive introduction, "Please Read Close," written by T. D. Allen, (the corporate name of a husband and wife writing team) prepares the young reader for the style in which the book is written. Very little editing has been done so that, like poetry, the sensitivity and feeling of the material is retained. Because most of the text is not grammatically precise, some of it may be difficult to follow, particularly for the reader who expects such perfection. The book seems most suitable for oral reading and discussion purposes for the younger reader, and for silent reading for the older reader. The story begins with young "Broneco" (the author's pen name) living with his grandparents near Four Corners and continues until the boy finishes school. The story is poignant; the author identifies with, and reacts to, his environment, including the land, sky, and his white and Indian surroundings. For this reason, young readers unfamiliar with the Four Corners vicinity may need supplemental material and maps. Good.

579. Molloy, Anne Stearns.
FIVE KIDNAPPED INDIANS: THE TRUE
ACCOUNT OF THE 17TH CENTURY
ACCOUNT OF FIVE EARLY AMERICANS:
TISQUANTUM, NAHANADA,
SKITWARROES, ASSOCOMOIT AND
MANEDAY.
New York: Hastings House, 1968.
(6–8)
Most history books casually mention that Squanto learned English on a journey to England before the Pilgrims came to New England. This is the true story of what happened to him. In 1605, Captain Gurge Waymouth was dispatched from England to sail to the coast of New England, where he was to kidnap some natives to take to England to provide the British with information on the New World; or, failing this, another Englishman, Owen

Griffin, was to stay alone in New England to pick up any information he could until another ship was dispatched to bring him home. The English managed to kidnap five Indian men: Tisquantum (Squanto), Nahanada, Skitwarroes, Assocomoit, and Maneday. The resulting subsequent journeys, encounters, and adventures that happened to these men is detailed in full as they traveled individual routes in England, Spain, and America. Tisquantum is examined more extensively by the author than are the other four, probably because of his historical importance. At first, he apparently regarded the Pilgrims almost as helpless, slightly foolish children, and helped them in the same ways he would have assisted any other children in the same circumstances. Later, his rivalry with other Indians over the Pilgrims is detailed. The author pictures him as an incredibly brilliant, versatile, and complex person. The research involved in a book this thoroughly documented must have been monumental; the author does a fine job. One wishes she had not fallen into the practice of using certain words that irritate many readers, such as *squaw* (see page 11) and *savage*. There is an interesting discussion of the author and her New England origins, maps of New England and the various voyages discussed in the book, a bibliography, and an index. Advanced junior high school students should find this book of interest, and teachers dealing with this subject matter should find the book invaluable. Writers, historians, anthropologists, and other professionals can all gain something from the book—perhaps one writer, some day, will receive enough inspiration from this volume to write the definitive book on Squanto. Good.

580. Momaday, N. Scott.
THE WAY TO RAINY MOUNTAIN.
Albuquerque: Univ. of New Mexico Pr., 1969. (7 and up)
This author presents the reader with an incredible privilege—the privilege of journeying with him into his explorations of himself, his people, his heritage. Momaday is so gifted a writer as to override

technique, politics, beliefs—everything but the experience of moving along with him in a flow of language that begins with his words but soon has the reader wondering where Momaday's thoughts and feelings and words leave off and where those of the reader begin. The book furnishes the reader with an exploration of self, the Kiowas, and N. Scott Momaday, intertwined and inseparable. A classic. Good.

581. Momaday, Natachee Scott.
AMERICAN INDIAN AUTHORS.
Boston: Houghton, 1972. (7 and up)
Natachee Scott Momaday (N. Scott Momaday's mother, to avoid confusion) presents here a collection of writings by various authors analyzing the literature and oral traditions of the American Indian. A good collection, it includes a diverse group of articles, speeches, and stories, from Chief Joseph to Vine Deloria. Momaday obviously intends this book for instructional purposes; she includes questions for the reader at the end of most chapters. The reader is presented with some interesting analyses by the various writers represented in this collection: (1) Momaday's description of English as a basis for Indian creativity; (2) Black Elk's thoughts on one significance of feathers, "I painted my face all red, and in my hair I put one eagle feather for the One above" (p.44) (quite at odds with the casual use of feathers in some illustrations for children's books); and (3) Vine Deloria's discussion of the lowering of academic standards for Indian students by some bureaucrats as an act of paternalism that wrecked a model educational program he designed. There is a section listing the major Indian tribes by state, a map, introductions by Momaday for each article she includes, and black-and-white photographs as illustration. Good.

582. Momaday, Natachee Scott.
OWL IN THE CEDAR TREE.
Boston: Ginn, 1965. (2–4)
One of the titles in the Ginn reading series, this book uses good language patterns in spite of having to work with a controlled vocabulary. It presents the life of

a Navajo boy who loves horses and drawing; and other than a rare, innocuous stereotype or two (for example: "Hashe was a Navajo boy and all Navajo boys love horses"), treats its subject matter and its characters with respect, such as the old one who might die in the hogan and the actions the Navajo take as a result. Good for Indian and non-Indian children alike, this book is well illustrated by Don Perceval's gold-, black-, and-white drawings. Good.

583. Monjo, F. N.
  INDIAN SUMMER.
  New York: Harper, 1968. (K–3)
  Indians are portrayed as the enemy ("Suppose it's Indians! We might get scalped" [p.14]) in this story basically concerned with a white settler family on the frontier during the Revolutionary War. The father is away fighting in the war, and so it is up to the mother and children to rout the Indians who attack. With no more than feathers from a quilt, the family successfully battles the whole war party. This is the type of book that presents a purchaser with a real problem: while it is true that an important part of the Revolutionary War was the battle for the frontier, and that pioneer families faced and met hardships, some of which were aggravated by the Indians of the region, it is equally true that many of those same white settlers were on their land illegally, even under white laws, and that it was, no doubt, harder to fight and defeat the Indians protecting their land than this story would indicate. The "Indian Summer" of the title is, according to the book, that time in September and October after harvest but before first frost when Indians were likely to attack. Anita Lobel's black-, brown-, and-white drawings are good, but deserve more emphasis. Story development: Adequate. Portrayal of Indians: Poor.

584. Monjo, F. N.
  THE SECRET OF THE SACHEM'S TREE.
  New York: Coward-McCann, 1972.
  (2–4)

A retelling of the legend of the Charter Oak (Connecticut's favorite story, according to the author), this book tells how a charter granting the colony special freedoms was hidden in an oak tree when British soldiers came to take it away. This book limits its concern with Indians to a brief commentary on King Philip's War, to a crazy woman in the plot whose husband was killed in the war, and to King Philip's head looking like a Halloween pumpkin, on page 19. The story does not mention that King Philip's family was sold into slavery in the West Indies by the Pilgrims. Margot Tomes's black-, white-, and-orange illustrations look as if they were designed for Halloween. One section is on both the writer and the illustrator. Writing: Good. Portrayal of Indians: Poor.

585. Montgomery, Elizabeth Rider.
  CHIEF JOSEPH: GUARDIAN OF
  HIS PEOPLE.
  Champaign, Ill.: Garrard, 1969.
  (3 and up)
  Consistent with the format of all of the Garrard Indian biographies, the author introduces Chief Joseph's story with background information and a map illustrating the trail of the Nez Percé, and the general area in which they lived. The author begins with a few events that affected Chief Joseph's early years. Unlike most stories about Indian leaders, in this book the author describes no remarkable feats performed by Chief Joseph as a child. In fact, he is depicted as a quiet, serious boy who preferred learning from and being with his father; however, he "was a good hunter and strong athlete." The young reader might wish to compare this conflict to that between whites and the Cherokee Nation, although that struggle is not alluded to in this book. Divided loyalties existed in both nations, and both were forced to take a long and arduous journey. The frequent and varied illustrations by Frank Vaughn are in color. Good.

586. Montgomery, Elizabeth Rider.
  CHIEF SEATTLE: GREAT STATESMAN.
  Champaign, Ill.: Garrard, 1966. (2–5)

A small, seldom-mentioned tribe of Pacific Northwest Coast Indians, the Suquamish, one of the tribes from the Puget Sound area, is introduced by the author in the usual Garrard series format. Some background information regarding the wealth and culture of these Indians and a map showing several numbered events described in the book are provided in the introduction. Several customs are presented and descriptions of Suquamish life, such as the long house and a "potlatch," a special kind of party, are touched upon briefly. Although rather stilted and somewhat stereotyped (both Suquamish and white women, when referred to at all, are depicted as good and kind), both good and bad white and Suquamish men are presented, giving the reader a more balanced view of the relationship between Seattle and his tribe, other Puget Sound Indians, and several white leaders. Once again, and consistent with other books in the Garrard series, the colorful illustrations by Ross Hoover distinguish the Suquamish Indians from other tribes described in the series and assist in clarification for the young reader. Adequate.

587. Montgomery, Jean.
THE WRATH OF COYOTE.
New York: Morrow, 1968. (7 and up)
This adventure story uses Miwok culture before and after the arrival of the Spanish as the background for historical fiction. The scene is the world of the Miwok during the lifetime of the protagonist, Kotola. Kotola witnessed the coming of Spanish explorers and the changing pattern of life in the region north of San Francisco Bay. Coyote is a god of the Miwok Nation, and when the laws of Coyote are violated, Kotola believes all subsequent misfortunes are caused by his wrath. This book could be read aloud to younger children, but the vocabulary is more suitable for junior high. Good.

588. Moon, Grace.
CHI-WEE.
New York: Doubleday, 1925. (6–8)
The story of Chi-Wee, a Pueblo Indian

girl, is told through a recounting of her adventures, such as her trip to an ancient ruined pueblo, an accidental excursion into the kiva, and a kidnapping. The book is arranged in episodes which lend themselves well to reading aloud. In reality, it is a moot point whether a traditionally raised Pueblo girl would go into a ruined pueblo and enter a kiva. There are some who would; perhaps, there are more who would not. Certainly at the time of publication, there were many more who would not. The book does have historical value; few authors in 1925 would have attempted a book detailing Pueblo life. Look before buying. Adequate.

589. Moon, Grace, and Moon, Carl.
ONE LITTLE INDIAN.
Chicago: Albert Whitman, 1967.
(K–2)
This is the story of a small Navajo boy written in easy-to-read language so simplified that, at times, it is not especially informative: "He lives in a different kind of house from the one most children live in. His clothes are not like theirs. Almost all of the things he does are different things." Primary-age average readers can read this book for themselves, for the most part. The illustrations, in full color and in yellow-, black-, and-white, are of the "cute children" variety. While the writing is not particularly inspired, it is adequate, and the whole idea behind the book is a good one. Adequate.

590. Mooney, James.
THE GHOST DANCE: RELIGION AND THE SIOUX OUTBREAK OF 1890.
Chicago: Univ. of Chicago Pr., 1965.
(7 and up)
This book provides a graphic account of the Ghost Dance, a ceremony based upon the revelations of two patriot prophets, Tavibo and Wovoka, who preached that the dead were soon to return and that the whites and their culture were, at the same time, to be destroyed by a natural cataclysm. The book is marred by the author's tendency to editorialize, and there is much sentimentality. Other books

should be included in a collection to offset this problem. The book is vividly written, however, in great detail. Adequate.

591. Morgan, William.
COYOTE TALES.
Washington, D.C.: U.S. Dept. of the Interior, Bureau of Indian Affairs, Div. of Education, 1949. (2–5)
Intended for Navajo children to allow them to use familiar materials in their schooling, or to allow Navajo children lacking a traditional background to become more familiar with the oral literature of their culture, this book presents a series of Navajo tales about Coyote. The book provides an introduction to Navajo storytelling traditions and stresses the several purposes these stories served; that is, recalling history, telling of ceremonials, teaching right and wrong, and explaining natural phenomena. Andrew Tsihnahjinnie's black-and-white drawings are good but poorly reproduced here. The whole book deserves a better format. There is a vocabulary section. Good.

592. Morris, Richard B.
THE FIRST BOOK OF THE INDIAN WARS.
New York: Watts, 1959. (4–6)
This book concentrates primarily on the Indian wars in the eastern part of the United States from the coming of Europeans to the Revolutionary War. Although the view the author gives is largely of the various Indian groups as warriors, he is careful to make clear that this was not their entire life. However, typical of most books written at this time (1959), he does concentrate on men:

> Now, this is by no means a fair picture of the Indian. He was a man of peace as well as a fighter. He passed the pipe of peace at his councils as often as he raised the tomahawk. He was an explorer, a discoverer, a hunter, a trapper, and a farmer. He was the first to discover America, the first to learn the secrets of this vast continent. [p.1]

The introductory section is sketchy, but the author writes well. The book itself is limited mostly by a "history as war" theme, which prevents the reader from gaining a view of the overall quality of a group's history and its people. The sections dealing with post-Revolutionary War times are brief and incomplete:

> In fact, wars between Indians and white settlers continued until 1890. Since then peace has existed. Indian reservations are Indian country where the Indians govern themselves. The federal courts see to it that the rights of Indians are protected. Since 1924 citizenship has been extended to all Indians. And that is as it should be. For are they not truly the very first Americans? [p.81]

The black-and-white illustrations by Everett Fisher are good, albeit fierce and warlike; Mildred Waltrip's maps are informative; and the author includes an index that would be easy for elementary school-age children to use. Adequate.

593. Morrow, Suzanne Stark.
INATUK'S FRIEND.
Boston: Atlantic Monthly Pr., 1968. (1–3)
It is almost impossible to differentiate between text and illustration in this book in which the text is so much a part of the design format. The story is concerned with a young Eskimo boy, Inatuk, who has to move with his family to Point Barrow because of his father's inability to find adequate food for his family in the wilderness. The family, especially Inatuk, hates to leave the country for the slums of the city. The various ways Inatuk says goodbye to his friends are presented in a warm, compassionate way by Morrow. She includes in her text such diverse points about modern (1968) Eskimo existence as the fact that most live in sod huts, and she gives a view of the Eskimo carving craft as partly based on intuition: "It [soapstone] almost whispers and tells you what shape will be set free" (p.44). Ellen Raskin's white-, black-, and-orange illustrations are excellent and an integral part of the story. Good.

594. Myers, Elizabeth.
MARIA TALLCHIEF: AMERICA'S PRIMA BALLERINA.
New York: Grosset, 1966. (7–9)

This biography follows the development of Maria Tallchief's career as a ballerina from childhood to her retirement in 1966. Except for several asides, the author includes few comments about Tallchief's relationships with others except in connection with her struggle to become a ballerina. The author also makes a few questionable generalities about Osage beliefs with respect to dancing: for instance, "it could work miracles," "it was as necessary to them [the Osages] as breathing." In addition, the author ascribes a rather negative comment about Osages and work to Tallchief's father, supposedly made when she told him she would be paid to dance: " 'If you are paid, you will be the first Osage to earn a living.' " Nevertheless, the author explains how the affluence of the Osages helped them adjust to the white, middle-class way of life much easier than other tribes, a point not all readers—especially Osage readers—will agree with or accept. While the author makes an interesting comment about the federal government's injunction against tribal dancing because it "feared the emotions" dancing "could arouse," she does not elaborate upon this policy and its effects on Indian life and culture except to say that Tallchief's grandmother, who had lived through this time, hoped to "imbue her with the spirit of tribal dances." In all, the young reader will learn more about ballet and the probabilities (both in terms of hard work and luck) of becoming a prima ballerina than about either the Osages in general or an Indian woman in particular. Some readers may get bogged down in the somewhat confusing chronology of the various ballet companies, and how Tallchief fit into these. The theme of women, in general, having problems combining a career with a family (as Tallchief chose not to do) may raise questions from some readers. Adequate.

595. Myron, Robert.
MOUNDS, TOWNS, AND TOTEMS.
Cleveland, Ohio: World, 1966.
(5 and up)
From the early cultures of Mound Builders to the Reorganization Act of 1934, which returned the reservations to the Indians, this book traces the cultures and lifestyles of the original inhabitants of the North American continent and their descendants. The scope of civilizations in North America is described dramatically and factually. The various cultures which built mounds; the many bands who built pueblos in valleys, on mesas, and in cliffs; the seven tribal groups of the Northwest; the Plains tribes who followed the buffalo; and the Six Nations of the Northeast; all these and more are included in this book. After the last chapter, there is a comparative chronological chart for North America, Central and South America, Europe, and the Near East and Asia, spanning the years from 50,000 B.C. to 1962 A.D.— 51,962 years of human development. Good.

596. Myron, Robert.
SHADOW OF THE HAWK; SAGA OF THE MOUND BUILDERS.
New York: Putnam, 1964. (7 and up)
After giving a comprehensive summary of the coming of people to the Americas, this book pieces together the evidence of the culture of the Archaic Indians in the Ohio Valley. The hawk mentioned in the title is the peregrine falcon, the creature portrayed most frequently in the sculpture of the Mound Builders, whose culture has been dated between 100 and 1000 A.D. Another name for these people is the Hopewell Culture. Maps, sketches, and photographs illustrate the book, and many examples of the hawk motif are shown. Very impressive is the sculpture and copperwork found in some of the mounds and pictured in the book. The style will appeal to young people, and the mystery of the people who chose the hawk for a favorite symbol is better than a fiction plot. Good.

597. Navajo Community;
Roessel, Ruth, ed.
NAVAJO STORIES OF THE LONG WALK PERIOD.
Chinle, Ariz.: Navajo Community College Pr., 1973. (7 and up)
This is a collection of forty stories, retold by living Navajo men and women as

169

they had heard them from grandparents and great-grandparents or other relatives. The stories deal with the personal experiences of Navajo men, women, and children who were subjected to the "Long Walk" or forced dislocation from (and/or escape back to) their homes. As the author carefully points out, some storytellers place the blame for the Long Walk at the feet of the Navajos themselves; others point the finger at the U.S. government, the Mexicans, or other Indian tribes. Nevertheless, one cannot help but empathize with every person described in each of the stories. In addition to a brief description of each narrator, the editor explains the Navajo concept of time and provides definitions of five levels of Navajo kinship: the biological family, extended family, outfit, clan, and linked clans. There are numerous pencil sketches by Raymond Johnson, which are extremely well done and complement the text. In addition, a map of the Navajo Reservation is reproduced on the inside covers, front and back, of the book. Good.

598. Nee, Kay Bonner.
POWHATAN: THE STORY OF AN
AMERICAN INDIAN.
Minneapolis, Minn.: Dillon Pr., 1971.
(3–5)
This biography of Powhatan concentrates as much on his tribe's history and customs (e.g., "The Powhatan were very clean people. They bathed in the river every morning, even on the coldest days of winter" [p.6]) and on his daughter, Pocahontas, as on Powhatan the man. The legend of Pocahontas, the "young princess" as she is called by the author, is set forth as fact, although many historians do not believe it to be true. The book also deals with Thomas Rolfe, son of Pocahontas and John Rolfe. The book is characterized by good, sparse writing. Adequate.

599. Nelson, Mary Carroll.
ANNIE WAUNEKA: THE STORY OF
AN AMERICAN INDIAN.
Minneapolis, Minn.: Dillon Pr., 1972.
(4–9)

As is true of much of Nelson's work, (such as her earlier biography of Pablita Velarde), the author once again has captured the essence of her subject, Annie Wauneka, as a living, real individual, as well as presented an objective view of her tribal group, the Navajos. Beginning with an introduction describing the Navajo nation, or "the Dineh" (The People), the author presents some historical background leading up to Chee Dodge's (Wauneka's father's) leadership and eventually into Ms. Wauneka's own accomplishments. Widely acclaimed and recognized as a leader of her people, Ms. Wauneka's achievements are described in the context of believable situations, which need no further literary embellishments. Consistent with the earlier work, the book includes photographs of Ms. Wauneka as well as amplifications or explanations of Indian concepts and practices. The photographs in the book are from R. A. Brown of the *Albuquerque Journal*; Martin Link, the Navajo Tribal Photograph Collection; and Annie Wauneka. Good.

600. Nelson, Mary Carroll.
MARIA MARTINEZ: THE STORY OF AN
AMERICAN INDIAN.
Minneapolis, Minn.: Dillon Pr., 1972.
(4–6)
Maria Martinez is a famous Pueblo Indian potter, and this is her story. She has lived a long life in which
> it is traditional that all people in the pueblo live on one social level. No one is expected to do outstanding things or to be too much of an individual. Persons who are unusual in any way are still looked on as somehow dangerous to the group. [p.11]
and yet has prospered. The book gives good explanations of Pueblo customs and interests. A realistic view of Pueblo women is presented. Non-Pueblo or non-Indian readers may need help understanding her husband's giving her his money and her dividing it with both groups of parents: "In the pueblo, it was felt that everyone worked to help everyone else in their family" (pp.34–35). Other items for discus-

sion with young readers might be church influences, alcohol, changes in Pueblo life. The author occasionally uses the word *American* where she means non-Indian: "The teacher was an American woman named Miss Grimes" (p.25). An excellent discussion of pottery-making is given. Good.

601. Nelson, Mary Carroll.
MICHAEL NARANJO: THE STORY OF AN AMERICAN INDIAN.
Minneapolis, Minn.: Dillon Pr., 1975. (4–7)
Michael Naranjo is a Pueblo sculptor blinded in the Vietnam War. In this biography of his life, Nelson presents, in addition to a fine delineation of the man and his accomplishments, a short but good history of the Pueblo Indians; an excellent section on the relationship of Naranjo to his work:

When Spirit was completed, Michael knew it instinctively. There was nothing left for him to do on it. He talked to the statue and felt a companionship with it. The connection between him and his statue had lasted close to a year. [p.51]

and photographs of some of Naranjo's sculpture. This is a good book to use with all children, Indian and non-Indian, and it is especially good material to use with handicapped children or children who are close to handicapped people. Good.

602. Nelson, Mary Carroll.
PABLITA VELARDE: THE STORY OF AN AMERICAN INDIAN.
Minneapolis, Minn.: Dillon Pr., 1971. (4–9)
In one of the more objective examples of the writing of biographies, Nelson presents Velarde's life story in text written simply and with great sensitivity. There are neither stereotypes nor romanticized characters here. Absent, too, are the stilted or unreal individuals often found in biographies. Beginning with the birth of Tse Tsan, or "Golden Dawn" (the name "Pablita" was given to Ms. Velarde by the nuns when she was at school), the author introduces both the Santa Clara Pueblo people and the Pueblo culture. Just as Pablita Velarde learned Anglo ways and eventually married a white man, Herb Hardin, the author weaves Indian and non-Indian life into her book in much the same effective way as Pablita apparently was able to combine the two ways of life into her own life style. Always an individual, separate from others (both Indian and white), Pablita emerges as a unique, talented person. Several photographs of Ms. Velarde and examples of her art are included. Good.

603. Nequatewa, Edmund.
TRUTH OF A HOPI: STORIES RELATING TO THE ORIGIN, MYTHS AND CLAN HISTORIES OF THE HOPI.
Flagstaff: Museum of Northern Arizona, 1967. (8 and up)
These Hopi stories of creation, origins, and beliefs are deceptively simple: they are not easy to understand, just as some segments of the Judeo-Christian Bible are difficult to interpret. In an involved explanation, Nequatewa informs the reader how it is possible for him to share stories intended only for Hopis with non-Hopi readers: in an attempt to record the stories before they are lost as traditions change, Nequatewa, as a member of a clan permitted to share with outsiders, is allowed to write the stories. For the most part, the original language patterning of the author is kept to insure the authenticity of the feel and content of the stories. Also included is an interesting account of Dr. Fewkes, pioneer ethnologist, as a part of the legends. The printing is difficult to read in the section devoted to the author's notes. Good.

604. Newcomb, Charles G.
THE SMOKE HOLE.
San Antonio, Tex.: Naylor, 1968. (5–8)
The plot of this story has an unusual twist. Yazzi, a young Navajo orphan, is sent by his beloved grandfather to live with and learn from a white trader. Yazzi learns well; and, secure in the affection of

his grandfather and the trader, bridges both Navajo and white world. Customs, ceremonials and family ties of the Navajo are described, and various portrayals of the whites acquaint the reader with several types, from the empathetic trader to the insensitive federal agent. The story is limited by routine writing and one-dimensional characterizations. Adequate.

605. Newcomb, Franc Johnson.
HOSTEEN KLAH: NAVAHO MEDICINE MAN AND SAND PAINTER.
Norman: Univ. of Oklahoma Pr., 1964. (7 and up)
This is an extremely well-written and informative documentary, in which some less sophisticated readers may get bogged down with facts and details. The feelings and attitudes of the characters (in an interpretive sense) have been most carefully omitted. The story of a modern Navajo, the author traces Hosteen Klah's background from his grandmother's grandfather, who was a chief, to his grandmother's history, through his own boyhood and ultimate achievement as medicine man and sand painter. The author describes the education of a Navajo medicine man and his relationships with the white world, and includes good, illuminating photographs at appropriate places throughout the book. (On page xxvii the author provides an interesting explanation regarding the distinction between the two spellings *Navaho* and *Navajo*. Apparently *Navaho* is the preference of the University of Oklahoma Press, while *Navajo* is the Indian preference.) Good.

606. Newcomb, Franc Johnson.
NAVAJO BIRD TALES.
Wheaton, Ill.: Theosophical Publishing House, 1970. (4–adult)
Published under a grant from the Kern Foundation, this collection of folk tales for children conveys the color and atmosphere of Navajo tribal lore and customs. The reader is drawn into the culture by the literary device of a narrator, an old medicine man who passes on the oral tradition of his people to a Navajo shepherd boy and his companions. Many of the values and ethics of the Navajo people are conveyed through tales of animals and birds. Lovely black-and-white sketches by Navajo artist Na-Ton-Sak-Ka whet the appetite for more illustrations than are included. Good.

607. Newell, Edythe W.
THE RESCUE OF THE SUN AND OTHER TALES FROM THE FAR NORTH.
Chicago: Albert Whitman, 1970.
(3 and up)
An extensive introductory section, taking up almost half the length of the book, prepares the reader for these tales of the Far North which are apparently of both Indian and Eskimo derivation, something which the author never makes clear in spite of the lengthy introduction. Much of the work is based on that of Boas and other early ethnologists, and the author has obviously done a good deal of research. Modern as well as older cultural patterns are described: "Nowadays, the people of the Far North live in towns, fly in airplanes, drive tractors, and race in snowmobiles. When they hunt, they use the best weapons" (p.23). Sources are listed immediately after each story, and there is a glossary of Eskimo words. The illustrations were done by Franz Altschuler, who makes good use of white lines etched or scratched on black shapes. Adequate.

608. Newman, Sandra Corrie.
INDIAN BASKET WEAVING: HOW TO WEAVE POMO, YUROK, PIMA AND NAVAJO BASKETS.
Flagstaff, Ariz.: Northland Pr., 1974.
(7–9)
Each chapter of this book discusses the history, uses, materials, making, and designing of the baskets of the Indian tribes listed in the title of the book. The pictures of basket making are most graphic, and procedures describing their manufacture are clear. Included in the book is a glossary of terms and a list of suggested readings. Interspersed throughout are authentic facts about the Indian peoples, themselves. The book is well written. Good.

609. Nooyéét, Bit Haz'áadi.
NÁSHDÓI YÁÁZH.
Washington, D.C.: National
Geographic Soc., 1972. (1–3)

A book completely in Navajo about African lions, this is a National Geographic Society publication for teaching Navajo children to read Navajo. The format is beautiful, and the photographs meet the usual technically competent National Geographic standard. This book demonstrates how bright, professional-looking books can be produced for different ethnic groups for a reasonable price. All the publisher needs to do is replace the Navajo segments with English or Swahili or Danish to have a book that can cut across cultures. Whether or not a book on African lions is appropriate for use with young Navajo children is the kind of argument that can never be ended, with some educators maintaining that materials should be relevant and specific to a culture, while others argue that one purpose of reading is to extend student horizons beyond what they see every day. Neither side is wrong, but they both can get mighty heated in their discussions. This book could be used as is, written in Navajo, to teach non-Navajo children to interpret picture content, to demonstrate to non-Navajo-speaking parents the difficulties encountered in a child's beginning to learn to read a printed page, and to help Navajo children realize that their native language can be written down and read, among other uses. Good.

610. Norbeck, Oscar E.
BOOK OF INDIAN LIFE CRAFTS.
New York: Association Pr., 1966.
(5 and up)

With a map for a frontispiece, this book is careful to distinguish between Indian nations in respect to costumes, ornaments, decorations, weaving, music, and other cultural elements. The illustrations in black-and-white show how to make different objects from original American cultures, using the same materials originally used by Indians, as well as substitute materials. The book is designed for use by youth groups interested in developing projects on Indian culture. Although many Indian nations are mentioned, the author has emphasized Plains Indian crafts. Good.

611. Norbeck, Oscar E.
INDIAN CRAFTS FOR CAMPERS.
New York: Association Pr., 1967.
(5 and up)

This is a small, pocket-sized condensation of Norbeck's previous work, *Book of Indian Life Crafts*. Refer to that review, #610.

612. O'Connor, Richard.
WAR CHIEF OF THE SIOUX:
SITTING BULL.
New York: McGraw-Hill, 1968.
(5 and up)

This book covers Sitting Bull's life from his babyhood until his death, which partially precipitated the massacre at Wounded Knee. Beginning with the explanation of how Sitting Bull earned his name, the author emphasizes his early life in the "last carefree years left to the Indians" when the boy grew up in "complete freedom" and where he was "nourished on rich soup and broth, pemmican larded with buffalo tallow, buffalo hump, haunch of venison," and so on. However lengthily the author explains his views of the "free, careless days of the child of nature," he is less expansive in his descriptions of the constant fear of attack from other Indian tribes; he does state that Sitting Bull's mother put moccasins on his feet each night because there might be a night raid, giving him further instructions, in the event of an attack, to run and hide until the fighting was over (pp.15–17). O'Connor's treatment of the moves from camp to camp, following game, the raids and counter-raids where every Indian man, woman, and child were often killed seem almost glamorous when compared to his comments about white duplicity and treachery. He provides details of Sitting Bull as a young boy and recounts his early brave deeds, such as counting coup at age fourteen, fighting a grizzly bear, and killing a Crow chief after being shot in the foot. The author's treatment of women is derogatory, when they are mentioned at all. With the exception of Catherine Weldon, the white woman who preached against the Ghost Dance, the author seldom refers to any women by name, including Sitting Bull's mother, described early in the book. However, he does give an authentic report of the various historical events surrounding Sitting Bull's life. In addition, he correctly points out that major decisions rested with elders and warriors, not with one or two great chiefs or other important individuals. The black-and-white "drawings" by Eric von Schmidt border on the grotesque. However, since the story deals mainly with violence and death, it may be consistent to illustrate the characters described as if they were in the intermediate stages of decomposition. Adequate.

613. O'Dell, Scott.
ISLAND OF THE BLUE DOLPHINS.
Boston: Houghton, 1960. (6–9)
This is a most unusual story, based upon the recorded incident of an Indian girl whose tribe was evacuated from its California island home. For eighteen years, Karana lived a female Robinson Crusoe existence. Once some Aleuts came to the island, but she hid until they left. Year after year she kept herself alive by building a rude shelter, creating tools and weapons, finding food, and fending off the wild dogs, her ever-present enemies. Told in the first person, Karana's story is a convincing one of survival in an adventurous setting that will appeal to adolescents and preadolescents who spurn romantic teenage stories, and to girls seeking identity and feelings of independence. This book is a Newbery Award winner. A classic. Good.

614. O'Dell, Scott.
SING DOWN THE MOON.
Boston: Houghton, 1970. (2–6)
This is a story of a young Navajo girl in 1864, when Kit Carson invaded Canyon de Chelly and started the Navajo on the "Long Walk" to Bosque Redondo, New Mexico. The story moves along briskly, aided by language that flows and by accurate details of Navajo customs (for instance, women owning sheep, talk of ghosts, the warrior tradition of the Navajo, girls running in the morning); however, there are a few places where the text does not quite sound Navajo: "I know it is bad luck to be so happy. The gods do not like anyone to show happiness in this way and they punish those who do not obey them" (p.2). This was a 1971 Newbery Honor book. Adequate.

615. O'Dell, Scott.
ZIA.
Boston: Houghton, 1976. (6–8)
This is a strange tale. Zia is Karana's niece, and this story continues Karana's adventures after she leaves the Island of the Blue Dolphins. Zia and her brother find a boat on the beach near where they live at the mission at Santa Barbara, California. They repair the boat and attempt to rescue Karana, but weather, distance, whalers, and shipwrecks interfere. Finally, Karana is rescued and finds life at the mission too confining. She goes to live in a cave on the beach where she becomes ill. Zia tries to nurse her, and as Karana becomes weaker, Zia tries to get help at the mission. The padres refuse unless Karana will return to the mission, which she will not do. She dies, according to Zia, because she misses the island and the animals and because she sees no place for herself in mission life. At Karana's death, Zia also leaves the mission to return to her home with the Pala Indians. O'Dell writes beautifully, and, in spite of the tangled plot described above, manages to provide readers with an understanding of a dilemma that is not easily solved. Good.

616. O'Kane, Walter Collins.
THE HOPIS: PORTRAIT OF A DESERT PEOPLE.
Norman: Univ. of Oklahoma Pr., 1953. (7 and up)
This is an illustrated series of "portraits," or vignettes, about living (as of

1953) Hopi Indians. Except for four pictures, the portraits are almost exclusively of elderly men. However, the text describes both men and women. The book reflects the attitudes of the author and includes a great many stereotypes and role assignments; for instance, page 242 describes four-year-old Margaret, pictured on the opposite page in a clean, frilly green department store-type dress and modern hair style, as the granddaughter of one of the previously shown elderly men, one who "knows how to do her part in household duties." The other three women pictured in the photographs are similarly described as daughters or wives, while the men who appear in photographs are described in terms of their own merit. Nevertheless, the color photographs are worth seeing; not all, however, are described in the text. Adequate.

617. Olds, Elizabeth.
FEATHER MOUNTAIN.
Eau Claire, Wisc.: Hale, 1951. (1–4)
This is a good story, an adaptation of an Iroquois legend about how various birds got their colored feathers. The author's color illustrations are well displayed by a fine, eye-pleasing format. There is nothing in the story to identify it as Iroquois or even Indian; adults will have to identify it as such for the child reader. Good.

618. O'Meara, Walter.
THE SIOUX ARE COMING.
Boston: Houghton, 1971. (4–6)
O'Meara uses an Ojibwa family preparing winter food, forced to flee from the threat of a Sioux raiding party, as a backdrop for this story of the Ojibwa son, who grows up and takes his share of family responsibilities, symbolized by his building of a canoe for escape under almost impossible conditions. The author is obviously well acquainted with the minutiae of Ojibwa life—foods, harvest, and so on—and includes a detailed account of how to build an Ojibwa canoe. O'Meara's writing and Lorence Bjorklund's black-and-white illustrations are certainly competent, but nei-

ther author nor illustrator create much excitement in this book. Adequate.

619. Overholser, Wayne D., and
Patten, Lewis B.
THE MEEKER MASSACRE.
New York: Cowles Book, 1969. (5–9)
A fictionalized account of the so-called Meeker Massacre of 1879, in which the killing of Indian Agent Meeker and the capture of his wife and children, among others, led to the displacement of the Utes from their Colorado homeland and the opening of the land to white settlement, this book won the 1969 Spur Award for the best western juvenile book. The story is told through the adventures of two teenage boys, Dave Madden, a white, and Tono, a Ute. The two friends witness or participate in an assortment of events during the uprising, including Meeker's attempt to plow under the Ute horse pastures and race tracks, and various scenes of slaughter and capitivity. The authors write well. However, occasionally their characterizations miss: for example, Colorow, the Ute chief, is pictured primarily as a big, greedy beggar, and the white boy, Dave, is almost too smart, forgiving, and aware. Dave's thoughts at the end of the book smack of paternalism:

Suddenly Dave knew what he wanted to do when he was old enough. He would work with the Indians, wherever they were when that time came. He wanted to understand and he wanted them to understand white people. If he were successful, things like the Meeker massacre would never need to happen again. [p.133]

The authors provide the reader with a fine introductory section and a map of the story's setting. Good.

620. Palmer, William R.
WHY THE NORTH STAR STANDS STILL.
New York: Prentice-Hall, 1957. (3–8)
A recounting of a Paiute (spelled "Pahute" in the text) legend explaining natural phenomena, this book is well illustrated by Ursula Koering's brown-and-white sketches. The author was made a

tribal member for various services he provided on land disputes, and states that at first he was denied permission to "make a book" about Paiutes, but later received the necessary approval. He includes an interesting section on Paiute astronomy and a glossary of Paiute words and names. His explanation of the Paiute's lack of standards of measurement will not be considered valid by many linguists or semanticists due to his limited interpretation of the term *measurement*, nor will his statement, "the Pahutes are animists" (unpaged) be considered a complete explanation of Paiute religion by many specialists on Indian religions. Good.

621. Parish, Peggy.
GOOD HUNTING, LITTLE INDIAN.
New York: Young Scott Books, 1962.
(K–2)
A story of an Indian boy (tribe unspecified) who goes hunting, has various adventures, and comes home on the back of a wild hog (a rather dangerous method of transportation, to say the least, even in fiction), this book is saved neither by good writing nor by "redeeming social qualities." Although illustrator Leonard Weisgard's technique is good, his picturing of a Pueblo pot in a Plains tepee and a mixture of tribal dress styles further complicates the book's stereotyping problems. Poor.

622. Parish, Peggy.
GRANNY AND THE INDIANS.
New York: Macmillan, 1969. (1–3)
In this humorous, thirty-page story, the illustrations depict Indians in settings that might be interpreted as stereotyped, and the characterization of a gun-toting granny who is totally fearless may be too ridiculous for some readers. Granny Guntry is a spunky old lady who lives alone in the woods. She frequently pilfers the rabbits, turkey, and fish that the Indians (tribe unspecified) had intended for their own meals. This upsets the Indians, but Granny doesn't change her life style until her house burns down; then she decides to "move in" with the Indians. In response

to this, the good-hearted Indians decide to build Granny a new house. Her gratitude is boundless; in repayment she vows to cook all their meals, every day. As this is too much meddling, the Indians finally make a deal with her: if she will stay out of the woods, they will supply her meat every day. The story ends happily. This is a humorous, and entertaining, if not factual, story. The large print and delightful three-tone illustrations by Brinton Turkle suggest that a primary grade audience is intended. Story development: Adequate. Portrayal of Indians: Poor.

623. Parish, Peggy.
LITTLE INDIAN.
New York: Simon & Schuster, 1968.
(K–2)
This is the fantasy story of a little Indian boy (tribe unspecified) who is searching for a name. He finally chooses Snapping Turtle when one catches on to his trousers and hitches a ride home. Needless to say, the story has little to do with the traditions of any tribe regarding naming customs. However, the book was probably never intended as a serious treatise on American Indian naming practices and rituals. Nevertheless, it is just such unconscious practices on the part of authors and illustrators (in this case John E. Johnson, who has provided typical "bow, arrow, and feather" fantasies in color) to which many Native American groups object. Parish and Johnson both demonstrate plenty of talent; a little research would make their efforts more fruitful. Poor.

624. Parker, Arthur C.
SKUNNY WUNDY.
Chicago: Albert Whitman, 1970.
(4–7)
A collection of Seneca Indian tales, this book is a revised edition of Arthur C. Parker's 1926 book. The author, whose Indian name is Gawaso Wanneh, is descended through his father's family (his grandfather was a leading sachem, or chief) from the Senecas. In this collection of twenty-eight tales, told to the author by his "uncles" ("Every old Indian expected

to be called 'uncle' " [p.10]), Mr. Parker reports the more frequently repeated tales of the old tribal storytellers. The story about "Skunny Wundy" begins the series. Skunny Wundy is a stranger or an extremely intelligent being who puts all the stories told to him each night by the Fox (under circumstances reversed from those of Scheherazade), into an otter skin bag to be discovered by boys and girls when they arrive on earth. The stories are each about animals with specific personality traits; for example, Fox and Raccoon are clever, Rabbit is easily fooled, Bear is brave but stupid, Wolf is often a villain, and Turtle is considered the best or most important animal, according to the author. The book will interest most young readers and can be compared with Aesop's fables, which these tales resemble closely in moral tone as well as in content. The illustrations by George Armstrong are in black-and-white, interesting as well as surprising and startling. Good.

625. Parker, Mack.
THE AMAZING RED MAN.
San Antonio, Tex.: Naylor, 1960.
(5–8)
The reminiscences and interests of an obviously sincere and admittedly self-educated man, this book is filled with a poorly written, unrelated assortment of his thoughts and beliefs about American Indians. Some samples:

I am proud of the fact that I have never had any trouble with the Indians. [p.vi]

When this country was discovered, the American Indian excelled all nations in the science of medicine and drugs and in agriculture. [p.xi]

Chief Victor Griffin, Quapaw Tribe, was a great leader of his people, a good man and a fine neighbor. I was proud to call him friend as well as a brother Mason. He is now deceased. [p.2]

Having been raised among the Indians and the different tribes, I know from experience many of his characteristics. [p.13]

I have known many full-blooded Indians of many tribes. They were not deceitful or egotistical. Proud, yes, but not the haughty pride; theirs was a humble pride of a great race. [p.15]
Various chapters detail such various subjects as "Great Chiefs I Have Known," "Let Us Save America," and the like, and frequently consist of nothing more than lists of names. The chapter on Indian women, for example consists of one paragraph which begins, "An Indian woman, Mrs. Sacajawea, of the Shoshone tribe. . . ." (p.48). There is an index. Poor.

626. Parkman, Francis.
THE OREGON TRAIL: SKETCHES OF
PRAIRIE AND ROCKY MOUNTAIN LIFE.
Boston: Little, 1937. (5 and up)
Written in the florid but courtly style of writing popular at the turn of the century ("The Wild West is tamed, and its savage charms have withered" [p.xi]), this book is illustrated by the great sketches of Frederic Remington. Basically a story of pioneer life on the Oregon Trail, the book treats Indians as incidental or as obstacles. This is a historical classic, first issued in 1892, and reflects some of the common prejudices of the time, not only about Indians, but about Indian women, termed *squaws*, and about Mormons, also seen as fearful obstacles. There is an index. Good as history, but does not include a detailed or particularly accurate picture of American Indian groups of the time.

627. Parnall, Peter.
THE GREAT FISH.
Garden City, N.Y.: Doubleday, 1973.
(K–2)
The illustrations by the author, which, incidentally are the best part of a fine book, show modern pollution and what it does to tribal salmon fishing grounds. He almost makes pollution pretty, so well does he draw and so skillfully does he compose his pictures. The reader is hit with great design, and it takes a moment to realize that the subjects Parnall draws are tin cans, trash, "gloop." In the story, in which the Indian grandfather recounts tales to

his grandson of other, better times, the language flows smoothly. Adults who look at this book in a superficial manner may wrongly conclude that this is a fine, beautifully illustrated book to help children learn about the fine, beautiful life of the American Indian. This would be a mistake; much hidden depth is to be found. Be prepared for intense discussions about the issues the author raises as the child reader is struck with the same paradox of technique and subject. Art and literature teachers can use this book as an object lesson on the author-illustrator. Although recommended for grades kindergarten through two, the book would be of interest to many mature readers in grades three and four or even higher because of content and illustration. Good.

628. Parsons, Elsie Clews.
AMERICAN INDIAN LIFE.
Lincoln: Univ. of Nebraska Pr., 1967.
(7 and up)
This book uses as its format a series of fictional stories detailing white observations of various Indian groups: for instance, "She [the Indian subject of this conversation] always says she will come, and sometimes she comes and sometimes she doesn't come. I was so surprised when I first came out here to find that Indians were like that" (p.1). Parsons writes and edits well, and the list of cautions A. L. Kroeber offers in the introduction about religion and the limitations placed on Indian groups by economics and government are still applicable; as he states, humor is not a part of this collection, at least not intentionally. The book is illustrated by C. Grant La Farge; there is an appendix giving notes on various Indian tribes; and some brief, interesting notes on the illustrator. This book is a well-written example of white reaction reporting, and, although now dated, it still has historical value. Good.

629. Payne, Elizabeth, and Davis, Jack.
MEET THE NORTH AMERICAN INDIANS.
New York: Random House, 1965.
(3–5)

A description of five tribes (Makah, Hopi, Creeks, Penobscot, and Mandan) at the time of Columbus, illustrated with black-, white-, and-brown drawings, this book emphasizes hunting, gathering food supplies, dress, climate, tools, war; all more or less readily accessible information. For the most part, social and family patterns are not covered. The inclusion of a Northwest tribe is unusual for a book of this sort, and the writer gives a good description of language and custom changes before the introduction of white culture patterns and a good, simple description of the "Hopi way." Some controversial items are stated as fact; for example, that scalping preceded the white men, that the Makah were much richer than the Hopi, that Columbus discovered America, that Creeks were more warlike than other tribes, or that Mandans are representative of Plains tribes. Sometimes Indian customs are represented from the author's viewpoint: "They [Creek women] made the boys do all kinds of jobs they did not like to do" (p.47). Supplement with other books on these subjects to avoid a one-sided view. Adequate.

630. Peake, Katy.
THE INDIAN HEART OF CARRIE HODGES.
New York: Viking, 1972. (6 and up)
Not really a book about Native Americans, except for brief references to Zuñi fetishes and the carrying of a fetish-shaped rock by the main female character, this is a satisfying portrait of an adolescent white girl. Well written in noncondescending fashion by a writer who obviously believes teen-agers deserve good, intelligent materials, this book tells of the friendship of the girl and an old trapper. From the opening scenes of the girl mirroring the movements of the flight of a hawk, through the detailing of the friendship between trapper and girl, and, later, between the girl and dog and the girl's reaction to the hunting of coyotes, this is a book most cattle-country kids, especially, can appreciate—it presents an accurate picture of ranch life. The writer's use of words is precise and appropriate: "In the way that dogs

learn such things, Tippy immediately adopted for himself the limitations of Carrie's personal territory" (p.16). Thomas B. Allen's black-and-white illustrations, that suggest rather than detail exact images, fit very well the mood of the story. Good.

631. Pearson, M. J.
PONY OF THE SIOUX.
Garden City, N.Y.: Doubleday, 1961. (4–6)
Apparently set during the so-called Spirit Lake Massacre, judging from contextual clues, this book is about an Indian convert who warns a town about danger, becomes friends with a white boy, and is adopted by a white family as one of their own. Indians are treated primarily as a danger and a worry, except for the boy who saves the town. The book is illustrated in black-and-white by Carl Pfeufer. Story: Adequate. Portrayal of Indians: Poor.

632. Peck, Leigh.
DON COYOTE.
Eau Claire, Wisc.: Hale, 1941. (2–4)
A good book about coyotes but not particularly about Indians, except for the inclusion of several Indian tales about Coyote (tribal sources unspecified), this book is concerned with the effect coyotes have had on humanity—white ranchers, Indians, Mexicans, and others. Virginia Lee Burton's color illustrations are excellent. Good.

633. Peck, Robert N.
FAWN.
Boston: Little, 1975. (7–9)
This slightly farfetched story of Fawn, the son of a scholarly French Jesuit and the grandson of a Mohawk warrior, is well written and well paced. Women receive short shrift; Fawn's mother is ordered to be Black Robe's woman. Since the book presents a story of Indian life dominated by war, male concerns, and revenge, it should be supplemented with other views of Mohawk life. Adequate.

634. Penney, Grace Jackson.
TALES OF THE CHEYENNES.
Boston: Houghton, 1953. (5–7)

Using an interesting organizational concept, Cheyenne legends recounted as if they belonged to one person, this book presents a good picture of Cheyenne old-time storytelling practices. Readers will be surprised at the similarity of these stories to those of the Greeks, Romans, Hebrews, and other peoples: for example, the story "How Dry Land Came to Be" shares many parallels with Genesis, and other stories remind the reader of Velikovsky's cataclysmic theories. Walter Richard West's black-and-white illustrations are good, but reproduced here in much too small a format. The book—stories and illustrations, alike—is good enough to warrant reissuing with a more modern format. Good.

635. Perkins, Lucy Fitch.
THE ESKIMO TWINS.
New York: Walker, 1969. (2–4)
With an original copyright date of 1914, this book was one of Perkins's well known twin series, popular in children's literature up through the 1930s. The story contains a series of adventures, each episode complete in a chapter. Written on an approximately second-grade reading level, the book is too long by today's standards. The text contains a surprising amount of accurate material, but is, for the most part, a fantasy that has little to do with Eskimos, who are made to behave as if they were the white, middle class kids next door at the start of the century: "They waved their hands as it [the sun] slipped out of sight. 'Good-bye, old sun,' they shouted, 'and good-bye, Shadow, too! We shall be glad to see you both when you come back again'" (p.192). Perkins is also the illustrator, and her line drawings seem dated and cute, picturing as they do the twins with their twin pups. The book is of historic value because of its contribution to children's literature. Story: Adequate. Portrayal of Eskimos: Poor.

636. Perkins, Lucy Fitch.
THE INDIAN TWINS.
New York: Walker, 1969. (2–4)
Those adults raised in the 1930s will doubtless remember Perkins's twin series

books. This one, about a tribe the author calls Leaf Dwellers, is the Indian volume of the series and reflects the sentimental prose often considered appropriate for children's books at the time of its copyright, 1930: "Far away in the golden West there is a snow-capped mountain, and on its eastward side, sloping toward the sunrise, there is an ancient forest" (p.vii). The writing contains passages that stereotype the behaviors of boys and girls:

> "I believe I'll creep under my mother's blanket," he thought to himself. "She is only a woman, and I'm almost sure she would feel more safe if I were with her." [p.9]

> She did not wait to find out what it was —she didn't remember that little Indian children must never, never cry—she just opened her mouth wide and let out one great, big, round scream. [p.13]

The old-fashioned black-and-white illustrations are the author's. Of historical interest though dated. Poor.

637. Perrine, Mary.
NANNABAH'S FRIEND.
Boston: Houghton, 1970. (2–4)
This story has a universal theme—the necessity of children assuming responsibility for themselves and others and replacing some of childhood's isolated reliance on the family with more reliance on self and outsiders. A young Navajo girl is sent out alone by her grandmother to herd the family sheep. She is afraid and lonely and makes herself some dolls that she plays with as a substitute for her family. Another Navajo herder girl comes along, and they become friends. This theme applies across cultures. The solution to the girl's problem, the rapid appearance of another girl who becomes a friend, causes the reader to wonder what would have happened if, as is often the case in real life, no one had appeared. How would the girl handle her loneliness then? Leonard Weisgard's black-, white-, gold-, and-violet illustrations are beautifully done and help carry the story; unfortunately, the people he draws do not look Navajo. Good.

638. Perrine, Mary.
SALT BOY.
New York: Houghton, 1968. (3–4)
This is the story of an Indian named Salt Boy. Salt Boy wants to learn how to rope. His father promises to teach him how, but tells him not to practice on his mother's sheep. While tending the sheep, he finds a rope and is forced to use it to save one of the herd. In taking the risk of using it, he demonstrates his responsibility to his father, and is allowed to learn how to rope the big, black horse. The book makes clear the fact that the herd belongs to the mother. Although this appears to be a Navajo story, no reference to a tribe is made. This is a good example of rounded characterization and good plot development. The writing is well done. The illustrations are fine and accurate, although the father's hat in the drawings is not the type of headgear Navajo men usually wear on the reservation. Good.

639. Philbrook, Cleve.
CAPTURED BY THE ABNAKIS.
New York: Hastings House, 1966. (6–8)
This fictionalized account of two white boys, ages fifteen and eleven, who were captured by Abnakis, lived with the Indians for several months, and then escaped, is a typical captivity story. The author does a good job of describing settler life in 1695 and includes such details as how to fell backlogs (notching trees so they fall in a line). However, he sometimes stereotypes the Abnakis: "It was well that he did, for Kohokas now revealed that vacillation of character Ike knew was typical of the red man" (p.37); presents a hard-to-believe picture of running a gauntlet: "He reached the end of the line without a blow landing squarely" (p.50); and offers a casual, but not necessarily accurate, picture of violence and brutality:

> He was sure if the situation were reversed, he and Joe would not exactly coddle an Indian prisoner. [p.26]

> Biting his lip, he put the whip to Joe without mercy, lashing him to his feet.

The Indians back at Pigwacket had done this to both of them sometimes, when he and Joe were fatigued or rebellious, but Ike never dreamed he would ever have to use such desperate measures. [p.131]

The writing is average in quality, although the author does offer interesting comments in the author's notes section. Adequate.

640. Pietroforte, Alfred.
SONGS OF THE YOKUTS AND PAIUTES.
Healdsburg, Calif.: Naturegraph, 1965. (4–8)

In an attempt to save some of the music of the California Indians, the author, who describes himself as more of a researcher than a musician, may have used too scholarly an organizational pattern for most fourth through sixth graders. He presents each song, including musical notations and translations, in conjunction with a short story—possibly the best part of the book for elementary school-age children. Tapes are available to accompany the text. The book presents material of value to Indian and non-Indian reader alike. Unfortunately, the type used in printing the book is crowded and hard to read, the format is badly done, and the reproduction of photographs is of poor quality. There is a bibliography. Book format: Poor. Contents and writing: Good.

641. Pine, Tillie S.
THE INDIANS KNEW.
New York: McGraw-Hill, 1957. (1–4)

This presents an interesting array of some of the things Indians (never fully specified) knew, such as the fact that wood could be bent to make things go rapidly through the air, and the like. The format is organized in such a way that each thing "the Indians knew" is also given an application that holds true today (1957) in the readers' lives, and appropriate experiments based on the scientific fact under discussion are described. This is an interesting tie-in and helps children understand that Indians were scientists, too. The problem with the book, however, is

two-fold: (1) in terms of science, the reader could conclude that the Indians under discussion never carried the scientific principle to a high level of application and that only non-Indians completed the process. This, of course, is not valid—applications now being made of the various scientific discoveries are far from perfect or complete; and (2) there is confusion on what constitutes science and progress. Instead of emphasizing that a jet plane does not constitute something more progressive and scientific than finding a way across unmarked prairie, the book gives the impression one lifestyle is superior to another. Ezra Jack Keats's color illustrations are good, although he mixes up a variety of Indian hair, dress, and living styles. Adequate.

642. Pistorius, Anna.
WHAT INDIAN IS IT?
Chicago: Follett, 1956. (2–3)

Pistorius uses a question and answer format ("What Indians built skyscrapers 1000 years ago?" "What Indian invention was used by the Navy?" "What was the Supermarket of the Plains?") for this general book about American Indians for primary-age children. The writing is simplistic: "Some of these people lived very simply. Others were great builders and artists, whose works still remain after thousands of years." She does not differentiate adequately among various tribal groups beyond a superficial type of classification ("Woodlands Indians," "Plains Indians," and the like). The title was one in a series of books similarly labeled and is an unfortunate choice, adding more stereotyping to a field already full of misunderstanding. Poor.

643. Place, Marion T.
RETREAT TO THE BEAR PAW: THE STORY OF THE NEZ PERCÉ.
New York: Four Winds Pr., 1970. (7–11)

A well-written and well-researched account of the fight and the flight of the Nez Percés under Chief Joseph, this book gives the reader a fine analysis of Nez Percé tactics. Place delineates clearly the controversies among the Nez Percé over the Dreamer faith, the decision to rest at Bear Paw and wait for Sitting Bull's relief party, and what to do after the surrender. The aftermath section describes the splitting of the Nez Percé, with some fleeing north, where they met a Sioux rescue party who took them to Sitting Bull in Canada, and others being shipped to Bismark, North Dakota; Ft. Leavenworth, Kansas; Indian Territory; and other places over General Miles's protests. At the end, "The reservation doctor said simply, 'Joseph died of a broken heart' " (p.185). Good.

644. Pogue, Joseph E.
    TURQUOIS: MEMOIRS OF THE
    NATIONAL ACADEMY OF SCIENCES.
    Vol. 12, pt. 2, Second Memoir, Third
    Memoir.
    Glorieta, N. Mex.: Rio Grande Pr.,
    1972. (5 and up)
The definitive book on turquoise, first published in 1915, this is a reissue featuring updated material and color photographs. The contents cover the history and the uses of turquoise all over the world, with special attention to the relationships between turquoise use and American Indian groups. Various types of turquoise are described and pictured; there is a bibliography, an index, maps of turquoise mines and formations, and pictures of turquoise fetishes, figures, and jewelry. The book is intended for adult readers, but, in spite of its small print, upper elementary-level and young adult readers can use selected portions. A classic. Good.

645. Potter, Robert R., and
    Robinson, H. Alan, eds.
    MYTHS AND FOLK TALES AROUND
    THE WORLD.
    Baytown, Tex.: Globe, 1971. (7–9)
This book contains myths from Greece and Rome, Northern Europe, Eastern Europe, the Near East, the Far East, Africa, and from America, complete with vocabulary lists, discussion questions, and editorializing. Three of the American myths concern Indians: "The Daughter of the Stars," "The Blue Man of the North," and "How Pocahontas Saved My Life." Although most of the myths predate Columbus, the Plains Indians, in "The Daughter of the Stars," demonstrate knowledge of oceans on both sides of the continent, and that the earth was round. "The Blue Man of the North" is a myth explaining seasonal change. "How Pocahontas Saved My Life" is John Smith's exaggerated version of the saving of his life by Pocahontas. It is adapted from Smith's *General Historie of Virginia, New England and the Summer Isles*, 1624. The few illustrations are in black-and-white. The writing is simplified, but the stories are interesting. The interest level of the book is junior high school, and the vocabulary level is approximately grade four. Good.

646. Powers, Mabel.
    STORIES THE IROQUOIS TELL THEIR
    CHILDREN.
    New York: American Book, 1917.
    (2–4)
An old classic collection of Iroquois tales, probably not as suitable for children, today, as for adult researchers and writers interested in the history of children's literature due to old-fashioned language and the questionable paternalistic attitudes of the writer (who calls the Iroqucis her "Red Children"), this book has an introduction written by various chiefs of the Seneca, Onondagas, Tuscaroras, Oneidas, Cayugas, and Mohawks. An attempt to save Iroquois stories for future generations, the book uses some Iroquois words in the story. Chiefly of value for historical reasons. Poor.

647. Powers, William K.
    INDIAN DANCING AND COSTUMES.
    New York: Putnam, 1966. (4–6)
This text is characterized by stiff writing and stereotypes: "Many years have passed since the American Indian donned his buckskin moccasins, breechcloth, and blanket, and strode from his painted tipi to hunt for buffalo, or seek vengeance against an enemy" (p.11). It details Indian dance information for the reader,

such as the May-September powwow circuit; singing and drumming accompaniment; basic body steps; old time, fancy, and modern dance; costuming; how to run a powwow; sources of information; and an index. The dancers pictured in the black-and-white instructional photographs do not look Indian. "How to do it" information: Adequate. Portrayal of Indians: Poor.

648. Pugh, Ellen Tiffany.
THE ADVENTURES OF YOO-LAH-TEEN: A LEGEND OF THE SALISH COASTAL INDIANS.
New York: Dial, 1975. (3–6)
Good black-and-white drawings by Laszlo Kubinye illustrate legends recorded by an unknown missionary more than 100 years ago, adapted by Pugh for upper elementary school children. A monster tale similar in many ways to a fairy tale, the story is well written and imparts a good feeling. The book would be good for reading aloud to younger children. Good.

649. Qoyawayma, Polingaysi [Elizabeth Q. White] as told to Vada F. Carlson.
NO TURNING BACK: A TRUE ACCOUNT OF A HOPI INDIAN GIRL'S STRUGGLE TO BRIDGE THE GAP BETWEEN THE WORLD OF HER PEOPLE AND THE WORLD OF THE WHITE MAN.
Albuquerque: Univ. of New Mexico Pr., 1964. (6 and up)
This is the autobiography of a Hopi woman who became a Christian, went to white schools to learn to teach, taught Indian children on the Navajo and, later, the Hopi Reservations, and retired to become a potter and educational consultant. According to the author, this book was a difficult one to write: "It has been painful to recall my long-drawn-out struggle in living. Many of the episodes, buried deeply, emerged slowly" (foreword). She tells of her conservative Hopi childhood, when children were often hidden to keep them out of school, and where the group was often a potent force in life: "To live away from the Hopi village, bereft of the daily companionship of her friends, un-

able to take part in the Mazhrau dances and witness the Kachina ceremonies? Unthinkable!" (p. 167). The author presents a history of the Hopi during her lifetime. She does not attempt to speak for all Hopis, recognizing the factional and regional differences in beliefs:

I have had three different answers to the same question from three different Hopis. This is not to say that each was not convinced that he was telling the truth. It was merely that they were of different ages and from different villages, where rituals varied. [foreword]

She details her rejection by many Hopis, often caused by her religion, her teaching beliefs, or her uniqueness: " 'Polingaysi! Oh-ee-e! You are the little one who wanted to be a white man.' The words were spoken matter-of-factly and without censure, but they brought tightness to the woman's throat and sadness to her mind" (p.3). Her attempts to make education more meaningful for Hopi children, establishing a curriculum that was neither insultingly easy nor inappropriately difficult, are described; and she presents a realistic scene of despair when she journeys out on the sand dunes to think. A chronicle of what it means to be different in a culture that is highly group-oriented, this is not the story of a woman lacking in character —anyone who had the strength to be herself and alienate many whites and Hopis, alike, is not going to write an autobiography with which all will agree. This book will be a source for controversy in any collection. Good.

650. Radford, Ruby L.
SEQUOYA.
New York: Putnam, 1969. (2–4)
This story concentrates upon Sequoyah's development of a written Cherokee "alphabet" (not called "syllabary" in this book, as it should be). Departing somewhat from other stories dealing with Sequoyah's "talking leaves," the author describes how Sequoyah became feared and was made an outcast by his own people, as well as by his wife. The author treats Sequoyah quite objectively as an unusual

person who seemed strange to his peers. One of the better books about Indian leaders, this one is illustrated by Unada, whose Indians, unfortunately, have the distinction of all looking alike. It is interesting to note that in all but four of the forty-four illustrations, Sequoyah is the only male to be shown wearing a turban. Despite its several weaknesses, the book is well written and has few, if any stereotypes, other than those conveyed by the illustrations. Good.

651. Randall, Janet.
THE BUFFALO BOX.
New York: McKay, 1969. (6–8)

This fictitious story is set at the time the Nez Percés, under Chief Joseph, attempt to flee to Canada, pursued by General Miles and the U.S. Army, and are overtaken at Bear Paw. In the story an old Nez Percé medicine man gives Willow Girl, a twelve-year-old Nez Percé girl, a magic box for safekeeping. The girl has been called home from the missionary school to accompany her parents on the journey. The box will grant wishes to its bearer, and the girl uses it to try to get her wishes for safety to come true. Instructed to turn the box over to the proper persons, the girl comes to feel that there is no magic in the box and drops the contents of the medicine bundle it contains into the river. At the end, the girl turns away from her people to white ways as she says to the children, "I will tell you a new story that you have never heard before. I will tell you one of the stories I learned at the mission school" (p.118). The book is written in a stiff, cliché-filled style: "If only staunch Two Forks had not been killed at Big Hole!" (p.88), and is unnecessarily harsh toward "Indian" customs: "The medicine bundle had only one power, the power to make young braves dream foolish dreams and believe that they could not be beaten in battle" (p.117). The author creates her own version of Nez Percé beliefs, which actually have little to do with the Dreamer faith; in short, her main character disagrees with something that never was. Poor.

652. Raphael, Ralph B.
THE BOOK OF AMERICAN INDIANS.
New York: Arco, 1973. (5 and up)

A good, basic, general reference book on American Indians for upper elementary school-age children, this is a thorough, well-written presentation of Indian history from antiquity to modern (1973) times. The author's clear, concise style of writing does not intrude upon the reader's main task—that of gaining useful information—even though the type the book is set in is too small for use with children of this age. The book does not restrict its contents to dates and wars, as do so many books on Indians, but also deals with customs, social life, everyday activities, communications, and trends. Among other good features, there is a section on infant treatment; a realistic description of the lives of women in various tribes: "In most tribes the woman was the head of the house and she had a great influence in deciding on major problems of the tribe" (p.112); and an unusual presentation of the relationships between some tribes and their horses: "Horses were considered capable of taking care of themselves. They were neither stabled nor was any food stored for them" (p.126). In some instances, there are unfortunate choices of language on the part of the author: "Grinding flour was a woman's chore. Here a Pima squaw works on a metate in Arizona, 1902" (p.2); and a stereotype-invoking chapter heading: "Happy Hunting Grounds" (p.134). The book is profusely illustrated in black-and-white, and there is a map of Indian reservations. Good.

653. Raskin, Joseph, and Raskin, Edith.
INDIAN TALES.
New York: Random House, 1969. (3–5)

A collection of Indian legends from the tribes who lived around the Hudson River, this book needs a more precise and more interesting title. The book is written in language most third graders can easily read, and Helen Siegel's green-, black-, and-white crayon-resist illustrations provide good line effects for the viewer. The various descriptive and introductory passages delineate important details of origin, place, and setting for the reader. Good.

654. Rasmussen, Knud.
BEYOND THE HIGH HILLS: A BOOK OF ESKIMO POEMS.
Cleveland, Ohio: World, 1961.
(K and up)
Guy Mary-Roussiliere's color photographs are incredible. His excellent use of space in composition, unexpectedly combined with color, is enough to give even accomplished photographers fits of envy alternating with questions of "How did he do it?" When one considers the technical difficulties of taking the photographs (for instance, how did he keep the camera warm enough to work?), one is overwhelmed with the unbelievable results. The Eskimo chants were collected by Knud Rasmussen and fit the illustrations perfectly. The format does both collector and photographer justice. Good.

655. Rasmussen, Knud.
THE EAGLE'S GIFT: ALASKA ESKIMO TALES.
Garden City, N.Y.: Doubleday, 1932.
(3 and up)
A classic collection of Eskimo tales recorded by Rasmussen on his 1921–24 expedition across Arctic America, these stories were translated into English by Isobel Hutchinson. Rasmussen writes of Eskimo reaction to his efforts to record the legends: "You ruin our stories entirely if you are determined to stiffen them out on paper. Learn them yourself and let them spring from your mouth as living words" (p.vi), and of his observations of the importance of words: "Festivity cannot be enjoyed with dance and song alone. The most festive thing of all is joy in beautiful, smooth words and our ability to express them" (p.vi). The tales were set down as he heard them, and no effort was made either to abridge or adapt them for children's use. The reading level of the story text is upper third grade, while that of the introductory section is adult. A classic. Good.

656. Reeder, Russell Potter
(Colonel Red).
THE FRENCH AND INDIAN WAR.
Nashville, Tenn.: Nelson, 1972. (7–9)
A book that basically is concerned with the effects the French and Indian War had on various white groups, this text deals with Indians only as they were of service to the French or English. It makes much of Indian brutality:

The Iroquois had killed two hundred French, roasted and eaten five children, burned fifty-six of seventy-seven houses, and taken ninety prisoners. [p.22]

Three stragglers were quickly, and brutally murdered. [p.73]

Iroquois screamed when the red flag went up, and prepared to tomahawk and scalp prisoners. General Amherst balked. Sir William warned that over-control would make the Indians quit, Amherst told Johnson that his army was sufficient without Indians, that he wanted their help but would not purchase it at the expense of barbarities. [p.158]

The author seems puzzled by the apparent reluctance of Indians to jump right in to fight for whites:

And who, outside of a very few frontiersmen, knew how to lead Indians? Even the outstanding American leader, George Washington, had arrived at the stage where he was willing to admit that he did not know how to motivate Indians and make them eager to carry out missions. [p.67]

and gives the reader little reason to understand the Indian side. This is a well-written, "army, wars, and battles" book, beginning with the struggles at Deerfield and Lachine. It is illustrated by Edward J. Krasnoborski's maps. There is a reference list of books for further reading, an index, and an appendix giving an explanation of terms and a resume of four colonial wars. Organization and writing: Adequate. Portrayal of Indians: Poor.

657. Reichard, Gladys A.
DEZBA: WOMAN OF THE DESERT.
Glorieta, N. Mex.: Rio Grande Pr.,
1971. (7 and up)

This is a beautifully, intelligently, and precisely written book about the life of a middle-aged Navajo woman in the 1930s. The author's phrasing, choice of words, use of punctuation, and concise language patterning is a joy. The introduction by Charlotte J. Frisbie, Ph.D., Assistant Professor of Anthropology at Southern Illinois University, sets the stage. Frisbie writes in a style remarkably similar to Reichard's and equally as readable and scholarly. The publisher has allowed Frisbie a free rein, and she has responded with an introduction that is literate and professional; she justly praises Reichard, points out changes in Navajo life since the thirties when the book was published, and criticizes the book's design where appropriate:

> Technically, Blessingway should not be termed a "chant." The poetic license utilized by Reichard in describing the Dawn Songs of the Girl's Puberty Rite as being accompanied by "rattles" which "beat excitedly" should be labeled as such since technically this is inaccurate. Furthermore, in deference to the anthropological principle of cultural relativism, the songs should not be described as "monotonous," since they are far from such. Finally, all cultures, including that of the Navajo, are constantly changing and because of this, some of the descriptions . . . are no longer accurate.

The book itself is fun, but not easy, to read. The author tends to long dissertations about customs and events set into an unwieldy dialogue pattern that may cause the reader to lose track of the action and even of who is talking. The concept of the extended, matriarchal Navajo family is firmly established in the story:

> Living theoretically at Dezba's was Alba, the oldest of Loco's children. It was difficult to say where she really lived, for she was with her aunts as much as she was with her grandmother. No outsider would have guessed who was the blood mother of any of the children at Dezba's for, although each woman had a favorite child, that child was usually not her own, but rather her sister's or brother's. Little Policeman was a general favorite. He was the son of Tuli, Dezba's son, who was living with his mother for some time. Tuli's wife had tuberculosis, and since she was a "returned student," that is, had been to school for some years, she had been persuaded to go to one of the Government hospitals for treatment.

The book is illustrated by black-and-white photographs by the author and her sister, Lillian Reichard, not technically or artistically especially well done, but informative and interesting. Good.

658. Reichard, Gladys A.
SPIDER WOMAN.
Glorieta, N. Mex.: Rio Grande Pr.,
1968. (7 and up)

An autobiographical account of the three years Reichard spent on the Navajo Reservation learning to weave Navajo rugs, this book opens with an interesting introduction that sets the scene for the reader, and an acknowledgment section that is a virtual roll call of the knowledgeable writers, traders, and anthropologists of the period. There is a great, soft flow and cadence to the language of the book; it is easy to see this writer loved the life she was leading and tremendously enjoyed the adventures she had. In those days a trip on the Navajo Reservation involved sand, dirt, and mud roads, with subsequent breakdowns and flats. This woman evidently loved the adventure, the isolation, and the people. As part of the story, she details the various steps, processes, and differences among weavers in making a rug, as well as the different customs from Navajo family to Navajo family and geographical section to geographical section. The part of the book devoted to setting up a loom is difficult for nonweavers to understand. Navajo life, as this woman saw it, was idealistic, and her writing reflects this romanticism in her:

Fire gleams through the cracks of the shade made of odds and ends fitted about the pinon tree where Maria Antonia does her summer work. She is out at the woodpile making the chips fly. Her beehive of activity is within calling, but not within talking, distance of me. The smoke of her cedar fire, mingled with the pungent odor of the sage stirred up by the chewing goats, and with the dust of their pawing, is wafted to me on the gentlest and coolest breezes. Along the old road from the north a rider appears. He is Curley's son, Altnaba's husband, Tom's brother. Tired with the day's farming, he sings a weird song for company as his white horse lopes through the gathering darkness. A dog, tail between legs, in sneaky quiet, makes a foraging tour of my fireplace. The sheep, protesting or conversing ever more quietly, snuggle contentedly into the dust of the corral behind me. [p.14]

The book is illustrated by black-and-white photographs. Good.

659. Reit, Seymour.
CHILD OF THE NAVAJOS.
New York: Dodd, 1971. (3–6)
The story of the daily life of a Navajo boy, as seen through the eyes of a boy named Jerry Begay, this book contains photographs which are excellent and quite relevant to today's Navajo child. The print is clear and can be easily read. The structure of the sentences are, on the whole, simple and should be easily understood. The story presents a positive self-concept to the Indian child, as well as much information for a non-Indian. Good.

660. Rice, Josiah M.
A CANNONEER IN NAVAJO COUNTRY:
THE JOURNAL OF PRIVATE JOSIAH M.
RICE.
Denver, Colo.: Old West Publ. Co. for the Denver Public Library, 1970.
(7 and up)
Edited by Richard H. Dillon, this is a reproduction of the journal of a private in the army who went along on Sumner's campaign to Cañon de Chelly. Rice describes the Mexican and Spanish settlers in much more detail than he does the Navajo, and he points out the fear the Navajos inspired:

They [the Navajo] had become the rulers of New Mexico so perfectly that they had nothing to do but go into a town and supply themselves with what they wished most. . . . The word "Navajo" will create the most terror, and gloomy feelings, to a Mexican, you can imagine. [p.58]

Rice's drawings are very good and his writing one of the few examples we have of journals kept by soldiers in the Indian campaigns of the Southwest, in contrast to the many available on the campaigns on the Plains. There is an index. A classic. Good.

661. Richards, Cara E.
THE ONEIDA PEOPLE.
Phoenix, Ariz.: Indian Tribal Series, 1974. (4–6)
This is one of the Indian Tribal Series on various American Indian tribes, and true to the format of other books in the series, opens with a brief biography of Purcell R. Powless, at the time of publication the chief of the Oneidas. The author explains in an interesting fashion why the Oneidas are so little known among whites:

In one of the ironies of history, the Oneidas, who died with the colonists during the Revolution, are less well known to modern Americans than their brother nations in the famous League of the Iroquois, the Mohawks and Senecas who fought for the British crown. Because the Oneidas were on the winning side, they did not figure in the heart-rending accounts of massacres nor in the exciting accounts of captives. No American novels dwelt on their viciousness and ferocity. With casual disregard, white historians of European descent are too taken up with the saga of their colonial and pioneer ancestors to bother acknowledging their debt to the only true Native Americans. Such historians pass over lightly Oneida heroism and courage. [pp.1–2] A history and summary of customs, European contacts, land losses, religious beliefs, recent happenings, and future possibilities, this book is invaluable for young researchers and adult instructors alike. There is a short list of suggested readings, a few photographs and a brief description of the author. The format, using adult layouts with easy-to-read language, also makes this book a good choice to use with slower junior high and high school readers. Good.

662. Richter, Conrad.
A COUNTRY OF STRANGERS.
New York: Knopf, 1966. (6 and up)
A companion story to his more famous *The Light in the Forest*, this is in some respects a better book. The story of a white woman captive who is returned to the whites against her will along with her half-breed son, this is a better treatment of women on the author's part. Richter writes well, especially in his description of the whites attempting to prompt the woman to remember her childhood. At the end of the story, she and True Son (hero of *Light in the Forest*) go back to their Indian life. There is a brief description of the author and the type used in printing the book. Good.

663. Richter, Conrad.
THE LIGHT IN THE FOREST.
New York: Knopf, 1953. (6 and up)
The story of a white boy, captured at age four, who is adopted into the Delaware tribe, this well-written book presents his dilemma as he tries to decide which he is. He finally decides to try living as a white. Richter does his best characterizations here of men and boys; his delineations of the characters of white women do not come off as well. Good.

664. Robinson, Dorothy I.
NAVAHO INDIANS TODAY.
San Antonio, Tex.: Naylor, 1966. (3–5)
Dorothy Robinson's simply written re-

source book traces the early history of the Navajos and the era of resettlement on the reservation. She acquaints the young reader with the 1966 scene through a chapter dealing with changing patterns of life in terms of education, economy, government, arts, health, and so on. A final chapter on religious beliefs and ceremonies clarifies the complex relationship between the Navajos and their religions, explains the function of the medicine man, and gives insight into ceremonials attached to initiation rites, marriage, and death. Dated. Adequate.

665. Robinson, Maudie.
CHILDREN OF THE SUN. THE PUEBLOS, NAVAJOS, AND APACHES OF NEW MEXICO.
New York: Messner, 1973. (3–5)
This is a textbook-style book, chiefly concerned with New Mexico Indian customs, history, and daily life. Fictional excerpts are interspersed to illustrate the factual sections. The author tells of boarding schools, discusses the lives of both boys and girls, explains women's ownership of property, talks of the problems of Indians trying to gain control of their schools, includes a description of tribal business enterprises, and mentions the Four Corners power plant. There are some inconsistencies; for instance, one picture shows a woman identified as Apache in Pueblo dress, which, of course, is possible but perhaps confusing to children. The writing suffers from an "Indians are just like the people down the street" syndrome: of course they are, and, at the same time, of course they are not. The overgeneralizations that crop up in the text may be due to the necessity of using simple vocabulary for elementary-age children, but they do detract from the quality of the book. Few people could quarrel with the intent of statements such as, "The churches and the government wanted to make the Native Americans like the white man." The fact that, for years, Indians have had to bear the brunt of similar, all-enveloping generalizations does not excuse an author's making this same kind of statement

about other groups. The book would be useful for reference for school work and vacation planning; it is illustrated in black-and-white. Adequate.

666. Robinson, Sandra Til.
ALMANSOR.
Los Angeles: Nash, 1974. (7 and up)
The poetic and rhythmic writing style of a not particularly realistic story of a half-white, half-Indian California ranch woman makes this a book not everyone will like. It is not an easy book to read, mostly because of the uncommon amount of dialogue. It mixes Indians, whites, conservationists, industrialists, and ranchers in a way that makes a good story, but that does not give an especially revealing picture of the lives of the majority of California Indians today. The author's style may be as much a discussion point as the characters. Good.

667. Robinson, Tom D.
AN ESKIMO BIRTHDAY.
New York: Dodd, 1975. (3–5)
This is a current view of the life of modern Eskimo children. The author's note section is particularly descriptive: "There are some old people who speak very little English and who wear tennis shoes, and young people who speak very little Eskimo and wear caribou mukluks. It is, perhaps, the best of both worlds" (p.40). Glo Coalson's black-and-white illustrations are excellent and give a feeling of space, and her picture (on page 13) of a modern Eskimo family living in a new house, with a nonfat dried milk carton used as a cradle for the dog and a picture of John F. Kennedy on the wall, gives an especially accurate view. Good.

668. Rockwell, Anne.
THE DANCING STARS: AN IROQUOIS LEGEND.
New York: Crowell, 1972. (K–2)
An Iroquois legend explaining the Pleiades constellation, this is an easy-to-read story in an excellent format for primary school children. The author's simple color drawings fit the mood of the story, al-

though the people pictured may be overly "cute" for some tastes. The author provides a good, brief introduction to the story to help readers orient themselves. Good.

669. Rockwood, Joyce.
LONG MAN'S SONG.
New York: Holt, 1975. (6–10)
This novel, set in pre-Columbian times, is the story of a young Cherokee apprentice medicine man. Good, detailed descriptions of life patterns are worked into the plot, and the writing is better than average. Good.

670. Roessell, Robert, and Platero, Dillon, eds.
COYOTE STORIES OF THE NAVAJO PEOPLE.
Rough Rock, Ariz.: Board of Education, Rough Rock Demonstration School, Navaho Curriculum Center, 1968. (3–6)
This book was prepared primarily as a reader for Navajo boys and girls. It is one of a series by the Rough Rock (Arizona) Demonstration School depicting Navajo life and culture, and was designed to develop a positive self-image and affirmative sense of identification among Navajo children in the primary grades. The book contains fourteen stories about the principal character, "Trotting Coyote," each of which can be read aloud to younger children. George Mitchell uses ink outlines filled in with crayon as the technique for illustration, a procedure that can inspire young artists because of its similarity to their own work. Good.

671. Roland, Albert.
GREAT INDIAN CHIEFS: THE STORY OF THE INDIAN PEOPLE'S STRUGGLE FOR SURVIVAL, TOLD THROUGH THE LIVES OF NINE COURAGEOUS LEADERS.
New York: Macmillan, 1969. (7–9)
The book chronicles the influence of the American Indian culture in shaping the American political system. The book is an introduction to the study of Indians through some of their best-known chiefs:

Hiawatha, Powhatan, Philip of Pokanoket, Popé, Pontiac, Maquinna, Tecumseh, Sequoyah, and Sitting Bull. Junior high students should find the book stimulating. Good.

672. Rothenberg, Jerome.
SHAKING THE PUMPKIN: TRADITIONAL POETRY OF THE INDIAN NORTH AMERICAS.
Garden City, N.Y.: Doubleday, 1972. (7 and up)
An excellent discussion of modern trends in cross-cultural literature is contained in the preface of this collection of American Indian poetry:

> The awkwardness of presenting translations from American Indian poetry in the year 1971 is that it has become fashionable today to deny the possibility of crossing the boundaries that separate people of different races & [sic] cultures: to insist instead that black is the concern of black, red of red, & [sic] white of white. Yet the idea of translation has always been that such boundary crossing is not only possible but desirable. [p.xix]

Rothenberg has an interesting style of translation, more modern in format than most, although occasionally he comes up with an almost Biblical feel to his phrases. Some of the poems could be read aloud to younger children, but some of the poems do deal with sex (see page 116) and might not be appropriate for younger readers. Readers can understand the feelings in back of the comment of one of Frank Boas's sources in 1920, who said, "Long ago her mother had to sing this song and so she had to grind along with it. The corn people have a song too, it is very good. I refuse to tell it" (p.3). Good.

673. Running, Corrine.
WHEN COYOTE WALKED THE EARTH: INDIAN TALES OF THE PACIFIC NORTHWEST.
New York: Holt, 1949. (3–6)
Plunging right into the tales with no introductory remarks, the author presents some of the Northwest Indian tales about seasons and animals. Story sources and origins are discussed in a section at the end of the book; Running bases much of her work on the Melville Jacobs project. The language of the writing flows well, the stories are short and succinct, revamped for a non-Indian audience and to fit better into a written form. Adults may wish to read original text translations to compare the two. The book is illustrated in black-and-white, but the book's format suffers from its old-fashioned layout. Good.

674. Rushmore, Helen.
THE MAGNIFICENT HOUSE OF MAN ALONE.
Champaign, Ill.: Garrard, 1968. (3 and up)
This is the story of how one old Osage man managed to deal with his new-found oil money, please others, and remain himself. The book does not preach, nor does the author strive mightily to make a laborious moral about the evils of materialism or about the virtues of those who resist the temptation to own worldly goods. The book is funny, humane; chuckling a little, perhaps, at all of us. In the short space of the book, the author manages to provide the reader with characters of depth—Man Alone, the old Osage, and his friends, War Eagle, another old Osage, and Little Hair, the white trader. There are no real characterizations of women because the story is mostly concerned with the three men mentioned above, although the author may be giving a false impression of the docility of Osage women when she has the main character reflect, "This thought was not good. Men must lead. Women must always follow meekly in the tracks of their husband's moccasins. The grandfathers had so decided" (p.22). A classic. Good.

675. Rushmore, Helen, with
Wolf Robe Hunt.
THE DANCING HORSES OF ÁCOMA AND OTHER ÁCOMA INDIAN STORIES.
Cleveland, Ohio: World, 1963. (3–7)
This is an interesting collection of tales from the people of the Ácoma pueblo, which the author erroneously locates in

southwestern New Mexico, rather than the west-central portion of the state. There is an informative section devoted to changes, to the Ácoma way of life, and the like, although there is occasionally a judgmental quality to the use of words, such as the word *primitive* in the statement, "Until recent years furnishings were primitive" (p.160). The stories are well written, and the book is illustrated by Wolf. Good.

676. Russell, Don.
SIOUX BUFFALO HUNTERS.
Chicago: Britannica Books, 1962.
(2–4)
Using color photographs of modern-day (1962) Sioux and color illustrations by Bob Glaubke to explain the text, this book presents the importance the buffalo had to the Sioux in the old days through means of the fictional story of a young Sioux boy. The wigs worn by men and boys in the photographs are obvious and distracting, and the history of the Sioux is presented in a sketchy fashion; but, all in all, the book is informative. Adequate.

677. Russell, Solveig P.
NAVAHO LAND—YESTERDAY AND TODAY.
Chicago: Melmont, 1961. (2–3)
A simply told description of Navajo life, concerned with the importance of sheep, dwellings, clothing, food, ceremonies, and silver work, this book also gives information on government schools. Descriptive poems follow various subjects, conveying some feeling for the dignity and beauty of the Navajo life style. The material is now dated: "Most of the Navahos of today are herders" (p.8), and has a tendency to stereotype: "Navahos love horses and usually own more than one" (p.13), or, "A Navaho woman ties her long black hair into a loop at the back of her neck" (p.19). Baida Whitebead's black-, white-, and-orange illustrations are simple and well done and reflect the style of drawing prevalent at the date of publication. There are short descriptions of the author and illustrator. Dated. Poor.

678. Ryan, J. C.
REVOLT ALONG THE RIO GRANDE.
San Antonio, Tex.: Naylor, 1964.
(6–8)
The revolt of the Pueblo Indians along the Rio Grande is presented in a series of separate but related vignettes of the men involved. The author's opinion and bias are evident, making this a good object book for educators to use to teach critical reading skills. The account is written in an interesting, albeit rather florid, fashion:

The real characters of the two men were as different as their garb. Marcos, the humble servant of the Lord, walked in true humility, the shapeless, sober habit of gray cloth prescribed by his order covering his person from shoulders to ankles. Nobody suspected that under that somber garb moved a strong, firm-muscled body that gave the priest his great physical stamina. Estevánico, in contrast, pushed forward with a lusty stride and the haughty mien of one who knows his strength and revels in it. [p.75]

The author overgeneralizes and stereotypes: "Estevánico, a child of nature whose ancestors had but lately come into association with the culture of civilized man" (p.5), and women are seldom mentioned, but the momentum of the book as a whole makes it worth consideration in spite of the inadequacies of its parts. The author presents imagined conversations and thoughts in literary form; it might be well to supplement this work with more straightforward, factual accounts. Good for pleasure reading, as well as for instructional work. Good.

679. Saloman, Julian M.
BOOK OF INDIAN CRAFTS AND INDIAN LORE.
New York: Harper, 1928. (5 and up)
This is a very early (1928), comprehensive reference work pertaining to many North American cultures. Detailed information is provided on many aspects of Indian life. The author has gathered together information about music, dance steps, food, clothing, shelter, and lan-

guage, and gives a detailed bibliography about most North American cultures. The book is a useful resource, a trailblazer at the time of its publication. Some more recent publications have supplanted it, but teachers and children can still find usable information on specific subjects in parts of the book. Adequate.

680. Sanders, Ruth Manning.
RED INDIAN FOLK AND FAIRY TALES.
New York: Roy, 1960. (4–6)
An unfortunate choice of title (*Red Indian* is hardly descriptive of the Native American peoples) and lack of an introductory section to establish some sort of reader background about the tribes involved mar this otherwise excellent, readable collection of Indian legends. The stories are written in a fashion children can understand. The black-and-white illustrations by C. Walter Hodges are fine, but there are not enough of them. The stories and the illustrations deserve a better format. Adequate.

681. Sandoz, Mari.
THE STORY CATCHER.
New York: Grosset, 1963. (7–10)
The setting of this story is Nebraska, where Mari Sandoz lived as a child. Lance, a young Sioux who, like his father, has the courage, daring, persistence, and ability needed for earning great honors as a leader of his tribe, enjoys drawing—making pictorial records of the history of his people. Buffalo hunting, ceremonials, and home life are all recorded in the dust, on skins, or in his memory. Although Lance participates in all the necessary activities of the tribe, he is only fulfilled when capturing the beauty, simplicity, and color of Indian life in pictures. Years pass, with adventure, hardship, and sorrow. Finally, Lance's talents are recognized and he is publicly acknowledged as "The Story Catcher"—the recorder of the history of the Sioux tribe. Preadolescents, adolescents and adults can all enjoy this well-written book, showing the scope of activities available for Sioux boys in a nonsexist way. Good.

682. Sandoz, Mari.
THESE WERE THE SIOUX.
New York: Hastings House, 1961.
(6 and up)
Mari Sandoz describes here her life as a child living near the Sioux Reservation. In the process she explains many of the customs she observed, including child-rearing practices, the selection of second parents for the child, marriage and divorce customs, the buffalo hunt (with detailed descriptions of the preparation of the meat), and the belief that the future and prosperity of the tribe depended on the virtue of the women. The book is written with understanding, knowledge, and warmth. Sandoz is a brilliant writer, and it is obvious she knows and loves her subject matter. The picture she presents is of the life of a past day, interesting in itself, and vital in its role of clarifying present-day Sioux life, with its many variations. Her description of Indian reaction to white child-rearing practices is typical of her insight:

> The American Indian considered the whites a brutal people who treated their children like enemies—playthings, too, coddling them like pampered pets or fragile toys, but underneath like enemies to be restrained, bribed, spied on and punished, or as objects of competition between the parents. [p.25]

The black-and-white illustrations by Amos Bad Heart Bull and Kills Two are well done, and the reader will wish for more. Full of wisdom, warmth, and love, the book is a classic. Good.

683. Scheele, William E.
THE EARLIEST AMERICANS.
Cleveland, Ohio: World, 1963. (5–8)
Illustrated by the author, this text, in combination with his pictures, creates a vivid portrait of the archaeologist's search for evidence about prehistoric Americans. He sketches both in words and drawings the fragments of evidence that have so far been discovered. "Figgins' Bison" and the Folsom projectile point embedded in its ribs are shown with the caption: "The turning point in American prehistoric

studies." The discipline of archaeology is explained in a manner that will convince children that no artifact should be touched until a scientist can study it in the proper way. Scheele closes with the thought that a "new" earliest American will be discovered some day. Good.

684. Scheele, William E.
THE MOUND BUILDERS.
Cleveland, Ohio: World, 1960.
(3 and up)
This short, easy-to-read, and vividly written book about the Hopewell culture is illustrated by the author. He combines information about the Hopewell culture in the Ohio Valley with maps and illustrations, giving a realistic picture of the lives of these ancient people. The beauty of their artwork has inspired the author to create sketches in the same style showing activities in a day's work. He considers them the most interesting of all the Mound Builders. Good.

685. Scheer, George.
CHEROKEE ANIMAL TALES.
New York: Holiday House, 1968.
(3–5)
Based largely on James Mooney's report to the Bureau of Ethnology in 1900, *The Myths of the Cherokee,* this is a collection of Cherokee animal tales that are in easy-to-read, primary, and fairly literate language. The main problem with the book is Scheer's editorializing in the introductory sections. Not too many people would disagree with his calling the U.S. government's Indian policies, "brutal, deceptive, and disillusioning" (p.13). But he wrongly attributes to the Cherokees a fascination with war and misinterprets its importance to them:

> Their first devotion was to warfare, which they called their "beloved occupation," and they did everything to aggrandize it by dances, honorary titles, and tribal prestige. But when they were not at war with neighboring tribes or invaders, their men were on the hunt for the game of the highland. [p.10]

His description of Cherokee women is incomplete and confusing: "To their women they left food, cooking, rearing of children, clothing" (p.10). He uses the phrase "they realized" throughout the book, leaving the reader puzzled as to the antecedent of "they." His description of Sequoyah is meager:

> . . . a crippled hunter named Sequoyah. So entranced were the Cherokee with the idea of a written language of their own and so eager for learning that in a few months after the publication of Sequoyah's alphabet in 1821, thousands of former illiterates were able to read and write. [p.13]

Adequate.

686. Schellie, Don.
ME, CHOLAY & CO.: APACHE WARRIORS.
New York: Four Winds Pr., 1973.
(6 and up)
An excellent story of the friendship of two young teen-age boys, an Apache and a white, this book is set in Arizona in 1871, during the time Tucson townspeople and Papagos raided a peaceful Apache settlement set up under the protection of the U.S. Army at Camp Grant, killed 125 Apaches, mostly women and children, and carried away 28 other children as slaves, only 6 of whom were ever returned to their people. In the story Cholay is one of the captured children. He escapes, and with Joshua, the white boy, frees some of the children and escapes with them back to the Apaches. The story is well written in a sparse, realistic style:

> Laying a palm against the rough trunk of a mesquite tree, I leaned over and throwed up. I puked till I feared my innards would follow next. My body were wore out and I dripped that cold sweat that comes of vomiting and I stumbled about the ruins of the village some more and finally sprawled to the ground. And then I buried my face in my hands and wept. I wept for Charlie. [p.1]

Schellie has captured the feel and the dialogue of the time. He writes in an intelligent fashion for his young readers: for instance, "I lifted my head and smiled what I suppose were a weak smile—the kind you read about in the romantic novels. I wished Miss Consuela had been there to see it" (p.233). He has done a masterful job of characterization. There is a fine introductory section to orient the reader. Good.

687. Schmucker, Barbara C.
WIGWAM IN THE CITY.
New York: Dutton, 1966. (6–8)

The story of an Ojibwa girl whose family left the reservation to live in Chicago, this book gives readers the feeling that there are valid reasons for choosing a life style based on a mixture of cultures and values, and that this choice of priorities is each person's right; an obvious enough thought, not particularly startling or original, but a thought few books (or people, for that matter) truly share. This book is noteworthy for presenting a divergence of views, and validating each choice. In the story, an Ojibwa girl challenges the white boy who has been teasing her to a race. He has been teasing her about her moccasins and about her Indian ways. She wins, and he asks her father to make him a pair and to allow him to learn how to make them. The plot is slight, but the emotions and feelings expressed are realistic and lifelike. The book stresses the importance of Indian Centers to the urban American Indians. One minor discrepancy in the book is the picturing of the harvesting of wild rice from a motorboat; this is a point of controversy owing to the backwash if handled improperly, and some Ojibwas prefer nonmotorized boats. Good.

688. Schultz, James Williard.
MY LIFE AS AN INDIAN.
Morristown, Me.: Corner House, 1973. (7–12)

This story, first published in *Forest and Stream* in 1907, describes the life of the author among the Blackfoot Indians. The story gives a frank, sympathetic, and warm portrayal of the Blackfoot Indians, including foraging for food, buffalo hunts, battles with other tribes, and daily customs, through the eyes and ears of a white man who chose to live among them as an Indian. The few pictures are of Indian life at the time of the story, 1881–1907. The book is authentic. There is some editorializing, but it is minimal. Good.

689. Schultz, James Williard.
WITH THE INDIANS IN THE ROCKIES.
New York: Houghton, 1911. (6 and up)

An account of life with the Blackfoot Indians in the old days, this book has passages highly reminiscent of the writing style of Saint Exupéry:

So I went back to my studying and my parents kept me closer at home than ever. [p.5]

I am going to pass over what I have to say now as quickly as possible, for even after all these years, and old as I am, the thought of it still hurts. In February of the following winter my father fell ill of the smallpox and died. Then my mother and I took it, and my mother died, also. [pp.5–6]

Schultz is a romanticist, but he knows his subject. This is a well-written story that gives insight into the lives of white and Blackfoot alike. The book is illustrated in black-and-white by George Varian in the popular style of the time. Good.

690. Schweitzer, Byrd Baylor.
ONE SMALL BLUE BEAD.
New York: Macmillan, 1965. (1 and up)

The unusual concept of using one small blue bead from a prehistoric culture as a focus for speculating about what might have been, adds much to the effectiveness of this outstanding book about prehistoric times. Upon learning about strangers who live in other places, one of the old men of the village wants to go to see their life for himself. To allow him to go, a boy who has been known for his laziness offers to do the old man's share of work. The man goes, then returns with information that helps the whole tribe. Schweitzer uses superb phrasing, poetic and lyrical:

> I think that there is something
> That just tells a man to go
> In search of people who may not be,
> In search of places he may not see.
> Still he has to search.
> That's clear to me. [p.14]

Her words could inspire older students in their own writing. There are many opportunities for serious human relation discussions in this material. This type of writing may extrapolate slightly beyond the anthropological and archaeological data the writer used, but the story does show these sciences as offering materials for creative purposes. Symeon Shimin's illustrations are exquisite. Good.

691. Scrivner, Fulsom Charles.
MOHAVE PEOPLE.
San Antonio, Tex.: Naylor, 1970.
(7 and up)
A record of the Mojave people and their contacts with explorers, trappers, miners, Mormons, settlers, and soldiers, this is a thoroughly researched account of their history through the end of the nineteenth century, with comments and asides concerning their social, familial, and economic structures. Occasionally pedantic in tone:

> When Spaniards came into the Colorado River basin, they found several thousand people living in what is now the Needles, California, area. It could rightfully be called the "Valley of the Mohaves." This valley contained the largest concentration of people in what is now the southwestern United States. [p.1]

this author often includes his personal evaluation of the events he records: "Fortunately for the Maricopa, the Pima warriors began to arrive on horseback, with their lances" (p.131). There is an excellent analysis of the Oatman children's captivity, as well as of other events affecting the Mojaves. Each chapter contains footnotes and references. Good.

692. Searcy, Margaret Zchmer.
IKWA OF THE TEMPLE MOUNDS.
University, Ala.: Univ. of Alabama Pr., 1974. (2–5)
Searcy builds this book on an unusual plot device, writing as if she was talking to the present-day child reader and asking him or her to pretend to be living at the time of the story. The story itself is basically only a vehicle to carry facts about the Mound Builders' customs, life, and artifacts, and is written in a satisfactory but not inspired way. This book could be read alone by a bright seven-year-old; it might have to be read aloud by an adult for younger children. It is recommended that the reader do some preliminary research about Mound Builders, since it takes time to know the "who, what, when, where, and why" of this prehistoric group from this author's presentation. The forcing a girl into marriage as a second wife in the story was not a usual custom among Indian groups as recorded by later Indian and non-Indian chroniclers. This point may need to be clarified for child readers. Adequate.

693. Seibert, Jerry.
SACAJAWEA: GUIDE TO LEWIS AND CLARK.
Boston: Houghton, 1960. (4–6)
In the first five chapters, the author describes Sacajawea's birth, her childhood, a few extraordinarily brave deeds she performed, and her abduction by a Hidatsa warrior (in this book the capture is described as a sacrifice to save other members of her tribe). One chapter presents the events that led to the Lewis and Clark expedition, and includes a brief description of each member of the group who went. The remaining chapters are devoted to Sacajawea's feats as guide to the explorers and include some background information regarding the habits of the frontiersmen, hunters, trappers, and voyagers who accompanied Lewis and Clark. While the information about the men, expedition accouterments, geography, and weather are accurately and artfully described, Sacajawea appears some-

what unreal or remote by comparison. Except for Clark, however, Sacajawea is the only character who is given any depth. Consistent with other stories about her, Charbonneau, Sacajawea's owner, is scarcely mentioned. The illustrations by Lorence Bjorklund contain sufficient detail to contribute to the descriptions included in the text. There are four maps illustrating the United States and its territories in 1801 and the routes taken by the explorers to and from the Pacific Ocean. Good.

694. Seymour, Flora Warren.
   BIRD GIRL: SACAJAWEA.
   New York: Bobbs-Merrill, 1945. (3–7)
   Although somewhat stereotyped and modernized, this story of Sacajawea's childhood is sufficiently adventuresome to hold the interest of most young readers. Certainly the frustration of being a female, wishing to join in the hunts and exciting games with the boys, is a continuous theme throughout this story. However, some of the family conversations seem more like the social interchanges between modern brothers and sisters or children and their parents, misplaced in an Indian setting of almost 200 years ago. Sacajawea's attachment to her doll, "Quiet Child," and her relationships with other children seem more in tune with the present. Young female readers may identify with her spirit of adventure, when she sneaks out to join her older brother in a hunt and when she saves her little brother from drowning. The last chapters in the book, describing Sacajawea's capture by the Minnetarees and her trip, as guide, for the Lewis and Clark expedition, may be less rewarding for the young reader. Not as well written, and rather confusing, the writing of these experiences is greatly condensed. The illustrations by Edward C. Coswell, composed of black-and-white sketches, with filled-in shadow people, neither distract from nor really contribute to the text. Adequate.

695. Shannon, Terry.
   LITTLE WOLF, THE RAIN DANCER.

Chicago: Albert Whitman, 1954. (2–4)
   This book features a plot based on erroneous interpretations of Zuñi culture and ceremonials, especially the reasons given for dancing, the descriptions of ceremonials, and the behavior of participants. The story involves a young Zuñi boy participant who is not supposed to eat during a ceremonial, but does. He performs various actions before he can compensate his people for this violation. The book is written through a screen supplied by the author's cultural expectations: "The song sounded more like a wail, while the dance looked as though Little Wolf was just stomping his feet. But that is the way Indians dance and sing and Little Wolf was happy and pleased with himself" (p.8); and Charles Payzant's illustrations show idealized, amorphous faces that, except for their darker shading, could have been used for the Dick and Jane series. Poor.

696. Shannon, Terry.
   RUNNING FOX: THE EAGLE HUNTER.
   Chicago: Albert Whitman, 1957. (2–3)
   The story of a young Hopi boy and his adventures, which include having a vision, learning from the men in the kiva, hunting turtles, and capturing an eagle, this book details the Hopi life of an earlier time. The book contains a surprising amount of information about Hopi customs, such as boys learning the secrets of their mother's clan, and boys learning to weave. Charles Payzant's color illustrations are well done, although his pictures of people are idealized, sort of a Hopi Dick-and-Jane type of illustration. Adequate.

697. Shannon, Terry.
   STONES, BONES, AND ARROWHEADS.
   Chicago: Albert Whitman, 1962. (4–8)
   Written expressly for children in intermediate grades, this book is also suitable for reading aloud to second or third graders. Children who have visited a museum and are motivated to learn more about early civilizations will find this book an

interesting supplement to their field trip. The content is general, with simple illustrations depicting everything from invertebrates to Homo sapiens. The account is simplified, perhaps oversimplified, and covers very briefly a great number of facts. The best part of the book is the description of fourth, fifth, and sixth grade students working with an archaeologist at a site uncovered by a bulldozer. The careful discipline of archaeology is meticulously described, as the children are involved in salvaging as much as they can before the onslaught of earthmoving equipment. Working an archaeological site in road-beds before construction begins is a common means of excavation today. The description of this method is particularly appropriate for this reason. Good.

698. Shaw, Anna Moore.
PIMA INDIAN LEGENDS.
Tucson: Univ. of Arizona Pr., 1974.
(4 and up)
A collection of Pima legends adapted for children by Shaw, a Pima woman, this book has a thoughtful, intelligent analysis of Pima oral literature by Bell King, former superintendent at Salt River reservation King reminds the reader of the condescension a non-Indian can display when admonishing a tribe to keep its culture:
Many of us—even some from the Indian Southwest—assume that the cultures of at least some of our Indian neighbors have all but died out. We regret this and baffle our Indian friends by exhorting them to "preserve" that of their tradition which we see as remaining. This narrow view of Indian "culture" is usually viewed in aesthetic terms. Basket weaving, pottery making, silver work—even certain of the techniques of graphic arts taught in Government boarding schools during the 1930s—are commonly seen as just about all that is meaningful left to certain tribes. These, along with traditional dances, fragments of music and tribal legends, we feel, should be preserved at all cost. However well-intentioned are these salvage efforts by non-

Indians, they are indeed arrogant in that they tell Indians which aspects of their lives (if any) are truly "Indian." They are also mistaken in that they assume that elements of culture can be "preserved" as one preserves the head of a buffalo through taxidermy. [p.xii]
Later King suggests that
This little book shows something of the process of cultural change. For these legends, learned more than sixty years ago in the then conservative Pima village of Gila Crossing, have been modified over the years as a reflection of changes in the cultural traditions of those who learned them . . . notwithstanding, the legends remain every bit as much Pima as the versions told at the turn of the century. [p.xii]
and tells how the author's old grandfather "improvised the stories to hold the grandchildren's attention" (p.xiv) so that "Coyote . . . was dressed . . . in cowboy clothes with boots, spurs and a bright red necktie" (p.xiv). Included, too, is an excellent (and controversial) dissertation on change, customs, authenticity, and Pima oral traditions. Shaw does use certain words that many non-Indians consider "Indian," such as *squaw*, *great spirit*, *many moons*, and so on, since she feels it impossible to find exact translations in English of many Pima words. One wishes she had found better English words in these cases. Good.

699. Shaw, Anne Moore.
A PIMA PAST.
Tucson: Univ. of Arizona Pr., 1974.
(5–7)
This autobiography of Anna Shaw, a Pima woman, tells the story of her family from the time of her grandfather through her own children. Unevenly written, the book nonetheless is a fascinating glimpse of the adjustments one family made to the Pima/non-Pima worlds they lived in. Shaw is a Presbyterian, and this often colors her interpretations of events. The book details her early life and her views concerning old versus new customs, as in this picture caption:

This picture of the Sacaton cemetery was taken around the turn of the century. Yellow Leaves was buried in such an unmarked grave. Now we have beautiful stone monuments for our departed loved ones, but the grief we feel is no greater than that of the Pimas of old. [p.23]

She presents an interesting look at what it means to be female in the Pima world and gives a matter-of-fact account of a girl entering puberty. She gives equally detailed views of what it is like to have a Pima heritage, never claiming that hers is the definitive experience. Her tales of her school days provide homey little episodes that a person who had not lived there could never have written:

You see, in those days most of us spent two years in each grade in order to master the difficult English language along with the subject matter. Indian students most often would be from eighteen to twenty-one when they graduated from eighth grade, old enough for marriage. [p.137]

From time to time in the book, she gives her views of the Apaches, calling them "marauding Apaches" on page 7, and states in a caption for a picture of her husband on page 138, "Once he beat an Apache boy in a track-meet dash, much to the delight of us Indians from other tribes. We were so tired of hearing the Apaches brag about their running ability." The book is illustrated with black-and-white photographs and contains an epilogue devoted to short biographies of people the author considers of importance to Pimas. This is the highly personal story of one woman, and in spite of the awkwardness of some of the writing and the controversial nature of some of her views, well worth reading. Good.

700. Sheppard, Sally.
INDIANS OF THE EASTERN WOODLANDS.
New York: Watts, 1975. (5–8)
A factual textbook or reference work, this book is illustrated with black-and-white pictures and drawings. It has an index and a bibliography. The author

deals in a knowledgeable way with the customs of these Indians, describing matriarchal societies, kinship and clan relationships, and the importance of women in choosing leaders. She explains in detail how a son inherits, but not how a daughter does. The discussion of reservation life today and in the future is excellent. Readers will find the book useful for reference and study before and during a vacation. Good.

701. Shor, Pekay.
WHEN THE CORN IS RED.
Nashville, Tenn.: Abingdon Pr., 1973. (1–4)
On reading this adaptation of a legend of the Tuscaroras, it is difficult to tell which of the opinions expressed are the author's and which are part of the legend. This is important, since the story states that the coming of whites is a punishment for the "evil ways" (unpaged) of the Tuscaroras, that red corn turned white as a result, and that it will not turn red again until the Tuscaroras mend their ways and the whites leave. This would be a difficult concept to teach Southwestern youngsters who have probably seen multicolored corn all their lives. The author is, no doubt, incensed about the treatment of Indians by non-Indians, but her writing on this subject is sometimes indefinite; for instance, in speaking of the Indian's self-image, she states that it will "surely one day translate itself from the real to the ideal, and thus compensate them [the Indians] for the heavy dues which the long memory of misery has exacted" (introduction). Gary Von Ilg's color illustrations are beautiful and technically impressive; Shor writes well; and the book has a fine layout. Adequate.

702. Showers, Paul.
INDIAN FESTIVALS.
New York: Crowell, 1969. (2–3)
This is a simple, at times simplistic, easy-to-read book about the special tribal festivals, including those of the Seminole, Zuñi, Plains, and Eskimo. Locations of various powwows and intertribal events

are listed, including Anadarko, Oklahoma; Gallup, New Mexico; and the like. This is a research type of book, good for instructional use and for background for any of these ceremonials. Lorence Bjorklund's illustrations are informative. Adequate.

703. Siegel, Beatrice.
INDIANS OF THE WOODLAND.
New York: Walker, 1972. (3–5)
In a question and answer format, this book covers such topics about "Woodland Indians" (the Indians of New England at the time of the Pilgrims, according to the author) as appearance, food, hunting, farming, villages, children, language, travel, and the current scene. The writing is simplistic and textbook-like in tone: for instance, "The land was fragrant with blossoms and the thick forests were alive with animals and birds" (p.11). Occasionally the author states a concept well for young readers:

> Indians find life a little easier on reservations. They have a sense of freedom on land that is theirs. They can live a little as their ancestors did. They take care of each other and still share everything even though there is not much to share. [p.79]

These Indians are treated as a group; consequently, the reader does not get a feel for them as individual tribes. The black-and-white line drawings by Baptiste Bayhylle Shuntona, Jr., are well done. The author includes suggestions on places for children to visit and to write to, and ideas for further reading. Adequate.

704. Sine, Jerry, with Klinger, Gene.
SON OF THIS LAND.
Chicago: Childrens Pr., 1970. (6–8)
The story of a modern Winnebago man, Jerry Sine, told in his own words, this book describes his life from his childhood as an Indian dancer, through school and the army, to his career as a commercial artist. It demonstrates to young readers that every person has a story, that it is difficult to generalize about the modern-day Indians, and that a career such as that of commercial artist is open to people with a variety of backgrounds. It pictures the successful adjustment of an Indian man to adversity and to challenge. The section on the career possibilities for commercial artists is a welcome addition to the literature on career guidance. The black-and-white photographs are often of the family album type, but this very nonperfection is an asset. A text of this sort is especially useful for junior high and high school students who do not read well; it combines high content interest with low reading vocabulary level. Good.

705. Skinner, Constance Landers.
BECKY LANDERS: FRONTIER WARRIOR.
New York: Macmillan, 1926. (5–7)
The story of a young Kentucky pioneer girl, this book includes several actual historical characters of the period as part of the plot, but the tale has little do do with American Indian groups except as enemies of the white characters:

> Whole settlements had been wiped out, men, women, and children slain or carried away to whatever fate the whim of their captors might dictate—some to be murdered on the march in a moment of angry caprice, others to be burned in the Indian towns in celebration of the victory, and a few to be saved and adopted into the tribe. [p.2]

The girl's brother is a captive, and she goes with the George Rogers Clark expedition to Vincennes to help free him. The writer correctly details the many responsibilities most pioneer children had. Her writing is rather old-fashioned for current day reading. Portrayal of Pioneer Life: Adequate. Portrayal of Indians: Poor.

706. Sleator, William.
THE ANGRY MOON.
Boston: Little, 1970. (K–3)
This Tlingit legend was adapted by the author from the tales recorded by John R. Swanton in 1909 for the Bureau of American Ethnology. The moon becomes angry at a girl who laughs at his face. He captures her as punishment, and she has a number of adventures before she is freed. The format and book layout are excellent;

both help carry part of the story. Blair Lent's color illustrations are "elaborations on original Tlingit motifs, and are not meant to be authentic" (back of frontispiece). The book needs a more thorough introductory section. Good.

707. Smith, Theresa Kalab.
WIKI OF WALPI.
Austin, Tex.: Steck-Vaughn, 1954.
(4–6)
The author makes use of fine poetic imagery to tell the story of an albino Hopi boy, his differences, his trying to live in a group where he appears to be strange, and his eventual emergence as a medicine man. His mother and father are portrayed as equally important in his growth, a fact feminists will appreciate. For the most part, the story stays true to Hopi tradition, with some minor errors; for instance, the author implies that the flocks of sheep belong to the father; the pueblo governor is shown as having greater authority than reality warrants ("'Oh, yes, you will,' Povi said, shaking his head North and South. 'I am the governor of this pueblo. You will do as I say'"); and the description of the friendship between Navajo and Hopi sheepherders may not reflect the reality of the two tribes' current dispute over grazing lands. Teachers and parents may wish to supplement this with other books and discussions of what happens to children who are born different and do not have the advantage of the fortunate, indeed, almost magical, appearance of a Navajo medicine man (or anyone else) who understands and helps solve problems instantaneously. Adequate.

708. Sneve, Virginia Driving Hawk.
BETRAYED.
New York: Holiday House, 1974.
(7 and up)
This is an uneven work of fiction. The book uses an interesting and elaborate plot to make a point about some of the reasons many Sioux often feel desperation and despair, both in the Dakota uprising of 1862 and today. The provocations for the uprising are clearly delineated, but much of the story remains obscure and the reader may lose track of the chronology of events, of why one group of Sioux interfered with another, of what happened to both white and Sioux survivors, and of the sequence of the hangings at the end. This obscurity could have been overcome with more definitive transitional passages. In the story some whites are captured by the Santee Sioux in 1862 at Lake Shetek. A young Teton Sioux half-breed has a vision, barters for the captives, and returns them to their homes. The book closes on a scene in which many Sioux are hanged. The writing itself is awkward in places:

> All was calm in Sioux country, and the United States was fully occupied with its Civil War. Therefore, on August 18, 1862, great shock reverberated in the East with the news that the passive Santee, who had been exposed to Christianity and civilization longer than the other Sioux tribes, had started a ruthless war. [p.14]

but the writer has done her research and she has a feel for the emotions she engenders in both her readers and her characters. There is a glossary. Adequate.

708a. Sneve, Virginia Driving Hawk.
HIGH ELK'S TREASURE.
New York: Holiday House, 1972.
(5–8)
This story of a Dakota Sioux ranch family concentrates, as do many of Sneve's stories, on the young son of the family, and the book features her usual, careful attention to authentic details of the present-day reservation life characteristic of unbroken, more successful Dakota families. She adds such accurate details as the adult responsibility Indian children often assume at an early age, the grandmother's fear of ghosts, and the Indian family's more sophisticated handling of artifacts that formerly might have been sold to whites at give-away prices. Sneve's character delineations of men and boys tend to be fuller and more convincing than her portraits of girls and women. The young boy is portrayed as idealistic and inventive, and the father as under-

standing and wise, while the sister is pictured as helpless and dependent, and the grandmother as fearful and nagging. In the story Joe High Elk has hopes of renewing his ancestral herd of fine horses. In the process of looking for a lost horse, he encounters thunderstorms, horse thieves, greedy whites, a long-lost family member, and a relic that sheds light on the death of Custer. Sneve provides lessons in Dakota customs, history, and language along the way. She occasionally resorts to a positive form of stereotyping of the Sioux: "High Elk (whose name had originally been Steps-High-Like-An-Elk) loved horses, as did all of the Sioux. Sioux horsemen had been the bravest, most daring, and most agile of all the Plains Indians" (p.12); Cheyenne, Comanche, and Arapaho, among others, might disagree. Her writing also sometimes suffers from a pedantic quality as she attempts to pack a large number of facts about a certain style of present-day Sioux family life into her narrative and dialogue passages; Sneve does present in this book a convincing picture of a Dakota family living a successful, fulfilling life. Oren Lyon's fine black-and-white illustrations add much to the narrative through their dramatic and sharply focused composition. There is an illustrated family tree for the story characters, and the author gives a short glossary of Dakota words. Good.

708b. Sneve, Virginia Driving Hawk.
JIMMY YELLOW HAWK.
New York: Holiday House, 1972.
(3–5)
The story of a successful, middle class Dakota ranch family, this book is a step ahead of most children's books about Native American family life because of the author's ability to utilize effectively her own Dakota childhood experiences to make the book more authentic. Sneve writes knowingly of South Dakota thunderstorm violence; of the annoyance of mosquitos; of middle class Indian home life that includes a grandfather who prefers to spend his summers in a tent; and of less successful neighbors who accuse

the family of trying to be *wásicus* (whites). She gives a realistic picture of ranch life that would be familiar to any children raised in the country, such as ordering clothing from a catalog, or enjoying hamburgers and malts on a visit to town. The characterizations are well done, especially that of the father, who emerges as a likable man who wants the best for his family; that of the Dakota school teacher, who has fun with her charges and expects them to excel, while, at the same time, giving them a great deal of freedom; and that of the grandfather, who is an example of how one lives his or her own life without condemning or condescending to others who choose other ways. The dialogue passages are well done, especially those between the teacher and her students. Occasionally the speeches attributed to the grandfather bog down in the author's attempt to provide too much detail about the old days. However, the interest and authenticity these details add are worth this price. In the story, Little Jim is discontented with his name, and takes steps to secure a new one in the old way. After many adventures and misadventures, his father understandingly names him Jimmy Yellow Hawk. Oren Lyon's black-and-white illustrations are accurate in detail and appropriate in feeling, adding a sense of movement to the story without being so explicit that they limit the reader's own imagination. This book won a first prize in the 1971 Council on Interracial Books for Children contest. A short glossary of Sioux words and phrases is included. Good.

708c. Sneve, Virginia Driving Hawk.
WHEN THUNDERS SPOKE.
New York: Holiday House, 1974.
(6–8)
This book is an uneven product. On the plus side, the author writes from an informed stance based on her Indian background about a close Dakota Sioux family, providing the reader with a realistic sense of the conflicts between the mother and father over old values, Christianity, aged parents, and raising children. Sneve de-

tails carefully the conflict between old and new ways in the action between the mother and the grandfather. And her first-hand knowledge of the violence of South Dakota storms enhances the reader's sense impressions and visualization processes. Oren Lyon's black-and-white drawings are dramatic, well composed, and authentic in feel, although disappointingly few in number. On the other hand, Sneve presents, for the most part, cardboard characters that show little depth; for instance, the white trader is a cheat given relentlessly stereotyping lines: " 'Bah!' exclaimed Mr. Brannon scornfully. 'You Indians are just a bunch of superstitious heathens' " (p.93); a white tourist is characterized by stereotypic adjectives: "When he turned back to Norman the white man's pale blue eyes looked shifty and greedy" (p.79); and, just in case the reader fails to appreciate the point, the author comments through the main character, "Norman's mouth tightened in anger. This white man felt free to take the Indians just the way all white people did" (p.79). The father emerges as the one character with any depth and understanding of the conflicts the author presents. Sneve deals in a one-sided manner with Christianity, showing Indian converts as uniformly misguided and intolerant. Another value, the desire for money, is portrayed as categorically evil: "But Matt Two Bull was looking sadly at Norman. 'You are talking like a white man,' he softly reprimanded. 'Being rich isn't important to an Indian' " (p.74). Materialism, of course, is an issue that non-Indian and Indian young people alike struggle with as they develop their value systems. This author, as is her right, has a definite point of view, and, although she tends to portray materialism and other "bad" values as being white, she does make an effort toward evenhandedness:

"Do you mean that all of the white man's ways are bad?" Norman asked.

Matt Two Bull shook his head from side to side. "Sitting Bull, one of our old chiefs, told the people, 'When you find something good in the white man's road, pick it up. When you find something bad, or that turns out bad, drop it and leave it alone.' " [pp.75–76]

Sneve's writing, especially her dialogue passages, tends to tediousness at times. This, her advocacy of a certain value system, and her lack of depth in characterization are flaws that a purchaser may feel are more than compensated for by her familiarity with her subject, by her accurate depiction of the region's geography and climate, by her inclusion of authentic Dakota customs, and by her presentation of a successfully operating, present-day Dakota family. In the story: a fifteen-year-old Dakota boy finds an ancient coup stick that changes magically from old to new as the family fortunes improve. This stick is a source of conflict, particularly among the mother, the paternal grandfather, and the young boy as they argue over what to do with it. At the end, the boy and the grandfather "give the *coup* stick back to the earth" (p.94). There is a short glossary of Sioux words. Adequate.

709. Squire, Roger.
WIZARDS AND WAMPUM: LEGENDS OF THE IROQUOIS.
New York: Abelard-Schuman, 1972.
(3 and up)
This is a collection of seven stories drawn from the folklore of the Senecas. The stories are dissimilar, and yet there is a thread of continuity; in each, there are characters, both human and animal, that undergo sudden transformations, from "the depths of despair" to the "heights of success." These changes are usually due to the good will of the Great Spirit or the wrath of the Evil One. The stories have been adapted for young children, yet there are some surprisingly adult and effective asides: for instance, "He was a big boy, but slow in thinking, with awkward hands and feet" (p.17); or "And Turtle: He had lived a long time and knew that life held many disappointments" (p.42). The writing itself is uneven and at times pedestrian: "Strong and intelligent, the Iroquois were a happy people, advanced in religion and government" (p.13). Charles Keeping's illustrations are

superb. A combination of techniques such as rubbings and outline drawings, including hidden images such as the face in the tree trunk on page 24, makes the pictures useful for teaching skills such as visual closure and visual figure-ground. Good.

710. Stands-in-Timber; Liberty, John; and Liberty, Margot.
CHEYENNE MEMORIES.
New Haven, Conn.: Yale Univ. Pr., 1967. (8 and up)
A beautiful, moving opening statement by Fred Last Bull, Keeper of the Sacred Arrows, sets the tone for this book in which the authors share with the reader the meaning of being Cheyenne. The book includes such diverse elements as a history of the Cheyenne from prehistoric times until they were moved onto various reservations; shares some of the earlier Cheyenne tales; explains some of the Cheyenne ceremonials; and gives anecdotes about Stands-in-Timber's family. The authors write well, combining research, scholarship, and precision with words to form a work suitable for serious students as well as for readers in search of a book strictly for pleasure reading. There is a good bibliography and an index. Good.

711. Steele, Mary Q., and Steele, William O.
THE EYE IN THE FOREST.
New York: Dutton, 1975. (5 and up)
Although this story presents a clear picture of the Mound Builders of the Ohio River valley, the tale seems forced. The plot, about the quest by a young priest candidate for the Sacred Eye of Adena, gives the authors chances to detail pre-Columbian life. In this example of adequate but uninspired writing, present-day motivations are given to story characters. The main girl character is a stereotype: she causes trouble, she is portrayed as a slave, as dirty, as a witch, and has other equally negative characteristics. The anti-woman stance of the main character seems rather extreme: "A woman should not hunt and bring meat to our cooking fires" (pp.54–55). Poor.

712. Steele, William O.
THE MAN WITH THE SILVER EYES.
New York: Harcourt, 1976. (5–8)
This book is centered around a theme of conflict of cultures. A young Cherokee boy is sent by his grandparents to spend a year with a Quaker trader at the time of the Revolutionary War. During the year, he discovers that he is the Quaker's son. After burying his father, he goes back to live as a Cherokee. Steele infuses the characterization of the boy with depth in an intelligent manner and weaves Cherokee customs into the tale in an effortless, appropriate fashion. Good.

713. Steele, William O.
WAYAH OF THE REAL PEOPLE.
New York: Holt, 1964. (7–9)
This is the story of a Cherokee boy, Wayah, who is preparing to leave for Williamsburg to study, part of a trading agreement between the Cherokees and the settlers. His grandfather warns him that he will become like a tree split by lightning, divided by white and Indian ways. At school his only real friend is a white boy named Duncan. There are four other Indian boys attending school, but he cannot relate to them. When he returns home after a year he has a better understanding of the white world that is helpful to his people. This book can serve as a focus for discussions, or can be used simply as a book to read for pleasure. Good.

714. Stefansson, Evelyn.
HERE IS ALASKA.
New York: Scribner, 1959. (7 and up)
Factual information about Alaska up to, and including, its admission as the forty-ninth state in 1959 makes this book valuable as history. Rewritten as a statehood edition, this reprint of a 1943 commentary on Alaska is of historical interest. There is no effort to use a vocabulary appropriate for children, but the author has an easy, natural style that appeals to all ages. She dispels stereotypes and misconceptions and corrects the nonsensical cliches that are applied to Alaska. Her emphasis is on problems and trends that were

newsmakers in the 1940s and 1950s. Of course, there is no mention of the disastrous earthquake of March, 1964, or of Alaska's petroleum reserves and the pipeline. For the time in which it was written, the information is helpful. Dated. Good.

715. Steiner, Stan.
THE NEW INDIANS.
New York: Harper, 1968. (7 and up)
A treatise on issues and people of importance at the time of publication, this book would be difficult for all but the best junior high readers to handle, but would be invaluable for those who can manage the vocabulary and the contents, written primarily for adults. Stan Steiner has been active in many of the current crises for Native American groups, and has been instrumental in encouraging many young Indian and non-Indian writers. The viewpoint Steiner presents here is definitely and admittedly biased. He has emphatic views on what courses of action Indian and non-Indian groups should take. He documents here, over and over again, that American Indians are not "crushed," as they are so often presented, but are involved in the most vital, invigorating, exciting social processes of our times. He presents a good example of brilliant, angry, biased writing and is so forceful that young readers (adults, too, for that matter) need to know that there are other, equally legitimate, points of view on the topics he covers. Good.

716. Steiner, Stan.
THE TIGUAS.
New York: Crowell-Collier, 1972.
(5–8)
Stan Steiner is a romantic. This fact is reflected in the way he puts words together:

> In the gentle wind that blows down the highway the lone feather in the headband of the War Captain of the Tigua Indians sways like a radio antenna. He grins. He squints at the diesel trucks that roar past him on Highway 80, on their way to El Paso, Texas. [p.1]

He shows it in the way he writes of an Apache raid on the Tiguas in the old days: "In hunger and frustration the Apaches raided the farms of the Pueblos, for they too were starving" (p.26). And the all too short book he has produced on the Tiguas, that tribe of city Indians who live in El Paso, Texas, is an incredibly effective blend of realism and poetry. He details the Tiguas leaving Gran Quivera, New Mexico, in 1675, and their changing of details and substances (cigarettes for peace pipes, for example) without changing the process of the spirit of their ceremonies, beliefs, and customs. Steiner gives the reader a rare insight into chronology and into the definitions of the word *civilization*, as he compares European scenes and Tigua:

> When most of Europe was inhabited by wild and primitive tribes the forefathers of the Tiguas were living in towering apartment buildings in the Mountains of the Apple. They had built great cities when London was still a village and New York was mostly a swamp. [p.21]

and he writes of an item that many who have lived in the desert have always wondered about—the effect of heat on Spanish armor: "Laughter greeted the conquerors. The people of the pueblos thought the weary knights in their sweaty armor who marched back and forth through the sweltering deserts were fools" (p.25). This fine writer also knows when to quit; this book is only eighty-eight pages long. Steiner could have included more details about women and about tribal factions and how differences are resolved. This book will probably be of most interest to fifth through eighth graders. There is an index, and the book is illustrated by black-and-white photographs. A classic. Good.

717. Stephens, Peter J.
TOWAPPU: PURITAN RENEGADE.
New York: Atheneum, 1966. (4–8)
A fictionalized story of the adventures of a Puritan youth at the time of King Philip's War, this well-written book manages to give the young reader a lot of his-

tory painlessly. Timothy Morris and his father, more sympathetic than the rest of the Puritans believe they should be to the Algonquins, are arrested by Puritans, and escape to the Indians. At the end of the war, the boy and his father sail south, to live where they hope they will share more completely the beliefs of the settler population. Stephens writes well and presents an unsparing picture of Puritan customs, such as their flogging practices, and their treatment of the Algonquins:

> The English victors showed no mercy. They shot their prisoners or sold them into slavery—men, women, and children. Those Indians who escaped such a fate ran the gauntlet across hostile Iroquois lands to lose their identity among the friendly tribes to the west. Behind them, the white settlers squabbled over Philip's lands. [p.246]

William Moyer's black-and-white drawings are appropriate; there is a good historical comment section and an interesting, short section on the author. Good.

718. Stevenson, Augusta.
SITTING BULL: DAKOTA BOY.
New York: Bobbs-Merrill, 1956. (3–7)
This book presents an extremely romanticized, stereotyped account of Sioux relationships between parents and children. A typical episode begins with Sitting Bull's sister telling her mother that Sitting Bull is being called "Slowpoke" by the other boys because he runs so slowly. After overhearing this, his father responds that the name is "a shame both to him and to me." The family is presented in a modern, nuclear family arrangement (a mother, father, and sister); and subsequent relationships and people, while introduced as "braves," "cousins," "uncles," and "nephews," are detailed in such a way as to suggest neighborhood situations not unlike the early Dick and Jane readers. Written in an almost entirely conversational style, concerned mostly with dialogue between Sitting Bull and his family or his friends, the story deals primarily with Sitting Bull's early boyhood until he is about thirteen years old. After some forty intervening

years (indicated briefly by the author in the comment, "many years passed"), in the last chapter the author condenses Sitting Bull's life into a few tersely presented encounters with the whites. She also describes a conversation between President Grant and some of his army officers, in which they decide, in a rather cavalier fashion, the fate of Sitting Bull and his people. The book may be very unsatisfying, if not misleading, for some young readers because of this incompleteness. The illustrations by Harry Lees are in black-and-white. Poor.

719. Stone, Buena Cobb.
SON OF THE LAKES: A STORY OF THE KLAMATH INDIANS.
Klamath Falls, Ore.: Smith-Bates Printing Co., 1967. (2–4)
Primarily designed for instructional purposes, this fictionalized account is so full of facts that, regardless of their accuracy, the reader has difficulty figuring out the plot. The story consists of the involved adventures of several young Klamath children. The dialogue passages are labored, full of supposed Indian-style wording: "'But you have only thirteen summers,' she replied" (p.1); and rather sexist ideas:

> "You are just a girl, and easily full of pity," scoffed Ke-how-la. [p.4]

> "Girls cannot climb kosh, the pine," teased Ke-how-la, "but Plu and I will climb for moss." [p.5]

The book includes a bibliography and a map. The format suffers from poor printing. Margie P. Newman's black-and-white line drawings are informative, even if not earthshaking in their technical production. Adequate.

720. Stoutenburgh, John L., Jr.
DICTIONARY OF THE AMERICAN INDIAN.
New York: Philosophical Soc., 1960. (4 and up)
A dictionary of simple, basic definitions of American Indian terms from *Aatsosni* to *Zuñi Pueblo*, this book is primarily useful for upper elementary school

children. It is worth having for the reference purposes for which it was designed, but would need much supplementation for a scholar interested in in-depth research. Good.

721. Stuart, Gene S.
THREE LITTLE INDIANS.
Washington, D.C.: National
Geographic Soc., 1974. (2–4)
An instructional-type book written in basal reader style, this is the story of three young Indian children: a Cheyenne boy, a Creek girl, and a Nootka boy. Young readers will probably receive the most information from the pictures, rather than the writing, which is often composed of simplistic prose: "A fine potlatch with many presents showed how important the chief was. And the party gave everyone a chance to have a good time" (p.30). Louis S. Glauzman's color paintings are up to the usual high standards of most National Geographic Society book illustrations. Adequate.

722. Stull, Edith.
THE FIRST BOOK OF ALASKA.
New York: Watts, 1965. (4–6)
This book gives information on many aspects of Alaskan history, ethnology, geography, agriculture, transportation, economics, and politics. Written in a style easily assimilated by children in the middle elementary grades, the articles are short and illustrated with black-and-white photographs. The author calls herself a "cheechako" in the foreword, and tells the reader on page 3, "*cheechako* . . . That is you. 'Cheechako' means newcomer." The text is appropriate for tourists, including as it does many anecdotes comparing the differences between what the Alaskan likes and what the reader likes. There is much useful information for people who have never been to Alaska, or who are visiting for the first time. The articles on each subject are brief, and are dated before 1965. The statistics also pertain to this era. Students using this book need to be reminded that the book was not written primarily for Alaskans, that many things have changed since 1965, and that the author writes from the tourist's point of view. With that in mind, children can gain interesting ideas. Adequate.

723. Suggs, Robert C.
THE ARCHAEOLOGY OF NEW YORK.
New York: Crowell, 1966. (7 and up)
In this book, a great population center is explored for archaeological data, as artifacts and linguistics are used as clues about the ancient people who once lived along the Hudson River. The author develops an overview of Paleo-Indian culture by piecing together fragments of archaeological data from the New York area. He tells how the fragments were found, and hypothesizes an interpretation. He traces the cultures that succeeded one another and concludes the book with the coming of the Europeans and the drastic changes that occurred when they "discovered" this part of the world. Good.

724. Suggs, Robert C.
THE ARCHAEOLOGY OF SAN FRANCISCO.
New York: Crowell, 1965. (7 and up)
Archaeological discoveries near San Francisco are described and used as clues to interpret the daily life of prehistoric peoples. This fast-paced, fascinating account is written by a practicing archaeologist. He makes the discipline of archaeology more appealing than detective fiction as he unravels the mysteries of the Paleo-Indians, the Early Horizon, the Middle Horizon, and the Late Horizon. He concludes with the coming of the Spanish missionaries, who, in a very short time, eradicated much of the cultural differences in California, replacing Indian ways with Mission life. Good.

725. Sutton, Felix.
THE HOW AND WHY WONDER BOOK OF NORTH AMERICAN INDIANS.
New York: Grosset, 1965. (2–4)
This book presents an overall, survey view of various American Indian and Eskimo cultures, now dated due to the 1965 publication date. The writing style uses a question format which is sometimes pe-

dantic: "For the most part, the Indian languages are melodious and pleasant to the ear. Their style is very eloquent, full of fine phrases and involved descriptions" (p.9); simplistic: "Although the Indian braves were usually much too busy hunting, fishing, and fighting to have time for sports, they did occasionally pass the time by playing games" (p.11); and judgmental:

> When the first white hunters and prospectors explored the southwestern deserts, they found the poorest, most miserable tribes of Indians on the North American continent. . . . But the Southwest Indians have a glorious past. [p.44]

All in all, the writing is adequate for the task and time. The illustrations, in color and black-and-white, are informative. Adequate.

726. Sutton, Felix.
INDIAN CHIEFS OF THE WEST.
New York: Messner, 1970. (4–6)
This book includes brief biographies of Sequoyah, Crazy Horse, Chief Joseph, Sitting Bull, and Geronimo. The format and the title are misleading; the introduction, "The Plains Indians," gives readers the impression that all these men were Plains Indians. Crazy Horse and Sitting Bull were; however, Geronimo was Apache, Chief Joseph a Nez Percé, and Sequoyah was, in reality, a member of an eastern tribe, the Cherokee, and not technically a chief in the sense that the rest of the men in the book were. The author's dividing line between settler and army, on one hand, and the federal government, on the other, is not so precise as he indicates in the following excerpt:

> As a rule, the white settlers and most army officers tried to deal fairly with the Indians. But the government in Washington—the Agency for Indian Affairs, in particular—cheated them, lied to them, stole from them, and broke the treaties they had made with them. [p.17]

Russell Hoover's black-and-white illustrations are well done. Poor.

727. Syme, Ronald.
OSCEOLA: SEMINOLE LEADER.
New York: Morrow, 1976. (3–6)
The author begins this biography with background information regarding Asi-Yahalo's (Black Drink's) English father, William Powell, and Creek mother, Polly Copinger, even though not all historians are convinced Powell was Osceola's father. Syme places Osceola's life and times in the context of contemporary events of the time and U.S. governmental edicts that directly affected the Seminole Indians. Included, too, are Seminole and black relationships, and some of the more widely known Seminole customs. The author's style is consistent with most good biographers, in that he writes objectively and provides sufficient factual information to support his inferences. Although he speculates ("William Powell was an independent sort of fellow, who took life very easily"), he does so with feeling and dignity. The black-and-white illustrations by Ben F. Stahl add a sad, almost awesome, dimension to the book. All Indian, black, and white individuals have sober, almost formidable, or angry expressions. Good.

728. Tamarin, Alfred H.
WE HAVE NOT VANISHED: EASTERN INDIANS OF THE UNITED STATES.
Chicago: Follett, 1974. (3–6)
An excellent, well-written social studies type of text, this book would be equally good for classroom reference or for a vacation guide. The emphasis is on Indians of today, and present-day eastern Indian reservations are described. An especially well done section tells of Indians who cannot prove they are Indian:

> Indian communities can appear exactly like every other community around them and still be Indian. The people can vary in skin, hair, and eye coloring, with some being dark and straight-haired and others fair and blue-eyed. Yet all are Indian. [p.20]

The book gives the reader a picture of the "we," not "I," of family, clan, tribe, and nation that often pervades Indian actions. Illustrations are in black-and-white. Good.

729. Tamarin, Alfred, and
   Glubok, Shirley.
ANCIENT INDIANS OF THE SOUTHWEST.
Garden City, N.Y.: Doubleday, 1975.
(4–6)
This book, with its careful description
of the history and archaeology of the ancient Indian cultures of the Southwest, is
a good book for a budding anthropologist
or archaeologist. Color and black-and-
white photographs show tools, pottery,
and archaeological sites of the peoples
who once lived in present-day New Mexico, Arizona, Nevada, and California. The
writing is better than the average social
studies or reference text style, and is limited to assumptions and conclusions based
on archaeological findings. Use the book
for background for teachers, for a travel
reference by children, for students who
live in the Southwest who want to know
more about their area, and for Indian children who want to learn about their history.
Good.

730. Tanner, Clara Lee, ed.
ARIZONA HIGHWAYS INDIAN ARTS
AND CRAFTS.
Phoenix, Ariz.: Arizona Highways,
1976. (6 and up)
A collection of various articles written
by different authors, this book deals with
Southwest Indian art work, including basket making, weaving, kachina designing,
and jewelry-making. It covers its material
thoroughly, presenting a rounded, historical view of Indian crafts; for example, it
mentions the comparatively recent origin
of silversmithing, and comments on design:
   Collectors have inadvertently produced
   another effect on doll carving by paying exorbitant prices for pornographic
   dolls. Pornography as such did not
   exist among the Hopi until a generation ago. [p.95]
The color photographs are excellent and
show fine examples of each craft. Good.

731. Tanner, Clara Lee.
SOUTHWEST INDIAN PAINTING:
A CHANGING ART.

Tucson: Univ. of Arizona Pr., 1973.
(7 and up)
An outstanding commentary on American Indian art, this book is invaluable for
art instruction, information, and appreciation purposes. Tanner's points of view
are her own, and are highly personal. She
ties together cultures, history, and art, and
deals effectively with change: "Should the
Indian change in his art expressions? It is
sheer sentimentality to expect him not to
change, for when he reaches a static point
he is dead" (p.435). She is occasionally
guilty of some positive stereotyping:
   Not only do the ceremonies give the
   puebloan peace of mind, but they also
   reflect his unity of purpose, his one-
   mindedness, his cooperative effort for
   the common good. [p.433]
The book details the old and new in American Indian painting. It is true that the art
work she selects to illustrate the book
leans to the traditional, the popular, and
the best known, but she does know her
field. The pictures in the book could be
used with younger children. Good.

732. Tanner, Clara Lee, and
   Kirk, Richard.
OUR INDIAN HERITAGE: ARTS THAT
LIVE TODAY.
Chicago: Follett, 1961. (2–5)
This book deals primarily with Southwest Indian art, and the color reproductions of paintings used as illustrations are
beautiful, reflecting the cooperative work
between the author and Arizona Highways magazine on the book's publication.
The pictures, indeed, are the most important part of the book; the text represents
a beginning, a good reference for a vacation, a survey type of look at the art involved. Tanner's interpretations are highly
personal and reflect a view that is not necessarily shared by others as she explores
the history of Indian art: for instance, "It
was the problem of getting enough to eat
that caused them to develop the first
crafts. They needed better ways to get and
prepare food" (unpaged). In spite of the
publication date, much of its contents still
remain relevant. Good.

733. Taylor, Paula.
JOHNNY CASH.
Mankato, Minn.: Creative Educational
Soc., 1975. (5–8)
With a vocabulary and reading level of
about fifth grade, a good format which
makes intensive use of graphics, and an
interesting subject, this book would be a
good choice for junior high (and even senior high) students who are slow readers.
They could read the text, enjoy the concepts presented, and appreciate the higher-
grade layout level of the text. Basically a
story about part-Indian, country-western
singer Johnny Cash, the book details his
early life and struggles, tells of his Indian
heritage, and presents other relationships
between popular music and the Indian
heritage, such as the song written about
Medal of Honor winner Ira Hays. Good.

734. Tebbel, John.
A COMPACT HISTORY OF THE
INDIAN WARS.
New York: Hawthorn, 1966.
(7 and up)
Tebbel makes an attempt to present the
history of the Indian Wars period in a fair,
impartial style:

As always, brave men fought and died
on both sides. Their leaders were sometimes brilliant and courageous, sometimes stupid and cowardly. Neither side
enjoyed a monopoly of good or evil.
[p.10]

Carleton did what he could at the beginning, even putting his own troops
on half-rations to save the Indians
[Navajos] from starvation. [p.213]
Occasionally, however, his horror asserts
itself in stereotyping adjectives such as
"gold-greedy Spaniards" and "gold-crazed
Spaniards" (p.11); and his recoiling at
certain events is obvious:

It is helpful to recall, for example, that
one of the first acts of those who came
to explore the New World was to enslave some of the trusting natives and
take them back to Europe, either as
proof of their voyages, or to work in
European mines, or both. [p.10]

In one senseless show of force, De
Soto's men killed a hundred helpless,
sleeping warriors in a village. [p.11]
His comments about modern conditions,
while representing the period of publication, often still hold true: "And to the
hopelessly huddled and often starving
survivors in the concentration camps we
choose to call reservations, it is a war that
has never ended" (p.10), or, "The white
man's road, for the Indian, had no ending.
He has, as the government so aptly puts it,
been terminated" (p.306). All in all, this
is a surprisingly compact, well-written reference on the Indian wars from the time
of Columbus through Wounded Knee.
There is an index and a bibliography, and
the book is illustrated by black-and-white
drawings. Good.

735. Thomas, Estelle Webb.
GIFT OF LAUGHTER.
Philadelphia: Westminster, 1967.
(7–9)
Somehow, whites often feel that they
will be the ones the Indians like and
choose as friends; that they will be greeted
with Indian smiles, gratitude, and thanks;
and stories like this one promote the fallacy. In it, a young white woman is sent to
a remote part of the Navajo Reservation
to teach. She has a series of adventures,
wins the children's love and the parents'
gratitude, and takes an Indian baby with
her to care for when she goes home for the
summer. The romantic element of the
story concerns a young doctor. The writing is uneven; sometimes breathless, sometimes naive: "The only Indian in sight was
certainly not dangerous-looking. At least
he was fully clothed, with no paint or
feathers showing" (p.29); sometimes
stereotyping:

"They are the least-civilized Navajos on
the reservation," she looked madden-
ingly smug as she added, "They have a
special grudge against all Government
employees and consider only the Traders their friends." [p.27]
sometimes ethnocentric:

"The children who presently emerged
were certainly not the same who had

gone in. They were shining little Americans, with freshly laundered garments from the skin out, teeth brushed, shoes brushed, hair wet and sleeked down [p.44]

sometimes condescending: " 'He say he not need money if Washingtone [sic] and you and John Collier leave his sheep and horses alone' " [p.115]; and occasionally, thoughtful and intelligent. There is no doubt that the story will be of interest to many young readers who will relate to the romanticism and idealism expressed and will be carried along by the author's organizational ability and, no doubt, well-meant paternalism (maternalism?). This book presents the purchaser with a dilemma. Book organization and author's writing skill: Adequate. Portrayal of Indians: Poor.

736. Thompson, Eileen.
THE GOLDEN COYOTE.
New York: Simon & Schuster, 1971.
(7–9)

The plot of this story is an interesting one of loneliness that could have been written about any culture. Little Otter, a young Pueblo Indian boy, is rejected by his tribe because his mother is a member of a different tribe, and is lonely after the death of his godfather, the person he held in the highest esteem. He finds an injured coyote pup and nurses him back to health. The pup and the boy both become outcasts and set out to find a new home. While searching for the new home, Little Otter learns of Navajo raiders who plan to attack the village. He returns to warn and help his people. In the conclusion, Little Otter discovers where he belongs, and learns what he must do with Willow, the golden coyote—he sets him free. The story is interesting and well illustrated, but many readers familiar with Pueblo culture, with its many kinship and clan groupings, may wonder at the authenticity of a story that portrays a child rejected simply because his mother is from a different tribe. Even Pueblo people disagree about this, some saying it could happen, others feeling that it would depend on the Pueblo involved, and others rejecting it as completely contrary to Pueblo tradition. A controversial book. Adequate.

737. Thompson, Hildegard.
GETTING TO KNOW AMERICAN INDIANS TODAY.
New York: Coward-McCann. (2–4)

This book will provide young children with a general overview of the life of various American Indian groups at the time of publication. The book offers some good insights; for example, it talks of both reservation and nonreservation life, and presents an interesting, if controversial, interpretation of Navajo life: "The newer life of the people [Navajo] is in its towns and villages" (p.28). It treats the BIA with surprising gentleness:

However, our government protects their right to what remains through the Bureau of Indian Affairs, a Bureau in the U.S. Department of the Interior. The Bureau also advises Indians on business affairs, helps them govern themselves, and sees that they get the kind of education they need to live in today's world. [p.10]

At times the book is inaccurate and misleading, as in comments dealing with the Menominees and the Klamaths:

Others, like the Menominees of Wisconsin, have turned their reservation into a state county, or like some of the Klamaths in Oregon, have sold their land. These tribes no longer need the help of the federal government, and the government has therefore given up its supervision of them. [p.11]

Thompson presents a thorough look at schooling, and includes the description of a day at boarding school and the offer of one Indian to educate a dozen white boys. She gives a good analysis of Navajo familial and kinship relationships for young readers. Adequate.

738. Time-Life, ed.
THE LIFE TREASURY OF AMERICAN FOLKLORE.
New York: Time-Life, 1961.
(8 and up)

Like mythology makers the world over, the Indians of North America developed legends to explain things they did not understand, and to render less frightening the vast forces of nature. They told tales to explain how the world was created, how life began, how plants grow, how the mountains and lakes were formed. In these myths, natural phenomena were personified, and Sun, Sky, Earth, Winds, and Thunder became supernatural beings. Indian groups were conscious of the importance of storytelling: the sacred legends were often acted out in ceremonial dances filled with violence, awe, and pathos. Included in this book are fifteen myths from the following tribes: Seneca, Zuñi, Five Nations (Mohawk, Onondagas, Cayugas, Oneidas, Seneca), Blackfoot, Menominee, Fox, Pueblo, Eskimo, Tachi, Pascagoulas, Cherokee, Paiute, and Navajo. Some of the legends are violent, with much blood in evidence. They are true to the old-style, traditional pattern. The stories are well written. Good.

739. Tobias, Tobi.
MARIA TALLCHIEF.
New York: Crowell, 1970. (2–5)
Although many biographies about Tallchief describe her father as an easy-going man who enjoyed the outdoors (and, therefore, as someone who never worked), this book depicts him as downright lazy (as opposed to his wife, who was "strict and full of energy"). Similarly, Gerald, Tallchief's older brother, is described briefly in the same vein. No author, however, could deny Tallchief's persistence, hard work and astounding achievements, nor the fact that being a child of an Osage family with money contributed significantly to provide many opportunities, such as the Tallchief family's move to Los Angeles so that the girls could "find better music and dancing teachers." The young reader interested in the activities and contributions of present-day Indians should read other biographies about both those who stayed on the reservations and those who left, as Tallchief's family did, but not necessarily under such good economic conditions. The color-accented illustrations, several of which appear to have been copied from actual photographs, are nicely done. Adequate.

740. Tomerlin, John.
PRISONER OF THE IROQUOIS.
New York: Dutton, 1965. (4–7)
This is a fictionalized account of a white boy who was taken and raised by the Onandagas during colonial days. Nursed back to health and treated as an Onandaga, he returns at the end of the book to warn his white parents about the British. Tomerlin writes extremely well, but he gives an erroneous impression about Onandaga women when he seems to accept them as docile and cites such evidence as the following:

Like the Oneidas, when the Onandaga men went out to hunt they never brought game back with them. This was the women's task. A brave would return to the village and say to his wife, "I have killed." Then she, by following his trail, would go and find the deer or elk or bear, or whatever it was, and bring it into camp. If the animal were large, she might have to cut it up and make several trips, but that was her job. [p.69]

What he writes was often true, but this does not, contrary to what he seems to think, mean that the women were slaves; on the contrary, in all these tribes, women had immense power. The book does need more of an introduction or a preface; the jacket cover states the book is nonfiction, but this is never clarified in the text. There is a brief section describing the author. Adequate.

741. Tomkins, William.
UNIVERSAL SIGN LANGUAGE OF THE PLAINS INDIANS OF NORTH AMERICA.
San Diego, Calif.: William Tomkins, 1937. (5 and up)
This book combines beautiful, poetic writing with surprising facts about sign language:

There is a sentiment connected with the Indian Sign Language that attaches to no other. It is probably the first American language. It is the first and only American universal language. It may be the first universal language produced by any people. It is a genuine Indian language of great antiquity. It has a beauty and imagery possessed by few, if any, other languages. It is the foremost gesture language that the world has ever produced. [p.7]

However, it also combines an unfortunate print job and choice of type face that make the book hard to read. Originally directed to Boy Scouts, the book is staggeringly comprehensive. Among other topics it includes lists of work, codification of pictographic symbols of Sioux and Ojibwas, the history of sign language, smoke signaling, idioms, synonyms, and so on; enough to gladden a linguistics professor's heart. The material is accurately and thoroughly presented, and if someone reissued the book, minus its Scout format and with more modern illustrations, it would make a fine children's book. Good.

742. Trapp, Dan L.
JUH: AN INCREDIBLE INDIAN.
Southwestern Studies, Monograph No. 39. El Paso: Univ. of Texas at El Paso, 1973. (7 and up)

Juh was an Apache contemporary of Victorio's, and this book details his accomplishments in war and in leadership. Trapp presents Juh's story in straightforward prose: "Juh was a prominent and important Apache, of singular capacity and ruthlessness, deserving to rank with Cochise, Mangas Coloradas, Victorio and well above Geronimo in accomplishment" (p.5). The book features plain, unadorned, subtitles: "His Rise to Leadership," "His Physical Appearance," "His Early Encounters," and so on. He includes extensive references in this biography of a great, often unknown, Apache. Good.

743. Turner, Frederick W., III.
THE PORTABLE NORTH AMERICAN INDIAN READER.
New York: Viking, 1974. (7 and up)

This book is not portable; it weighs too much to be slipped into handbags and pockets, and the print is too small for quick reading by tired vacationers. But it should be read. Turner is erudite, perhaps too much so for recreational or vacation reading, and has much to offer. The acknowledgements are impressive and the introductory comments insightful. The book itself is divided into four sections: "Myths and Tales," "Poetry and Oratory," "Culture Contact," and "Image and Anti Image," each of which has an introductory section, and was designed for adults. Still, it can be useful for advanced junior high school readers and for adults who work with Indian students or with non-Indian students studying American Indian cultures. This collection includes some of the usual, good writings and some works that are not typically presented in an anthology, such as a journal entry about the Lewis and Clark expedition and two realistic, unromanticized captive stories. Turner presents an analysis of Indian women-men relationships. He labels Indian cultures sexist; not all would agree with him (see pages 375–77). For example, he refers to modern American Indian life as follows:

> The typical situation then finds the man idle, out of work, and the woman providing both support and some semblance of household order. In this way the Indian woman has begun to emerge as at least an equal sharer in the new tribal culture, a privilege which ironically and symbolically came to her in some tribes only with the death of her husband and her own menopause. [p.377]

Other author comments are equally thought-provoking. Good.

744. Udry, Janice May.
THE SUNFLOWER GARDEN.
Irvington-on-Hudson, N.Y.: Harvey House, 1969. (3–4)

The characters are Algonquin in this involved fictional story, and the author gives them present-day motivations that would probably not hold true for Algonquin society:

> Pipsa's father was like most Indian fathers. He taught his son to do the things he could do, and he often praised him. He never thought of praising a little girl.
>
> But Pipsa's mother was proud of her and sometimes said, "Well done, my little Pipsa!" [p.10]

In the story, Pipsa, a young girl, longs for her father's praise. He praises only her brothers, and her mother's praise is not enough. She grows sunflowers for the tribe to use. Finally, in an involved ending, Pipsa kills a rattlesnake, her father orders her brothers to help guard the sunflower garden, and Pipsa wins the praise of her father and of her tribe. The book assumes that the feelings of modern girls would also be true for this girl, but with the variance in kinship groups between cultures and with fathers assuming a different series of roles in Algonquin society, the book's major premise is doubtful. However, the author writes adequately, and her illustrations, although the people do not look particularly Indian, show good technical skill. Adequate.

745. Underhill, Ruth M.
FIRST PENTHOUSE DWELLERS OF AMERICA.
Santa Fe, N.Mex.: Laboratory of Anthropology, 1946. (7 and up)

One of the most thorough of the popularized anthropological studies of its day about the Pueblos, this book still has much to offer readers, although the more modern sections are limited, of course, to periods before 1946, the date of publication: "However the people of Taos to this day cut the seat from trousers, to make them as much like the old leggings as possible, and wear special herbs in moccasins" (p.18). Underhill, anthropologist though she is, is still a romanticist and writes like one:

> Down there, among the cactus and the shimmering lizards, lies another land with another history. But he who follows the history of the Pueblos prowls

through the canyons of the waterless plateau with its brilliant sky, wild thunderstorms, glaring heat and windy chill. [p.1]

She can effectively use the "literary" writing style popular at the time of publication and make it into effective prose, instead of the pretentious pieties her less-gifted contemporaries produced. She presents in this book a readable survey of the Pueblos, much of it still relevant. And she reminds the reader that, unlike most American Indian groups, "The Pueblos had status as property holders" (p.19). She concentrates in this book on prehistory, the Hopi, the Zuñi, the Keres, the Tewa, and Taos Pueblo. She includes a well-selected bibliography, now dated. Good.

746. Underhill, Ruth M.
HAWK OVER WHIRLPOOLS.
Locust Valley, N.Y.: J. J. Augustin, 1940. (7 and up)

A well-written story about the Papago, or Desert People, this book tells the story of a family, particularly one member of the family, a young man at the time schools were being built on the reservation and white culture was beginning to make inroads into the old ways. Underhill writes well and presents here an idealistic, romantic, yet accurate view of the Desert People and their customs, as she traces this young man's life through white schools, white cities, and back home to become Keeper of the Smoke for his people. A typical passage:

> "He is the father of the people. Of course he must care not only for our work, but for our sacred things." He paused. Only later Carmelita understood that the revelation he made next was an honor rarely shown to a woman. It was a stately form of lovemaking. "My father is one who has dreamed." [p.6]

The sections describing the confusions of children who spoke little or no English at boarding school and the elaborate forms of address to fellow kinship and clan members are especially well done. Good.

747. Underhill, Ruth M.
INDIANS OF SOUTHERN CALIFORNIA.
Washington, D.C.: U.S. Dept. of the
Interior, Bureau of Indian Affairs, Div.
of Education, 1941. (7 and up)

A reference type of book, this volume
is a well-written, well-researched analysis
of the history of the Indian peoples of
California, including daily life, familial
patterns, religion, and history. Occasionally the author includes some stereotyping
in her comments: for example, "When the
Spanish missionaries first came to southern California, at the end of the eighteenth
century, they found a peaceful, good hu-
mored people moving about" (p.5). The
section on California Indians of today is
severely limited by the publication date,
thus restricting the book's usefulness to a
presentation of history up through the
1930s. The book is illustrated by interesting photographs and Velino Herrera's
good black-and-white illustrations. There
is a map of the reservations of Southern
California, and the author lists a bibliography. Underhill's work in popularizing
anthropology was a pioneering effort, and
this book will serve to acquaint readers
with her style. However, other than the
historical material, there are more complete modern treatments available on
Southern California Indians. Adequate.

748. Underhill, Ruth M.
RED MAN'S RELIGION.
Chicago: Univ. of Chicago Pr., 1965.
(7 and up)

This book is intended for the mature
reader making an initial acquaintance
with the religious practices of the "First
Americans," their history and their status
as of 1965. The book is written in non-
technical language and is exploratory in
nature. It raises questions of origin and
relationship, rather than proposing solutions. The scope of the volume is limited;
some areas, such as ceremonial development, have been left for future workers in
the field. The author repudiates the stereotype of the Indian seeking the Great Spirit
and the Happy Hunting Ground. She
makes it clear that the Indian's ("Red

Man" is an unfortunate title choice, due
to its sexist tone and inadequate description of Native Americans) religions were
quite complicated. Various tribes and
groups differed in their beliefs; for instance the reigning deities ranged from a
Great Holy Flame of Life to the California
condor. Religious ceremonies constituted
the very core of Indian existence, according to the author, but their purpose was
not worship as whites know it. Indian religion was a partnership between man and
the supernatural, and this partnership, it
was felt, benefited both. The book is well
written and interesting. It lists extensive
references. Good.

749. Van der Veer, Judy.
HIGHER THAN THE ARROW.
San Carlos, Calif.: Golden Gate Junior
Books, 1969. (6–8)

Van Der Veer has the knack of writing
realistic dialogue that sounds as though it
might be spoken by a modern California
Indian girl, a girl who is an average
enough teen-ager to be glad when the hair
fashions change to straight, and who
might say, "I don't think that I'd ever get
tired of television" (p.7), unusual enough
to say, "Some people like to say that the
teachers pick on the Indian and Mexican
children more than the others, but I'm not
positive" (p.8). In the story, the girl wants
to make a statue of St. Francis when her
sick coyote pet dies, and she is helped by
a teacher to see the advantage of working
with a white girl to make the statue. They
become friends. The story is paced well,
and Van Der Veer writes in a straightforward fashion. However, the ending may
be too pat for some tastes. F. Leslie Matthew's woodcuts are competent. Adequate.

750. Varga, Judy.
THE BATTLE OF THE WIND GODS.
New York: Morrow, 1974. (K–3)

Childlike word patterns and illustrations contribute much to a story less adult
in concept than many myths. Easy to read,
the book explains weather in mythological
terms. Good.

751. Vaudrin, Bill.
TANAINA TALES FROM ALASKA.
Norman: Univ. of Oklahoma Pr.,
1969. (5 and up)
This author obviously enjoyed immensely his work researching and writing
this book, as indicated in his comments:

> No words on a printed page could hope
> to recapture the spirit and immediacy
> of a firsthand telling of these stories by
> the people themselves. Steambaths and
> fish boats have played their parts for
> me—and gas lamps and Swede stoves,
> log houses and long winter nights.
> Many of my favorite hours were spent
> in the preparation of this collection of
> stories. [p.x]

His enthusiasm shows in the book; he provides a good introductory section, he uses
language easy to read and understand,
and he writes well, with zest for recording
this series of Tanaina Indian tales. He
makes sidetrips in his writing that enhance reader enjoyment of the stories, as,
for example, when he reminds us that the
Russians were the first whites the Tanai-
nos saw, and as he explores the intricacies
of the geographic status of the Athapas-
can language. The stories, themselves, are
primarily animal tales and, had they been
given an easier format, would be read by
even younger children. Kenai Buck Hay-
den's illustrations are appropriate, and
there is a glossary. Good.

752. Velarde, Pablita.
OLD FATHER: THE STORY TELLER.
Flagstaff, Ariz.: Northland Pr., 1960.
(3 and up)
This book is unbelievably good. The
author's paintings are exquisite, the writing is lyrical, and everything fits together
as it should in this collection of Pueblo
legends. D. Hancock provides a thoughtful
introductory section and presents cogent
reasons for reading the book: "Because of
this book we are richer when we look at
Orion and Long Sash as well" (p.15).
There is an index. A must for every library, this book is a classic. Good.

753. Villaseñor, David.
TAPESTRIES IN SAND: THE SPIRIT OF
INDIAN SANDPAINTING.
Healdsburg, Calif.: Naturegraph,
1966. (4 and up)
The format of this book is miserable;
there is simply no other word to describe
it. The printing is bad, even blotted in
places; the reproductions of sand paintings are poor, the type unsuitable, and the
layout atrocious. The writing itself is, to
say the least, uneven, ranging as it does
from unusual bits of information ("The
Indian awarded everyone in the tribe.
Children and women alike could claim
coups for feats of unusual dancing, with
these honors included in their dress"
[p.4]) to personal asides that are almost
too much to expect strangers to read
("Many have touched my heart with help
and encouragement throughout the long
period of research and struggle" [p.111]).
Still, the book has something, an intrigu-
ing quality that slips up on the reader and
that is really rather hard to define. The
author exerts much personal charm. He
shows that sand paintings are not limited
to Navajo groups alone (Zuñi, Hopi, Papago, and many Southern California Indian groups, among others, have a tradition of sand painting). It is true that his
explanations of sand paintings are highly
personal and probably do not provide a
defiinitive picture of what they actually
represent to various Indian groups in reality, but his explanations are fun to read.
He willingly experiments with the sand
painting medium (or media, as he does
it). The main problem (and the main
pleasure) with the book is separating author opinion from fact, a task complicated
by his extensive use of references. Probably, the book would work best for those
readers who have some sort of sophistication in this area and who can enjoy with
(and also become angry at) the author in
his recapitulation. Controversial. Good.

754. Vizenor, Gerald.
THE EVERLASTING SKY: NEW VOICES
FROM THE PEOPLE NAMED THE
CHIPPEWA.

New York: Macmillan, 1972.
(7 and up)

This is an angry, bitter, sensitive, loving, thoughtful account of the Chippewa, or Ojibwa, Indians, the Oshki Anishinabe (new people of the woodland). The author is an Ojibwa, and he writes from personal experience of home, family, city, reservation, BIA and public school education, and the harassment and prejudice of law enforcement personnel against the Anishinabe. He tells of elders who resist change, of women who hold the people together, of young people who have little knowledge of the old ways, and of men and women militantly fighting to assert Anishinabe identity and to attain justice for their people: "'Who am I?' he asked himself, '—something the white man named and made up . . . I was chained in a dream and thought about us all being named by a psychopath like Columbus'" (p.15). The book is beautifully, sophisticatedly written; some non-Indian readers may find their consciences and complacency pricked too sharply (or not sharply enough, depending on their viewpoint). (Note the acknowledgment to Stan Steiner.) An excellent, meaningful treatment. Good.

755. Vogel, Virgil J.
THIS COUNTRY WAS OURS.
New York: Harper, 1961. (8 and up)

This history of American Indians is broad in scope. Starting with the Aztecs, Incas, and Mayas, it presents the Indian side of history from 1492 to 1958. Each period of United States history is summarized and documented, with the role of the Indian emphasized. This book is an excellent reference, and would help to balance books written from the viewpoint of the Indian as merely one who reacts to white takeover and white civilization. Good.

756. Voight, Virginia Frances.
THE ADVENTURES OF HIAWATHA.
Champaign, Ill.: Garrard, 1969. (1–3)

This is a version of the Hiawatha legend, well written in primary-grade language. The black-, white-, and-tan illustrations by Gordon Laite are excellent, combining Indian design, Art Deco, and Art Nouveau processes in perhaps the most important part of the book. The layout is especially effective—pretty, well illustrated, with easily readable type. The content of the book continues Longfellow's distortions of the legend of Hiawatha. The original Hiawatha was an Iroquois (this book implies he was an Ojibwa) and one of the founders of the Iroquois League. The author has Minnehaha going to live in Hiawatha's house when they marry; in actuality, as a Dakota, she would probably have insisted he move into her lodge. A short introductory statement could have taken care of these criticisms. Still and all, the legend as it is presented is well done. Adequate.

757. Voight, Virginia Frances.
CLOSE TO THE RISING SUN:
ALGONQUIAN INDIAN LEGENDS.
Champaign, Ill.: Garrard, 1972. (2–5)

A collection of Algonquin legends, this book centers around the exploits of Gooscap, a larger-than-life superbeing. The tales presented include creation myths, explanations of natural phenomena, and exploits of the Little People. The text is easy to read, averaging about third-grade level in difficulty, including the sections on the author and the artist. Gordon Laite's illustrations have almost an Art Nouveau feel, alternatingly black-white-brown; black-white-green; black-white-red; or any color combined with black and white. They fit well the content of the stories. Good.

758. Voight, Virginia Frances.
RED CLOUD: SIOUX WAR CHIEF.
Champaign, Ill.: Garrard, 1975. (3–6)

A Garrard publication, this book begins with a brief history of the Oglala Sioux and a map showing the various locations where Red Cloud's people lived. There are many similarities to other biographies about Indian leaders during the Indian Wars; for example, the recounting of a legend similar to one of Sitting Bull's boyhood, when the author elaborates upon a fight between Red Cloud and a grizzly bear and the ultimate reward of his "man-hood name." The typical stereotype of the "brave warrior in battle" and a "respected chief in peace" prevails in the story. Red Cloud was, of course, all of this. But there was more to him than his fighting ability. The author correctly includes the factual importance of horses and buffalo to all Sioux tribes. Red Cloud's visit to Washington, D.C., to meet the President is described, as is the contrast between the amount of wealth and power of the Indians and that of the other people of the United States. As with most of the other Garrard titles about Indian leaders, the illustrations by Victor Mays aid the reader in understanding and clarification. Adequate.

759. Voight, Virginia Frances.
SACAJAWEA.
New York: Putnam, 1967. (2–4)
This book is reminiscent of a fairy tale. It presents its characters as bland, sweet people who lived a bland, sweet story—a disservice to all of them, and perhaps especially to Charbonneau, Sacajawea's "husband" or "owner" (he has been given both epithets and euphemisms; perhaps he was, in reality, either, both, or neither). Typical descriptive passages include:
One of the best dancers was York, Captain Clark's Negro servant. York had taken care of Captain Clark for many years. Now he did many things to help the Indian mother and her baby. [pp. 30–31]

But Pompe cried all night long and kept the captains awake.
They didn't really mind. All the men were glad to have Sacajawea and her baby with them. [p.37]

How proud she felt to be the first woman to cross the mountains and see these things. [p.55; Flathead women, among others, had crossed these mountains many times.]
The illustrations by Erica Merkling continue the theme, showing as they do the people involved dressed in the fashionable outfits of the late 1960s, here modified to

include clean, untouched people wearing the inevitable feathers. This is not to say the book is not factual as it describes Sacajawea's childhood or her capture by the Minnatarees; it is rather that the book is typical of many volumes written about American Indians—acceptably accurate, acceptably written, acceptably illustrated—but that do not give much of a feel for the people themselves. Sections describe the author and the illustrator, and another lists key words. The book ends with the journey with Lewis and Clark. Adequate.

760. Voils, Jessie Wiley.
SUMMER ON THE SALT FORK.
New York: Meredith Pr., 1969. (5–7)
Primarily concerned with a white family who spends the summer camping, hunting, and grazing stock on the Salt Fork, this book deals with Indians, in this case the Nez Percés, primarily as background material that provides some elements of danger and suspense to the plot. The descriptive passages devoted to the Indians are not particularly accurate:
She wasn't sure she wanted to go. Indians were partial to red hair and had been known to scalp white people. . . . If she went to the territory, she must wear her sunbonnet all the time to hide her hair. [p.3]

"I doubt it. From what I hear, they're [Nez Percé] a sorry lot. Half of them are down sick. And the government took all their horses away from them. The Indians who came were mounted."
Ma said, "The government doesn't take an Indian's horse unless he's done something pretty bad." [p.119]
The story is centered on the thoughts and adventures of the young daughter of the family. The author certainly knows Midwestern ways; her descriptions of spreading clothes on the grass to dry, washing feet at bedtime, and swinging up to "let the old cat die" all ring true for those raised in this tradition. Leonard Vosburgh's black-and-white illustrations are adequate. Portrayal of white settlers: Adequate. Portrayal of Indians: Poor.

217

761. Voss, Carroll.
WHITE CAP FOR RECHINDA.
New York: Washburn, 1966. (6–8)
An example of awkward writing and plot design, this book still has some features the potential buyer may wish to consider: (1) it does, to some extent, hold reader interest, particularly for escape reading purposes; (2) it does portray, however romantically, a young Sioux girl who is a student nurse; (3) it shows the academic problems caused by limited educational background of some Sioux young people who want to be professionals; (4) it contains enough love interest to satisfy even the most romantic teen-age reader, as the girl decides between a white lab technician and an Indian intern; and (5) it does present the dilemma many Sioux adolescents face, whether to continue their education or drop out. Adequate.

762. Wallower, Lucille.
THE HIPPITY HOPPER; OR WHY THERE ARE NO INDIANS IN PENNSYLVANIA.
New York: McKay, 1957. (2–4)
First, there are American Indians living today in Pennsylvania (consult the U.S. Census report). However, this book's title concerns a Lenape (Delaware)-Shawnee legendary argument over women, children, and grasshoppers which led to the "Grasshopper" War. The writing is simplistic and lacks depth: "They were strong, brave Lenape Indians who lived a happy life" (unpaged); and, "The women of the village kept house" (unpaged). The book needs a table of contents and page numbers. There is an explanatory author's note at the end of the book, and the graphics and layout design are good. Poor.

763. Walton, Elizabeth Cheatham.
VOICES IN THE FOG.
New York: Abelard-Schuman, 1968. (5–7)
Primarily the story of two twin white girls in the 1840s who go to Cape Cod with their family, where they meet and have some adventures with some Gay Head Indians, this book has a naive, simplistic approach to the Gay Heads involved in the plot; "Tammy was a little startled to find that Indians said thank you, but she tucked it away in her mind as one score against Aunt Delia and one for her father" (p.51); and the white characters are made to say transparently absurd things: " 'I don't care how civilized Indians are,' replied Aunt Delia. 'I bet there's a tomahawk hidden some place' " (p.30). The plot involves the girls' helping a Gay Head girl with a broken leg, helping catch some white thieves whose villainies are blamed on the Indians, and helping reform the "superstitious" Gay Heads (one white girl informs the Gay Head girl that there are no ghosts). Many times the story seems a chronicle of willful twin brats. Shirley Hughes's black-and-white illustrations are acceptable. Story development: Adequate. Portrayal of Indians: Poor.

764. Waltrip, Lela, and Waltrip, Rufus.
INDIAN WOMEN.
New York: McKay, 1964. (6–9)
Despite the early publication date, this book has a lot to offer readers about the women it describes, including Big Eyes, Pocahontas, Sacajawea, Winema, Cynthia Ann Parker, Sarah Winnemucca, Indian Emily, Tomassa, Neosho, Maria Martinez, Annie Dodge Wauneka, and Pablita Velarde. An interesting juxtaposition of writing involves the description of the contrast between white and Indian women: "Like many other primitive peoples, a large number of American Indians gave women a higher position in their way of life than women enjoyed among white societies until recent times" (p.xi); followed immediately by Oliver LaFarge's no doubt well-meant sexist remarks about white women, even though he is more accurate in his descriptions of Indian women: "The conquering of the white man's West was men's business chiefly but keeping their country was the task of the whole Indian family and the women often were stauncher and braver than the men" (p.xiii). The book is well written and as interestingly paced as a good novel. There is fascinating speculation on the life of Sacajawea after her journey with the

Lewis and Clark expedition. While the Waltrips do repeat as fact the legend of Pocahontas and John Smith, they do give much accurate information about various tribal customs, such as the mother's oldest brother serving as disciplinarian for the children, or the fact that children belonged to the mother's clan. Many of the women described here aided the whites in some fashion, which no doubt resulted in their being included in white chronicles and remembered; too bad there are so few records of other Indian women who did not necessarily become involved with whites. The authors include a fine bibliography. Good.

765. Waltrip, Lela, and Waltrip, Rufus.
QUIET BOY.
New York: Longman, 1961. (7–9)
The story is about a modern Navajo boy, Quiet Boy. It begins when some sheep are stolen from the boy's family flock, and Quiet Boy, who believes he knows who the thieves are, becomes a detective; following a series of adventures, he solves the crime. While the story will hold the interest of most young readers, in some respects it has a Hardy Boys quality that places it in the category of a typical detective story about a young boy (not necessarily restricted to an Indian; any young boy). In this case, however, the action takes place on an Indian reservation. The plot centers about this young boy and his conflicts as he continually strives to please his grandfather, who questions white ways, and his father, who wishes him to accept the new world. In this respect, the authors attempt to demonstrate the struggle between two cultures and how one boy tries to adapt to one, yet integrate as much as possible of the other. The authors' style, almost exclusively consisting of conversational exchanges between characters, helps move the story along at a rapid pace. The black-and-white illustrations by Theresa Kalab Smith are interesting and detailed. Adequate.

766. Warren, Betsy.
INDIANS WHO LIVED IN TEXAS.

Austin, Tex.: Steck-Vaughn, 1970.
(2–4)
A straightforward, historical account with no literary pretensions, this book details the history of many of the Indian tribes who lived in Texas at one time or another, including the Caddoes, Wichitas, Jumanos, Karankawas, Atakapans, Tonkawas, Coahuiltecans, Kiowas, Lipan Apache, Comanches, Alabama-Coushatta, and Tiguas. The author, who also illustrated the book with black-, white-, and brown drawings, presents some insightful data: "Not all of the men in a tribe were warriors—only those who chose to be" (p.13); although at times she reduces some interpretations to banality: "Texas Indians did not write down stories of their history because none of the tribes had alphabets" (p.3). Good.

767. Warren, Mary Phraner.
WALK IN MY MOCCASINS.
Philadelphia: Westminster, 1966.
(4–6)
This is the story of five Sioux Indian children who are adopted by a childless white teacher and his wife. The title of the book is the theme of the story. The two oldest girls go to their new home in a small Montana town before the others so that a family routine can be established. The girls appreciate the greater material advantages of their new home, but are bothered by all of the washing, cleaning, bedtime, and other rules set down for them. The oldest girl, Melogy, especially resents the loss of freedom and feels the inherent disapproval of how her own, poorer family lived. The rest of the children arrive in August before school starts. There are some raised eyebrows in the community and some unstated disapproval, but no overt hostility is expressed toward the children before they enter school. By the time school starts the children have two good white friends, and some Spanish-speaking friends with whom they identify because they, too, are dark-skinned and as poor as they once were. In school, certain children call them names, wreck some of their playthings, and generally make life miserable

for them. The children learn that the mean white children have personal problems, too, which are affecting their behavior (although this is, no doubt, a heavy thought for children who are being discriminated against to have to learn). Almost all of the adults are pictured as understanding people who appreciate cultural differences and encourage the children to be proud of their Indian heritage. The story is a little idealistic, but it presents a sensitive and positive outlook. Good.

768. Waters, Frank.
BOOK OF THE HOPI.
New York: Viking, 1963. (8 and up)
Waters wrote this book with the help of thirty-two Hopi elders. It talks about the history, art, and religion of the Hopis. Deep spiritual meanings of religious rituals and ceremonies are revealed. Photographs and drawings help illustrate these ideas as they are expressed by Hopis as part of myths, legends, dances, and mystery plays. One of the classics of literature concerned with Indian culture. Good.

769. Waters, Frank.
PUMPKIN SEED POINT.
New York: Viking, 1969. (8 and up)
This is an autobiographical account of Frank Waters's stay on the Hopi reservation while he was researching their mythological beliefs. This well-written book tells of the author's reactions to the ideas of Hopi culture. Good.

770. Webb, George.
A PIMA REMEMBERS.
Tucson: Univ. of Arizona Pr., 1959. (5 and up)
A priceless, childlike book, this volume records the reminiscences of George Webb, born in 1893 at Gila Crossing, Arizona, on the Gila River Reservation. He has a great style that flows along with simple phrasing, then kicks at the reader with an unexpected change in pace, like the timing pattern of a good actor. Some examples:
These forefathers of mine never had

any of the whiteman's education. They were educated in the ways of nature and used natural resources for food and clothing. This may have something to do with their long lives as they lived to be very old. [preface]

Some of our white neighbors seem to think that our farms ought to be taxed the same as theirs. But so far as I remember we have never received any payment for some good land which is no longer ours. [p.120]

I was glad they came to me and not to some other Indians I know because some of them would take an offer for less. [p.119]

I have heard several white men say that the pace of what is called progress today is almost too much for *them.* Think how it must seem to a simple Pima who remembers the Gila River when it was a running stream. [p.126]

There are some very smart white operators coming into this desert country these days with money and influence. Not all of them can write their name. They have a string of lawyers to do that for them. [p.125]
Good.

771. Webb, Nancy McIvor.
AGUK OF ALASKA.
Englewood Cliffs, N.J.: Prentice-Hall, 1963. (2–4)
The story of Eskimo children who go hunting and find polar bears, this fictional account contains some facts that will tell the young reader about (1963) Eskimo life: "Aguk and Siksigak have never seen a walrus. Aguk and his father cannot hunt walrus for the great herds no longer come near their home. Hunters have killed them all" (p.7). However, much of the writing is simplistic and banal: "Here the sun does not shine at all in the winter, but the stars and moon are very bright." The author's woodcuts are informative, although the people in the illustrations do not look particularly Eskimo. Adequate.

772. Welch, James.

RIDING THE EARTHBOY 40.

New York: Harper, 1971. (8 and up)

A collection of poems written by Native Americans, this book provides a good sample of current American Indian literature. Many of the poems could easily be read by advanced upper elementary and junior high school readers. An introduction and more information on the poets would have been helpful. Good.

773. Wellman, Paul I.

INDIAN WARS AND WARRIORS EAST.

Boston: Houghton, 1959. (6 and up)

This is a well-researched, thorough, carefully documented, well-written book. Wellman is a realist, a tough writer who isn't afraid to remind the reader that the penalty for Indians for failure in the hunt was starvation. He presents many little-known Indian leaders, such as Opechan-canough, in this book. The purchaser should be aware that Wellman advocates unpopular opinions and that his books are sure to cause controversy. He does, however, represent a legitimate viewpoint and may serve to round out a collection likely to be skewed the other way. Some samples of his opinion:

> However, within the area now contained in the United States, with which this book is chiefly concerned, the tribes were savages—virile and admirable in many respects, barbarous in others. And they were so spectacularly different from the Europeans that they caught the imagination of the world. [pp.13–14]

> Cruelty was common among Indians, and to show pity was often considered weakness. Frequently—though not always—war prisoners were tortured to death. Yet the red man had no copyright on cruelty. In supposedly civilized Europe more persons died by fire for religious differences, or superstitious charges of witchcraft, or various crimes than were burned to death in all the Indian Wars put together. [p.20]

> We think of America as belonging to the Indians before the white man came. This was true only in the sense that a very thin population of natives hunted over it and occupied it. From the wide view—the view of the human race as a whole—it is not right for a vast area of productive land to be kept as an unused wilderness. Too badly does the world need food and materials. Where they are, men will go and make that land productive, at any cost. It has been so since history began.

> So perhaps the chief, and almost the only, justification of the white man's driving of the Indian from his hunting grounds is this: where once the area of the United States harbored no more than a few hundred thousand Indians, warring against each other, hunting and sometimes starving, it now supports in unequaled prosperity more than 173,000,000 people of all races—including more persons of Indian blood than were alive when Columbus first saw the New World. [p.180]

The book is illustrated with black-and-white photographs and excellent illustrations by Lorence Bjorklund. Good.

774. Wellman, Paul I.

THE INDIAN WARS OF THE WEST.

Garden City, N.Y.: Doubleday, 1974. (7 and up)

This book is a combination of two previous Wellman books, *Death on the Prairie*, 1934, and *Death in the Desert*, 1935, and deals with the Indian Wars of the West, giving special attention to those involving the Apaches and the Sioux, but also detailing the wars involving the Cheyenne, Comanche, Nez Percé, Utes, Modocs, and Kiowa, among others. Wellman writes angrily about past injustices—not a common practice in the 1930s. Some quotes from this book serve to establish his position:

> Between these two extremes of human culture there was no common ground. The Indian could not understand the palefaces' land hunger. But the white man's greed was all-consuming. [p.7]

We did not put Indians in gas chambers or crematories. But we did shoot down defenseless men, women, and children at places like Camp Grant, Sand Creek, and Wounded Knee. We did feed strychnine to red warriors. We did set whole villages of people out naked to freeze in the iron cold of Montana winters. And we did confine thousands in what amounted to concentration camps. [p.8]

He is fair, however, in giving some of the army officers of the time credit for their help and compassion for their Indian charges, and in condemning those officers who mistreated their prisoners, captives, and adversaries. There is a particularly well-written delineation of the Apache chief, Nana. The author gives a thorough index, bibliography, and introduction. The book is illustrated with black-and-white photographs. Although the most recent material is limited to events before 1947, there is much here for the young reader interested in history. Good.

775. Wentworth, Elaine.
MISSION TO METLAKATLA.
Boston: Houghton, 1968. (6–9)
The author tells the story of an English Christian missionary who established what she terms a model Christian community at Metlakatla among the Tsimshians, still inhabited today. She writes of the Tsimshians in a paternalistic fashion:

The captain, however, was filled with sympathy for these wild, superstitious children of the forest. It was easy to see that the white men had greedily taken advantage of these Indians for many years. [p.9]

Captain Prevost, besides being a valiant naval officer, was also a concerned Christian gentleman, and he angrily realized that no effort was being made to counteract the Indians' tragic moral and physical decline. He was keenly aware that a missionary could do more than guns to transform the savage natives into happy peaceful human beings. [p.11]

Highly oriented to Christianity, as are many Indians and non-Indians, this author presents a legitimate viewpoint, but the quality of her writing and the apparent condescension with which she speaks of the Tsimshians shows the reader how Christianity and cultural destruction erroneously become synonymous in many people's minds. The author's illustrations are the best part of the book, and there is a bibliography. Poor.

776. Wetmore, Ruth Y.
FIRST ON THE LAND.
Winston-Salem, N.C.: Blair, 1975.
(6–8)
A good, simple, straightforward textbook about the Indians who inhabit or have inhabited North Carolina, this book would be good for slower junior high school readers who need a simple vocabulary and an easy-to-read text. The author stresses that there is no single way of life for North Carolina Indian groups, either before or after the coming of the non-Indian settlers. She describes daily life, ceremonials, customs, and the like, for each of the tribes, sometimes in as few as one or two pages. The black-and-white photographs help inform the reader about more current conditions, and there is a bibliography and an index. Adequate.

777. Wheeler, Ruth.
BRIGHT SUNSET: THE STORY OF AN INDIAN GIRL.
New York: Lothrop, 1974. (3–8)
Sensitive, though overworked, is nevertheless appropriate for describing this outstanding story of the ambivalence about coming of age of a young California Indian girl. With good illustrations by Dorothy Matteson, the story flows well, telling about a girl's life in an older era. Surprisingly, because usually the reverse is true, the language used to write the story is easier than the concepts involved. For this reason (low vocabulary and high interest level), the book would be useful with slow readers of intermediate elementary grades and junior high age. The readability level is approximately third to fifth

grade, while the concepts would appeal to sixth, seventh, and eighth grade students. A good plot shows that girls were important and could solve their own problems. The story is perhaps as much about adolescence as about Indians. Good.

778. Whiteford, Andrew Hunter.
NORTH AMERICAN INDIAN ARTS.
New York: Golden Pr., 1970.
(5 and up)

This recent publication (1970) brings together a wealth of information on Indian arts. A compact reference book, profusely illustrated in color, this volume emphasizes the variety and creativity of Indian art forms. Whiteford is always careful to distinguish between cultures. However, so much information is crowded together on each page that a reader who scans quickly or a young reader might get a jumbled impression. It is useful as a reference work only on a very casual level, and would serve as an introduction to further research. Adequate.

779. Whitney, Alex.
STIFF EARS: ANIMAL FOLKTALES OF THE NORTH AMERICAN INDIAN.
New York: Walck, 1974. (2–5)

A collection of animal tales from various Indian tribes, including the Hopi and the Pawnee, this book gets its name from a Hopi story. Each tale is introduced by a short, helpful summary of the legends and the storytelling customs of the tribe represented. Written in textbook style, the book is illustrated by the author's black-, white-, and-blue-green drawings. Adequate.

780. Whitney, Phyllis A.
SECRET OF HAUNTED MESA.
Philadelphia: Westminster, 1975.
(7–9)

This is primarily a mystery story involving a teen-age white girl who is visiting New Mexico, and concerns American Indians because it makes use of Zuñi ceremonials and customs and modern-day Indian activities as part of an unbelievably complicated plot. Some quotes from the jacket cover:

From the moment she arrives with her family at Haunted Mesa Ranch, where her father is lecturing at a conference, things begin to happen. But for once they are happening to *her*–not to her older sister. What is moving mysteriously high upon the mesa? Why does the strange Indian boy, Charlie Curtis, take Jenny's precious roadrunner carving and leave, instead, a crudely whittled wooden snake? Why is her new friend, Greg, so belligerent? Who steals the Zuñi drum from the ranch museum? Or the kachina doll from the collection of the beautiful Consuelo Eliot, the friend of the Indians? And can it really be a giant with a blue head that Jenny glimpses on the rim of the dangerous mesa? . . . Why are the elders of the San Angelo pueblo so angry with Harry Curtis, Charlie's activist brother? It is not until an ancient Zuñi drum beats out the rhythms of the age-old festival of Shalako, calling the spirits of warrior ancestors to gather on the mesa in the white moonlight. . . .

The book features a subplot involving the main character's celebrity sister that is almost embarrassing to read, capitalizing as it does on the feelings of sibling rivalry most adolescents have at times. The sullen, sulky pouting and pettiness of Jenny's actions are hard to stomach. As to the treatment of the Zuñis–occasionally the author has some of the characters say sensible things about Zuñi culture and about some of the conflicts between old and new ways, although the chasm is not nearly so precise or so impossible to bridge as she implies. The Shalako ceremonial is generally held in December, as she has a character state on page 107, not in the summertime, as in the book, and is held for entirely different reasons from those given here. Her writing style has a gushy quality: "The red heart of the campfire centered the night scene and made it pulse with a crimson glow. Juniper wood gave off a pungent scent that was pleasant on the air" (p.7). As to the book's merits, Whitney has a way of carrying the young reader along on adventures that have just enough of reality to be barely plausible, making this a good book for escape reading. In this instance, it is a shame that the providing of such books must be done at the expense of changing the concept of Zuñi ceremonials. Story: Adequate. Portrayal of Indians: Poor.

781. Williams, Barbara.
LET'S GO TO AN INDIAN CLIFF
DWELLING.
New York: Putnam, 1965. (2–4)
A simple book written in textbook style: "Not all of the rooms contain fireplaces. The Indians probably found that it was better to be cold than to breathe in the smoke from a fire in a closed room" (p.35), this book would provide background for young children actually going to visit a cliff dwelling or interested in Indian ruins. A survey type of book, not an in-depth study, the text provides a pronunciation guide as each new word is introduced. The black-, white-, and-tan illustrations by Robin King are poorly done. The book contains a glossary, a section of things to do while reading the book, and a bibliography. The material is dated. Poor.

782. Williams, Barbara.
THE SECRET NAME.
New York: Harcourt, 1972. (6–9)
A well-written fiction book, this is the story of a Navajo girl who goes to live with a white family, told in the first person by the white daughter. The Navajo girl and the white girl have difficulty getting acquainted, but they become friends. The Navajo has trouble with white ways, and she is blamed when a rabbit dies, but gradually understanding prevails. The Navajo girl returns to the reservation and, as a present, tells her secret name to the white girl. The author is careful to point out that, "This book depicts only one of the many present-day attitudes that Navahos display toward their secret war names since contemporary observances vary widely" (back of frontispiece). She has a real flair for teen-age dialogue: "I wanted to leave right away for school. But you know how

mothers are about breakfast. They think you'll die or something if you don't get something hot" (p.35). She pictures well the white girl's dilemma about whether the Navajo girl likes her, because the white girl can't understand the Navajo girl's manner of thoughtful quiet. In short, this story genuinely strives to present a fair picture of the difficulties Navajo children often meet in their contacts with whites, and, except for some editorializing along the way, generally succeeds. Jennifer Perrott's illustrations do not look particularly Navajo, although she demonstrates good technical skill. Good.

783. Williams, Dorothy Jeanne.
NEW MEDICINE
New York: Putnam, 1971. (6–8)
This story of the Comanches, set at the time the whites were taking over their territory, is concerned with Walker, the least favored son of a Comanche chief. In the story the Comanches organize a Sun Dance to protect them from bullets. The subsequent attack against the whites fails, and First Son, his father's favorite, dies. Walker and his father go off on a journey to diminish his father's grief. Along the way he begins to practice Comanche medicine. After the Comanches surrender and go to Fort Sill, Walker gets a chance to become a doctor. This is a highly romanticized book, filled with improbable subplots, such as the test to see which of two women—one white, one Comanche—a small Comanche child will choose as mother. The author's occasional use of the word *squaw* is annoying. She does, however, often use insightful bits of information in her writing:

> The spirit who gave power told how to take care of it, what you must do and could not do. Some kinds of medicine had so many rules and were so hard to keep that the owners had taken the medicine back to the place where they got it, thanked the spirit, and respectfully given back the spirit. The stronger medicine was, the harder it was to live with. [p.8]

Adequate.

784. Williams, Frances.
RED MOUSE.
Austin, Tex.: Steck-Vaughn, 1967.
(K–2)
No tribe is specified for the Indian boy featured in this book. The boy doesn't like his name; he wants a better one. He wins the name of Wise Owl by shooting down a hornet's nest to rout a bear. The author uses a controlled vocabulary, and her writing suffers accordingly. Ellen Goins's brown-, white-, and-red illustrations are of the "cute kids" type—stereotyped feathers, buckskin fringe, and the like. Poor.

785. Williams, Jeanne.
TRAILS OF TEARS: AMERICAN INDIANS DRIVEN FROM THEIR LANDS.
New York: Putnam, 1972. (7–9)
Divided into five sections, this book gives details of the displacement of the nations of the Comanche, the Cheyenne, the Apache, the Navajo, and the Cherokee. It includes bibliographies for each section, and a detailed index. The author likens the placement of the Bureau of Indian Affairs under the jurisdiction of the Department of the Interior to "setting the wolf to guard sheep." She points out that Indian traditions, values, and life styles, which had been in harmony with the environment, were ignored when they hampered the ambitions of newcomers of European heritage. This happened not once, but many times, and she carefully documents and maps the points of conflict. But this is not simply a "bad white man" book; the author notes that this clash was not as simple as that, and she includes many comments similar to the following:

> Americans are descendants of survivors of persecution or hardship in their homelands—survivors of voyages as different as those of the *Mayflower* and slave ships out of Africa.
> There is also another group of American descendants of survivors— Indians who suffered the seizure of their lands by strangers and endured soul-bruising, body-maiming forced migrations. [p.7]

Good.

786. Wilson, Charles Morrow.
GERONIMO: THE STORY OF AN AMERICAN INDIAN.
Minneapolis, Minn.: Dillon Pr., 1973.
(5–9)
This biography of Geronimo details his life from childhood to death, often in simplistic terms: "Geronimo began his life in full freedom in the rugged terrain of the Southwest" (introductory statement). At times, Wilson interprets customs inadequately; for example, the usual Apache custom of a man living with his wife's family is misconstrued as follows:

> Geronimo, as a fourth child, would have succeeded his father as chief. But when Takleshim decided to marry Juana, a Bedonkohes Apache, he had to agree to join her tribe and gave up his right to the chieftainship. [p.2]

He also makes imprecise use of words; for instance, *Wickiup* is the usual name for the Apache dwelling, not *wigwam*, as used in this excerpt which also presents the author's judgments about Apache death customs:

> But following the burial in a secret cave, Apache custom had to be observed. It was grim and hard. In the presence of the tribal council of elder warriors and the chief, the dead man's wigwam and all his belongings were burned and his horses were turned free. [p.13]

There are some photographs of Geronimo included in the book, and the author does give an accurate picture of Apaches imprisoned without trial, and other injustices. Adequate.

787. Wilson, Dorothy Clarke.
BRIGHT EYES: THE STORY OF SUSETTE LAFLESCHE, AN OMAHA INDIAN.
New York: McGraw-Hill, 1974. (6–8)
Susette LaFlesche was an Omaha Indian who talked on the Boston lecture circuit, testified before Congress, and enjoyed the friendship of such celebrities of the day as Longfellow and Niehardt. She won a surprisingly large amount of issues for her people. This story of her life is well written and features an excellent bibli-

ography. The description of LaFlesche's involvement at Wounded Knee is most graphic and compelling. A good story, featuring a genuine heroine, the book is better than most social studies texts for facts and information about the era. Young readers may want to discuss the differences they see in the appropriateness of her actions in her time as compared to the present day. Good.

788. Wilson, Holly.
DOUBLE HERITAGE.
Philadelphia: Westminster, 1971.
(6 and up)
Set in Detroit in 1832, this lightweight story about a half-breed Ojibwa girl suffers from mediocre writing: "The blizzard roared on for three endless days, and Ma was very sick" (p.32). The type of story often referred to as a "girl's book," this is highly romanticized and hardly concerned at all with Indians, set as it is in a French settlement. In the story a half-breed Ojibwa girl suffers discrimination when she wants to marry a white man. She has several adventures, such as being accused of immoral behavior when she and her boyfriend are caught out inadvertently after dark alone, and being involved in a cholera epidemic. She marries the white man, convinced of his love. Adequate.

789. Witheridge, Elizabeth.
JUST ONE INDIAN BOY.
New York: Atheneum, 1974. (6–10)
This book is based on the lives of several young Ojibwa men. It tells of conflicts between the Ojibwa and non-Indian cultures, and the problems of schooling, courtship, and marriage in a well-written fashion. Teen-agers, both Indian and non-Indian, are given many opportunities to identify with the problems of the novel's characters. Although the characterizations are developed in a convincing manner, the author makes no claim that they are typical of Ojibwa youth as a whole—a good social studies class discussion point. The book should be supplemented with stories of other modern-day Indian young people who made other choices. Good.

790. Witt, Shirley Hill.
THE TUSCARORAS.
New York: Crowell-Collier, 1972.
(5 and up)
Shirley Witt has written a beautiful, poetic story of the Tuscaroras, the sixth nation to join the Iroquois confederacy. She tells of their forced migration from North Carolina to upstate New York, their legends, clans, the selection of the chiefs by the women, the Long House religion, contacts with Christianity, and the first Mohawks to work on skyscrapers. The cadence of the language is moving and suggests the imagined natural rhythms of the Tuscaroran language. The book is a delight. It is an education for non-Indian readers. Good.

791. Witt, Shirley Hill, and Steiner, Stan.
THE WAY: AN ANTHOLOGY OF
AMERICAN INDIAN LITERATURE.
New York: Knopf, 1972. (8 and up)
Included in this book are prophecies, songs, prayers, poems, legends, essays, proclamations, parodies, and satires from American Indian literature. Selections from the Navajos, Sioux, Ojibwas, Wampanoag, and Dakotas, among others, are included. The writings vary greatly in intensity and purpose. Some are humorous, others tragic: but the book presents a seldom discussed side of the Indian. The book is pro-Indian. The writing may be too sophisticated for many junior high readers, but more advanced readers will be able to profit from various selections. Good.

792. Wolf, Bernard.
TINKER AND THE MEDICINE MEN.
New York: Random House, 1973.
(4–7)
This story describes one week in the life of a modern, six-year-old Navajo boy who lives on the reservation. Black-and-white photographs show the boy at diverse activities: working at school, eating ice cream sundaes at the local Holiday Inn, living in a trailer in winter and a hogan in summer, participating in a peyote ceremonial. The book gives a description, with

few editorial comments, of one of a variety of possible current Navajo life styles. Purists who don't want to hear about Indians who have adopted some mainstream ways may be disappointed. It deals briefly but effectively with the concept of extended Indian families (all aunts and grandmothers are called "mother"); gives a good feeling about women and the aged; and states that the peyote ceremony is relatively new to the Navajo, introduced in 1930. Be prepared for questions about peyote from young readers. Good.

793. Wondriska, William.
    THE STOP.
    New York: Holt, 1972. (K and up)
An outstanding book featuring an unusual visual concept—the author/artist illustrated the book with the same landscape scene, painted over and over, from the same point of view at different times of the day in different weather—this book is a must for all readers interested in the illustration of children's literature. Dots are used in the pictures to represent characters and animals, making the paintings good materials for teaching various visual perception skills, especially form constancy and visual discrimination. The story involves two small Navajo boys who help an injured pony. One of the boys has to stay overnight alone in the desert while the other goes for help. This is great reading. Good.

794. Wood, Nancy.
    HOLLERING SUN.
    New York: Simon & Schuster, 1972.
    (7–9)
Good black-and-white photographs by Myron Wood illustrate beautiful translations of Taoseño poetry and sayings suitable for reading silently or aloud. The introduction tends to state qualities of Indians and whites as though they were separate species who have nonidentical traits; for example, all whites are only interested in facts, while all Indians are not: "Glottal stop? You might as well talk to the Taos about a hypothenuse"; or that Indians exhibit "simplistic faith that good

was rewarded and evil punished, that all things were a part of nature and therefore part of God." White Mountain Apache and Shoshone, among other tribes, might quibble with the author's evaluation that the Taos land "just happens to be the most productive, beautiful and pristine of any Indian reservation." And stereotypes are still stereotypes, even when they flatter; for instance, "They love to dance, these Indians, and they beat their drums and sing the soft, melodious words of the Tewa language." If this book is selected, children who read it also need access to books that tell of cross-cultural influences, of the shrewd Taoseño fight for Blue Lake, and of the Taos who do not live in the Pueblo. Good.

795. Wood, Nancy.
    THE MAN WHO GAVE THUNDER TO THE EARTH: A TAOS WAY OF SEEING AND UNDERSTANDING.
    Garden City, N.Y.: Doubleday, 1976.
    (8 and up)
A personal, mystical statement by the author, this could become a cult book similar to *The Prophet* or *Jonathan Livingston Seagull*, if it were given the chance. The book is written for adults, but it could be enjoyed by junior high readers and up, especially college students. It gives a delineation of Taoseño life and presents an explanation of the Old People versus the New People, with the author obviously on the side of the New People. Good.

796. Wood, Nancy.
    MANY WINTERS.
    Garden City, N.Y.: Doubleday, 1974.
    (K and up)
Excellent black-and-white and color drawings and paintings by Frank Howell illustrate Pueblo prose and poetry collected by Nancy Wood. The wording is sparse, musical, and effective, and shares equally with the illustrations in making this an effective book. Wood uses the word *Anasazi* to mean elders. More common usage reserves the word to a prehistoric Pueblo group. The Pueblo views of the whites, as quoted in this book, are revealing: "They

admire our children but they feel sorry for them" (p.7); and "The white man will not get down on his knees to look at the earth" (p.7). Readers will find many uses for this book other than the obvious, and important, one of reading for pleasure, including study of oral literature, of unusual use of language, and of the art of fitting prose and illustration together to make an insightful piece of literature. The book would be useful at all grade levels: the pictures with elementary-age youngsters, and the entire book for junior high level and above. Good.

797. Woodyard, Darrel.
DAKOTA INDIAN LORE.
San Antonio, Tex.: Naylor, 1968.
(7 and up)
A fascinating, strange work, this is the script of a four-night pageant written by the author at the request of the Ponca tribe for them to perform, although why he wrote the play about Dakotas is a puzzle. This is not written by an Indian, but the feeling is definitely Indian, as the author uses poetry and language in unusual and pleasing ways. There is a flow here, a mystique worth exploring, in spite of (yet sometimes because of) the personal references sprinkled throughout: "The Dakota are a serene people. They were extremely cordial to my wife and me" (p.xvi); and of the inclusion of segments such as "Faithless Women" and "Good Women." Good.

798. Worthylake, Mary M.
CHILDREN OF THE SEED GATHERERS.
Chicago: Melmont, 1964. (2–4)
This is a good, read-aloud fiction book about Pomo Indians. Based on factual information about these California Indians, the story is told in a style that will fascinate children. The daily life of Pomo Indians is seen through the eyes of a young Pomo boy. The dignity, resourcefulness, and beauty of Native Americans in California are portrayed simply and effectively. The book will appeal to young children, and also to older readers. Worthylake

taught in Lummi Day School on the Lummi Indian Reservation before moving to Laguna Beach, California. Good.

799. Wright, Wendell W.
NAHA, BOY OF THE SEMINOLES.
(no city): Esquire, Inc., 1957. (K–2)
An easy-to-read book about a young Seminole boy, this volume is written in textbook format, with questions for the young reader at the back of the book, such as "Where did Naha live?" and the like. The color illustrations by James Black are good and displayed to advantage by the format design. Limited concepts of Seminole life styles, compounded by the early date of publication, result in a sort of "father fishes—mother pounds corn" explanation of Seminole customs. Adequate.

800. Wyatt, Edgar.
COCHISE: APACHE WARRIOR AND STATESMAN.
New York: Whittlesey House, McGraw-Hill, 1953. (5–8)
Wyatt begins this book with background information regarding the relationships between the Apaches and whites, in general, and Cochise's branch of the tribe and American whites, specifically. He explains how Cochise wished to remain friendly with Americans, while other Apache tribes were less inclined to this, although they all agreed about Mexicans. Concentrating upon poor attitudes held by both white and Apache leaders, the author expands upon the deterioration of white and Apache relationships despite futile efforts of Cochise and Nantan Jeffords, the only white man who maintained Cochise's friendship. Unlike many books written about white and Apache leaders and the relationships between them, this one seems relatively free of stereotypes; however, it contains few references to women, except as someone's wife or mother. The illustrations by Allan Houser, an Apache descendant of Geronimo, are black-and-white sketches, drawn in the primitive style. Both the author and artist collaborated on another biography, *Ge-*

ronimo. There is a guide at the end of the book to the pronunciation and definitions of Indian and Spanish words. Good.

801. Wyatt, Edgar.
GERONIMO: THE LAST APACHE WAR CHIEF.
New York: McGraw-Hill, 1952. (5–8)
This book is one of the few biographies written at the time to have been reviewed and approved by an American Indian. Also noteworthy, the reviewer, Allan Houser, who did the black-and-white illustrations, claims to be a descendant of Geronimo. While the book is well written, it seems somewhat limited in that few descriptions of tribal life are provided, except in connection with preparation for war and brief forays against small ranchers and supply trains. Another disappointment, one that dates the book severely, is the absence of any role or description of women (except as children, and in a brief statement that Geronimo married his childhood friend, Aeope, and lost her and his three children about four years later when they were killed by Mexican soldiers). The book follows fairly closely the facts regarding various battles, treaties, and other historical information found in other biographies about Geronimo and his contemporaries. A glossary of terms, mostly names of people and places, is provided at the end of the book. Adequate.

802. Wyss, Thelma Hatch.
STAR GIRL.
New York: Viking, 1967. (5–8)
Based on a Bannock legend about a young girl who talked to the stars and disappeared, this book is the result of the author's speculation about the details of the legend. A young Bannock girl grows up happily and has many friends and one special girl friend. She is always curious, however, and one day she gets in a tree that grows tall, and takes her to the sky. There she finds the magical band of the Cheyennes in the sky, grows up, marries, and has children. Later she returns to the Bannocks. She has a happy life both places. Improbably enough, the author

makes this seem logical and almost real by her skills in organization, dialogue, characterizations, and attention to small details:

> Linking arms the two girls hopped into camp, telling everyone who would listen that they were twin jack rabbits joined together forever, looking for food—preferably roasted salmon. [p.19]

There is a brief introduction and a section describing the author. Good.

803. Yazzie, Ethelou.
NAVAJO HISTORY. Vol. 1.
Many Farms, Ariz.: Navajo Community College Pr., 1971.
(6 and up)
Perhaps few groups other than American Indian tribes would begin a history book, as do the Navajos who wrote this book, with what non-Indians would call legends or creation stories. A book written to be used by the Rough Rock Demonstration School students, this is a fine example of the tribe's attempt to provide a rich cultural background for Navajo young people. There is an English-Navajo glossary. The book is illustrated by color and black-and-white drawings and pictures. Andy Tsihnahjinnie does a fine job as illustrator. Be sure to see his interpretation of the various worlds on page 8. This is a good book to use with both Navajo and non-Navajo students, and adults will find much of value here. Good.

804. Yellow Robe, Rosebud.
ALBUM OF THE AMERICAN INDIAN.
New York: Watts, 1969. (2–6)
An amazing book, in that it offers elementary-age children a reasoned, fair, intelligent, well written, general introductory text on American Indian life, this would make a beautiful gift. It is almost impossible to review this book without sounding like one of the more gushing book jacket comments, but this is truly an impressive work. Some of its pluses: (1) easy-to-read language that presents complex concepts in simple terms, such as:

> [John] Eliot [a missionary] was a good friend to the Alqonkin people, but he

also spread the idea that to "educate" the Indian meant to replace his way of life with the white man's. This attitude damaged the Indian's respect for himself and his own culture and is perhaps responsible for the conflict between the Indian and the white man which continues to this very day. [p.35]
(2) emphasis on everyday life of many groups; (3) details of events seldom included in children's books on Native Americans, such as reporting that Pocahontas was held hostage by the British to insure the Indians' good behavior; (4) telling more about Indian help to whites than most books, regardless of the age of the intended reader; (5) plays on words that most adults think children incapable of understanding: "The French and Indian War was really the French and English War" (p.42); (6) unusual use of phrases and terms, such as calling Osceola's battles "guerrilla warfare campaigns" (p.45); (7) a reservation life section written in simple, clear, erudite language, such as the caption on page 62: "A modern Navaho hogan. The Indians are dressed in blue jeans and dresses such as any farm family might wear"; (8) indepth exploration of Indian feelings about television and movies; (9) a famous Indians section; (10) a willingness to write about controversial issues for young children; (11) bountifully illustrated by prints, maps, and drawings; and (12) good format and layout. Good.

805. Yolen, Jane.
RAINBOW RIDER.
New York: Crowell, 1974. (K–3)
An original creation legend written in the style of the creation legends of various American Indian groups, this book features effective language patterns and pacing: "In the time before time, the Rainbow Rider lived near the edge of the desert by the foot of the painted hills" (unpaged). In some places, the writing seems too consciously precious, but the writer's excellent feel for rhythm never falters. Michael Foreman's watercolor illustrations make effective use of space and gentle color, and

fit well into the patterns of the words; even the movement in the pictures draws the reader on—left to right, page after page. Not a bad idea for a book designed for an age level when children are learning correct reading eye movements and how to read a book from front to back. As to the propriety of the author's borrowing of a Native American format—why not? After all, to put together two old sayings, "Imitation is . . . in the eye of the beholder." Good.

806. Ziebold, Edna B.
INDIANS OF EARLY SOUTHERN CALIFORNIA.
Los Angeles: Sapsis, 1969. (2–4)
A book written about an area in which materials designed for primary children are scarce, this text presents a discussion of early Southern California Indians. The text is unnecessarily simplified: "They were usually happy and friendly. In spite of local quarrels they were peaceful people and there were few large wars among them" (p.8); but it does contain such little-known information as the fact that California Indians made sand paintings. The book contains a glossary, a bibliography, and an index sufficiently simple for children to use. In fact, the index is well designed for use for adults who want to begin teaching index use skills to children. The book is illustrated with black-and-white pictures, maps, and the like, typical of social studies texts, and includes many pictures of museum dioramas. Adequate.

807. Zuñi People; Quam, Alvina, tr.
THE ZUÑIS: SELF-PORTRAYALS.
Albuquerque: Univ. of New Mexico Pr., 1972. (7 and up)
This book presents views of Zuñi society, history, fables, morals, religion, war, and defense strategies, among other topics, all in the words of the Zuñis themselves. Robert E. Lewis, governor of the Pueblo, writes the introductory passages in poetic form. (What other governor would attempt this?) Several maps are included. This is a rare, beautifully written treat for the reader. A classic: Good.

How to Use the Index

Primarily a listing of tribes, persons, and events, the index for this book is designed to help readers locate information quickly and easily. To use the index, look up a subject alphabetically, then read the listing according to the following code symbols:

1. The numbers preceding any punctuation correspond to the numbered entries in the Annotated Bibliography. If the number alone is given, the whole book refers to the subject.
2. If a number is followed by a colon, the numbers after the colon refer to page numbers. Example: 38:14–15, 29–34, is read as entry number 38 in the Annotated Bibliography, of which pages 14 through 15, and 29 through 34 contain information on the subject.
3. The abbreviation (*fic*) in a listing means the book is fiction. Examples: 43:19–42(fic) or 48(fic).
4. The letters *sr* mean that the book contains scattered references not sufficient to justify a page-by-page listing. Example: 502:sr.

Subject Index